Learning Identity

*The Joint Emergence of Social Identity
and Academic Learning*

This book describes how social identification and academic learning can deeply depend on each other, through a theoretical account of the two processes and a detailed empirical analysis of how students' identities emerged and how students learned curriculum in one classroom. The book traces the identity development of two students across an academic year, showing how they developed unexpected identities in substantial part because curricular themes provided categories that teachers and students used to identify them and showing how students learned about curricular themes in part because the two students were socially identified in ways that illuminated those themes. The book's distinctive contribution is to demonstrate in detail how social identification and academic learning can become deeply interdependent.

Stanton Wortham is Professor and Associate Dean for Academic Affairs at the University of Pennsylvania Graduate School of Education. He also has appointments in Anthropology, Communications, and Folklore. His research applies techniques from linguistic anthropology to study interactional positioning and social identity development in classrooms. He has also studied interactional positioning in media discourse and autobiographical narrative. His publications include *Acting Out Participant Examples in the Classroom* (1994), *Narratives in Action* (2001), *Education in the New Latino Diaspora* (2001; coedited with Enrique Murillo and Edmund Hamann) and *Linguistic Anthropology of Education* (2003, coedited with Betsy Rymes). More information about his work can be found at http://www.gse.upenn.edu/~stantonw.

Learning Identity

The Joint Emergence of Social Identification and Academic Learning

STANTON WORTHAM

University of Pennsylvania

CAMBRIDGE UNIVERSITY PRESS
Cambridge, New York, Melbourne, Madrid, Cape Town, Singapore,
São Paulo, Delhi, Dubai, Tokyo

Cambridge University Press
32 Avenue of the Americas, New York, NY 10013-2473, USA

www.cambridge.org
Information on this title: www.cambridge.org/9780521608336

First published 2006

A catalog record for this publication is available from the British Library

Library of Congress Cataloging in Publication data
Wortham, Stanton Emerson Fisher, 1963–
Learning identity : the joint, local emergence of social identification
and academic learning / Stanton Wortham.
    p.   cm.
Includes bibliographical references and index.
ISBN-13: 978-0-521-84588-5 (hardback : alk. paper)
ISBN-10: 0-521-84588-2 (hardback : alk. paper)
ISBN-13: 978-0-521-60833-6 (pbk. : alk. paper)
ISBN-10: 0-521-60833-3 (pbk. : alk. paper)
1. Educational sociology.   2. Social psychology.   3. Identity (Psychology)   I. Title.
LC192.3.W67   2006
306.43 – dc22   2005017962

ISBN 978-0-521-84588-5 Hardback
ISBN 978-0-521-60833-6 Paperback

Transferred to digital printing 2010

Contents

Acknowledgments

The ideas and empirical analyses in this book have taken more than a decade to coalesce in this form. I would like to thank the many teachers, colleagues and students who have contributed to this work over the years. Karen Detlefsen, Jay Lemke, Ritty Lukose, Alexandra Michel, Judy Robbins and Michael Silverstein made useful comments on the manuscript. Kara Jackson, Michael Lempert, Kristina Wirtz, Teresa Wojcik and Todd Wolfson provided invaluable help as research assistants. Susan Fuhrman and the Penn Graduate School of Education provided financial, administrative and personal support. Asif Agha, Kathy Hall, Ritty Lukose, Greg Urban and other Penn colleagues have supplied an unusually stimulating intellectual environment. Fred Erickson, Ken Gergen, Sophie Haroutunian-Gordon, Phil Jackson, Jay Lemke, Ray McDermott, Rick Shweder and Michael Silverstein have provided crucial advice and mentoring over the years. Phil Laughlin shepherded the manuscript through the editorial process. Betty Deane skillfully and patiently produced the manuscript. I also owe thanks to the administrators, teachers and students at Colleoni High School who allowed me into their school, and to Denise, Ben and Rachel for their love and support.

1

Self/Knowledge

In functioning classrooms, as paradigmatic sites of rational activity, we expect to find focused and productive cognitive processes. Irrational and irrelevant things happen in classrooms, of course, but when teachers and students are doing the primary business of schooling – reading, writing, discussing, experimenting, calculating – we expect to find subject matter, argument, evidence and academic learning. As more sociological and anthropological studies of classroom practice have been done over the past three or four decades, however, it has become clear that social identification, power relations, interpersonal struggles and other apparently non-academic processes also take place during the primary business of schooling (e.g., Cazden, John and Hymes, 1972; Gee, 1989; Varenne and McDermott, 1998). Furthermore, these apparently non-academic processes cannot easily be separated from the academic activities that go on in classrooms. Subject matter, argument, evidence and academic learning overlap with social identification, power relations and interpersonal struggles (e.g., Leander, 2002; Lemke, 1990; Mehan, Villanueva, Hubbard, Lintz and Okamoto, 1996; Wortham, 1994).

Although many have pointed out the co-occurrence of academic and non-academic activities in classrooms, significant dispute remains about how to conceptualize relations between the two. Some continue to revel in demonstrations of non-academic activities in classrooms, claiming that ideologies of academic learning merely distract from the real social business of schooling. Some treat the two types of activities as concurrent but separate and continue to maintain that schooling is primarily about academic learning. More promising accounts have begun to explore the complex interrelations among academic and non-academic activities. This book describes one way in which academic and non-academic activities can overlap in classrooms. It focuses on social identification and academic learning, sketching an account of how these two processes can overlap and partly constitute each other. Through empirical analyses of social identification and academic learning in one classroom over an academic year, the book shows how subject matter, argument, evidence and academic learning sometimes intertwine with and come to depend upon social identification, power relations and interpersonal struggles in classrooms.

STUDENTS AS BEASTS

On January 24, in their joint English and history class, Mrs. Bailey and Mr. Smith discussed Aristotle's *Politics* with their ninth grade students. Aristotle argues that people who live outside society, who do not experience natural interdependence with others, are not fully human: "He who is unable to live in society, or who has no need because he is sufficient for himself, must be beast or god" (Aristotle, *Politics*, 1253a, line 29). This claim puzzles the late twentieth-century American students, who conceive of "humanness" as lodged in individuals' agency and inalienable rights. In order to help the students understand Aristotle's conception of human nature, the teachers give two examples. They imagine two students in the classroom as hypothetical "beasts," and they discuss how these hypothetical beasts might differ from humans who live in society.

Early in the discussion, Mrs. Bailey singles out Maurice as a hypothetical beast. ("T/B" is Mrs. Bailey and "FST" is an unidentified female student. Transcription conventions, a list of classroom participants and a key to abbreviations are in the appendices.)

315   **T/B:**   I mean think of what- he's saying
there. he's saying if Maurice went <u>out</u> and lived in
the <u>woo:ds</u> (4.0) [some laughter]
FST: °they're talking about you°
T/B: and <u>never</u> had any <u>contact</u> with the <u>rest</u> of us,
320   he would be- uh- like an <u>animal</u>.

With this example of Maurice, Mrs. Bailey uses the common pedagogical strategy of building an analogy between students' actual or hypothetical experiences and the curricular topic. Such analogies make familiar concepts available to students as they develop their own models of curricular topics. Mrs. Bailey probably hopes that students will better understand Aristotle's conception of human nature through a discussion of how Maurice the beast would differ from students who belong to society. Students' experiences as members of productive groups – perhaps their understandings of collective goals or shared responsibilities – might help them understand why Aristotle believed humans to be essentially social. By imagining how Maurice's dispositions and opportunities would be different if he lived apart from society, they might explore Aristotle's view of humans who do not live up to their social nature. With substantially more discussion, the example of Maurice the beast might contribute to students' learning about Aristotle.

The teacher's use of Maurice as an example may also help to socially identify him. Mrs. Bailey's hypothetical example separates Maurice the beast from "the rest of us" – the teachers and other students who remain part of "society." "The rest of us" are social beings, working together in society as Aristotle envisioned it. Maurice the beast does not participate in this society, living instead like an animal out "in the woods." Did Mrs. Bailey choose Maurice for this role because he himself is separated from the rest of the class in some way? Is she implying that Maurice sometimes behaves like a "beast?" As described in Chapter 5, the teachers and the girls who dominate discussion in this classroom often exclude Maurice from classroom interactions. They also sometimes identify him as resisting school and as unlikely to succeed in later life. In this context, the discussion of Maurice as a beast may not be merely hypothetical. Teachers and students may be commenting on Maurice's own social identity, as they draw a tacit analogy between his identity as a student excluded from classroom activities and his hypothetical role as a beast. Chapter 5 analyzes the "Maurice the beast" example in detail, showing how teachers and students do in fact use his hypothetical identity as a beast to reinforce Maurice's own identity as an outcast from the classroom "society."

Later in their discussion of Aristotle, the teachers and students switch from discussing Maurice to discussing Tyisha as a beast. Right before Tyisha enters the discussion, teachers and students have proposed that humans differ from beasts because humans have "goals." Tyisha offers her cat as a counterexample, arguing that her cat has goals just as people do – for instance, trying to jump onto the counter. Mrs. Bailey then inserts Tyisha (TYI) into the example.

T/B: let's- let's- let's take what- (3.0) let's take
675 what your <u>cat's</u> doing that every day he sees that-
<u>counter</u> that he wants to get on, and every day when
he passes that <u>counter</u> he tries to get up there. that's
a goal. ok[ay
FST: [yeah.
680 **T/B:** how is that different than your <u>goal</u>, the <u>goal</u>
that you might have had last night when you had
this reading, or
TYI: °I don't know°

Here Mrs. Bailey again uses students' own experiences to teach the curriculum. Aristotle distinguishes between uniquely human and other goals. Mrs. Bailey asks students to consider the differences between Tyisha's goals and her cat's goals. By exploring the differences between Tyisha and her cat, perhaps the students can better understand Aristotle's distinction between humans and beasts.

As the discussion continues, this seems to happen.

> **FST:** humans can do more things than cats can do, like they can <u>build</u>
> **TYI:** no that's not- just a goal. my <u>goal</u> is to <u>win</u> in Nintendo and
> 695 [laughter by a few girls in the class]
> **FST:** that's your <u>goal</u>?
> **TYI:** it's a go:al, so
> **T/B:** okay maybe winning at Nin<u>ten</u>do is like your <u>cat's</u> goal of getting on top of the-
> 700 **TYI:** right
> **T/B:** the- the counter. but aren't- don't we have more [long=
> **FST:** [better
> **T/B:** =ranged goals than your <u>cat</u> getting on
> 705 top of the <u>counter</u>, or you winning Nintendo?

Acknowledging Tyisha's valid argument that humans have some beast-like goals, Mrs. Bailey distinguishes between two types of human goals: uniquely human ones and more instrumental goals that we share with other species. As they pursue it in subsequent discussion (analyzed in Chapter 4), this distinction seems to help students understand something about Aristotle's account of human nature.

This discussion also has implications for Tyisha's social identity. In arguing that her goals are the same as her cat's, Tyisha describes herself as having the intellectually and morally uninspiring goal of winning Nintendo video games. This provides teachers and students an opportunity: in addition to addressing her argument about goals, they go on to criticize and tease Tyisha herself for having beast-like goals. Right before the next segment, Mr. Smith tries to convince Tyisha that she has uniquely human goals, like the desire to get up in the morning, get to school and pursue her education. Tyisha then tries to undermine the distinction between uniquely human and beast-like goals.

> **T/S:** so <u>you</u> had goals even before you s[tarted
> **TYI:**   [but not in
> 735 the summertime. I just got up, see, just like
> **T/S:** <u>ah</u>, and in summertime when you got up because you <u>had</u> to come to school, what was your goal or was it to sleep until three in the after<u>noon</u>? or to get up and play with your friends?

740   **TYI:** the same goal my cat had, to go to <u>sleep,</u>
      and get up and <u>eat</u>.
      T/B: ahhh, isn't that interes [ting? [increase in pitch,
      "mocking" effect]
      T/S: [ahhhh
745   **T/B:** same goals as her (1.0) [cat=
      FST: [cat had
      T/B: =had. wow.
      FST: so you are like an animal.
      T/B: so you <u>are</u> like an <u>a</u>nimal.

The teachers and students use their discussion of beasts and goals to tease Tyisha here. They imply that the rest of us have both uniquely human and beast-like goals, while Tyisha has mostly beast-like goals. The full analysis of this discussion in Chapter 4 will show, however, that the teachers and students are not simply teasing. By this point in the year they habitually exclude Tyisha and identify her as less promising than other students. When they identify Tyisha as a beast in this example, they reinforce her social identity as an outcast in the classroom.

These brief segments by themselves did not establish anything definite about Tyisha and Maurice's social identities, nor did they allow students to learn key concepts from the curriculum. But the detailed analyses in Chapters 4 and 5 will show that, together with other discussions, the examples of Tyisha and Maurice as beasts did contribute both to identifying these two students socially and to helping some students learn about the curriculum. Over several months, both Tyisha and Maurice were themselves identified as "beasts" of a sort – as students excluded from the core group of cooperative students and considered less likely to succeed in school. Over several months students also learned about the curricular issue of what "beasts" or social outcasts are, and about how different intellectual traditions have conceived the appropriate relation between individuals and society.

The examples of Tyisha and Maurice as beasts contributed both to social identification and to academic learning. Students and teachers used the examples to reinforce Tyisha and Maurice's social identities as outcasts in the classroom. At the same time, they used the examples to explore and ultimately to learn something about Aristotle's distinction between humans and beasts. These examples show how both processes can go on simultaneously in classrooms. The rest of the book looks in detail at Tyisha, Maurice, their teachers and their classmates over an academic year, in order to explore how these students' social identities overlap with the subject matter they learned. To frame the problem initially, it will be easier to conceive of separate processes – social identification and academic learning – that occur simultaneously and interconnect. As the book proceeds, however, I will argue that it is more productive to reconstrue social identification and academic learning as inseparable parts of more general processes.

Chapters 4 and 5 trace the identity development of Tyisha and Maurice in Mrs. Bailey and Mr. Smith's classroom over the academic year. The analyses show how both students were sometimes identified as "beasts" or outcasts in the classroom. It took many events of identification, across several months. But eventually Tyisha was routinely identified as a disruptive outcast, as someone who had rejected the teachers' authority and who had given up on the promised benefits of schooling. Maurice also came to be identified – although only sometimes, and only partially – as an outcast who refused to join the teachers and the cooperative students in their academic community. Thus Tyisha and Maurice *enacted* the analogy between their hypothetical behavior in the examples and Aristotle's account of society. In the classroom itself these two students were identified as beasts who allegedly refused to follow the rules of classroom "society."

Based on this brief sketch of Tyisha and Maurice's emerging identities, it may look as if they were being stereotyped based on their race. Both were African American students in an urban public school classroom at the end of the twntieth century. Although teachers and students did not use these terms, Tyisha became in some respects like the "loud black girls," and Maurice became in some respects like the "resistant black males" described by Signithia Fordham and others (1996; Anderson, 1999; Fordham and Ogbu, 1986). In the examples of Tyisha and Maurice as beasts on January 24, teachers and students did in fact draw on widely circulating models of identity that involve race – models that label some African American students as more likely to reject mainstream institutions like school – as they identified these two students as outcasts. But we will see that these racial models do not by themselves explain what happened to Tyisha and Maurice. These widely circulating sociohistorical models only contributed to the students' social identities as they were mediated through more specific local models of identity.

Denaturalizing Models of Identity

By "model of identity" I mean either an explicit account of what some people are like, or a tacit account that analysts can infer based on people's systematic behavior toward others. Models of identity develop historically. "Loud black girls," "resistant black males" and "disruptive students" can be intelligibly used as categories of identity only by some groups of people at specific sociohistorical moments. Hacking (1990) describes how such models and categories of identity emerge over decades and centuries.

During the nineteenth century in Europe, for instance, it became possible to conceive of people as "normal" and "deviant" in new ways. As the concept of probability emerged and was applied to people, it became routine to classify individuals as normal or deviant along various dimensions. Bureaucracies arose to gather and tabulate statistics on different types of people – focusing especially on deviance like suicide, crime and prostitution – and it became natural to categorize some people as deviant in ways that had not been possible earlier. Before the concept of probability was developed, there had been "human nature," and aberrations from it, but not normals and deviants along bureaucratically and scientifically established dimensions. Afterwards, both laypersons and experts had available what Hacking calls new "human kinds," new models of identity to apply to each other. Hacking argues that societies "make up people" as they develop models, categories and technologies for social identification.

Foucault (1966/1971; 1975/1977) offers a similar analysis, in some respects, showing how models of identity and institutionalized practices of identification developed over the last few centuries in Europe. He traces a larger historical shift – from identifying people based on their behaviors to classifying and disciplining them according to their mental and spiritual dispositions – and he describes how institutionalized technologies for classification developed, first in the church and then in government. He shows how schools, for instance, developed elaborate classifications of students as promising, normal, resistant, impaired and the like – classifications that have been institutionalized in grading practices, in disciplinary procedures, in the spatial arrangement of students in classrooms and through other techniques. He also describes how the social sciences have been crucial in developing classifications of identity that bureaucrats employ and that laypeople apply to themselves and others. Foucault would agree with Hacking that, after this historical shift, we are able to identify deviants in ways that had not been possible before. Foucault adds a more detailed and more menacing account of the practices of surveillance through which institutions and people now monitor themselves and others for deviance.

By providing compelling historical accounts of how models of identity emerge over decades and centuries, Hacking and Foucault denaturalize what seem to be inevitable ways of identifying people. Of course, it seems to us, there are deviants. Surely all societies have had people exhibiting non-normative desires, behaviors and attitudes. But Hacking and Foucault show how, although there may always have been people we would call deviants, those in other places and times have identified such people using very different models of personhood. There has not always been a concept of the human "norm," defined in probabilistic terms. There have not always been bureaucracies and social sciences to provide categories for sorting individuals and pathologizing some of them. There have not always been processes of surveillance, in which institutions and individuals make visible the normativity or deviance of their behavior.

I will pursue Hacking and Foucault's denaturalizing argument further than they do. Models of identity are contingent not only at the level of sociohistorical epochs, but also at more local levels. We must explore the local "spaces" (Blommaert, Collins, and Slembrouck, 2004) and shorter "timescales" (Lemke, 2000) in which widespread practices and categories get contextualized. Although Hacking and Foucault acknowledge that models of identity are not uniformly applied across contexts, their analyses present contemporary European-influenced society as if we have now adopted the models of identity that they describe. They do describe widespread ways of thinking and acting, of course, ones that are becoming even more widespread through media and other globalizing technologies. But, as Agha (in press) argues, models of identity always have a "social domain." Models of identity spread over time and space, through many types of events, but even the most widespread are only used by a particular subset of people in a given and time place. Furthermore, models of identity change as they move across time and space, and they are applied in contingent, sometimes unpredictable ways in actual events of identification.

Just as Hacking and Foucault show that apparently natural models of identity in fact emerge historically, over decades and centuries, I will show how apparently widespread sociohistorical models of identity vary as specific versions emerge locally. There is not one model of "loud black girl" and "resistant black male" in the contemporary United States that recurs in the same form across contexts. It does not suffice to argue simply that Tyisha and Maurice were identified as typical black girls and boys. Other African American students in the classroom did not get identified as outcasts, and Tyisha and Maurice did not fit the typical models in important respects. In order to provide a more adequate analysis, we must investigate empirically how a model of identity can take distinctive form in local contexts and how that locally inflected model is applied to individuals in specific ways. To apply sociohistorical models of identity uncritically, as if they "naturally" have the same form across contexts, would fail to explain how social identification actually happens in context.

Timescales of Identification

Lemke's (2000) concept of "timescales" helps clarify the relation between widely circulating models of identity, like those described by Hacking and Foucault, and the versions of these models that occur in local contexts like Mrs. Bailey and Mr. Smith's classroom over an academic year. Processes relevant to understanding meaningful human action take place across various characteristic time intervals – from the milliseconds required for neuromuscular activity, to the seconds required for ritualized interactional coordination, to the days or months required for group consensus-building, to the years required for the development of neuroses, to the centuries sometimes required for transformation in socioeconomic systems. Social scientists often represent these as different levels of explanation and argue that different phenomena can be explained at different levels. Lemke presents an alternative approach. He argues that any phenomenon is constrained and made possible by processes at several disparate timescales.

To understand how Tyisha was ultimately identified as a disruptive outcast in Mrs. Bailey and Mr. Smith's classroom, for example, we need to explore "cross-timescale relations" – the set of linked processes across several timescales that collectively explain how this phenomenon occured. As I argue in more detail in Chapter 4, it will not suffice simply to argue that she is an African American girl who was tarred with the longer timescale stereotype of being a "loud black girl." Her social identification as a beast, in the example of Tyisha and her cat, did happen only as teachers and students presuppose longer timescale models associated with her race and gender. But these longer timescale models were mediated through and changed by processes at shorter timescales.

As has been described by Garfinkel (1967), Rampton (1999), Schegloff (1988) and many others, widely circulating sociohistorical models of identity only take effect as they are successfully applied in events of identification. The application of such a category in practice is a contingent accomplishment that can misfire or take unexpected form. Analyzing Tyisha's social identification thus requires both attention to sociohistorically emergent categories of identity and interactionally emergent applications of these categories in events of identification. But I argue that, as illustrated by the cases of Tyisha and Maurice, we must attend to *other* timescales *beyond* sociohistorical and event-level emergence. In this case, we must also study how *local* categories of identity emerge in the classroom over the academic year.

In order to analyze the social identification and academic learning that occured in Mrs. Bailey and Mr. Smith's classroom over the academic year, we must attend to a months-long timescale across which classroom-specific habitual patterns of social identification and academic learning developed. Teachers and students developed local models of identity and habitually apply these to students like Tyisha and Maurice over the academic year. They also developed local models of curricular topics and used these as they worked to understand the subject matter. "Disruptive outcast," for instance, meant something particular to these teachers and students because they developed a local model of this identity that drew on their own experiences and discussions. This local model was constrained by longer timescale processes, but it cannot be fully predicted from those longer timescale processes. The local model was also constituted by shorter timescale processes, like the use of certain categories to identify Tyisha or

Maurice in particular classroom discussions. The local model emerged from but cannot be reduced to event-level processes.

Hacking and Foucault demonstrate the historical contingency and trace the emergence of models of identity across decades and centuries. Similarly, I will show the contingency and emergence of models of identity in local contexts like this one classroom over several months. Tyisha was not simply a loud black girl and Maurice was not simply a resistant black male. The analyses in Chapters 4 and 5 show them getting identified as somewhat familiar and somewhat peculiar versions of these categories. The social identification that actually happened to Tyisha and Maurice in this classroom cannot be understood without attending to contingent models of identity local to this classroom, because these local models emerged from but partly transformed more widely circulating models. Students and teachers could not have developed the local models they did without using sociohistorical models as resources. But they used these resources to build context-specific local models.

The social identification of students like Tyisha and Maurice, then, depends on contingent models of identity that emerge historically, locally and interactionally. Models of identity emerge at all three timescales (and across other timescales as well), and adequate empirical analyses will trace the emergence and reveal the contingent character of models at each timescale. My analyses in this book attend to emerging local models in particular, because of the central role these models play in explaining students' social identification in this classroom. I also attend to the contingent use of both sociohistorical and local models of identity within minutes-long events. Thus I analyze the interplay of emerging local models and the contingent events in which these and other models are used and sometimes transformed. I do not trace the emergence of sociohistorical models of identity like "resistant black male" across decades, although such models have emerged historically. One analysis cannot document all relevant timescales. I rely instead on others' descriptions of how these sociohistorical models have developed and are commonly used in contemporary America.

Close attention to the local timescale in this case also makes visible the intertwining of social identification and academic learning. By tracing the distinctive local models of identity that emerged in this classroom, as these teachers and students talked to each other over several months, we can see overlaps between social identification and academic learning that would not be visible if we attended only to isolated events or to more widely circulating sociohistorical models. Processes at other timescales played an important role in both social identification and academic learning in this classroom, and I attend to some of these processes in the analyses below. But I focus on the local timescale of these teachers' and students' interactions over an academic year, because this makes visible a distinctive way in which subject matter, argument, evidence and academic learning intertwine with social identification, power relations and interpersonal struggles in classrooms.

In addition to attending to models of identity that developed locally in Mrs. Bailey and Mr. Smith's classroom, the analyses in this book also attend to the trajectories of identification traveled by particular individuals across the academic year. Just as attention to the local timescale shows how apparently uniform sociohistorical models of identity can take on unexpected, context-specific forms as they are applied locally, attention to the social identification of individuals across events shows how both sociohistorical and local models of identity can be applied to individuals in distinctive ways. In other words, there are two relevant processes happening at the local timescale in Mrs. Bailey and Mr. Smith's classroom. Local versions of the "outcast" and "disruptive outcast" identities emerged over the academic year, as teachers and students transformed sociohistorical models and constructed distinctive local models of identity. At the same time, Tyisha and Maurice developed their own specific identities over several months in the classroom and these identities were not fully predictable from the local models. The local models of identity were shaped in part by the presence of Tyisha and Maurice as instances of them, and Tyisha and Maurice's social identities took on their particular form in part because of the local models that the class happened to be developing. But Tyisha and Maurice did not become canonical instances of the local models. In fact, they both violated central tenets of those local models. In order to understand the emergence of the local models, we must attend both to the locally typical identities attributed to students and teachers over the year and to the distinctive identities of Tyisha and Maurice. By attending both to emerging local models of identity and to how teachers and students applied these models in unique ways to Tyisha and Maurice as individuals, we will be able to explore one way in which social identification and academic learning can become inextricable.

LOCAL POWER/KNOWLEDGE

When we look at the local models of identity that developed in this classroom over the year and at the distinctive individual trajectories of identification traveled by Tyisha and Maurice, two things come into view. First, the social identification of these two students was non-normative in more than one way. It was not predictable from more widely circulating sociohistorical models of identity, although it drew on them. It was also not predictable from local models of identity that emerged in this classroom, although it drew on these as well. The non-normative, contingent character of the social identities actually inhabited by students in this classroom was complex – drawing on familiar models in some respects, but sometimes employing them in unusual ways. By attending to local timescales and to individual trajectories, we can see empirically how social identification actually unfolded in practice and we can generate a more nuanced account of how processes at different timescales contributed to students' emerging social identities.

Second, attention to local models and individual trajectories also makes visible how heterogeneous resources contribute to both social identification and academic learning. Social scientists and educators often assume that apparently non-academic resources like practices of social exclusion and xenophobic stereotypes are relevant to social identification, while assuming that academic resources such as students' background knowledge about curricular topics are relevant to academic learning. By looking closely at the local timescale in Mrs. Bailey and Mr. Smith's classroom, we will see that academic resources can be deeply implicated in social identification and that apparently non-academic resources can be deeply implicated in academic learning. Social identification and academic learning both depend on contingent, heterogeneous sets of resources, and the relevant sets of resources will vary across cases. To understand how students actually get identified and learn in classrooms, we must look across the typically segregated processes of social identification and academic learning and analyze how academic and non-academic resources can play essential roles in both processes. When the same resources contribute both to social identification and to academic learning, as they do in this case, the two processes deeply depend on each other.

Beyond Dualism

But we tend to resist seeing such interconnections, "purifying," as Latour (1993) says, the apparently non-academic and apparently purely cognitive realms. Despite the fact that social identification and academic learning can deeply interrelate, we tend to construe them as separate processes. Even though teachers and students might have taken advantage of the academic example of Tyisha as a beast to pursue their ongoing social identification of her as an outcast and an unpromising student, we normally think that Tyisha's emerging social identity as an outcast from the core group took shape apart from students' understandings of the curriculum. We normally think that students' emerging understandings of the curriculum – although they may be interrupted or occasionally facilitated by the social identification of students – generally take shape independent of students' social identities. After all, Tyisha could have been socially identified as an outcast even if they had been discussing a radically different curriculum, and students could have learned about the curriculum even if Tyisha and Maurice were not in the class. Social identification and academic learning may occur at the same time and through the same talk, but they seem essentially separate processes.

Why do we normally think of these two processes as separate? Latour (1993; 1999) and others argue that we are influenced by an unrealistic conception of knowledge, dating back to the Enlightenment, in which true knowledge is grasped by the individual mind as objective and certain. According to this conception, knowledge must be purged of all connections to social identities, power relations and subjective biases. Aristotle had a view of human nature, independent of what we might think of that view and how it might serve our purposes. If social identification and academic learning are mixed together, our interpretation of Aristotle might be polluted with our personal and political biases. The knowledge we aim to teach in school must be separated from subjective factors associated with our selves and our politics, the argument goes, and thus we should not mix together social identification and academic learning. Advocates of this conception acknowledge that social identification and learning sometimes go on simultaneously. Energetic social identification in a classroom may also block learning by distracting teachers and students,. But genuine learning must be analyzed as the purely intellectual process it is. Whatever their social identities may have been, students either developed representations that reflect Aristotle's views or they did not. Analyses of academic learning in this classroom must bracket any social identification that may have occurred and focus on academic processes alone.

Despite the power and ubiquity of this sharp distinction between social and subjective "pollutants" and objective knowledge, many philosophers and social scientists have argued against the Enlightenment conception of knowledge (e.g., Bickhard, 1993; Cavell, 1979; Haraway, 1991; Latour, 1999; Putnam, 1998). Some have focused on language. From an Enlightenment standpoint, language stands apart from and represents the world. "Ordinary language philosophy," from Wittgenstein (1953) and Austin (1956/1975) to Cavell (1979), explores how language gets used as part of social activity in the world. These philosophers break down the distance between language and the world by describing the immediacy of relations between words and world, as words are used in ordinary contexts. They show how everyday actors cannot, do not need to and would not want to establish definite, fixed relations between their words and the world. The words and representations involved in knowing are intertwined with practical activities in ways that allow ordinary people to go on unproblematically with everyday life. Only philosophers craving disembodiment could overlook the smooth function of everyday knowledge and yearn for the inhuman purity of objective knowledge.

Such alternatives to the Enlightenment view argue against what Bickhard (1980; 1993) labels "encodingism:" the picture of knowledge as a set of representations that encode a world that is separate from those representations. The alternatives also argue against classic oppositions like subjects/objects and humans/nature, which split the knowing subject from the known world (Haraway, 1991). Instead of splitting the knower from the world, we must embed the knower in the social and natural world. Bickhard's (1993) "interactivism" does this. In his account, representations emerge only within goal-directed action, within organism/environment relations. People learn as part of the same activities through which they act in the world, while performing social actions like identification. The resulting knowledge should not be extracted from activity and assessed objectively, if that means purged of all connections to the world. Knowledge exists only in activities, and it is only Enlightenment yearning for purity that drives us to epistemological anxiety. As Putnam (1998) puts it, body, mind and world are "braided" together, such that knowledge functions only through interactions among these intertwined components in practice. Such alternatives to the Enlightenment view of knowledge do not deny that people learn about the world. They argue that knowledge of the world does not involve a lone, disembodied thinker whose representations either correspond to the world or do not (Shweder, 1991).

Many alternatives to the Enlightenment view acknowledge that social identities and power relations play an important role in human cognitive life. Human activities, including academic and cognitive ones, both presuppose and create social identities. As Latour (1999) shows, if we trace the processes relevant to the development, validation and use of scientific knowledge – a type of knowledge typically considered "pure" – we quickly discover that social identities, institutional arrangements and power relations are bound up with that knowledge. In order to understand how people learn and use the resulting knowledge, we must explore how scientific learning and knowledge are intertwined with social identities and power relations in the world. Conversely, in order to understand how people get socially identified, we must explore how identities are bound up with and constrained by insights into the real world. But the involvement of social identity in cognitive practices like science does not undermine actors' claims to know things – if we conceive of knowledge as functioning in the social world as opposed to standing apart from it.

Power/Knowledge

Philosophers have provided abstract conceptualizations of how the mind and the world might be "braided," in Putnam's (1998) terms, but it has required empirical work by social scientists to describe more precisely how this braiding works. Many social scientific attempts to move beyond the Enlightenment conception of knowledge proceed from an alternative conception of human nature. Instead of a disembodied mind – or, in the philosophers' favored image, a "brain in a vat" independently cogitating about the world – many have proposed that human minds are essentially social (e.g., Bateson, 1972; Cole, 1996; Geertz, 1973; Tomasello, 1999; Vygotsky, 1934/1987). Humans differ from animals largely because of our ability to pass down increasingly complex tool use from generation to generation (Tomasello, 1999). At birth and throughout life we are dependent on others to provide us with physical and cognitive tools that we use to survive in and represent the world. By nature, then, humans are sociocultural. Without the tools provided to us by other members of our group, we would not be human – we would not speak or engage in sociocultural practices. Both our cognitive and social lives depend on tools we appropriate from others, and these tools help bind together mind, body, social practice and physical world.

By exploring how people actually use sociocultural tools in practice, social scientists have given empirical accounts of how processes like social identification and academic learning intertwine. Foucault (1966/1971; 1975/1977), for instance, describes how the development of demographic and other social scientific categories simultaneously afforded new forms of knowledge and new forms of power. Foucault traces how educational institutions, as one example, developed extensive taxonomies and practices for classifying students – with respect to their ability levels, special needs, attentiveness, obedience and so on. These systems of classification facilitated knowledge of students that was impossible without such taxonomies, by making visible new types of people. Educators could subsequently know what kinds of students they had and how these students were likely to behave, in ways that had been unavailable to them before.

Foucault shows how the acts of classification that these categories made possible simultaneously involve academic and bureaucratic cognition as well as social identification and the exercise of power. By virtue of separating off and making visible categories of "special needs," "gifted" and other types of students, for instance, the new systems of classification allowed educators to identify and enact surveillance over students in ways that had not been possible before. This surveillance is a kind of power according to Foucault because it allows institutions and individuals to label and normalize people's behavior. Events of classification – examining students, deciding which academic sections students will attend, labeling students as disruptive or not – make visible the kind of person a student is seen as and allow the institution to treat him or her accordingly. Foucault (1975/1977; 1994/2000) has a distinctive theory of power. It is not possessed by individuals, but acts on and through people as it circulates through social relationships. Whether we use Foucault's account of power or not, however, he makes a convincing case that the elaborate systems of social classification that developed over the last two centuries in Europe accomplish both academic and bureaucratic cognition as well as social identification and power relations.

Foucault does not argue that these systems of classification play one role in the academic/bureaucratic processes of sorting people and another role in the social processes of identifying and exerting power over people. He claims that any act of classification *simultaneously* involves knowledge and power. When we develop or implement a category for classifying people, we both understand them in a new way and we engage in a power relationship. The social act of regimenting their identities within a system of social value – of making both the subjects of our classification and others attend to the "normal" or "deviant" categories that they occupy – is *the same act* as the cognitive one of knowing them as a certain kind of person. The cognitive effect of the classification depends on making visible and normalizing their identity within a taxonomy, and this process of making visible is both a matter of cognition and power. Social classification is inextricably both the development of cognitive representations and the exertion of power.

The process of social classification illustrates how the development and use of a tool can knit together mental, bodily, social and physical aspects in one integrated practice. When Europeans began implementing more elaborate bureaucratic systems of social classification a few centuries ago, they developed tools that changed how people thought about themselves and others (by, for instance, distinguishing between "disruptive" and "gifted" students), tools that changed how people oriented and disciplined their bodies (by, for instance, making some students stand in the corner or do repetitive tasks) and tools that changed how people used physical objects and space to create and reinforce classifications (by, for instance, having different types of students sit in different places in the classroom). By tracing the power and knowledge involved in social classification, as classificatory practices developed in prisons, schools and other institutions in Europe, Foucault explores empirically how knowledge and social identification mesh in one important set of practices.

Foucault's translators use the term "power/knowledge" to capture the inextricability of social and cognitive processes in practices like social classification. Many acts of power are simultaneously and inextricably cognitive acts, and vice versa. The title of this chapter self-consciously echoes Foucault's term because the book shows how "self/knowledge" implies a similar sort of inextricability as the one Foucault describes with "power/knowledge." In Mrs. Bailey and Mr. Smith's classroom, many acts of academic learning were simultaneously acts of social identification and many acts of social identification were simultaneously acts of academic learning. As the teachers and students discussed Tyisha and Maurice as "beasts," they simultaneously identified Tyisha and Maurice and learned about Aristotle. The process of students becoming socially recognizable "selves" and the process of their learning the "knowledge" of the curriculum intertwined across the academic year in this classroom. At least in this case, the processes of social identification and academic learning were not even analytically separable, because the same acts simultaneously constituted both social identities and academic knowledge.

With the term "self/knowledge," however, I use the risky term "self." People often use "self" to refer to more private aspects of a person than I intend here. Sapir (1934b/1949) distinguishes between five selves: physical, physiological, psychophysical, sociological and psychiatric. Different types of analyses will be required to illuminate these various types of self, because different sets of interrelated processes typically account for these five types of consistent individual functioning. In this book, I address only the sociological self, or processes of "social identification." I do not deny the existence of individual-level physical, neurocognitive and unconscious processes. But I am interested in the intertwining between social identification and academic learning, and one book can examine only part of what happens when students are identified in classrooms. "Social identity/academic knowledge" might have been a more accurate title for the chapter, but "self/knowledge" preserves the analogy to Foucault and is more compact and suggestive.

Classroom Self/Knowledge

Foucault describes how social identification and cognitive classification intertwine through a set of practices involving the creation and use of taxonomies for classifying people. Social classification of the sort Foucault describes certainly occurred in Mrs. Bailey and Mr. Smith's classroom. Like Foucault, I will take a social scientific approach and describe empirically how social identification and academic learning mesh in practice. However, I will attend to a different mechanism than Foucault. Foucault describes taxonomies and practices of classification that develop over decades and centuries. I will describe how intertwining happens through models of personhood that develop over minutes, days and months. By looking at the local timescale, across several months in Mrs. Bailey and Mr. Smith's classroom, we will see how social identification and academic learning became as inextricable as "power/knowledge" does for Foucault. Teachers and students drew on and integrated both academic and social resources as they developed models of "self/knowledge," models that simultaneously helped identify individual students and helped students learn the curriculum. Chapter 4 will show in detail how teachers and students develop a local model of identity that both served to help them identify Tyisha and to construe one theme from the curriculum. Chapter 5 will show how the same thing happened with respect to Maurice and a second curricular theme. The empirical analyses in this book show how Foucault's insights about power/knowledge can be applied productively to the local timescale. The mechanisms are different, but social identification and academic learning overlapped just as robustly in Mrs. Bailey and Mr. Smith's classroom as power and knowledge overlap in Foucault's analyses of social classification.

Classrooms are strange social spaces, in part because of the discontinuity in relationships from year to year. Especially when starting their first year at a school, as happens with most American ninth graders, teachers and students do not know many of the others in the classroom. Thus, early in the year, teachers and students are often not sure how to identify individuals or what to expect about their academic knowledge. Because they lack more specific information about individuals, teachers and students must draw on more widely circulating models to interpret each other's behavior. Classroom identities early in the year are constrained by widely circulating presuppositions, like the institutionalized distinction between teachers and students and stereotypes about gender, ethnicity, style of dress, "disruptive" students and so on. But these widely circulating categories can be applied in various ways to particular individuals, as I argued above. Early in an academic year, students and teachers have more flexibility in identifying themselves and others, and there is more play in deciding how to implement sociohistorical categories of identity in context.

In other words, as the year begins teachers and students have not yet established local models of identity that include classroom-specific versions of available identities, nor have they developed robust models of many individuals' identities. As the academic year proceeds, teachers and students develop more robust local models of identity. These emerging local models are influenced both by longer timescale presuppositions about types of people and by particular events in which students have participated and been identified. If a student regularly raises his or her hand, answers teachers' questions and scoffs at others for refusing to answer, teachers and students might identify him or her more consistently as a "brown-noser" or a "cooperative student." Local identities almost always exceed more widely circulating expectations by being more specific and contextualized. Sometimes, as in the cases of Tyisha and Maurice, local identities are unexpected variations of both local and sociohistorical stereotypes.

As local models of identity and particular individuals' local identities develop over weeks and months, they relate differently to both longer and shorter timescale processes. Early in the year, more widely circulating sociohistorical models generally play an important role in establishing people's identities. Within particular events, teachers and students construct senses of who individuals are by presupposing and inflecting widely circulating categories. As local models of identity and individuals' identities solidify in their own right, over weeks and months, these become more important in mediating longer timescale processes. Instead of a widely circulating presupposition more directly constraining how teachers and students identify someone in an event, and instead of each event being a relatively autonomous arena for the construction of identities, as the academic year proceeds both sociohistorical models and the meaning of particular behaviors are increasingly mediated through robust local expectations.

Mrs. Bailey, Mr. Smith and the students, for instance, developed a robust local model of gender – put crudely, that girls are smart and promising while boys are unintelligent and unpromising (Chapter 2 provides a detailed account). This drew on some widely circulating assumptions about gender, but it contradicted others. Once this local model was established, it mediated how longer timescale processes took effect in this classroom, skewing them more toward the local model and screening out conflicting models of gender that might have applied to a given event. Whereas a particular event would make sense early in the year only as teachers and students drew on sociohistorical models that they shared, later in the year they could draw on robust local models to make sense of that event. As local models solidified, they also became more important in constraining shorter timescale processes. Even robust local models of identity only take effect in actual events, of course. Local models exist only as speakers presuppose them in practice, and local expectations can be ignored or modified in the context of actual events, but emerging local models often provide an important resource for social identification in practice.

This book shows in detail how such local models can play an important role not only in the social identification of students over time, but also in facilitating systematic overlap between social identification and academic learning. Academic and non-academic processes can mesh as emerging local models of identity play crucial roles both in identifying individual students and in students' emerging understandings of the curriculum. Resources from other timescales also play crucial roles in facilitating both social identification and academic learning. But the analyses of Tyisha and Maurice will show how systematic overlap between these two processes can depend on local models that emerge jointly through academic and social processes. When students and teachers create and use these local models, they engage in a hybrid activity that involves "self/knowledge."

Academic learning in the classroom generally depends on local cognitive models. Longer timescale cognitive models and tools initially play an important role in making sense of particular texts and events. Early in the year, teachers and students in most classrooms have to draw on and manipulate more widely circulating background knowledge that they share. As they work together over weeks and months, however, teachers and students often develop local cognitive models of curricular topics, and they use these to make sense of particular texts. Local understandings come to mediate their use of longer timescale resources, as teachers and students use robust local models of curricular topics to make sense of texts and to build their understanding of the subject matter. As described in Chapter 3, for instance, Mrs. Bailey, Mr. Smith and their students developed a local cognitive model of the relationship between individuals and

society that took social welfare as a key example. Henceforth, their understanding of curricular issues concerning individualism and collectivism,
and their interpretations of texts about these topics, were generally mediated through their local understandings of how a society should handle
social welfare programs. Thus local cognitive models can play an increasingly important role over the year, just as local models of identity do. The
analyses in this book will show how local cognitive models can systematically overlap with local models of identity, such that the processes of social
identification and academic learning mesh.

Of course, more than three timescales (sociohistorical, local and event)
are relevant to analyzing social identification and academic learning in a
classroom. The local level, for instance, would require finer distinctions to
capture the processes described in later chapters. As shown Chapter 2, the
robust local model of "promising girls and unpromising boys" developed
early and stayed consistent for the rest of the academic year. As described in
Chapter 4, however, Tyisha developed at least three local identities across
the year, one of which was eclipsed after two months and two others that
emerged and changed over periods of several months. It can be useful to
schematize classroom social identification and learning using three idealized timescales, but in fact relevant processes may be occurring across a
broad range of timescales. Specific phenomena will be best explained using
different configurations of relevant timescales. In some cases, decades-old
racial and gender stereotypes will be applied to individuals without much
local inflection, while in others, weeks-long local models will emerge and
change several times, transforming the impact of decades-long stereotypes.
The most productive configuration of timescales for analysis will differ
from case to case and must be determined for each setting and each phenomenon of interest.

I have been arguing, and the rest of the book will show, that social identification and academic learning can mesh at the local timescale across the
academic year. In general, there is some overlap between social identification and academic learning at many timescales. For instance, longer
timescale processes involving social identification and academic learning
intertwine in various ways. Categories used in enduring normative models
of society favor certain categories of identity. A society that understands
itself as composed of individuals competing with each other in a market that benefits all, for instance, may apply categories of social classification like "productive" and "unproductive" to people. Empirical studies of
such longer timescale intertwining between social identification and aca-
demic/bureaucratic practices would draw on historical and institutional
data, as Foucault (1975/1977), Popkewitz (2004) and others have done.
Such work is beyond the scope of this book. In the analyses below I note
how models from longer timescales constrained both social identification
and academic learning in Mrs. Bailey and Mr. Smith's classroom. But I
have not done the historical analyses necessary to show either how these

sociohistorical models emerge or how such models may facilitate overlap between social identification and academic practices at a timescale of decades or centuries.

Instead, this book analyzes how social identification and academic learning can also overlap systematically at the local level. As mentioned earlier, and as described extensively in later chapters (especially Chapter 3), local models of social identity and local models of the curriculum that developed in Mrs. Bailey and Mr. Smith's classroom shared several central categories. As they developed local models to identify themselves and others, students and teachers integrated academic concepts into these models of identity. As they developed local cognitive models to make sense of the curriculum, students and teachers integrated relevant categories of identity into their cognitive models. In fact, teachers and students did not develop one set of local models to accomplish social identification and another set to accomplish academic learning. Social identification and academic learning in this classroom drew on many of the same categories and depended on hybrid, overlapping models to accomplish both ends. The trajectory of their academic learning was shaped by models of some participants' identities, as aspects of these models opened up possibilities for understanding the curriculum in new ways. And the trajectory of some students' social identification was shaped by local models of the curriculum, as these models made available categories of identity that were applied to the students themselves.

Personalized Pedagogy

Subsequent chapters show how this overlap between local cognitive models and local models of identity depended in part on the "experience-near" or "personalized" pedagogy that Mrs. Bailey and Mr. Smith often used. These teachers often explored students' own experiences in order to help them understand the curriculum, by constructing examples from personal experience and building analogies between curricular topics and the classroom itself. In discussing Aristotle's *Politics* and other texts, for instance, the teachers and students explored a curricular theme about individualism and collectivism. This theme involved a fundamental question: whether individuals should limit their desires for the good of the group or whether society should facilitate individual autonomy. As they built local models of the curriculum to help them understand texts that take different positions on this question, teachers and students often used their own classroom as an example of a miniature society. Instead of asking how society in general should deal with questions about individual autonomy and the public good, they asked whether their own class should offer more autonomy or demand more sacrifice for the common good. The cognitive models of the curriculum that resulted from this analogy included categories of identity like "beasts" or disruptive outcasts who refuse to sacrifice for the good of the whole class and "cooperative" students who contribute productively to classroom discussion. At the same time that teachers and students were developing these cognitive models of the curriculum, using the analogy between their classroom and society in general, they were also constructing local models of identity and applying these to individual students and teachers. When a category like "beast" or outcast became available in their discussions of the curriculum, teachers and students sometimes applied it to students like Tyisha and Maurice during experience-near teaching. When they did this consistently, they inserted the curricular category into emerging local models that they were using to identify Tyisha and Maurice.

As more concepts like this were shared between local cognitive and social models, the analogy between the curricular topic and identities in the classroom became more robust. As shown in Chapter 4, Tyisha was regularly identified as a disruptive outcast through the same discussions in which students and teachers discussed Aristotle's and other conceptions of individuals who do not cooperate with society. As shown in Chapter 5, Maurice was regularly identified as caught between the "resistant" boys and the "cooperative" girls, at the same time as the class discussed whether citizens can legitimately resist those in power. Across the year, local models that teachers and students used to identify Tyisha and Maurice overlapped systematically with local models that they used to understand the curriculum. Thus social identification and academic learning became interdependent, as the local models that facilitated each process were woven together. This meshing was facilitated by the teachers' personalized pedagogy and by their use of students themselves as examples of curricular concepts.

The analogies between curricular topics and students' own identities in the classroom were particularly important to the meshing of social identification and academic learning in this classroom. These analogies were constructed through events of classroom discussion that occurred at a timescale of minutes – and especially through a type of event that I have called "participant examples" (Wortham, 1994). In a participant example, someone participating in the event of giving an example also becomes a character in the example. The examples of Tyisha and Maurice as beasts were both participant examples because the students themselves became examples of a beast. Participant examples sometimes propose or reinforce analogies between the social organization of the classroom and the topic being discussed. In the case of Maurice the beast, for instance, Mrs. Bailey separated Maurice off "in the woods" from "the rest of us" going about "our" business in the classroom.

Participant examples can facilitate overlap between emerging local models of the curriculum and emerging local models of identity because they apply the same categories of identity to the curriculum and to the participants included in the example. With the example of Tyisha and her cat, for instance, Mrs. Bailey both identified Tyisha herself as potentially a "beast" and helped students understand Aristotle's view of human nature. Thus she helped cement the category of "beast" or outcast into the emerging local model that teachers and students used both to identify Tyisha and to understand curricular questions about the relations between an individual and society.

As I have shown in previous work (Wortham, 1994; 1997; 2001b), participant examples often involve both social identification and academic learning. These examples can be useful tools to help students understand the curriculum because they apply familiar models and concepts to new subject matter. They can also be powerful devices for identifying students and teachers because they allow evaluative comments about participants who become characters in the example under the guise of discussing the example. In some cases, like the examples of Tyisha and Maurice as beasts, participant examples also connect social identification and academic learning. Because participant examples bring together the subject matter and participants themselves, teachers and students can use the same category of identity, like "beast" or "outcast," to construe the subject matter and to identify the participant with a role in the example. The analyses in Chapters 4 and 5 show how two series of participant examples, discussed on different days over several months, helped teachers and students build models of identity that they used both to understand curricular themes and to identify Tyisha and Maurice.

In previous work I have shown how single participant examples – at the minutes-long timescale of isolated events – can bring together social identification and academic learning when the examples allow teachers and students to use one model of identity that facilitates both processes (Wortham, 1994; 1997; 2001b). This earlier work on isolated classroom events has limitations, however. In order to make warranted conclusions about social identification and academic learning – processes that take place across events – I need concepts and data that allow me to follow students' identities and their academic learning across several months. This book goes beyond my earlier work by conceptualizing social identification and academic learning across events, at a local, months-long timescale. This makes visible the complex overlap between models of identity and models of the curriculum that this book analyzes in detail. It also opens up a more nuanced understanding of how apparently non-academic processes such as social identification and cognitive processes such as academic learning can become inextricable and depend on each other.

THE INEXTRICABILITY OF SOCIAL IDENTIFICATION AND ACADEMIC LEARNING

Throughout this chapter, I have moved back and forth between discussing social identification and academic learning as distinct processes that overlap, and arguing that they are inseparable parts of larger processes. Especially early in the book, I will often discuss the two as separate processes.

Chapter 2, for instance, develops an account of social identification, while Chapter 3 develops an account of academic learning. I have two reasons for analyzing the processes separately. First, in order to build up an adequate account of the integrated processes that in fact subsume social identification and learning, we first need to consider the subprocesses separately. Second, because everyday language and much social scientific research typically separate these two types of processes, it will be clearer to start with separate accounts and build to a more integrated one. Despite this initial separation of social identification and academic learning, one goal of the book is to develop a more adequate account in which the two processes cannot be separated.

I do not deny that some phenomena can be productively explained by positing a realm of relatively pure academic cognition. As Packer and Goicoechea (2000) point out, some social settings – for instance, many schools – deliberately separate cognitive contents from the bodies, identities and social positions of the people doing cognitive work. Ryle (1949) describes how educational institutions try to enforce an idealized image of "rational scientific man," acting as if "knowing that" is preferable to and purer than "knowing how." Writing about science, Latour (1993) describes the purifying practices through which we separate knowledge from the "pollutions" of context and the real world. Even the special cases of school and science do in fact contain social identification, power relations and interpersonal struggles. Nonetheless, in these special cases it may sometimes make sense to conceptualize academic learning as relatively independent of social identification and other apparently non-academic processes – especially when the phenomenon of interest involves academic cognition in a narrow sense.

However reasonable this strategy might be for some research questions, we must recognize that "pure" academic cognition is an idealization that obscures crucial and ubiquitous features of both academic and non-academic processes. Even in "purified" academic settings that aim for decontextualized knowledge, many apparently non-academic processes such as social identification nonetheless go on. Most phenomena of interest, even in academic settings, are interwoven with social identification, power relations and interpersonal struggles. To study these phenomena as if academic learning were separable from social context would be to miss important aspects of academic and scientific practices (Knorr-Cetina, 1999; Latour, 1999; Lemke, 1990). Many philosophical conceptions of human nature unwisely extrapolate humankind's central characteristics from the special case of decontextualized knowing – claiming, for instance, that logical reasoning about decontextualized problems is the mark of a human being. In order to develop a more realistic account of basic human processes, we must instead examine the more general situation in which activities like social identification, power relations and interpersonal struggles cannot be separated from subject matter, argument, evidence and academic learning. Note that I am not making the opposite mistake, claiming that academic "reason" is merely an illusion hiding the fact that human nature is all about power. We must acknowledge, instead, that neither reason nor power, neither social identification nor academic learning, exists in pure form. We must explore how both knowledge and power, both identity and learning, contribute to fundamental human processes.

Agha (in press) describes one fundamental human process that does not respect the habitual distinction between "pure" cognition and "polluting" social processes: the use of signs to establish social relations. Agha gives a general account of the creation and movement of the models through which we understand socially meaningful signs. He shows how all social relations depend on speakers' construction and circulation of mostly tacit models of personhood and relationship. And he shows how the representational function of language depends on the same general semiotic processes. Because all meaingful human activity depends on the interpretation of signs, both cognitive and sociological analyses must rely on the sorts of semiotic processes Agha describes. These general semiotic processes do not respect the boundary between power and knowledge because particular signs often depend on heterogeneous resources for their interpretation – both resources that involve representations of subject matter and ones that involve power relations and social identification. In order to understand the basic semiotic processes that underlie much of social and cognitive life, we must attend to interrelations among knowledge and power, academic learning and social identification.

Packer and Goicoechea (2000) describe another fundamental process that involves both knowledge and power: ontological learning, the process through which individuals create and transform themselves as they interact with others, sign systems and the world. Packer and Goicoechea describe how even academic learning is "ontological" and not "epistemological" because it involves changes in social being as well as changes in knowing. We are constantly and inevitably changing, even if in small ways, becoming different types of people as we learn new things. This process does not respect boundaries between the academic and the non-academic because academic learning changes who we are, and because knowledge is an integral part of the general process of ontological change.

There are other fundamental human processes, but the semiotics of social relations and ontological learning suffice to make the point. Basic human processes involve both apparently academic and apparently non-academic components, woven together into larger wholes from which "pure" components cannot be neatly excised. As humans act in the world, trying to make sense of and interact with people, objects, intellectual puzzles and other things, we interpret signs and become types of people. Semiotic activity and ontological development happen continuously, and they involve both resources that we tend to classify as cognitive and resources that we tend to classify as non-academic or non-cognitive. In most cases, these apparently different types of resources are woven together into configurations from which they cannot be abstracted if we hope to give adequate accounts of the human activity in question. Despite the fact that I begin by describing social identification and learning as apparently separate processes, then, I am working toward a more complex non-dualistic account. I intend my analysis of how social identification and academic learning participate in larger, integrated processes to illustrate how we need more complex accounts of reason and power, of identity and learning. If we rely on simple accounts of allegedly separate processes, we will fail to understand the human world.

OUTLINE OF THE BOOK

Before summarizing the contents of the book, I would briefly like to discourage premature judgments about the teachers. At some points in the analyses below, I describe Mrs. Bailey and Mr. Smith treating students in ways that seem inappropriate. Perhaps they went too far when they teased Tyisha, saying that she was in fact "like an animal," or in other cases when they explicitly called her a bad and disruptive student. I discourage quick judgments about the teachers, however, because such judgments would block adequate analyses of the data and oversimplify the complex moral judgments required to evaluate teachers' actions. It would be convenient but misleading to "explain" what happened to Tyisha and Maurice by citing the teachers' alleged prejudice, mean-spiritedness or lack of skill. Processes at several timescales played an important role in the phenomena that I will describe, and it would be poor analysis to attribute the bulk of it to some characteristic of the teachers. These were experienced teachers, using an innovative curriculum and skillfully managing a classroom. There are reasonable grounds to object to some of their actions, but I urge the reader not to let quick judgments of the teachers foreclose more nuanced analysis of the various factors in play. Chapter 6 returns to the question of the teachers' and students' responsibility for what happened to Tyisha and Maurice.

Chapter 1 has given an overview of the central argument. Teachers and students engage in social identification, power relations and interpersonal struggles that appear unrelated or even antithetical to academic learning. Instead of ignoring this fact, or erroneously concluding that academic learning is merely a front for power relations, we need more nuanced conceptual and empirical work on how apparently academic and apparently non-academic processes interrelate. This book looks closely at the social identification and academic learning that occurred in a ninth grade classroom over an academic year. By examining local models of identity that emerged over several months among these teachers and students, we will be able to see how both academic and apparently non-academic resources contributed to social identification and academic learning. The book describes in detail one way in which social identification and academic learning can mesh, focusing on local models that draw on both subject matter and students' identities. This demonstration makes it clear that social identification and academic learning should not be construed as separate processes, but instead as abstractions from more heterogeneous semiotic and ontological processes.

Chapter 2 has two sections. First, it develops an account of social identification. This account describes how social identification depends on configurations of resources drawn from several timescales. Our sense of naturally appropriate social identification is not constructed solely through socio-historical categories, event-level negotiations or local models, but through heterogeneous resources that work together. In different cases, different configurations of timescales are relevant to explaining successful social identification. Second, the chapter describes Mrs. Bailey and Mr. Smith's classroom and traces how the local model of promising girls and unpromising boys developed early in the year. This model provided important background for the development of Tyisha and Maurice's identities because each of them was the primary exception for her or his gender. Tyisha and Maurice each developed distinctive identities that were not simply aligned or simply opposed to each other, but they were nonetheless identified over time as the prototypical "unpromising girl" and "promising boy."

Chapter 3 has three sections. First, the chapter develops an account of academic learning. This account is parallel in important ways to the account of social identification developed in Chapter 2 – illustrating how the two processes might not be separable, but instead part of more general integrated processes. Second, the chapter describes Mrs. Bailey and Mr. Smith's curriculum and the students' academic learning. It introduces the teachers' pedagogical philosophy and goals. It then describes the two curricular themes that facilitated Tyisha and Maurice's emerging social identities, and it describes the local cognitive models that teachers and students developed to make sense of these themes. The chapter also gives evidence that students did in fact learn some of what the teachers intended. Third, using the accounts of social identification and academic learning developed in Chapters 2 and 3, the chapter then articulates more precisely how the two processes meshed in Mrs. Bailey and Mr. Smith's classroom.

Chapters 4 and 5 follow Tyisha and Maurice, respectively, across the academic year. By analyzing explicit statements that teachers and students made about their identities, the interactional positioning done to and by these students and many participant examples that included them as central characters, the chapters show how Tyisha and Maurice's social identities emerged and changed across the year. Each student's identity went through several phases. And each student's identity became increasingly intertwined with categories drawn from local models of the curricular themes. The analyses trace in detail the intertwining of social identification and academic learning, which occurred in its most complex form in these two cases.

Chapter 6 summarizes the argument and elaborates its implications. The empirical analyses show teachers and students developing local models of identity and using these local models, together with resources from other timescales, to establish distinctive individual trajectories of identification for Tyisha and Maurice. The importance of local timescale processes in this case illustrates how we must go beyond "macro" and "micro," beyond "structure" and "agency" in our accounts of social identification, power relations and interpersonal struggles. The empirical analyses also show how social identification and academic learning should not be construed as separate processes. We must move beyond the decontextualized thinker and beyond non-cognitive power relations as our idealized models of basic human processes. This book provides one model of how to analyze the complex interrelations between cognitive processes like academic learning and social identification, power relations and interpersonal struggles. The chapter ends by assessing the moral implications of teachers and students' actions in this classroom and by reflecting on the inevitably moral character of schooling.

2

Social Identification and Local Metapragmatic Models

In classrooms, the processes of becoming an identifiable type of person and learning the curriculum can mesh with one another. In order to analyze more precisely how this happens, we need specific accounts of social identification and academic learning. This chapter develops an account of social identification and Chapter 3 develops an account of academic learning. Drawing on these accounts, Chapter 3 goes on to describe how the two processes can be woven together, as happened in Mrs. Bailey and Mr. Smith's classroom. Chapters 4 and 5 analyze in detail how these two processes meshed over the year as Tyisha and Maurice developed their distinctive classroom identities.

This chapter first sketches a conceptual account of social identification. Resources at several timescales make essential contributions to social identification. An individual's social identity depends ultimately on phenomenally perceivable signs of identity given off in particular events. However, participants enact and interpret perceivable signs of identity only as they draw on models of identity that circulate more widely across time and space. In addition to event-level and sociohistorically circulating resources, social identification also depends on resources from intermediate timescales. In the classroom examined here, local models of identity emerged over several months and made key contributions to some students' identities. After developing this account of the heterogeneous resources that contribute to social identification, the chapter describes models of identity that crystallized in Mrs. Bailey and Mr. Smith's classroom over the academic year, focusing on the gendered categories of promising girls and unpromising boys. It then illustrates these gendered categories with respect to two students – Erika the stereotypical girl and William the stereotypical boy – tracing how their social identities emerged and solidified over time.

THE PROCESS OF SOCIAL IDENTIFICATION

Events of Identification

Individuals behave in certain ways or possess certain characteristics, and those behaviors or characteristics are interpreted by the individual and by others as signs of identity, as indications that the individual belongs to a recognized social type. We can identify people by referring to or by reacting to their characteristics and behaviors, but in either case all social identification happens in practice. Although models of identity may circulate widely across space and time, such models exist empirically only as people use them to identify themselves and others in actual events. Any account of social identification must explain how social identification gets accomplished in particular events as people react to or characterize others as having recognizable identities.

Even though countless events of social identification happen unproblematically in everyday life, it is not easy to explain how identification is accomplished. Any sign of identity can be interpreted in more than one way, and the behavior or descriptions of any individual contain many potential signs of identity that might support conflicting identifications of that individual. This complexity creates indeterminacy in social identification. Participants and observers might attend to different signs, or they might interpret the same signs differently. Given this indeterminacy, how are individuals routinely and unproblematically identified in practice? This is a deep philosophical and theoretical problem, and many have addressed it over the past half a century (e.g., Garfinkel, 1967; Silverstein, 1992; Wittgenstein, 1953).

In order to explore this problem, consider the following example from Mrs. Bailey and Mr. Smith's class. On October 9, the class was discussing creation myths. Prior to the segment below, Mrs. Bailey had claimed that myths explain universal human questions about creation, birth, death and similar experiences. Before the following segment they were discussing the role of goddesses in creation.

       T/B: okay, <u>gods</u> and <u>god</u>desses. why do we have
       goddesses?
       FST: to help um the gods create the earth.
       CAN: they know they need a woman, ah, they need a
5   woman
       T/B: they <u>need</u> a <u>wo</u>man's touch? why?
       [several students respond at once]
       FST: the basic needs, the basic needs
       T/B: well, wait a second. we don't usually hear from

10   William. come on, William? why a w̲oman's touch?
     WIL: [4 unintelligible syllables]
     FSTs: [1 second of laughter]
     T/B: does that make sense to you?
     FSTs: no.

At line 10 Mrs. Bailey singles out William, a student who will be described in detail later in this chapter. Lines 9–14 contain several signs that might be socially identifying William. For example, Mrs. Bailey says that "we don't usually hear from William." This group has been together as a class for one month, long enough for the teacher to assert that William does not often contribute to class discussion. What sort of identity is she attributing to William here?

In order to interpret this potential sign of identity, we need to know the significance of class participation. From background knowledge about the U.S. educational system in the late twentieth century, we know that many teachers valued class participation. Having observed Mrs. Bailey's classes for more than a year, I could provide substantial evidence that she and Mr. Smith valued it highly. So from the teachers' point of view, at least at first glance, Mrs. Bailey's "we don't usually hear from William" seems to identify him as inappropriately silent. The teachers might attribute more specific identities to William because of his inappropriate silence. He might be unintelligent, shy, resistant or various other possibilities.

"We don't usually hear from William" might be identifying him more positively, however. His silence might be valued by someone who considers the U.S. school system an instrument of racial or economic domination. Willis (1977), for instance, portrays some male working-class students' "oppositional" behavior as rational and even admirable. They recognize that the socioeconomic system is rigged against them, and they refuse to play along with the sham of meritocracy. In resisting school they also affirm their distinct working-class values. Willis thus identifies these male working-class students, at times, as admirable – although he also notes that their behavior undermines the limited but real chances they might have to improve their socioeconomic status through education. From Willis' point of view, then, William's lack of class participation might identify him as resisting the racial and economic domination that is legitimated through U.S. schools. If Mrs. Bailey were speaking as a champion of the oppressed, her comment about William's silence might identify him in this more admirable way. She might be gently coaxing him to participate, while acknowledging his identity as a disadvantaged black male student.

We could enumerate various other interpretations of this sign of identity as well. By saying that "we don't usually hear from William," Mrs. Bailey might be identifying him as inappropriately resistant, admirably resistant, shy, inattentive or in various other ways. Any potential sign of identity can be interpreted in multiple ways. In order to interpret a sign of identity more confidently, participants and observers must use relevant contextual information to infer the meaning of the sign. Participants and analysts search the utterance, and its discursive and physical surround, for "contextualization cues" that indicate what context might be relevant (Gumperz, 1982). Then they use that relevant context to infer the meaning of the sign. In this case relevant context might include, for instance, many contemporary American teachers' emphasis on classroom participation and their commitment to helping students improve themselves through schooling. These pieces of contextual information would probably lead us to identify William as behaving inappropriately and rule out the "admirable resistance" interpretation.

The first crucial principle about social identification, visible in this example, is that signs of identity do not directly establish given identities. Any sign might potentially help establish various identities for the individual in question. Participants and observers must attend to relevant context and thereby establish the sign's meaning. This process of inferring from and to relevant context has been referred to as "contextualization" (Gumperz, 1982; Silverstein, 1976, 1992) or "mediation" (Wortham, 2001a). No matter how good our ethnographic information, we cannot write a rule book for interpreting signs of identity. Instead of identifying an individual unambiguously, signs come to identify people only when participants and analysts infer relevant context and establish which of various possible identities is being enacted or described.

Agha (2004), Silverstein (1976) and Urban (2001) have made this point by arguing that a sign – any utterance or object that people find culturally meaningful – has meaning only with respect to a "metapragmatic" or "metacultural" model of it. A metapragmatic model is a model of recognizable kinds of people (e.g., inappropriately resistant students) participating in a recognizable kind of interaction (e.g., refusing to participate in class). Mrs. Bailey's comment, "we don't usually hear from William," in itself has indeterminate meaning. This sign gains meaning, in this case as a sign of William's identity, only with respect to more widely circulating metapragmatic models about why students should participate in class and what types of students do and do not participate. These models are "meta"-pragmatic because they frame the "pragmatic" or indexical signs of identity. That is, participants and analysts understand the meaning of a sign only as a relevant model constrains the possible meanings.

Metapragmatic models are ubiquitous in social life. For any sign of identity to make sense, the sign must point not directly to an identity for the focal individual but to a metapragmatic model that construes the sign in this way (Agha, in press; Bateson, 1972; Silverstein, 1976, 2003). For instance, William's silence before line 11 in the segment above allows teacher and students to identify him only insofar as this sign and others presuppose models of what silence might mean. Silence could mean that he is a shy person, a resistant student, a distracted person or other things. Such models make available the types of people that can be enacted in a given social context (Gee, 2001; Holland and Lave, 2001). Without them, we could not identify who people are or what they are signaling about themselves and others.

In Packer and Goicoechea's (2000) terms, metapragmatic models are not just "epistemological" but also "ontological." Social identification generally involves more than just inference to a cognitive model that *represents* the focal individual. Metapragmatic models are *lived* and *enacted* as well as represented. When socially identified, an individual often enacts a mode of being, and this enactment goes beyond merely representing oneself and others in characteristic ways. Metapragmatic models get established in particular events as participants come to inhabit or position themselves against enactable social types. We will see below, for instance, how William is identified as the prototypical "unpromising boy," resisting school and thereby doomed to low socioeconomic status in adulthood. The boys enact this model, and the girls enact contrasting ones, in embodied ways – responding to others with their bodies and verbal reactions, beyond what they or others cognitively represent (Bourdieu, 1972/1977; Dreyfus and Rabinow, 1993). When I talk about "models," then, I mean enacted models of identity that people orient to but often do not represent consciously. And when I discuss the process of inference to relevant metapragmatic models, I mean a tacit process of orienting oneself, not a purely representational process.

As we have seen, various aspects of the context might be relevant to interpreting Mrs. Bailey's utterance that "we don't usually hear from William." Like most contemporary U.S. teachers, Mrs. Bailey values class participation, and she might be upset by William's lack of appropriate participation. However, she also teaches in an inner-city school because she wants to help underprivileged students overcome the racial and economic discrimination they face, and her comment might indicate sympathy toward his reluctance to speak. These two interpretations of Mrs. Bailey's utterance – as condemning his inappropriate resistance or as sympathetic toward his understandable reserve – presuppose different metapragmatic models about kinds of students and how they should behave. If one or the other of these models (or a different one) has been made salient by signs earlier in the event, it will incline participants and observers to interpret the utterance in one or another direction. The metapragmatic model thus "regiments" the sign of identity (i.e., it makes clear which aspects of the context are relevant to interpreting the sign in this case) from among the various contextual aspects that might be relevant (Silverstein, 1993). Such regimentation by a metapragmatic model limits the possible meanings of the sign, making it easier for people to interpret or react to it.

Signs of identity and contextualization cues indicate that certain metapragmatic models are more likely relevant to interpreting a sign of identity. But metapragmatic models also regiment signs and cues, constraining which aspects of the context might be relevant to interpreting the sign in any particular case. Neither the sign nor the model has ultimate authority to dictate the correct interpretation. Instead, both participants and analysts face indeterminacy in interpreting or reacting to signs of identity. This indeterminacy gets overcome in practice as several signs or cues come collectively to presuppose a particular model. From Mrs. Bailey's utterance "we don't usually hear from William," taken by itself, we cannot tell what identity she is attributing to him. But as the interaction proceeds, teachers and students use other signs relevant to William's identity. In most everyday interactions – those that do not end with substantial indeterminacy – a set of signs collectively comes to presuppose similar relevant context and one metapragmatic model (or a small set) that would be appropriate for interpreting or reacting to the focal individual's identity.

In the brief example about William, there is another relevant sign in the utterance already quoted. Mrs. Bailey says that "*we* don't usually hear from William." Her "we" seems to mean "we others in the classroom," a group that includes at least some other students and the teachers but not William himself. Furthermore, her comment at line 13 positions the students who participate in class not only as members of "we" but also as empowered to judge the response William gives at line 11. Two girls act like authority figures and respond in line 14 that William's answer does not make sense. Mrs. Bailey's use of the pronouns "we" and "you," together with the girls responding as if they were the referents of "you," presuppose an interactional organization for the classroom.: There is a core group that includes at least the teachers and the two girls who spoke, and probably also other students who regularly participate in class (as we will see below, almost all members of this core group are girls – the girls dominate this segment and almost all other classroom discussion). William is excluded from this group. This separation of William from the core group of participants supports one of the interpretations of William's identity given above and not the other. If Mrs. Bailey were expressing sympathy for and admiring William's silence, she probably would not have separated him off from herself and the other students through this pattern of pronoun use, and she probably would not have allowed the other students to judge William's response as nonsensical.

Another piece of the segment may further support this interpretation of William's social identity in the classroom. At line 10, after urging William to "come on" and participate, Mrs. Bailey restates her question as "why a woman's touch." Given that these students are adolescents, and interested in intimate relations, Mrs. Bailey might be teasing William with this way of putting the question. "Woman's touch" might be a double entendre, presupposing not only the importance of goddesses in myths but also the sexual touching that a woman might do, perhaps to someone like William. At line 12 several female students laugh, and their laughter might indicate that Mrs. Bailey has been teasing William. The teacher thus seems to be taking advantage of his exclusion from the classroom to tease William, or she might be trying to entice him into joining the conversation by teasing him.

Although each of these signs of identity could be interpreted differently, the three together – Mrs. Bailey's "we don't usually hear from William," her use of the pronouns "we" and "you" to position William outside the core group of teachers and students and her question about "a woman's touch" – most likely cast his failure to participate in class as inappropriate. Rather than being sympathetic to William's reserve in class, the teacher seems to be indicating that he is inappropriately excluding himself from the core group of promising students who contribute. Individual signs of identity generally come to have more definite meaning, when viewed in the context of other signs, as several signs come collectively to support the same model of participants' identities. Like individual signs of identity, of course, patterns of signs can also be reinterpreted – and we will need substantially more evidence to make firm conclusions about William's identity in this classroom. But, in practice, social identities tend to solidify when patterns of signs together support a particular metapragmatic model as providing the most plausible social identity for the moment (Garfinkel, 1967; Silverstein, 1992).

Signs of identity thus do not directly establish social identities. In routinized cases, signs can of course have stereotypical meanings. But, in general, configurations of signs together limit relevant context and indicate which metapragmatic models are appropriate for interpreting or reacting to signs of identity. This has two methodological implications. First, analyses of social identification must not rely on signs of identity abstracted away from their contexts of use. A sign comes to indicate an individual's identity only when one metapragmatic model from among various possibilities comes to regiment that sign in a particular context. We cannot trust analyses that count or extract signs of identity without attending to how those signs come to have meaning with respect to relevant context. Second, discourse analyses of social identification must attend to mutually presupposing patterns of signs. A convincing analysis will trace the contextualization of a sign over time, showing how patterns of signs collectively come to indicate a particular identity for the focal individual. The analyses below illustrate this methodological approach. For a more detailed description of this methodology see Wortham (2001a).

The second crucial principle for interpreting signs of identity ("contextualization" was the first) has been called "entextualization" (Silverstein,

1993; Silverstein and Urban, 1996) or "emergence" (Garfinkel and Sacks, 1970; Wortham, 2001a). The indeterminate relation between signs of identity, relevant context and metapragmatic models is never overcome in principle – despite various proposed "grammars" meant to fix what a sign of identity means (e.g., Searle, 1969). Signs of identity only come to have determinate meaning in context through a contingent process in which relevant metapragmatic models emerge. As participants give off more signs of identity across an event, the signs tend to converge on one metapragmatic model as the most appropriate for interpreting or reacting to individuals' identities. When this happens, a recognizable "text" or organization for the interaction emerges, explicitly or implicitly, and corresponding metapragmatic models become appropriate for identifying or reacting to individuals.

From the short segment above, it looks as if William is being identified as an inappropriately resistant student, although we will have to examine more data to draw this conclusion with authority. The analyses later in this chapter will show how other configurations of signs did in fact collectively presuppose this identity for him. William's emerging identity was largely imposed on him by the teachers and the female students. In other cases, however, individuals actively adopt or transform the identities offered by others. Chapter 4 will show how Tyisha, for instance, sometimes embraced her emerging identity as an outcast in the classroom. Social identification always involves contributions from both the focal individual and others, but the proportion of these contributions varies from case to case.

Models of Identity

The process of social identification happens only in actual events, and signs of identity can be interpreted only with respect to particular contexts of use. Although it seems to participants as if certain models of identity naturally apply in a given context, participants do substantial work in any event to create unproblematic social identification (Garfinkel, 1967; Goffman, 1959). Only by attending to this event-level work – to how signs of identity come to have meaning within particular events – can we account for the social identification of students like William, Tyisha and Maurice. Nonetheless, in order to interpret or react to signs of identity as they occur in events, participants and observers must draw on metapragmatic models that specify characteristic types of people, actions and relationships. And these models must persist beyond specific events. Thus event-level analyses alone cannot explain the process of social identification. Identification lives only in actual events, but it necessarily presupposes models of identity that circulate across events. People accomplish apparently natural, unproblematic social identification not only through event-level work, but also through the longer timescale development of metapragmatic models.

Although it may seem obvious that event-level accounts of social identification cannot suffice, folk conceptions of language often essentialize particular signs as naturally connected to particular identities or characteristics. Agha (2003), for instance, describes the development of "Received Pronunciation" (RP) in Britain over two centuries, showing how people attribute naturally refined or superior qualities to certain sounds themselves. Similarly, people often interpret certain grammatical uses – preserving the accusative by saying "whom," for instance, or the anaphoric use of "they" to refer to a nonspecific singular subject – as indicating character, intelligence or the lack thereof, even though these uses have implications for social identity only with respect to broader models of who might speak this way. In fact, neither "accent" nor status is inherent in any sign of identity. The use of certain phonological features, for instance, becomes a sign of identity only when people interpret regular phonological contrasts with respect to a metapragmatic model of different kinds of people accorded differential social value (Agha, 2003). However nuanced our accounts of identities emerging within events, a full account of social identification must also analyze metapragmatic models that persist across longer timescales.

Many accounts of language, culture and education have described how social identification depends on such publicly circulating metapragmatic models. Gee (1999; 2001), for instance, refers to such models as "Discourses," presupposed ways of speaking and acting that are associated with certain types of people. Holland and her colleagues (Holland and Eisenhart, 1990; Holland, Lachicotte, Skinner and Cain, 1998) refer to them as "figured worlds," culturally shared, idealized types of events that involve recognizable sorts of people and characteristic actions. Bourdieu (1979/1984), Eckert (2000), Woolard (1989) and others refer to such models in terms of one or more "markets" of available identities. How one speaks or dresses gets evaluated with respect to a symbolic market that sets the value of certain identities, and one "buys" access and status by giving off signs that presuppose an identity of a certain value in the relevant market.

Sometimes speakers explicitly denote the metapragmatic model or category of identity required to interpret or react to a sign. In Britain, for instance, RP speech is sometimes called "public school pronunciation." More often, however, a set of signs implicitly indicates that a particular model is relevant for interpreting signs of identity and identifying an individual. When Mrs. Bailey said, "We don't usually hear from William," she did not say explicitly that William was a taciturn black male student who was unable or unwilling to take advantage of educational opportunities. But, together with other signs of identity from across the interaction and across the year, I argue that her utterance did turn out to presuppose this model of identity for William. Evidence of social identification, then, comes from both denotationally explicit and implicit signs of identity.

Social identification depends on publicly circulating models of identity, as these models get explicitly denoted or implicitly indexed in actual events of identification. Metapragmatic models are sociocultural phenomena – recurring across events and persisting across time and space. As Sapir and others have noted, culture and the models of identity that partly constitute it are "being reanimated or creatively reaffirmed from day to day by particular acts of a communicative nature" (1931/1949: p. 104). Urban (1996, 2001) and other contemporary anthropologists conceive of this process in terms of circulation. They conceive of social identification, and culture more generally, in terms of motion and trajectories, not in terms of objects and structures. Many competing models, categories and practices emerge and become recognizable, then get replicated, transformed or discarded. Such emergence happens, in practice, as metapragmatic models and other cultural phenomena circulate publicly. If a model ceases to circulate, it dies out and other ones take its place.

The identification of an individual requires the consistent circulation of certain signs of identity and certain metapragmatic models through events that include, refer to or presuppose that individual. For William to be identified as a resistant black male student, the teachers and other students, and perhaps William himself, would have had to label him this way and/or implicitly indicate that this category of identity applied to him across many events. Such acts of identification involved the simultaneous use of signs, like Mrs. Bailey's "We don't usually hear from William," and a metapragmatic model of identity that indicated how to interpret the signs. Some signs of identity recur consistently and can be systematically described – like the set of phonological variants associated with an "accent" like RP – while in other cases the signs of a given identity vary widely. But in both cases a metapragmatic model must be invokable or enactable, such that the model frames various signs, across events, as indicating a recognizable identity for the focal individual.

As William's identity emerged in Mrs. Bailey and Mr. Smith's classroom, the metapragmatic models used to identify him involved gender, race and school success. Over the last several decades in the United States, girls have overtaken boys in many areas. Girls receive better grades, outperform boys on standardized tests, drop out less, and enroll in and graduate from college at higher rates (Cole, 1997; Sum et al., 2003). Although sexism persists in schools and disadvantages girls in various ways (Brown and Gilligan, 1992; Holland and Eisenhart, 1990; Sadker and Sadker, 1994), boys face increasing challenges of their own (Newkirk, 2002), and their academic performance shows it. Teachers and students' gendered expectations for school success and the gender gap in school performance have been documented for both minority and majority youth (Lopez, 2003; Wortham, 2001c). In addition, popular culture circulates models of boys as not only less skilled in school but also as more susceptible to violence and other antisocial behavior, as well as circulating the stereotype that school success is unmasculine (Pottorff, Phelps-Zientarski and Skovera, 1996). Ethnographic studies have shown how such models filter down to teachers and students so that they often believe boys are less likely to work hard and succeed in school (e.g., Honora, 2003; Wortham, 2001c).

This metapragmatic model of boys – as uninterested in school, prone to antisocial behavior and less likely to succeed in school and life – is not only about gender but also about race because it is disproportionately applied to African American boys (Jordan and Cooper, 2003). Ferguson (2000) describes how black boys are disproportionately disciplined in school, labeled as "at risk" and as "failures." She argues that school rules "seem to be specifically designed to control, manage and channel the 'natural' behavior of boys [and black boys in particular], who are said to be more physical, aggressive, and sexual. Girls are believed to be more naturally agreeable, tractable, and able to tolerate the controlled atmosphere" (p. 42). This model of black boys at school fits with broader stereotypes of black men as aggressive, violent, overly concerned with respect, and irresponsible fathers (Anderson, 1999; Gadsden, Wortham and Turner, 2003; Nightingale, 1993).

William and the other black boys in Mrs. Bailey and Mr. Smith's class were at risk of being identified with this model of academically unpromising, antisocial boys. Because this model of male students – especially black male students – circulates so widely in the larger society, it would have been relatively easy for teachers or students to presuppose that William and his male classmates were resistant to school and unlikely to succeed. However, other potentially relevant models of identity circulate as well. There are models of successful black athletes and musicians. There are too few but increasing numbers of black professionals like Robert Johnson and Vernon Jordan, and heroic figures like W. E. B. DuBois, Martin Luther King, Jr., Ralph Ellison, and Booker T. Washington. William might have been identified using categories from these other available models, or from less widely circulating ones.

As Appiah (1992) and others have argued, models of identity linked to "major collective identities" like race and gender can be coercive when they are widespread and institutionalized. In fact, as shown later in this chapter, William ended up becoming a prototypical academically unpromising boy. But Chapter 5 shows that Maurice, another African American boy, often successfully struggled against becoming an unpromising boy. A dominant model may be more likely to frame an individual's identity, especially when race, gender, religion, ethnicity and other often-naturalized categories are involved. Nonetheless, despite the power of widely circulating models of identity, in most contexts several models are available to identify a given individual. Widely circulating sociohistorical models of identity often seem inevitable, as if members of a certain group always get socially identified in stereotypical ways. As argued in the last section, however, this sense of inevitability is constructed in particular events and in local contexts as participants work to establish one of several possible identities for an individual. The sense of naturalness in social identification is not only accomplished as widely circulating categories emerge over historical time, but also as participants in particular events and in local contexts maneuver to establish a particular model of identity for the focal individual.

Beyond Macro and Micro

Given the importance of both sociohistorical and event-level timescales, the most common account of how an individual like William actually gets identified involves a "dialectic" or an "oscillation" between publicly circulating models of identity and particular events of identification. "Dialectic" here refers to moving back and forth between two poles. According to this account, sociohistorical models of identity constrain events of identification, while at the same time particular events either reproduce or help to transform the sociohistorical models. This position is often credited to Giddens (1976), who called it "structuration," but many others in sociology, anthropology, education and related fields have adopted a similar position (cf., e.g., Blommaert and Bulcaen, 2000; Levinson, Foley and Holland, 1996; Linger, 2001). In order for William to get identified as a stereotypical resistant black male adolescent, this sociohistorical model would have to be invoked in particular events and, in a contingent process that might modify the model somewhat, get applied to William in context.

This "macro-micro dialectic" account of social identification captures some essential aspects of the process. As described in the last two sections, both particular events of identification and publicly circulating metapragmatic models play essential roles in social identification, and neither can be reduced to the other. Identification cannot occur unless people presuppose metapragmatic models that circulate beyond the speech event, but these models have actual effects only in particular events in which they are always recontextualized and sometimes inflected in specific ways. Our sense that certain social identities are "naturally" appropriate comes both from the sociohistorical emergence of models and categories (Hacking, 1990) and from the invocation of these models in events (Garfinkel, 1967).

Despite its strengths, however, many have recently criticized the macro-micro dialectic model (e.g., Bourdieu, 1972/1977; Eckert, 2000; Holland and Lave, 2001; Prior, 2001; Schatzki, Knorr Cetina, and von Savigny, 2001; Urban, 2001). Critics charge that, at its worst, the model assumes sociohistorical properties of groups or institutions without explaining how these are created and maintained – except by making the vague claim that they are constituted in actual events, a claim that simply means the broader properties repeatedly appear in actual events. But a deterministic macro-level account would also agree with this claim. Properties of groups or institutions must appear in events for them to be empirically available, but the fact of their appearance does not change the macro-level emphasis of such an account. Claims about the macro-micro dialectic often mask macro-level determinism with vague claims about the everyday constitution of social categories.

Many recent accounts seek to avoid such determinism, while preserving the strengths of dialectical accounts, by studying "practice." "Practice theory" centrally involves a critique of macro-level determinism, pointing out that models of identity can be transformed in practice and that we cannot know out of context what a "macro-level" model will mean for any individual or situation. Practice theory sometimes describes the "articulation between" (Bucholtz, 1999; Eckert, 2000), or the "co-development of" the widely circulating and the locally invoked (Holland, Lachicotte, Skinner and Cain, 1998), but such terms by themselves do not describe more precisely how publicly circulating models are contextualized in particular events so as to constitute social identification. I do not mean to denigrate the important point made by claims about practice – that we do not know what publicly circulating signs, categories and models mean in the abstract, but that we must also examine how they are contextualized in practice if we want to understand their role in processes of social identification. I am simply pointing out that "practice" must be explicated further in order to explain how processes like social identification work.

As Eckert (2000) notes, Dorothy Holland and Jean Lave (Holland and Lave, 2001; Lave and Wenger, 1991) have begun to do this with their concepts of "community of practice" and "history in person." Holland and Lave (2001) provide a useful overview, in which they describe the "mutually constitutive nature" of enduring social struggles, particular events and individuals' acts. Instead of describing individuals and events as already formed and "affected by" or "creating" social categories and institutions, they study the constitution of selves, events and institutions in practice. Practices are sociohistorically produced, but they are not merely derived from publicly circulating models and institutional processes. Holland and Lave redescribe sociohistorical models and structures in terms of "enduring struggles" between and among people, groups and institutions to emphasize how they are contested and constituted in practice. Events and actions can intervene in and transform these struggles, but such events and acts are always mediated by more widely circulating sociocultural patterns that are invoked in particular events.

This goes beyond a "dialectic" account because of its emphasis on "practice" as the leading edge of sociohistorical action and transformation. "Practice" overlaps with both enduring struggles and particular events because contestation in practices involves the production of both widely circulating and local categories and processes. Gregory (2001) illustrates this approach with his ethnographic account of how social class identities do not simply reflect preexisting categories, but are instead "formed and reformed through political and cultural practices that occur at multiple sites in community life" (p. 141). He describes how the social class identities of African American community activists emerged from contentious practices at church, in the neighborhood, in political organizations and elsewhere. The identities and experiences of particular individuals depended on the enduring struggles in play at a given time, but their "social class" took on particular meaning and force only in the context of the local practices and struggles in play at the moment. Gregory shows how an analysis that emphasized enduring struggles and/or contingent events, as givens apart from the local context, would fail to capture how social identification and other processes related to social class actually happened.

Practice theory thus promises a more specific account of how enduring struggles and particular events interrelate. By examining practices like the local political and civic activities described by Gregory, analysts can explore how categories of identity and events of identification are jointly produced in context. This approach only works, however, if "practice" can be more carefully defined. One sometimes hears the word invoked as if we have identified the fundamental level at which social life operates – even though the word is used to describe widely differing timescales, from types of human activities that recur over decades (e.g., Taylor, 1985), to sets of events involving a group of people that take place over months (e.g., Gregory, 2001), to particular events that take place over an hour or less (e.g., Rampton, 1999). "Practices" of the sort described by Taylor, Gregory and Rampton are certainly relevant to social identification in many cases. But if "practice" is the arena in which widely circulating and more local components come together to produce social identities, so that we can analyze how social identification actually works, we must know more precisely what it involves.

Social identification often relies on widespread, highly presupposable, sometimes coercive metapragmatic models – like those that identify black male adolescents as more antisocial and more resistant to school than other students. But no matter how widespread such models are, other models could be used to identify a student like William in any event of identification. How does "practice" explain everyday actors' resolution of this indeterminacy, such that students like William become clearly identified using one metapragmatic model or another?

Clearly "practice" cannot be one privileged timescale. "In practice" does not mean only events that happen across months but not decades, or only events that happen across minutes but not days. One could posit an indefinite number of intervening timescales, from the life of the universe to nanoseconds, and it would be obviously false to claim that some timescale or some particular combination was foundational (Lemke, 2000). Major sociohistorical identities are often important, but they do not always play the leading role in establishing the social identity of an individual. The active embracing of an identity by an individual sometimes plays an important role in social identification, but at other times it does not. Neither "structure" nor "agency" nor any other potentially relevant factor always plays a central – or even the same – role in social identification. Instead, different sets of processes, drawing on resources from various timescales, make possible different instances of social identification. If "practice" is to help us explain processes like social identification more precisely, it must be understood to mean the configuration of resources from relevant timescales that come together to establish identification in a given case.

Practice theory has the salutary effect of moving beyond two levels of explanation – "macro" and "micro," or "structure" and "agency" – to explore processes through which relevant models of identity are actually applied in context. However, we must not construe practice as one timescale, naturally basic to the others. Adequate analyses of social identification must do more than avoid the trap of essentializing sociohistorical categories. Adequate analyses must also attend to component processes at various timescales, with different focal phenomena demanding that we pay attention to different configurations of resources. We cannot establish in advance which timescales will be relevant to explaining human phenomena, for two reasons. First, in order to explain complex phenomena like social identification, analysts must attend to a configuration of interconnected processes across several timescales, not to one or two privileged timescales. Second, the relevant timescales will vary from phenomenon to phenomenon. Our sense of the unproblematic, "natural" establishment of social identity in a given case emerges from a contingent configuration of resources from heterogeneous timescales.

In William's case, for instance, the analysis below shows how locally circulating metapragmatic models of identity emerged in Mrs. Bailey and Mr. Smith's classroom and how teachers and students drew on these models as they identified him. These local models were gendered, identifying boys as more resistant to school and less likely to succeed. The models relied on more widely circulating models of gender and school success, which are shifting sociohistorically to portray boys as less academically promising. Mrs. Bailey and the vocal girls in the class developed an intensified local metapragmatic model of promising girls and unpromising boys. They could have drawn on other, even antithetical sociohistorical models of gender and school success, but in this case they developed an intensified version of the "unpromising boys" model. Then they applied this model to William across several months, so that he became the prototypical boy. We would misconstrue the social identification of William somewhat if we used only "macro-level" and "micro-level" analyses because this would miss the local model of gender and school success that Mrs. Bailey and the girls developed. This local model became established with what Agha (in press) calls a "social domain" that extended only to this classroom. In this case, the local emergence of the model and its application to William over several months is crucial to understanding social identification in this classroom.

By emphasizing the importance of the "local timescale" in this case, I seem to be confusing spatial and temporal dimensions. "Local," after all, refers more to space than to time. Furthermore, the relevant temporal and spatial extensions of human processes do not always correlate as they do in my case. Some processes occur at short timescales but have wide spatial extensions (stylistic fads), while others occur at long timescales with narrow spatial extensions (e.g., the development of unique practices within a family across generations). In this book I do not address these complexities. I use Lemke's "timescale" terminology because I find it useful, but I acknowledge that each relevant process has both spatial and temporal extension. When I discuss the "local timescale," I mean a spatiotemporal niche bounded spatially by Mrs. Bailey and Mr. Smith's classroom and temporally by the academic year in question.

Tyisha and Maurice's identities depended more deeply than William's on models established at the months-long local timescale. The analyses in Chapters 4 and 5 show that these two students were identified contrary to both the dominant societal and the local classroom models of typical male and female behavior, and that Tyisha and Maurice struggled both with and against their emerging, unexpected identities. These local timescale processes – the emerging gendered local model of identity and the months-long struggles over whether this model applied to Tyisha and Maurice – are necessary but not sufficient to analyzing social identification in this classroom. In order to understand the social identification of Tyisha and Maurice more fully, we must appreciate the widely circulating models of identity that concern race, gender and school success, the locally emerging models that drew on but inflected some of these, the months-long ontogenetic process in which particular students were identified with respect to (sometimes in concert with and sometimes contrary to) local versions of widely circulating models, and the particular events through which all this actually happened.

To focus on any one or two of these timescales alone would be to misconstrue the heterogeneous resources that made social identification possible in this case. By citing "configurations" of cross-timescale resources, I mean to emphasize that analyses at any one timescale do not suffice. The relevant timescales may vary with the phenomenon being explained, but almost all instances of social identification depend on configurations of resources. This means that the apparently natural character of social identification is not accomplished by emerging sociohistorical, local or event-level categories alone. Instead, categories and models emerge at different timescales and the trajectories of these emerging categories and models intersect so as to create apparently natural social identities.

Such configurations of cross-timescale components are somewhat analogous to the "epistemic cultures" described by Knorr-Cetina (1999). She describes the divergent social, physical and cognitive "arrangements and mechanisms" that facilitate the production of knowledge in different natural sciences. Warranted scientific knowledge is produced through complex configurations of individual actions, institutionalized statuses and practices, laboratory objects and other resources. Similarly, social identification depends on interrelated sets of heterogeneous resources. Knorr-Cetina also shows how epistemic cultures vary widely across natural sciences, such that they form "independent epistemic monopolies" (p. 4). Different sciences depend on very different components, ranging from individual laboratory work to collective consensus-building and from highly data-focused experiments to completely abstract theory. Similarly, I am arguing that the resources relevant to explaining different instances of social identification will vary from case to case and context to context.

In order to explain the spread of RP in Britain, for instance, Agha (2003) shows that the relevant processes took place over two centuries, with crucial developments (e.g., involving the increased circulation of popular novels containing extensive quoted speech) at the timescale of years and decades. Although some links could be made to both longer and shorter timescale processes, Agha shows that the key processes in this case involve centuries, decades and particular events of reading and writing. In contrast, I show that, in order to explain the emergence of classroom identities for students like William, Tyisha and Maurice, we must attend to a somewhat different set of timescales. We must attend particularly to the locally emerging models of identity in the classroom over the year, as these interrelated with more widely circulating conceptions of gender, race and schooling and with two particular kinds of events – explicit metapragmatic labeling of students and participant examples that included these students as characters. Determining the relevant timescales for explaining social identification (and other social phenomena) is an empirical process that will depend on the particulars of the case.

Just because I focus on the development of metapragmatic models within a particular classroom over several months, then, I am *not* claiming that local metapragmatic models always play a crucial role in social identification. In fact, the analyses of Erika and William (later in this chapter), contrasted with the analyses of Tyisha and Maurice (in Chapters 4 and 5), show that the social identification of different individuals in the same context can depend on different configurations of timescales. Nor do I claim to have analyzed all timescales relevant to the social identification of students in this classroom – to do so would require substantially more space and more detailed data from outside the classroom. I do claim to show that adequate analysis of social identification in this case must examine how processes at various timescales interconnected. I emphasize the local processes of teachers and students' social identification over the course of the school year in order to show how we must go beyond "macro" and "micro" to provide an adequate analysis in some cases.

In addition to identifying the timescales and resources most relevant to explaining a focal phenomenon, an analyst must describe how the various components interrelate. Lemke (2000) draws on Star and Griesemer's (1989) concept of "boundary objects" for this purpose. A boundary object participates in processes at more than one timescale and constrains them both. The spatial layout of a classroom (Leander, 2002), the textbooks (Apple, 1986) and the habitual embodied stances of teachers and students (Bourdieu, 1972/1977), for instance, both mediate longer timescale processes and constrain the emerging structure of particular events. Participant examples, as they were introduced in Chapter 1, can be boundary objects in this sense. Participant examples are particularly rich in their implications for social identification because they double participants' roles, making them both participants in the classroom interaction and topics of conversation within the example (Wortham, 1994). Such examples connect more widely circulating metapragmatic models, often drawn from the curriculum, with particular students' emerging local identities. Students in a local context like Mrs. Bailey and Mr. Smith's classroom can be identified across classes, in significant part, through participant examples that apply characteristic sociohistorical and local models to individual students. Chapter 3 describes in more detail how participant examples can not only help bring together heterogeneous resources to accomplish social identification, but also how they can facilitate the meshing of social identification and academic learning.

Agha (2003) describes another way in which cross-timescale components can interrelate. A "speech chain" is a linked series of speech events, in which the hearer in one event goes on to circulate a particular sign or model as the speaker in a subsequent event. This concept is related to, but makes more precise, Bakhtin's (1953/1986) concept of "intertextuality." Hearing someone associate a particular phonological form with a model of refined character, for instance, the hearer might go on to presuppose the same association in his or her own subsequent speech. As more hearer/speakers do this, especially as such linkages begin to circulate in the mass media, the sign/identity linkage circulates more widely and perdures over a longer timescale. The speech chain concept explains how a particular set of signs and metapragmatic models emerge, interactionally, socially and historically. Agha applies this concept to longer timescale processes – tracing, for instance, how readers of prescriptivist works that specified "correct" pronunciation in Britain in the nineteenth century went on to write novels that more widely circulated RP.

The concept of speech chain can also be applied to the events across which an individual is socially identified (Wortham, 2005). Teachers and students came consistently to presuppose certain metapragmatic models as they identified William, Tyisha and Maurice. Signs of identity came to index emerging local models of identity for these individual students, as teachers and students came habitually to use characteristic signs and models of identity while describing and interacting with them. The social identities of these individuals thus emerged over a chain of events in which they more consistently inhabited characteristic metapragmatic models that more and more participants came to recognize and assume. Chapters 4 and 5 describe in detail these "person-focused speech chains" (Wortham, 2005) or "trajectories" of identification (Dreier, 2000) – those series of events across which Tyisha and Maurice's social identities emerged in the classroom.

Trajectories of Identification

Any particular act of identification depends on the existence of metapragmatic models from longer timescales and on the emergent contextualization of these models in a particular event, but social identification happens to individuals. We must not focus on publicly circulating models to the exclusion of the individuals who are the objects and sometimes the agents of this process. Cohen (1994), Linger (2001), Rapport (1997) and Sökefeld (1999) argue that cultural analyses have inappropriately moved away from the individual to focus on the cultural possibilities available in any situation. By also attending to the individual across time we can trace the actual models of identity that are applied to individuals and that often could not be predicted out of context. These pleas for the individual do not advocate "individualism," but "individuality," as Cohen (1994) puts it. Publicly circulating metapragmatic models and interactionally negotiated events are essential to social identification, but a full account must also attend to individuals' trajectories over time.

At times, these accounts of the individual in social context fall into traditional Enlightenment conceptions of the autonomous subject, endowed with the agency to choose among culturally available alternatives. Rapport (1997) even argues for individuals' "radical" freedom, in an existentialist sense. Flax (1993), Hatgis (2003) and many others provide extensive critiques of such Enlightenment conceptions. I would prefer to explain historical change with reference to more complex cross-timescale systems, as Holland and Lave (2001), Lemke (2000) and others do. This is a complex issue, however, and a theoretical account of free will and the extent of individual autonomy is beyond the scope of this book – although I do discuss Tyisha and Maurice's "agency" in Chapters 4, 5 and 6. Here I want simply to follow Cohen, Linger, Rapport and Sökefeld's plausible argument that analyses of social identification must include as one relevant process the ontogenetic development of an individual's identity across events. In order to analyze the social identification of students like William, Tyisha and Maurice, we must attend to the ontogenetic emergence of individuals' social identities across months-long chains of events – in addition to the months-long emergence of shared local metapragmatic models in the classroom, the longer timescale emergence of sociohistorical models and the contextualized enactment of these models in events of identification.

Individuals' identities "thicken" (Holland and Lave, 2001) or become more consistently presupposable across a series of events, not usually in one pivotal event. Such thickening happens when publicly circulating models of identity are invoked in local contexts and come to circulate consistently through events of identification that include a given individual. William did not become a resistant male student because of that one comment by Mrs. Bailey about "not hearing" from him. Gendered models of identity and schooling, from among various models about male and female students that circulate more widely, came to circulate consistently in this classroom. These models were increasingly applied to William, framing him as a prototypical resistant male student across several events of identification. William's identity thickened across a chain of events in which he was consistently identified using a locally developed model of identity that drew on and contextualized more widely circulating models. In William's case, this social identification was mostly done *to* him. In Tyisha and Maurice's cases, the students themselves struggled with and partly shaped the models of identity that they came to inhabit.

The social self is, as Sapir said, "a gradually cumulative entity" (1934b/1949: p. 560), although there are sometimes ruptures and transformations as well. Stability in social identification occurs over time as an individual consistently inhabits a model of identity and as others interpret and/or react as if the individual has that identity. Dreier (2000) introduces the concept "trajectories of participation" to describe this process through which individuals develop identities across events. He insists that one cannot be or become a person in a single context. The relevant unit of analysis for social identification is not an individual event or an individual mind. Analysts must follow individuals' trajectories across events to see how individual modes of participation and social constraints help produce social identities.

According to Dreier, adequate analyses of social identification will study "personal life trajectories in complex social practices" (p. 257). Any given event involves more than publicly circulating models of identity, whether these circulate at sociohistorical or local timescales, because such models must always be recontextualized in particular events. Individuals' trajectories of identification intersect with events, and an analyst must understand these trajectories in order to understand the social identification taking place in that event and across time. Individual trajectories of identification thus represent another type of intermediate timescale pattern relevant to understanding social identification, in addition to locally emerging metapragmatic models. The analyses below will trace how individual trajectories of identification – both more typical (William and Erika) and less typical (Tyisha and Maurice) – and emerging months-long, classroom-specific models of identity intersected to constitute the social identification of these students in Mrs. Bailey and Mr. Smith's classroom.

Social identification happens across a trajectory of events as signs of identity and metapragmatic models are consistently applied to and inhabited by an individual. Widely circulating categories and models are essential to social identification, but only as they are contextualized within local settings and particular events. In settings like a classroom, local versions of more widely circulating models often develop and participants in these settings draw on those models as they identify themselves and each other. Individuals in those settings move along their own trajectories, which draw on locally and sociohistorically circulating categories of identity in some-times unique ways. We can only analyze the social identification that happened to Tyisha and Maurice by attending to the emerging cross-timescale configuration of models, trajectories and acts of identification. So my analysis attends to sociohistorical models of identity, the local versions of these that emerged in the classroom, the trajectories of individuals who were identified over time with respect to these models and the contingent events in which acts of social identification actually happened. The apparent naturalness of these students' social identities can only be explained with reference to all these relevant timescales. The next section traces the social identification of Erika the prototypical girl and William the prototypical boy, in order to introduce the gendered local model of identity that became pervasive and important in Mrs. Bailey and Mr. Smith's classroom.

GENDERED MODELS OF IDENTITY IN THE CLASSROOM

I gathered all the data from Mrs. Bailey and Mr. Smith's classroom myself. Talented research assistants helped by doing initial data analyses, but I did all final data analyses myself. I had become interested in Colleoni High because of the "Paideia" curriculum some teachers were implementing, and I was introduced to teachers and administrators by a colleague who had done research there. The administrative coordinator of the Paideia program at Colleoni introduced me to Mrs. Bailey, who was one of the faculty members most involved in the program. Over two years, I conducted intermittent pilot research in the classrooms of Mrs. Bailey and a few other teachers. In the third year I conducted more systematic research, observing and audiotaping Mrs. Bailey and Mr. Smith's classroom about fifty times, as well as making recordings and consistent observations in another classroom.

My access to the classroom was through the teachers, and this influenced the kind of data I gathered. I interviewed students outside of class, but not as much as I would have liked. I was able to interview the teachers more consistently, so I knew more about their point of view. Teachers and students both saw me as someone interested in the Paideia curriculum and instructional methods, someone who came from the university and thus shared a worldview with the teachers more than the students. Both teachers and students were accustomed to classroom observers, so I was not an anomaly or a large disruption. I was unusual in that I returned to the classroom consistently across the year. This proved to them that I was interested, it allowed me to build respectful relationships with the teachers and some students, and it allowed me to collect more detailed and accurate data than would have been possible with a shorter stay.

My initial interests as a researcher in Mrs. Bailey and Mr. Smith's classroom did not involve social identification. I was interested in Paideia teaching methods and the reduction of teacher authority these methods call for, but I did not design the study to explore individual students' social identities. It would be nice to have more data from students and teachers, such as interviews in which they explicitly assessed individuals' identities across the year. I did interview the teachers and a few students, but my questions focused on their reactions to the curriculum. Despite this gap in the data, however, I have enough information to draw robust conclusions about the social identities attributed to and inhabited by many students. In recorded classroom discussions, teachers and students often explicitly characterized the focal students' identities. These characterizations agree with the relatively few explicit characterizations they told me in interviews. Furthermore, I have extensive recorded evidence of students and teachers consistently positioning themselves and each other in ways that reveal the social identification that was occurring in the classroom.

I also have data, drawn from other researchers, on metapragmatic models that took hold in Mrs. Bailey and Mr. Smith's classroom. Any classroom contains habitual practices and models that constrain teachers and students' identities. Jackson (1968) usefully summarizes many common classroom practices and models with the terms "crowds, praise and power." Schools must manage large numbers of students with relatively few adults, and they must maintain discipline. So they adopt schedules, rules and disciplinary procedures to manage the "crowds." These rules and procedures offer categories for identifying teachers as "mean" or "nice," for example, and identifying students as "well-behaved" or "lacking in self-control." Schools also embrace explicit ideals for both academic and interpersonal behavior. Educators both informally and formally "praise" students who reach these ideals, identifying them as "cooperative," "intelligent," "hard-working" and the like. And schools enforce clear "power" relationships between educators and students. Because educators have the power to praise and discipline, they have available models of identity like "insubordinate" students, "deviant" and "inappropriate" student behavior. Eckert (1989), Willis (1977) and others have described how students respond with their own sets of practices and models, and these student-generated models also provide categories of identity – often categories that identify students as having values that either align with or contradict the school's.

Many practices and beliefs associated with crowds, praise and power circulate widely across space and time and have become deeply entrenched in classrooms. Mrs. Bailey, Mr. Smith and their students recognized and used many such practices and models in their classroom. The teachers maintained control of the class by exercising their power over students, and they expected students to meet typical academic and social standards of behavior. The teachers also identified students whose academic and interpersonal behavior merited praise or censure, sometimes tacitly and sometimes explicitly. Like most other students, those in Mrs. Bailey and Mr. Smith's classroom were being apprenticed into a type of institutional practice. This practice presupposed widely circulating models of both praiseworthy and deviant identities.

As mentioned in Chapter 1, however, these teachers organized their classroom in a distinctive way, following the Paideia philosophy. Adler (1982) argues that education must centrally prepare students to participate in democracy. The Paideia Group, on behalf of whom Adler wrote, envisioned an "educationally classless society" – with quality schooling for all and equal opportunities to participate in debating about and governing society. This belief undergirds the most distinctive aspect of Paideia pedagogy – "seminar" discussions that involve Socratic questioning by the teacher and aim toward "enlargement of understanding, insight and aesthetic appreciation" (Adler, 1982: p. 22). In seminar, the teacher "helps the student bring ideas to birth" (p. 29) instead of filling the student with preestablished knowledge. Paideia teachers, including Mrs. Bailey and Mr. Smith, want students to develop and analyze their own ideas, not simply to memorize others'. As Weltman points out, Adler was seeking to develop social cohesion through education, not just individual excellence. In seminar, "students share knowledge with each other and strive to elevate themselves by elevating the discussion level of the whole group" (Weltman, 2002: p. 76). Adler envisioned seminar discussions as paradigmatic sites of both individual and collective effort, with teachers and students offering their own opinions and evidence but also agreeing on terms and developing collective accounts.

Mrs. Bailey and Mr. Smith often followed Adler's lead, both in their espoused philosophies of teaching and in practice. They empowered students to offer and defend their own opinions, and they encouraged student-directed discussion. These Paideia practices made less widely circulating models of teacher and student identity salient in Mrs. Bailey and Mr. Smith's classroom. For instance, teachers and students could be identified as co-inquirers into essentially contestable questions, as well as experts and novices. The teachers' Paideia practices presupposed social and educational ideals that differ from those more common in classrooms: valuing open-ended inquiry in which teachers and students inquire together, respecting students as capable of developing and defending their own arguments, encouraging discussion in which students and teachers collaborate to advance their understanding of an issue, and so on.

Sometimes more widely circulating practices and models of classroom identity conflicted with Paideia practices in this classroom. The teachers most often defended Paideia ideals in such cases, overcoming typical ways of organizing classroom identities and activities by, for instance, pursuing a student's unexpected argument instead of rejecting the student's ideas and returning quickly to more conventional interpretations. Sometimes, however, Paideia practices gave way to more traditional practices and judgments. As we will see in the case of Tyisha in Chapter 4, Mrs. Bailey and Mr. Smith did use traditional categories of identity like "disruptive student" in order to manage some students' behavior. These teachers allowed students unusual freedom in proposing and defending interpretations that diverged from the teachers'. However, when they perceived a student straying too far from accepted ideas and standard practices, they used their authority to identify students as disruptive and to discipline those students. In my judgment, this was sometimes necessary in order to keep classroom discussions productive. But this circumstance reveals some of the heterogeneous resources teachers and students drew on to identify themselves and each other – including both widely distributed models of classroom power relations and "disruptive" students, more narrowly circulating Paideia models of appropriate student behavior, and local classroom versions of both kinds of models.

Promising Girls and Unpromising Boys

Many sociohistorical models might have been relevant to identifying the students in Mrs. Bailey and Mr. Smith's classroom. In addition to models typically associated with classroom behavior and with Paideia pedagogy, a variety of sociohistorical models occasionally became relevant: models of naïve religious believers (a large group of devout students) as opposed to rational skeptics (the teachers), of "high class" mainstream consumers (several of the students) as opposed to the unrefined lower classes (a few unfortunate students, plus people living in the neighborhood), of "decent" people who work within the system (many of the students and their parents) as opposed to "street" people who work outside it (people from the neighborhood; cf. Anderson, 1999), of blacks who continue to suffer from racial oppression (most of the students) as opposed to whites who benefit from it (the teachers and a few students) and so on. These and many other widely circulating models of religious beliefs, social classes, the social system, race and ethnicity, among others, could have become salient in the classroom. Some of these models of identity did in fact play a role at different times during the year. But teachers and students habitually came to presuppose one widely circulating model of identity more often than all these others: Girls are less troublesome, smarter and more promising than boys.

As described above, this model circulates somewhat widely across American society and American schools, increasingly so in recent years. But teachers and students developed a specific local version of this model. The local metapragmatic model emerged over the first two or three months of the academic year, with teachers and students habitually attributing different identities to boys and girls. They presupposed that girls cooperate more with the teachers, are more intelligent and will more likely succeed professionally and economically in later life. Boys, in contrast, more often resist classroom expectations, are less intelligent and will most likely not succeed professionally and economically in later life. More than any other category of identity, gender became relevant to the social identification of students. By the middle of the year, many students were routinely identified according to these gendered models – as promising girls and unpromising boys – and these categories of identity could easily be presupposed in almost any classroom interaction.

The teachers often referred to the class in gendered terms, especially when making comments about discipline. On November 30, for instance, Mr. Smith said, "I had to separate the young men because they were chatting over there. I can do the same thing for the young ladies." Mrs. Bailey also explicitly articulated the gendered model at times. Also on November 30, she characterized girls and boys this way: "Okay, that's one meaning of discrimination. I look and I see differences. . . . I see that Katina is a girl and William is a boy and I discriminate against William because he's a boy and girls are much easier to deal with." On February 18 she was even more explicit, echoing a comment by one of the girls: "That's how boys are, they're kind of stupid." (See Chapter 5 for surrounding context and more extensive analysis of this comment.)

Although Mrs. Bailey, and subsequently many of the girls, did sometimes explicitly articulate the model of promising girls and unpromising boys, they more often presupposed it in differential behavior toward girls and boys in the classroom. Before the following segment on January 25, Maurice had accused Gary of interrupting him. Mrs. Bailey and the girls then treated Gary in a way that they often treated the boys.

MRC: every time I <u>say</u>
something <u>you</u> got something to say about it
STS: [4 seconds of yelling]
110 FST: I'm sick of it. <u>he</u> get on my <u>nerves.</u>
STS: [4 seconds of yelling]
FST: he criticizing, but he don't say anything.
because [[4 unintelligible syllables]
T/B: ah [I think that maybe, <u>la</u>dies. I think then that
115 maybe because I'm not always picking up what
Gary's <u>do</u>ing over there, he kind of makes himself
invisible[to some extent=
<u>FST</u>:   [(hh)
T/B: =<u>if</u>, you know, <u>if</u> he is saying something that
120 you would <u>like</u> him to share with the <u>group</u> or you
think=
FST: [ah
T/B: =he[needs to share with the group, either
because it will contribute to the conversa<u>tion</u>=
125 FST: [oh I don't know
T/B: =[or because it will embarrass him, maybe we
should get it out, okay?

At lines 110 and 112, two girls characterize Gary as making unwarranted and unproductive criticisms. This characterization is not necessarily gendered. It was Maurice, after all, who initially complained about Gary at lines 107–108. But at lines 116–117, Mrs. Bailey says that Gary "makes himself invisible." This characterization fits with the metapragmatic model and the habitual behaviors that have developed over the year, in which the boys sit in the back of the room and refuse to say anything while the teachers and the girls dominate discussion.

More telling than what Mrs. Bailey and the girls say about Gary, however, is how they treat him. They enact the category of "unpromising boy" in how they behave toward Gary, even if they do not represent this category explicitly. Although Maurice referred to Gary as "you" in line 108, treating him as an addressee, the girls and Mrs. Bailey refer to Gary in the third person throughout the segment. They feel free to talk about him, assuming that he is not a participant in their classroom interaction. This presupposes that girls contribute to class discussion while boys like Gary do not. Mrs. Bailey further presupposes this when she presents the girls as controlling the conversation, at lines 119ff. Several of the girls (and sometimes Maurice, as we will see in Chapter 5) constitute "the group." Mrs. Bailey first casts these girls as representatives of the group, in a teacher-like role – empowering them to judge whether Gary should share something (at lines 119–127). At line 126 she even suggests that they might tease Gary, by saying that the girls could ask him to share something with the group in order to "embarrass" him. Mrs. Bailey often uses teasing in a pedagogically skillful way, to involve students or to defuse a tense situation. However, sometimes she and Mr. Smith join the girls in teasing one or more of the boys in ways that reinforce the category of unpromising boys.

The teachers and girls often positioned the boys as students who were habitually excluded from the classroom conversation, who became third-person objects of discussion and legitimate targets of the girls' teasing. This situation was made more difficult for the boys by their small numbers, ranging anywhere from 20 to 35 percent of the students in class on a given day (i.e., up to six boys out of a total class of up to 17). In this situation, it is not surprising that the boys, except for Maurice, huddled together and kept their heads down. The following type of event occurred often, with a boy refusing to answer the teachers' questions.

> **T/S:** what? (5.0) Gary? males are not going to attack
> 495   males, they've got this clan going.
> **MST:** tsh
> **FSTs:** [1 second of laughter]

Here Mr. Smith identifies the "males" as a group, and he remarks on their sticking together in a "clan." Gary characteristically refuses to answer.

These examples introduce the local metapragmatic model in which girls are cooperative, smart and promising while boys are resistant, dumb and unpromising. By the end of November, Mrs. Bailey had articulated this model explicitly, and several girls were beginning to treat the boys as if this model applied to them. Except for Maurice, the boys did not actively struggle against this social identification – although, as Foley (1996) argues, silence can be a legitimate form of resistance. The case studies of Tyisha and Maurice, to be presented in Chapters 4 and 5, depend on these two students being identified as exceptions to this local gendered metapragmatic model. Tyisha became the most obvious unpromising girl and Maurice became the one promising boy, though in both cases their identities were more complex than these simple characterizations suggest. This gendered model is one essential component of an adequate cross-timescale account of Tyisha and Maurice's social identities. But before turning to these atypical cases, we need to examine the gendered model in more detail. The rest of this chapter provides more robust evidence of the local gendered model by presenting two students who became the prototypical girl and boy in the classroom. Erika was identified as the smartest girl in the class and the student most likely to succeed, while William was identified as the most resistant and unpromising student.

Erika as Smart and Promising

Erika was a fourteen-year-old black female student. She had an unusually high score on the assessment test that teachers received as background information on their students – the only student in this class who was in the top quartile of students across the city. She did not contribute to class discussion as often as the half dozen most vocal girls and Maurice. This may have been because she was shy. Or she may have learned that academically successful girls, especially black girls, risk their academic status if they dominate discussion too much (Fordham, 1996). When Erika did speak, however, teachers and students almost always listened. Other students not only listened to her comments in class, but they also sometimes crowded around her before and after class asking for advice on homework or explanations of topics they did not understand. Both teachers and students treated Erika as the most academically successful student in the class.

This was clear in the teachers' evaluations of her contributions. They sometimes paraphrased or cited Erika's points in a positive way, as in the following segment from December 17.

81   **T/B:** so because as Erika says they- they have more in
       common than they do their
       MRC: [differences
       FST: [differences

At line 81, Mrs. Bailey's "as Erika says" both praises Erika by restating her comment and urges other students to attend because Erika is the one who has made this insightful comment. Maurice and another student are attending closely and jump in to complete the teacher's utterance.

The teachers also cleared space for Erika to contribute much more often than they did for other students. Other students often had to fight for the floor if more than one person wanted to speak, but when the teachers saw Erika trying to talk, they often intervened to give her an opportunity. On April 12, for instance, Mrs. Bailey said, "Okay, Erika. Let Erika explore this point a bit. Go on and say, everybody listen." The teachers also often counted on Erika to answer more difficult questions. On February 22, for instance, Mrs. Bailey asked students to find evidence from the text to disprove a claim Tyisha has made.

       T/B: find it and help her understand it. this is where your
       responsibility as students comes in. when somebody says,
815   hey, if I go into Athens and I'm, I'm from Africa, I'm
       going to be killed. find something that says that she's wrong.

After a couple of wrong answers, Erika speaks up.

       T/B: Erika's got it. where we read before.
       ERK: it says, our city is thrown open to the world and we
       never expel a foreigner or prevent him from seeing or

830   learning anything of which the secret if revealed to an
enemy might profit. that's why I was <u>say</u>ing that I <u>don't</u>
think just because they would be <u>black</u> they would be
<u>slaves</u>.

This passage shows the contrast in classroom identities between Tyisha, the most clearly unpromising girl, and Erika the prototypical promising girl. This is a typical instance of classroom participation for Erika, getting the right answer and receiving the teacher's praise for it. Although she did not speak as much as some of the other students, when Erika did speak the teachers' response was often something like "Erika's got it."

In addition to explicit praise and their efforts to clear the floor for her, the teachers sometimes used Erika as a participant example when they were discussing a successful or admirable person. Although she did not become a topic of discussion nearly as often as Tyisha or Maurice, Erika became an example of positively valued characters on a few occasions. On February 21, for instance, the class was discussing Pericles' funeral oration and Athenian democracy. Pericles describes the heroic Athenian citizens who had gone to war against Sparta in order to preserve the Athenian way of life. Mr. Smith tries to help students understand the text by proposing Erika as a participant example.

> **T/S:** oka<u>:y</u>. now, suppose I came up to you and said, Erika,
> in <u>or</u>der for this life to sur<u>vive</u>- in order for <u>Ty</u>isha to enjoy
> herself, in order for Brenna to <u>sit</u> there and <u>say</u> nothing, in
> 590   order for Katie to come in <u>late</u> every day, in order for <u>him</u>
> to do- droodles, [in order for <u>Gary</u> to fall <u>asleep</u>=
> **MST:**   [droodle (hhh)
> **T/S:** =in order for <u>Cordell</u> to <u>speak</u> lower, in order for
> <u>I</u>vory to say <u>nothing</u>, <u>you</u> have to go out and defend their
> 595   right and die. what do you tell me?

As illustrated extensively in Chapters 4 and 5, these teachers often nominate students as participant examples when those students' own social identities are analogous to the character being discussed. So Mr. Smith's selection of Erika as a participant example here may identify her as cooperative or heroic like the Athenian soldiers they are discussing. In this example, Mr. Smith also explicitly identifies various other students. Unlike Erika, who in the example is sacrificing herself for the good of the society, Mr. Smith takes the opportunity to point out other students' deficiencies. Tyisha, as we will see in Chapter 4, is the most stigmatized student in the class, and Mr. Smith says that she just wants to "enjoy herself." Brenna and Katie are white girls who rarely participate in class – as Mr. Smith says, Brenna "sits there and says nothing" and Katie "comes in late every day." Gary, as we have seen, is one of the stigmatized boys, and he spends more time and energy combing his hair and daydreaming than participating in class. Mr. Smith says that he just wants to "fall asleep." Mr. Smith also takes the opportunity to make negative comments on an unidentified male who doodles, on Cordell who talks too loudly and on Ivory who says nothing. This example identifies Erika as a good student, in contrast to the seven students whose negative characteristics Mr. Smith describes. The students he does not criticize in the example are Maurice and one other boy, the half dozen vocal girls who dominate class discussion and perhaps William (although William might be the "him" at line 590).

The example also shows that there are a few girls who do not often participate in class and who thus might not fit the model of promising girls – Katie, Brenna and Ivory. (Cordell normally fits the model, participating actively and receiving the teachers' praise, despite Mr. Smith's comment at line 593 about how she speaks loudly.) But the fact that all the cooperative, vocal students except Maurice are girls is still significant. Teachers and students presuppose that cooperative, successful students are girls, even if they do not consistently presuppose that all girls are successful. And Erika, as Mrs. Bailey makes clear again later in the discussion on February 21, is the paradigmatic cooperative and successful girl: "I don't see anyone writing that down, except Erika."

As described above, contemporary Americans are developing an increasingly robust sociohistorical model of gender and school success in which boys are less academically promising and less cooperative than girls (Newkirk, 2002). Mrs. Bailey, Mr. Smith and their students had this model available from the beginning of the year. If teachers and students had only drawn on this gendered metapragmatic model a few times across the year, there would not have been a robust local version of this model. Instead, the sociohistorical model itself would simply have been presupposed in separate events. However, in this classroom, across several months, Mrs. Bailey and the female students consistently drew on and intensified the sociohistorical model, creating a robust local model of gender and school identity in which the girls were habitually identified as cooperative, smart and promising. Despite the sociohistorical model of cooperative, successful schoolgirls, there are many other (often contradictory) gendered models that could have been used to identify students in any given event. In Mrs. Bailey and Mr. Smith's classroom, however, these other models became less likely to be relevant in any particular event as the robust local metapragmatic model of promising girls and unpromising boys became more entrenched.

William the Stereotypical Boy

On the other end of the spectrum from Erika was William, the prototypical boy, who was both explicitly characterized and interactionally positioned as resistant, unintelligent and unlikely to succeed. As the local model of promising girls and unpromising boys became more deeply entrenched, it became more likely that William would be identified as unpromising in any given event. The following sections trace how the teachers and the girls came habitually to presuppose this identity for him. William illustrates most vividly the gendered model of identity that developed locally in this classroom – a model that became important background against which Tyisha, Maurice and other students were identified across the year.

The analysis of William also illustrates three important aspects of social identification. First, it illustrates a "trajectory of identification," showing how an individual can develop a habitually presupposed local identity over several months in a classroom. Compared to Tyisha and Maurice, William's trajectory was relatively simple – he began the year as just another student, quickly became the prototypical unpromising boy and continued with this classroom identity for the rest of the year. But his social identity does nonetheless emerge and thicken across a trajectory of events. Second, the analysis of William shows how categories from the curriculum can be used to facilitate a student's developing social iden- tity. Unlike Tyisha and Maurice, William's identity does not systematically overlap with a curricular theme across the year. But teachers and students do opportunistically use curricular categories to reinforce his identity as an unpromising boy. Third, the analysis of William's developing social identity shows how participant examples can be particularly rich sites of social identification. William was identified in many other events as well, but participant examples played an important role.

William was a fourteen-year-old African American male who had poor test scores and was not doing well in school. Like almost all the other boys, William tried to sit in the back of the classroom and often talked surreptitiously with his friends during class. Increasingly over the year, he did not participate willingly in class, tended to give terse answers when called upon and sometimes refused to answer direct questions from the teachers. Both inside and outside of class, William appeared laconic. He was physically the largest student in the class, and he played football. He spent time between classes with a group of male friends that included Maurice. William sometimes got into shoving and teasing matches with the vocal girls before and after class. These matches were most often instigated by the girls. Once or twice, however, I did observe him retaliate by shoving a girl after she had teased him during class.

As I argued above, William's reserve in class could have had various implications for his social identity. He could have been identified as a stereotypical resistant black male student. But he could also have been identified as someone who legitimately refuses to join a system rigged against him (Foley, 1996; Willis, 1977). Or he could have been identified as a project for the teachers – someone they coaxed back into the academic mainstream. These and other possible social identities were potentially available for William when he began ninth grade in Mrs. Bailey and Mr. Smith's classroom, because these metapragmatic models existed at a sociohistorical timescale and could have been drawn on in class. Over the academic year, however, as teachers and students came to identify William as an unpromising boy, it became less likely that other potentially relevant models would be used to identify him.

William's identity thickened at the same time as Mrs. Bailey and the vocal girls developed their intensified local model about promising girls and unpromising boys. The teachers and the vocal girls often singled William out as the prototypical unpromising boy. He was both explicitly identified and interactionally positioned as resistant, unintelligent and unpromising, and he became a preferred example of characters that were backward or difficult. This started early in the year. On October 9, for instance, in a class about creation myths, Mrs. Bailey identified William as resistant and unintelligent. Right before the following segment, they were discussing the role of insects in a creation myth.

> **T/B:** what is the relationship between insects and the earth?
> **FST:** they're both living.
> 250 **T/B:** they're both living. hey come on, pay attention.
> William, what do you know about insects in relationship to
> the earth? (2.0) know anything about insects? tell me one
> thing you know about insects. (3.0) nothing?

At line 250 Mrs. Bailey asks students to pay attention. Several students seem distracted around this point in the transcript, as indistinct background conversation can be heard, but the teacher singles out William as the target of her question. Teachers often ask disruptive or distracted students to answer a question about what has just been said as a way of disciplining them or getting them to pay attention. By singling out William, then, Mrs. Bailey may be identifying him as a disruptive student.

William does not answer her question, which is not unusual. Mrs. Bailey responds by changing her question in a way that presupposes something else about William. At line 251, by phrasing her initial question as "what do you know," Mrs. Bailey presupposes that William knows something. At lines 252–253, she simplifies the question to "tell me one thing you know." Despite the simplification, this still presupposes that William knows at least one thing. When she waits several seconds and still gets no response, she changes her question to "nothing?". This presupposes that he does not know anything about insects. Because someone who truly knows nothing about insects would be unintelligent, in this segment the teacher acts as if William is not only misbehaving but also not smart.

This one incident by itself did not establish William as the prototypical unpromising boy. On October 10 they could have begun interpreting

William's resistance as legitimate, or they could have begun to coax him into becoming a model student. But as the local model of promising girls and unpromising boys became an increasingly salient resource for identifying boys and girls in this classroom, William was consistently identified as an unpromising boy. Across many events like this, his local identity thickened. The rest of this chapter follows William through several events across his trajectory of identification.

William Out of Control. On November 30, William was identified again as the prototypical unpromising boy, this time through a participant example. This class session focused on the concept of "discrimination." Mrs. Bailey gave two brief participant examples to illustrate the common meaning of "discrimination" as unjust treatment of someone based on irrelevant characteristics.

75   **T/B:** okay, that's one meaning of discrimination. I look and
       I see differences. I see Gary is white, and, and Eugene is
       black and I discriminate against Eugene because he's black.
       or I see that Katina is a girl and- and William is a boy and I
       discriminate against William because he's a boy and girls
80   are much easier to deal with. (2.0)

Mrs. Bailey reiterates her common judgment about girls and boys at lines 79–80: "girls are much easier to deal with," probably meaning that they are more cooperative than boys in class. While making this point, she singles out William as the example of a boy who is less easy to deal with. She also singles out Gary and Eugene, but as examples of their race and not their gender. William is the one she mentions as an example of how boys are harder to deal with, and this helps to establish his status as the prototypical resistant boy.

As class discussion continues on November 30, William becomes a character in an extended participant example. This discussion shows how the teachers and some of the female students continued to single William out as a resistant, unintelligent, unpromising student and how they used a curricular category to do this. The text on this day was from the *Upanishads*, and it focuses on a less common sense of "discrimination" – meaning "discernment." The text has two main characters. One shows discrimination by selecting a worthy goal and maintaining self-control on the way to reaching that goal. The other lacks self-control. As the text says, "He who lacks discrimination, whose mind is unsteady and whose heart is impure, never reaches the goal."

Mrs. Bailey notes that "self-control" is a category on some report cards, and she uses this as an example to explore the concepts of self-control and discrimination described in the text. William quickly gets nominated as an example of a student who received a "check" in self-control in prior years (i.e., who was marked down for failing to behave in class).

> **T/B:** so, the kid that gets the check in self-con<u>trol</u> is a kid who does what in the classroom?
>
> 140 **WIL:** doesn't behave.
>
> **FST:** don't behave
>
> **T/B:** like <u>what</u>, William, give me a specific.
>
> **FST:** William talks too much.
>
> **T/B:** <u>talks</u> too much? wait, that doesn't seem to be a
>
> 145 problem with <u>you</u> people.
>
> **FSTs:** [2 seconds of laughter]
>
> **T/B:** did <u>you</u> ever get a check in self-control? (1.0) for tal<u>king</u> too much? no?
>
> **FST:** he doesn't talk a <u>lot</u>.
>
> 150 **T/B:** well, what did you- [what did you- what did you do=
>
> **FST:**   [he talk a lot.
>
> **FST:**   [°he doesn't talk a lot°
>
> **T/B:** =that got you the check in self-control?
>
> **FST:** talk a lot.
>
> 155 **WIL:** tal<u>king</u> too much.
>
> **T/B:** you <u>played</u> around too much.
>
> **CAS:** and he <u>talked</u> too much.
>
> **T/B:** <u>talk</u> too much.
>
> **WIL:** <u>she</u> talked too much.
>
> 160 **FSTs:** [1 second of giggling]
>
> **T/B:** Cass<u>and</u>ra talked too much.
>
> **FST:** no:

At line 140 William offers an answer to Mrs. Bailey's question. Especially early in the year, he did sometimes answer questions, albeit tersely. Mrs. Bailey does not fully accept his answer, however. Instead, at line 142 she pushes him for more information. This is likely part of Mrs. Bailey's intermittent but ongoing attempts to involve William in class discussion. At line 143, however, a female student makes William himself an object of discussion by volunteering him as an example. Just as the character in the text lacks self-control, this girl suggests, William talks too much in class and thus lacks self-control. This does not fit with William's reserved behavior in Mrs. Bailey and Mr. Smith's class, which Mrs. Bailey and another student note at lines 144–145, 149 and 152. But it turns out that the female student who volunteered William at line 143 has in mind a case from several years earlier in which William did get in trouble for talking in class. Mrs. Bailey picks up on this at line 147; and at lines 151, 154 and 157 several female students claim that years ago William did talk too much in class. William himself admits this at line 155. So William is emerging here as a central character in a participant example, with his past self exhibiting a lack of self-control by talking in class. This comes to have implications for William's social identity in Mrs. Bailey and Mr. Smith's classroom, as characterizations of him as undisciplined in the example spill over into characterizations of William himself in the present.

The girls act in this segment as they typically do toward William and the other boys. By volunteering William in an unflattering example, a girl opens William up to teasing. And several other girls join her in describing William's past lack of self-control, using the third person and excluding him from the conversation. As we will see, this example facilitates teasing that gets quite heated and that goes on for almost twenty minutes. William himself is uncharacteristically active in this class discussion. He answers the teacher's questions at lines 140 and 155 even though the example is not flattering to him. And he also fights back against the girls, as we can see at line 159. This is still relatively early in the year, and William occasionally struggles against the girls' teasing and identification of him as an unpromising boy.

As Mrs. Bailey and the girls continue to discuss the participant example, they make it increasingly hard for William to avoid being identified as an unpromising boy. Cassandra goes on to narrate the specific events in which William used to bother her by talking in class.

      CAS: only time I talked when he bothered me. he sat right
      in front of me, and he always turned around, and talked.
165 **WIL:** °never said anything°
      FSTs: [2 seconds of overlapping chatter]
      FST: the poor thing
      FSTs: [1 second of laughter]
      T/B: why- why did the teacher say that was <u>bad</u>?
170 **CAN:** cause maybe
      WIL: she [4 unintelligible syllables]
      T/B: there's-
      FST: because he couldn't control it.
      FST: because he was doing something that he wasn't
175 supp<u>os</u>ed to be doing.
      T/B: what was he supp<u>os</u>ed to be doing? [instead of=
      FST: [sitting.
      T/B: =bothering Cassandra.
      CAS: doing his <u>work</u>.
180 **FST:** doing his work and paying attention to his teacher.
      T/B: okay, so when he: (1.0) instead of <u>do</u>ing his work
      decided to turn around and bother Cass<u>and</u>ra, then he
      wasn't cont<u>roll</u>ing himself. why'd you <u>do</u> that William?
      FSTs: [1 second of laughter]

185   **CAN:** because he wanted to be <u>bad</u>.
       T/B: oh, I don't think that William wanted to be <u>bad</u>. why,
       why did you turn around and bother her?
       WIL: °I didn't have nothing else to do°
       T/B: you didn't have [anything else to do?
190   **T/S:**   [umm-
       CAS: probably for attention.

After Cassandra describes his disruptive behavior at lines 163–164, William
objects at line 165. But Mrs. Bailey and the girls ignore his objection and
keep referring to him in the third person. At line 169 Mrs. Bailey treats
Cassandra's account as accurate and explores William's behavior as an
example of "bad" or undisciplined behavior. Then at line 173, a female
student follows the teacher's lead, using a category from the curriculum to identify William's behavior: "he couldn't control it." The teachers and the girls then discuss how William's lack of self-control under-
mined the goals that a good student would have had. Like the character
in the text, William failed to pursue worthy goals because he lacked self-
control. Cassandra becomes an authoritative commentator on William's
actions (and at line 191, on his motivations) as they discuss William's
shortcomings.

Note how Mrs. Bailey and the girls are beginning to use the curricular
categories of "self-control" and "goals" to help identify William. In this
discussion of the curriculum, mediated by the participant example, they
identify William as someone who violated classroom rules and failed to do
what teachers expected of him. As we will see, they may also be identifying
William himself, in the present, as lacking self-control and as unlikely to
reach his academic goals. By this point in the academic year William has
already been cast as an unpromising student who sits in the back of the
room and refuses to participate. As he did in the events described in the
example, then, William is still failing to pursue worthy academic goals.
Thus the participant example helps Mrs. Bailey and the girls draw categories from the curriculum and use them to identify William himself.

In addition to identifying him in this way, the girls and the teachers also
put increasing interactional pressure on William. From the beginning of
the example, the girls have all referred to William in the third person. That
continues in this segment, and Mrs. Bailey follows their lead up to line
183. Thus the teacher and the girls treat William as an object and talk about
his uncontrolled behavior. William tries to break in and defend himself at
lines 165 and 171, but Mrs. Bailey and the girls do not let him. Then at
line 183, Mrs. Bailey turns to William and addresses him as "you." By this
point, however, she has accepted Cassandra's side of the story – concluding
that "he wasn't controlling himself." When she asks, "Why'd you do that,
William" (i.e., why did you turn around and bother Cassandra), the teacher

seems to be teasing him as well as pursuing the discussion of self-control. Remarkably, given how the teacher and girls have been treating him in this segment, and given his tendency to remain silent, William answers her question at line 188.

Cassandra's comment at line 191, however, foreshadows how William's interactional position is about to get worse. The girls and Mrs. Bailey go on to speculate about William's motivation for bothering Cassandra.

> **T/B:** can anyone tell me why William was <u>bothering</u>
> Cassandra?
> **FST:** attention.
> **TYI:** he probably liked <u>her</u>.
> 210 **T/B:** he liked her?
> **FST:** no
> **STS:** [1 second of laughter]
> **T/B:** okay, so his <u>liking her</u> might have done what?
> **FST:** caused [the trouble.
> 215 **FST:**   [[6 unintelligible syllables]
> **FST:** got him uncon<u>trolled</u>. he couldn't <u>help</u> himself.
> **FSTs:** [1 second of laughter]
> **T/B:** he couldn't <u>help</u> himself. he liked Cassandra so much
> that he couldn't <u>help</u> himself.
> 220 **FSTs:** [4 seconds of laughter]
> **FST:** felt that he couldn't control it.
> **T/B:** [FSTs continue to giggle throughout T/B's turn] is
> it very clear? there- there was William and he knew he was
> supposed to be doing his <u>spelling</u> workbook, right? and fill
> 225 in those ten pages of spelling this week. <u>and</u> there's
> Cassandra, sitting be[hind him,=
> **FST:**   [doing her work
> **T/B:** =[and he:=
> **FST:**   [and all he could think of was-
> 230 **T/B:** =he had one thing he was sup<u>posed</u> to do and he had
> something else that he:?
> **FSTS:** <u>wanted</u> to do.
> **T/B:** <u>wanted</u> to do.
> **FST:** Mrs. Bailey
> 235 **T/B:** a:nd (1.0) rather than doing what he was sup<u>posed</u> to
> do he did what he:?
> **FSTs:** <u>wanted</u> to do.
> **T/B:** =wanted to do. and the teacher said that he what?
> **FST:** <u>lacked</u> self-control.
> 240 **T/B:** <u>lacked</u> self-control. okay, now does that start to, to- to-
> to bring us a little bit closer to this?

At line 209 Tyisha suggests that William bothered Cassandra because he liked her. Another girl makes the teasing even more pointed at line 216 by speculating that William was in the grip of uncontrollable urges such that "he couldn't help himself." This clearly suggests sexual desire, and it therefore generates substantial laughter from several female students. Mrs. Bailey aligns herself with the girls by repeating the comment at line 218. The class is still discussing the example of William and Cassandra in order to explore the concepts of self-control, goals and discrimination, but the girls and Mrs. Bailey are also teasing William about his alleged desire for Cassandra.

For the rest of the segment, Mrs. Bailey connects the example back to the curricular concepts, trying to make explicit the analogy between William and the undiscriminating character in the text. Just as the character in the *Upanishads* lacks self-control and fails to reach a worthy goal, William lacked self-control and failed to learn in class. When a female student tries to continue the teasing at line 229 by further describing William's obsession, Mrs. Bailey speaks over her and draws out the analogy between William and the character in the text. Mrs. Bailey and the girls thus do two things simultaneously in discussing the example of William out of control. They use the example in order to learn about the curriculum by exploring the analogy between William's lack of self-control and the character in the text. And they use the example to tease William about his alleged desire for Cassandra.

Because it doubles William's roles in the classroom – casting him as both an example of undisciplined behavior and a student participating in discussion of the curriculum – the participant example facilitates both the academic and the identity-related functions of this classroom discussion. The example also allows teachers and students to connect the academic learning and the social identification, as they use curricular categories as resources to identify William. Mrs. Bailey and the girls go beyond teasing him about past actions to teasing him about his emerging identity in the present. Like the character in the text, they imply, William fails to discriminate worthy from unworthy goals when he resists participating in Mrs. Bailey and Mr. Smith's class. The curricular categories of "worthy goals" and "lack of discrimination," mediated through the participant example, help the teacher and the girls to identify William himself as an unpromising student. If the class had not developed the robust local model of promising girls and unpromising boys, and if William had not already become a plausible example of an unpromising boy, the example of William out of control would not have had the same implications for William's identity. But given the robust local model and William's emerging identity, this example does help establish William's identity as the prototypical boy.

As the class continues to discuss the example, the implications of the discussion for William's own identity become more salient and more unpleasant. The example of William out of control has so far identified William as resistant because his undiscriminating behavior distracts him from worthy academic goals. But as discussion of the example continues, William himself begins to get characterized as unintelligent and unlikely to succeed.

310 **T/B:**   and, where are- did
the teacher hope William was eventually going to g<u>o</u>?
FST: high school.
FST: tsss [hissing sound produced by one student]
T/B: and from high school?
315 **FST:** coll[ege?
KAT: [probably college
T/B: and from college?
CAN: grad school.
FSTs: [5 seconds of laughter]

Many of these students plan to attend college and graduate school, but the female students' extended laughter at line 319 seems to indicate that they do not expect William to accomplish that.

This segment by itself might not have serious implications for William's identity, but a similar sort of laughter occurs about one and a half minutes later.

 T/B: so, it was di<u>stracting</u>
you from where you wanted to <u>be</u> [and, yet, you did it,=
345 **CAS:**   [yep
 FSTs: [giggle
 T/B: =didn't you? why do you suppose you did
    that, William?
 FSTs: [2 seconds of laughter]
 FST: you have to have a reason.
350 **FSTs:** [1 second of laughter]
 FST: °no self-control.°
 FST: °no self- control.°
 T/B: do you- do you- do you think that when William's
  <u>thir</u>ty, in <u>law</u> school=
355 **FST:** in law school?
 FSTs: [1 second of laughter]
 T/B: =and Cassandra is thirty and in <u>law</u> school, °yeah,
  they had to work a few years and that kind of stuff,° and
  the two of you are in <u>law</u> school, and William is sitting in

360 front of Cassandra, he's gonna to turn around and start
     bothering her in the lecture?
     FST: no.
     FST: no
     GAR: no.
365 **FST:** after work. like if the two of them are meeting
     T/B: is he, do you think he's going to be <u>punch</u>ing her
     during the- the- the lecture?
     STS: no.
     FST: no.
370 **T/B:** sending her <u>notes</u>?
     FSTs: [2 seconds of laughter]

At lines 343–347, Mrs. Bailey repeats the interactional pattern described at line 183, in which she moves from discussing William as "he" to a pointed question directed to him as "you." At lines 351–352, two girls again use the curricular category of self-control to characterize William. As Mrs. Bailey elaborates the example through the end of this segment, she also imagines William doing inappropriate things like "punching" Cassandra.

In addition to reinforcing the picture of William as disobeying classroom rules, Mrs. Bailey also raises the topic of graduate school in this segment. At lines 353–354 she imagines William in law school. This again elicits laughter from the girls, and this laughter might presuppose that William has little chance of making it to law school. It is possible that Mrs. Bailey brought up the prospect of William in law school in order to counter the girls' laughter about William in graduate school that happened at line 319 above. We could interpret her comments about William in law school as implying: When William is in law school, and he may well get there, he will of course be more mature and will not punch Cassandra. But we could also interpret her comments as implying: We all know that William does in fact punch Cassandra and others, and that he is a resistant and generally unsuccessful student, so it is not likely that he will ever make it to law school. With their laughter and teasing of William, the girls clearly support the latter interpretation. They build on the local model of promising girls and unpromising boys to identify William as unpromising. Given my observations in the class and my conversations with her, I believe that the teacher intended the former. She gets caught up in teasing William at times, and his reluctance to participate in class did frustrate her, but she also continued to try to reach him, on occasion, throughout the year. Nonetheless, the girls' strenuous identification of William as unpromising, and the teachers' general acquiescence to this, allowed William's identity as an unpromising boy to thicken further through this example.

Teachers and students continued to discuss this example for several more minutes, and the teachers and girls continued to tease William. At one point, for instance, while connecting the example to the Hindu concept of reincarnation, the teachers and girls decided that William would be reincarnated as a parrot, "something that talks a lot." William continued to resist such treatment, and Mrs. Bailey continued to take the girls' side in teasing him. In the following segment, for instance, they refer to a line from the text in which the character who lacks self-control is described as "living in an abyss of ignorance." Both Mrs. Bailey and Mr. Smith use the example of William to illuminate how those who lack self-control are "ignorant" because they lack the ability to discriminate worthy from unworthy goals.

> **T/B:** Mr. Smith addressed your attention to that, that little piece there in the beginning. and if we think about <u>William</u> here. (1.0) okay? (1.0) living in an a<u>byss</u> of ignorance. was
> 420   William living in an a<u>byss</u> of ignorance?
> **WIL:** [no.
> **FST:** [yeah
> **FSTs:** [some giggles]
> **FST:** yeah.
> 425   **WIL:** no, I wasn't.
> **FST:** °yes, you was°
> **T/B:** yet, wise in their own con<u>ceit</u>. (4.0) did you (1.0) <u>know</u> you were ignorant?
> **FST:** [4 unintelligible syllables]
> 430   **FST:** (hh)
> **T/B:** did you think you were <u>wise</u> in bothering her? do you think it was <u>wrong</u> to bother her? William? do you think it was <u>wrong</u> to talk to her and bother her and all that stuff?
> **FSTs:** [2 seconds of laughter]
> 435   **T/B:** Wi:lliam?
> **FSTs:** [1 second of laughter]
> **T/B:** do you think it was <u>wrong</u> to bother her?
> **WIL:** yeah.
> **CAS:** then why did you <u>do</u> it?
> 440   **T/B:** how many of you think William really thought it was wro:ng to bother Cassandra?
> **FSTs:** [2 seconds of laughter]
> **T/B:** okay, could it- could it be that Cassandra, excuse me, could it be that William was living in an- an abyss of
> 445   ignorance, yet <u>wise</u> in his own conceit, thinking that he was not doing something wrong?
> **TYI:** but, then, why would he keep talking to somebody that ignored him?
> **T/S:** then why don't you go back to the o<u>rig</u>inal paragraph

450   Mrs. Bailey <u>read</u>?
       FST: °you go round and round°
       T/S: when a <u>man</u> <u>lacks</u> discrimination, and his <u>mind</u> is
       uncontrolled, his <u>senses</u> are unmanageable=
       FSTs: [1 second of laughter]
455   **T/S:** =like the restive horses of a charioteer.
       T/B: Cassandra?
       CAS: maybe it's- maybe discrimination in that paragraph
       means, like, <u>not</u> knowing the difference between wrong or
       right.
460   **CAN:** but then when- but then- the <u>tables</u> turned on <u>him</u>.
       T/B: okay but let's- let's establish that <u>meaning</u> first.
       Cassandra was it- brought out another meaning of
       discrimination, and that's to be able to tell the difference
       between what is <u>right</u> and what is wrong. what is <u>good</u> and
465   what is not good. did William lack discrimination?

In this segment Mrs. Bailey once again assumes that categories from the text accurately describe William and confronts him with a pointed question about his behavior: "Did you know you were ignorant" (lines 427–428). Note that Cassandra asks a similar type of question at line 439, showing how the girls are imitating Mrs. Bailey's pedagogical technique in order to tease William. William resists the negative characterization at lines 421 and 425, but he does answer the teacher's question at line 438. Mrs. Bailey then addresses the rest of the class at lines 440–441, empowering them to make a judgment about him. As they have done throughout the example, in this segment the girls and Mrs. Bailey most often treat William as an object of discussion and tease him.

It becomes clear in this segment that the example also helps some students to learn about the curriculum. At lines 445–446, Mrs. Bailey points to William's alleged lack of recognition that he was doing anything wrong, and then Mr. Smith reads a passage from the text about "discrimination." Cassandra follows at lines 457–459 with an insight about the less common sense of "discrimination" that the teachers have been working on all through the class. The students may not have developed rich understandings of the concept "discrimination" here, but they do at least reach the insight articulated by Cassandra. Thus the example of William is not merely a vehicle for teasing and socially identifying him. By building analogies between curricular concepts and the students' own experiences, the participant example helps students learn something about these concepts. Chapter 3 provides more extensive evidence of how participant examples can simultaneously identify students and help students learn the curriculum.

This example of William out of control represents an important event relatively early in his trajectory of identification in this classroom. Before this example on November 30, he had been identified several times as resistant and unlikely to succeed. So students and teachers had begun to presuppose an identity for him, but this participant example helped his identity thicken. Before the example, Mrs. Bailey and the girls had also begun to establish the robust local model of promising girls and unpromising boys. Having this metapragmatic model available to identify boys like William made it easier for them to identify William as an unpromising boy while discussing the example. William's thickening identity and the emerging local metapragmatic model of boys and girls thus reinforced each other.

The analogy between William and someone unable to discern worthy goals helped identify him as a student who was not pursuing worthy academic goals but was choosing instead to resist school. Through the participant example, the teachers and the girls used curricular categories like "lacking self-control" and "unable to discriminate worthy goals" to identify him. When the girls joked about William being unlikely to make it to graduate school, they also reinforced his identity as a student who was unlikely to succeed. And their interactional positioning of William in the third person, as an object of discussion, helped establish him as a nonparticipant in the academic activities of the classroom. This one example by itself might not have had much impact on William's social identity in the classroom, but it did contribute to both the local model of promising girls and unpromising boys and William's local identity. It was an extended, lively, memorable conversation in which Mrs. Bailey and the girls connected William's emerging identity as an unpromising boy to the emerging local model of promising girls and unpromising boys. William could still have ended up with a different local identity, but after this conversation, that was less likely.

Mrs. Bailey's treatment of William here may seem inappropriate. She introduced and fostered the local stereotype of promising girls and unpromising boys. And sometimes she joined the girls when they identified William as unpromising. As I argue in Chapters 1 and 6, however, even if one should condemn Mrs. Bailey for treating William as she did, we should not let quick judgments about the teachers obscure the complex cross-timescale processes – not reducible to the actions or attributes of any individual – that created the social identities that William and other students came to enact. It is also not clear that Mrs. Bailey intended to identify William as an unpromising boy. Mrs. Bailey worked to be accessible and develop good relationships with her students. She used lighthearted teasing as one means to this end, and she may have seized on the participant example involving William to involve him more in class discussion. Her teasing about William's alleged desire for Cassandra was funny, and by itself it was not inappropriate. Furthermore, Mrs. Bailey may not have been aware of the implications that participant examples can have for students' identities. She and Mr. Smith focused on the cognitive implications

of such examples, and students did sometimes learn academically by using
their own experiences to help illuminate the curriculum. Nonetheless, seen
in the context of William's emerging social identity as an unpromising boy,
Mrs. Bailey's teasing of him in this case had serious negative consequences.
As I discuss more extensively in Chapter 6, I believe that we should hold
the teachers responsible for some of these consequences.

William the Slave. As the year went on, the interactional tension between
the boys and the girls increased. The girls dominated discussions, and
when a boy said something – sometimes even when he did not say anything – the girls, often, and the teachers, occasionally, disagreed with his
comments or teased him. This happened, for instance, on January 18 during a discussion of Aristotle's *Politics*. Teachers and students were exploring hierarchies that Aristotle sets up between opposing terms, including
man/woman and master/slave. They initially discussed the alleged superiority of men to women, and this generated some heated exchanges. Having the superiority of males as an explicit curricular topic led the boys and
girls to a few vigorous disagreements.

In the following segment, they discuss Aristotle's claim that, for women,
it can be courageous to obey. We normally think of disobedience as more
likely to involve courage, so Mrs. Bailey searches for an example to help
students understand Aristotle.

> **T/B:** let's see something. yeah. let's find something where
> it's pretty clear cut. it's pretty <u>clear</u> cut. I mean, think of
> your own lives. when have you had to do something that it
> 185 took courage to do and what you were <u>doing</u> was obeying.
> **CAN:** when teacher tells you to write a <u>paper</u>, an essay or
> something.
> **T/B:** ahh
> **STS:** [3 seconds of overlapping comments and laughing]
> 190 **T/B:** <u>Eugene</u>, what's your problem?
> **EUG:** that's cour<u>age</u>ous? to write a <u>paper</u>?
> **T/B:** well, explain to her why you <u>don't</u> think it is.
> **CAN:** yeah, explain it to me.
> **STS:** [4 seconds of overlapping comments]
> 195 **MRC:** maybe if he have to read it in front of the <u>whole</u>
> class, but just <u>writing</u> it is not being courageous.

At line 189 several male students object to Candace's answer with unusual
vigor. Mrs. Bailey singles out Eugene as someone who "has a problem" –
perhaps identifying his behavior as inappropriate in the classroom. But
Eugene and Maurice go on to offer plausible arguments. At line 192
Mrs. Bailey asks him to address his argument to Candace. At line 193
Candace adopts a confrontational tone, challenging Eugene to make the

argument. Maurice then answers for the boys, criticizing Candace's point, and the conflict continues. The boys participate more actively than usual here, perhaps because the topic of gender has increased tension between the boys and the girls.

In addition to illustrating the continuing conflict between boys and girls, the discussion on January 18 also includes another participant example that contributes to William's identity as the prototypical unpromising male student. The vocal girls continue to use the local metapragmatic model of promising girls and unpromising boys as one resource in their ongoing conflict with the boys. Later in the discussion on January 18, the conversation shifts from the man/woman hierarchy to the master/slave one. The teachers are trying to get students to imagine what it would have been like to live in a slave-owning society.

> **T/B:** <u>what</u> do you have to do in your head to get
> yourself to <u>own</u> another human being?
535 **FST:** be racist
> **MRC:** think you're superior
> **T/B:** you each have five hundred dollars and Erika's for
> sale.
> **STS:** [2 seconds of student laughter]
540 **T/B:** maybe we should make it William, we might get more
> work out of William.
> **STS:** [3 seconds of overlapping student comments and
> laughter]
> **T/B:** <u>five</u> hundred dollars, William is yours.
545 **STS:** [5 seconds of overlapping student comments and
> laughter]
> **T/B:** what would you have, what would you have to <u>do</u> to
> get yourself to <u>buy</u> William? what would have to be going
> <u>on</u> in your head?
550 **FST:** I would have to convince him to come and work for
> me.
> **T/B:** <u>you</u> don't have to convince him. he's for <u>sale</u>.

At lines 537–538, Mrs. Bailey initially offers Erika as an example of a hypothetical slave whom the students could own. But she quickly shifts to William, because "we might get more work out of William." Given their presupposed identities, this quick shift from Erika to William does not seem accidental. Being a hypothetical slave is not a desirable role, and William is more likely to get chosen for such a role. In saying that we would get more work out of him, Mrs. Bailey also alludes to William's physical strength. Choosing William instead of Erika draws on the brains versus brawn distinction central to Erika and William's robust local identities.

As the class continues to discuss this example, the teachers ask the students to imagine William as a slave. This is (happily) difficult for students, who keep imagining William as an autonomous human being with rights. In order to help them understand ancient Greece, however, the teachers need students to grasp the reality of slavery. So Mr. Smith elaborates the example, imagining William as a dehumanized slave. While pursuing his legitimate pedagogical goal in this way, Mr. Smith also reinforces William's identity as a physically imposing, unintelligent person and as a legitimate object of teasing in the classroom. This further solidifies both the local model of unpromising boys and William's identity as the prototypical boy. This example thus serves as another important event along William's trajectory of identification.

In the following segment, Mr. Smith describes William as strong and as suited to menial labor. He also continues to talk about William in the third person, excluding him from the conversation.

> **T/S:** okay? now there is William who is a <u>piece</u> of
> property=
> **STS:** [3 seconds of student comments and laughter]
> **T/S:** =[and, no, no, you've gotta, if you're not going to do
> 625 this mind sync, I can use you as well, you won't catch
> I think what she's, that's a piece of property, okay? that is not
> a human being. that's a <u>valuable</u> piece of goods.
> **JAS:** okay.
> **T/S:** how would you, <u>why</u> do you think you first of all,
> 630 would want him, why do you <u>want</u> property?
> **JAS:** to work the <u>land</u>.
> **T/S:** huh?
> **JAS:** never mind.
> **TYI:** cause I want it.
> 635 **STS:** [2 seconds of laughter]
> **T/S:** what about him would make William valuable? now,
> wait. ah ah. I know you're making jokes of this, but we
> could use you too, what about <u>that</u> person, <u>that</u> piece of
> property that's for sale that would make him valuable?
> 640 **JAS:** what would make him valuable?
> **T/S:** valuable.
> **FST:** °[4 unintelligible syllables]°
> **T/S:** uh, okay, I'm the, I own property, quite a bit, uh, well
> he doesn't look like he's crippled or injured. he has two
> 645 eyes that <u>see</u>, uh, he has muscles on his <u>hands</u>, fingers are
> intact, uh, uh, tends to keep quiet.
> **TYI:** (hh)
> **T/S:** uh, okay, I can use him. I umm, I'll make certain he's
> clothed so he doesn't get <u>frostbitten</u>, fed so he doesn't <u>starve</u>

650 to death, just the way you put your chain away in your
jewelry box. uh, I'll make certain that if he gets <u>sick</u>, uh I
will try to keep him relatively healthy and uh, in return, let
me see. well, I need the uh dog poop shoveled up and I
need the <u>leaves</u> cleaned, and I <u>don't</u> like to walk on the
655 roof, so that can be your job to shovel off the snow, uh, I
don't like taking out garbage, that'll be your job, and
otherwise, you will <u>not</u> interfere with what I'm doing.

At line 623 the students talk and joke in the background, as they have
been doing throughout this discussion of William the slave. The teachers
have a difficult time getting them to focus on the academic aspects of this
example. Mr. Smith responds by threatening that he will imagine them
in the role of slave, at lines 624–625 and 637–638. This makes clear that,
for Mr. Smith at least, being placed in the role of a hypothetical slave is
not desirable. Mr. Smith also reinforces the characterization of William
as strong, by mentioning his muscles at line 645. And he imagines some
unpleasant menial tasks for William at lines 653–657.

The students laugh about William in this role, at lines 623, 635 and 647,
presumably because they recognize some characteristics of William the
unpromising boy in Mr. Smith's description. Nonetheless, the girls make
fewer jokes and laugh less than one might expect, given their behavior
toward William in earlier classes. In fact, as the discussion continues, both
girls and boys refuse to imagine why they or others might want to own
William as a slave. The idea of slavery is so aversive for these African
American students that they will not engage with the topic or the example,
despite having William as a potential target for their teasing.

T/S: she said
670 you're all in agreement, you <u>can't</u> <u>own</u> William. why?
FST: [because
FST: [because he's a human being.
T/S: wait a second. we're in a [1 unintelligible syllable]
okay?
675 MRC: cause he, no.
JAS: he has a mind, he can think for himself.
T/S: now, come on, this is not funny. I am very <u>serious</u> in
what I just said. yeah.
LIN: because he's um, cause today during these days, we
680 don't need a piece of property because we have to do it
ourselves, in older times, they had like <u>big</u> plantations and
like <u>big</u> houses-
T/S: but I mentioned things that are not big, it's shoveling
the snow, taking out the dog poop, [sweeping=

685 **LIN:**   [oh, uh
     T/S: =sweeping the house out, uh keeping the sidewalks
     clean, raking the leaves, that's <u>not</u> big things. I just don't
     like doing them. and it just wastes my time [and I can=
     TYI: [isn't it against
690 the law to
     T/S: =use him.
     T/B: yes, it's against the law (hh) to own a slave (hh) now,
     Tyisha.
     STS: [1 second of laughter]
695 **T/B:** but the question is what- why is it that you all without
     even the <u>law</u> coming in here, would not con<u>ceive</u> of owning
     William?
     CAS: because he's a human being.
     T/B: he's a human being. so what? what does that have to
700 do with it?
     CAS: they have feelings, just like everybody else.
     T/B: just like everybody else, just like?
     CAS: me.
     T/B: just like <u>you</u>. you see William as what?
705 **STS:** a person.
     T/B: a person like?
     FST: you.
     FST: me.
     T/B: yourself.

Instead of joining Mr. Smith and Mrs. Bailey in teasing and perhaps also
identifying William here, the students take his side. Unlike the unpleasant
ways that the girls treat him in other discussions, here they defend William
as a human being who can think for himself, has feelings and is essentially
like everyone else. The teachers selected William for the role of a slave
and a menial laborer, probably because of his presupposed identity as a
physically strong but unintelligent student. However, the other students
refuse to accept this positioning of William. In this particular event William
unexpectedly fails to be identified as an unpromising boy.

I argue that the girls fail to take advantage of this opportunity to tease
William because his local identity as an unpromising boy is overshadowed
in this case by his identity as an African American. The teachers' example suggests an analogy between William's identity as a physically strong,
unintelligent, unpromising boy and his hypothetical role as a slave and a
menial laborer. And the curricular model of a strong, uneducated, dehumanized slave might have been used to identify William himself – just
as teachers and students used the curricular model of an uncontrolled,
undiscriminating person to identify William himself as they discussed the

example of William out of control. But for these African American students, the curricular topic of slavery strongly presupposes a different metapragmatic model. Most African Americans are descended from slaves and continue to feel the effects of slavery quite deeply. We can see that the history of American slavery is on the students' minds in the earlier segment at line 535, where a student describes slaveholders as "racist," and when they mention "plantations" and "working the land" at lines 631 and 681. All the students who participate in this discussion are black, and both teachers are white. In this context, then, despite having William as a tempting target, the girls are unwilling to imagine him as a slave and themselves as slave owners. Despite the robust local model of gender differences, and despite the robust identification of William as an unpromising boy, students feel so strongly about the sociohistorical models bound up with American slavery that on this occasion they ignore William's gender and his vulnerability to teasing. This one event does not transform William's local identity, however. In future discussions, as we will see, he continues to be an unpromising boy. But in this event the power of the sociohistorical issue of race preempts the local model.

Mr. Smith tacitly acknowledges that gender would be a safer topic than race when, immediately following the above segment, he says:

710   **T/S:** Mrs. Bailey, I have a better idea. since I can't buy
      William, I'll get married, get a wife, and have her do all of
      this since she's obviously inferior and she can do all of
      this=
      STS: [4 seconds of overlapping comments]
715   **T/S:** =[and it does say she's the manual to the mental
      worker, the barbarian to the Greek, and silence is a
      woman's glory and that woman is a maid. so I don't have to
      own her, since she is already, she can go ahead and do all
      the things that I don't like. I like, I like this idea.

Mr. Smith is probably being deliberately provocative with this comment about treating his wife as a servant, both to provoke student involvement and to change the topic away from slavery and race. Although Mr. Smith does not regularly take the boys' side in the same way as Mrs. Bailey takes the girls', he does make occasional provocative misogynistic comments like this. He thus contributes to the ongoing gender tension in the classroom. In this case, Mr. Smith's shift back to gender as a topic also acknowledges that the students will not discuss William as an example when race and slavery are the salient issues.

William the Spartan. As the year continued, William remained mostly silent in class. But when he did speak or became the subject of discussion, the teachers and girls continued to identify him as resistant, unintelligent and unlikely to succeed. In a short interaction on January 25, for instance, Mrs. Bailey tried to involve William. Earlier on this day, the teachers had students write down their answers to a discussion question. Mrs. Bailey asks William to refer to his written answer and outline the characteristics of a society described in Ayn Rand's *Anthem*, a society proposed by a character named "Equality."

> **T/B:** okay. William?
> **WIL:** I forgot.
> **T/B:** you forgot <u>what</u>?
> **FSTs:** [4 seconds of laughter]
> 135 **FST:** he says I a<u>gree</u> with Cordell's idea before.
> **T/B:** William? you forgot <u>what</u>.
> **FSTs:** [4 seconds of laughter]
> **T/B:** the idea is what kind of society is- shhh. the idea is, William?
> 140 **FSTs:** [7 seconds of laughter]
> **T/B:** kay. (1.0) William. the idea is what, what kind of society do you see <u>E</u>quality trying to develop. (3.0)
> **FST:** he always <u>do</u> this.
> 145 **FSTs:** [3 seconds of laughter]
> **T/B:** would you like <u>look</u> down at your response?
> **FST:** sit there be quiet.
> **T/B:** one of the reasons I wanted you to write something down is so when you got to seminar you
> 150 <u>had</u> it with you. so the next time I ask you to write something for the seminar, please <u>have</u> it, cause that <u>way</u> you don't have to feel like you're on the <u>spot</u>. you already <u>have</u> gotten something down on paper. okay, Martha?

Even with reserved students like William, the teachers periodically tried to engage them in academic discussions. At lines 133 and 136, Mrs. Bailey tries to involve William with an utterance that is perhaps unintentionally funny, asking him: "you forgot what." (If he has forgotten it, how could he answer the question?) So the girls laugh extensively at lines 134 and 137. At lines 138 and 141, Mrs. Bailey acts as if she was not intentionally joking by earnestly asking William to answer a question about the text.

The girls, however, continue to presuppose that they are laughing at William. Their extended laughter at line 137 is inappropriate, given Mrs. Bailey's goal of engaging William with the question, and thus the teacher hushes them at line 138. But the girls are used to laughing at William, and so they continue to laugh at line 140 as if Mrs. Bailey had been making a joke. After Mrs. Bailey restates her question to William and he remains silent, a girl characterizes him at line 144, saying that he always does this – she might mean that he forgets things or that he remains silent. This yields more laughter from the girls. Although Mrs. Bailey has been trying to involve William here, she ends the segment by pointing out how he has failed to write down his answer as she had asked, and she thus reinforces his identity as a student who does not do the assignments. So William is made an exhibit of how not to behave, even though the teacher probably did not intend this when she started the exchange.

In addition to being identified as an unsuccessful student, William also continued to be selected as a participant example when it fit with his class-room identity. On February 22, the class was discussing the Peloponnesian War and contrasting Athens and Sparta. As described more extensively in Chapter 3, they spent many class hours developing contrasting images of Athens and Sparta – casting Athens as a moderate democracy that pro-moted both community and freedom and Sparta as a draconian collectivist state that stripped away individual freedom by (for example) taking chil-dren from their parents at age seven and forcing them to live in military barracks.

In this particular class, Martha has been arguing that the Athenians have no chance of winning the war because the Spartans are a military machine. While responding to Martha's argument, Jasmine inserts William into a participant example in the role of a Spartan.

335

340

345

350

MAR: =yeah, going into a war, they going to face people whose experience in war, I mean, think, eat, feel nothing but military training-
T/S: what you're doing is calling Pericles a liar here.
T/B: (hh)
T/S: okay, we've got four hands at once. I don't know who's first.
FST: Jasmine.
T/S: Jasmine? okay.
JAS: now, Martha.
FSTs: (hh)
JAS: if you was about to fight William, he's bigger, he's taller than you, don't you think he'll beat you up?
MAR: cause he got the-
JAS: wait, wait a minute. don't you think he can beat you? yes or no?
MAR: but not [10 unintelligible syllables]
JAS: I'm sure that he could beat you. he's got more training than you.
[bell rings (3.0)]
FSTs: [5 seconds of yelling back and forth about William

355   fighting Martha]
       MAR: but then I just have to keep fighting, right?
       FST: that's what they're doing.
       MAR: they just keep fighting, but they would <u>n</u>ever beat
       Sparta.

At lines 343–346 Jasmine speaks like a teacher, offering a participant example as part of her response to Martha's argument. She presents William as
analogous to a Spartan soldier and Martha as analogous to an Athenian.
She apparently selected William for this role because he is "bigger" and
"taller" and could beat Martha up. Her selection of William as an example
here again foregrounds his brawn, as opposed to the brains or the moral
character that both the text and the students have been praising in the Athenians. The example is dropped quickly, but it reinforces William's identity
as a brawny and not a brainy person.

Despite the fact that Jasmine and others are talking about him, William
himself says nothing during the discussion of this example. The girls refer
to him in the third person and leave him out of the conversation, while
Martha speaks in the first person and Jasmine refers to Martha in the
second person. As we have seen, the girls and teachers typically talked
about William in the third person and he typically did not respond. On
February 22, however, the teachers had been making a special effort to
have all students participate. All but two students said something during this class, an unusually high level of participation. Mrs. Bailey did
entice William to contribute briefly, later in the discussion. The teachers
have asked students to name some activities that ancient Greeks participated in.

       T/B: and what, William? William, come on, what did you
420   just say?
       WIL: I said, fight lions.
       FST: (hh)
       T/S: <u>fine</u> <u>lines</u>?
       FSTs: <u>fight</u> <u>lions</u>.
425   **T/S:** no:, no that's <u>R</u>oman. that's Roman. <u>Greeks</u> didn't
       fight lions, that's the <u>R</u>omans. you've <u>got</u> the <u>wrong</u> place.
       T/B: well William you're <u>making</u> connections. okay,
       Jasmine or Martha?

William apparently said something difficult to hear before line 419, and
Mrs. Bailey takes the opportunity to involve him in class discussion. He
gives an incorrect answer, and Mr. Smith points this out. But Mrs. Bailey
praises him for trying at line 427, saying that he is "making connections."
Here Mrs. Bailey does not take the opportunity to identify William as a bad
student, but instead praises him for trying to participate. Together with

their occasional attempts to involve him in class discussions, moments like this show that the teachers did give William opportunities and would have liked him to do better. They were sometimes frustrated by his refusal to participate, disciplined him for his surreptitious talking with his friends, and reinforced his identity as an unpromising boy by talking about him in unflattering ways. But they also sometimes invited his participation and tried to encourage him.

William Content with Mediocrity. The most powerful events of identification involving William were participant examples in which students and teachers drew categories of identity from the curriculum and applied them to his hypothetical character, then transferred these categories onto William himself. Together with the girls and teachers' disparaging comments about him, and their interactional positioning of him as uninterested and unpromising, such examples identified William as resistant, unintelligent and unlikely to succeed. William became a participant example again on April 12 while the class was discussing a short story by John Steinbeck called *The Pearl*. In the story, an indigenous person named Quino finds a valuable pearl. He brings it to the Europeans who dominate the local town, and they offer him 1,000 pesos for it. This is a large amount of money for Quino, but not for the Europeans. He suspects that they are cheating him. The story explores whether Quino should be content with the 1,000 pesos, or whether he should make a dangerous journey to sell the pearl for a better price in a distant city.

Mrs. Bailey asks her guiding question at the beginning of the class.

```
       T/B: okay, my question to you, assuming that you've read
       the book, Katie. my question to you is should Quino have
       sold the pearl. it should come as no surprise because we've
10     had it on the back bulletin board since we started. should
       Quino have sold the pearl? so if you could take a moment to
       figure out what your answer is to that. (12.0)
       STS: [15 seconds of chatter]
       T/B: okay William, can we start with you? should Quino
15     have sold the pearl?
       WIL: [no audible response]
       T/B: why?
       WIL: cause.
       T/B: cause? you have to speak up a little bit. cause why?
20     WIL: cause he would have had a lot of money.
```

At lines 8–9, Mrs. Bailey asks the question. She starts with William at line 14, and he offers an answer. His answers at lines 16 and 18 are characteristically terse. (Given what teachers and students say subsequently, it is likely that William nodded his head, meaning "yes," at line 16). William elaborates

a bit in line 20. Mrs. Bailey then moves on to poll other students for their
answers, a pedagogical technique that she often used.

As the discussion proceeds, most students argue that Quino should not
sell the pearl to the Europeans for a low price. Mrs. Bailey and the students
explore various reasons why. They discuss, for instance, whether Quino
might have done something to change the Europeans' domination over
his people. During this discussion the teacher calls on William again, as
well as other students, and he changes his answer to match other students'
views – arguing that Quino should not have sold the pearl but should have
tried to change his situation. At one point Mrs. Bailey briefly points out the
contradiction between William's two answers, but she does not criticize
him or pursue his change of position.

Later in the class, Mrs. Bailey returns to and broadens her original question, asking whether Quino and disadvantaged people like him should be
content with low status or whether they should seek to change it.

> **T/B:** okay now, without screaming at one another, should
> Quino be content, or should Quino go after different things?
> **CAN:** he should go after different things.
> 1245 **FST:** go after other things.
> **FST:** go after other things.
> **IVR:** °go after other things.°
> **T/B:** pardon? (1.0)
> **IVR:** go after other things
> 1250 **T/B:** you don't know?
> **FST:** go after other things.
> **T/B:** Cordell?
> **COR:** go after other things.
> **T/B:** go after other things?
> 1255 **FST:** content.
> **T/B:** be content.
> **FST:** (hh)
> **T/B:** William. William, what's the problem? what, what
> complicates that question for you, William? (2.0)
> 1260 **FSTs:** [3 seconds of chatter]
> **T/B:** William are you content? shhh. William are you
> content? are you happy with what you have at the moment?

Mrs. Bailey is concerned with the students' misbehavior in this class, as
shown by her comment ("without screaming at one another") in line 1242.
She also said in lines 7–8 "assuming that you've read the book," a comment
that provides more evidence that she has been concerned throughout the
class with students' failure to follow standards of classroom behavior. It is
spring, and the weather is nice, and students have been speaking out of
turn and drifting off topic during the discussion. Mrs. Bailey is concerned

about this, and she wants to engage them with the important curricular question of whether oppressed people should be content with their place in society.

As shown at lines 1244–1253, most students in the class continue to argue that Quino should not accept the Europeans' low price and that he should not be content with his low status. Around line 1257 William must have said or done something that the teacher found inappropriate because at line 1258 Mrs. Bailey says, "William, what's the problem" and "what complicates that question for you, William." She then nominates William as a participant example by asking whether he himself is content. By examining William's level of contentment, the class can now explore, by analogy, whether Quino should have been content. Mrs. Bailey uses the participant example both to discipline William – he did something inappropriate, and so she makes him an example – and to draw the class back into discussion of her question about whether Quino should have been content. As usual, this participant example also tacitly opens the question of whether William himself is like Quino. Is he disadvantaged? Does he struggle enough to overcome that disadvantage? As students and teachers continue discussing the participant example, these questions get raised more explicitly.

Right after introducing it, Mrs. Bailey pursues the participant example.

> **FST:** no.
> **T/B:** do you <u>want</u> other things?
> 1265 **FSTs:** [1 second of laughter]
> **T/B:** (hh) okay, can we, can we do something besides <u>nod</u> your <u>head</u> up and <u>down</u>.
> **FST:** (hh)
> **T/B:** okay you're <u>not</u> content with <u>what</u> you <u>get</u>, you <u>want</u>
> 1270 other things. (1.0) does that make you <u>greedy</u>?
> **FST:** n[o
> **WIL:** [no.
> **T/B:** why not?
> **WIL:** °I don't know°
> 1275 **T/B:** you don't <u>know</u>?
> **FST:** cause it's good.
> **T/B:** are you gonna <u>work</u> for these other things?
> **WIL:** yeah.
> **T/B:** are you gonna, o<u>kay</u>, so you're gonna <u>work</u> for other
> 1280 things. does that make you <u>greedy</u>?
> **FST:** yeah.

This example might function both to advance the academic discussion and to identify William. By discussing William as an example, the class can explore both Quino's predicament and the larger curricular question of whether oppressed people should accept their social position. But the example may also have implications for William's own identity because he may or may not be content with his position in the class and in society. The teachers have made it clear over the year that they are not satisfied with William's performance. So this discussion could also be relevant to the question of whether William accepts his identity as an unpromising student. Thus the category of "being content," drawn from the curriculum, could be used to characterize William's own identity. As the discussion proceeds, the example does in fact help students and teachers both explore the curriculum and identify William.

William does not respond verbally to Mrs. Bailey's question at line 1264, but we can infer from lines 1266–1267 that he nods. As we have seen, the teachers and the girls habitually identify William and most other boys as silent, unintelligent and unpromising – for instance, as being limited to simply nodding instead of offering more extensive responses. One female student laughs at line 1268, thus acting as if Mrs. Bailey has been teasing William or as if his behavior is laughable. The teacher may have been teasing, either in an attempt to involve William or in an attempt to play to the audience of girls. In any case, at line 1269 she goes back to pursuing the academic issue.

Mrs. Bailey asks at lines 1269–1270 whether William's lack of contentment – and by analogy Quino's refusal to accept the 1,000 pesos for his pearl – is greedy. She repeats this question at line 1280. She is using a pedagogical strategy, forcing William to defend one of two apparently undesirable positions. If he claims to be content she may accuse him of complacency, but if he claims not to be content she accuses him of greed. The teacher probably intends for William to elaborate his position. She challenges William to develop a more extensive argument about the curricular issue. Mrs. Bailey pursued this strategy often, with many students, and often with pedagogical success. She probably hopes that William might argue, for example, that his lack of contentment stems not from greed but from a desire to overcome an unjust social order.

At lines 1277 and 1279, Mrs. Bailey introduces the idea of "working" to get what one wants. This fits with the curricular issue as she has formulated it: if you are not content, but willing to work to overcome your problems, you are not merely greedy. When Quino held out for more than 1,000 pesos, he might have been working to overcome injustice or holding out for a fair deal instead of merely being greedy. But the idea of "working" to attain things that would make you content might be relevant to William's own classroom identity as well as to the curriculum. The teachers' main complaint about William is that he does not work and that he is content to sit in the back of the room and say nothing. So Mrs. Bailey may also be asking him, implicitly, whether he is willing to work in school for what he wants. Thus Mrs. Bailey may be using the curricular categories of "being content" and "working" to attain one's goals, in order to point out that

William should stop being silent and work harder in the classroom. These implications for William's own identity are still merely potential. However, other signs of identity soon point to the same issues about William's own failure to work hard, such that these implications for William's local identity become more robust.

As the conversation continues, Mrs. Bailey asks William to name something that he might be willing to work for.

> **T/B:** name <u>some</u>thing that you want. (4.0)
> **MRC:** a brain.
> **FSTs:** [4 seconds of laughter and chatter]
1285 **T/B:** William, name <u>one</u> thing you want.
> **WIL:** a car
> **T/B:** you <u>want</u> a <u>car</u>. <u>okay</u>. do want a beat up old ja<u>lo</u>py?
> **FSTs:** [1 second of laughter]
> **T/B:** what <u>kind</u> of car do you want? (9.0) find a <u>car</u>. a
1290 1975 <u>Chev</u>y?
> **FSTs:** [1 second of laughter]
> **FST:** no, a <u>big</u> car.
> **T/B:** he doesn't have a <u>car</u> at the moment. <u>I'll</u> give you the
> 75 <u>Chev</u>y, are you gonna be con<u>tent</u>?
1295 **FST:** <u>I</u> would
> **MRC:** <u>I</u> would
> **T/B:** it starts, it starts when the weather <u>isn't</u> rainy and it
> <u>isn't</u> cold.
> **FSTs:** [3 second of laughter]
1300 **T/B:** and you can't really drive it at <u>night</u> because the
> <u>lights</u> won't stay on? [FSTs continue to laugh] and you can
> be, be, but what you've <u>always</u> <u>wanted</u> is a car?
> **FST:** <u>I'll</u> take it
> **FST:** <u>I'm</u> <u>sel</u>fish.
1305 **FST:** I don't <u>want</u> it (hh)
> **T/B:** uh, is <u>Will</u>iam being ungrateful?
> **FSTs:** no.
> **FST:** it's <u>his</u> money.
> **FST:** it's a <u>piece</u> of <u>junk</u>.
1310 **FSTs:** [1 second of laughter]
> **T/B:** but he's <u>always</u> wanted a <u>car</u>.
> **FSTs:** so?
> **STS:** [2 seconds of yelling]
> **JAS:** he said he wanted a <u>car</u>, he didn't say he wanted a
1315 <u>work</u>ing car.
> **FSTs and T/B:** [1 second of laughter]
> **JAS:** he just <u>said</u> he wanted a <u>car</u>.

T/B: to<u>mo</u>rrow, I can get you one of those <u>cars</u>, that, <u>you</u>
know, has the <u>four</u> wheels and no <u>en</u>gine
1320 **FSTs:** [2 seconds of laughter and chatter]
T/B: okay, shhhh. Gary, name <u>some</u>thing you want? (1.0)
Tyisha, what's something you want?

At line 1283 Maurice teases William, claiming that he wants "a brain" and
thus implying that he is unintelligent. Many other students show that they
get the joke by their sustained laughter. Mrs. Bailey then returns to the
example, and William answers earnestly at line 1286 that he would like a
car. Mrs. Bailey pursues William's idea here, in order to explore the concept
of being "content." She asks what kind of car he wants, at line 1289, but
then she waits several seconds with no response.

When William does not answer, Mrs. Bailey imagines a car for him – a not
very desirable old Chevy. Her example of the Chevy participates both in
their discussion of the curriculum and in the ongoing social identification
of William. By analogy with the story about Quino, William's being content
with the old car would be like Quino accepting the Europeans' low offer.
The class might discuss William's hypothetical choice about the car in order
to explore Quino's choice, and in order to explore the larger curricular
question about being content as opposed to working and improving one's
lot in life.

The example also presupposes something about William's own identity. Mrs. Bailey imagines an old, cheap car for William. She goes on to
characterize it as seriously defective at lines 1297–1301 and 1318–1319.
Mrs. Bailey is joking – successfully, as shown by students' laugher at lines
1299 and 1320. But her imagining William with such a low status car also
contributes to identifying William himself. William gets identified as a fool
who would end up with such a "piece of junk." At line 1314–1315, Jasmine
adopts the same role as Mrs. Bailey has been playing, using the example
to tease William. When Jasmine says "he said he wanted a car, he didn't
say he wanted a working car," she positions William as a sucker who got
what he asked for without realizing his mistake. They are talking about
the hypothetical example, of course. But characterizing William as a fool
and a sucker, even within the example, reinforces the local model of him
as an unintelligent and unpromising student.

The discussion of William's junk car may also presuppose something
about the consequences of William's classroom behavior. These teachers
and students know people who drive old, malfunctioning cars. These are
unfortunate, inner-city residents who have low-paying jobs or do not work.
They generally dropped out of school, and that partly explains their low
socioeconomic status. By explicitly labeling his refusal to participate as
inappropriate, and by developing the model of William the prototypical
unpromising boy, the teachers have suggested that William may be on his
way to failing out of school. So describing him as a hypothetical owner of

a junk car may also suggest something about his fate if he continues to be a silent and unpromising student. Mrs. Bailey's question about whether he is content, in this context, might be a question about whether he will continue to resist working in school. If he does, one might infer, he will end up among the group of people who drive junk cars.

Thus students and teachers' discussion of William as an example, and whether he would be "content," uses the analogy between William and Quino in order to reinforce his identity as an unpromising student. William himself acts as if he is content to stay at the bottom of the class and the bottom of society when he refuses to participate in school. Almost all the other students have said that Quino should refuse his low station in life and work hard to find something better. Most of the girls and Maurice act this way, by working hard in school, but William does not. The participant example allows Mrs. Bailey and the girls to point this out tacitly, as she uses the curricular categories of "being content" and not "working hard" to identify William himself.

Across the year, then, William was identified as the prototypical unpromising male student – resistant, unintelligent and unlikely to succeed later in life. Teachers and students identified him this way using three primary mechanisms. First, they sometimes explicitly described him as unpromising, in comments about his behavior or his potential. Second, they positioned him interactionally as an unpromising boy. For instance, they often talked about him in the third person, presupposing that he did not have anything constructive to offer classroom discussion. And the girls laughed at suggestions that he might succeed later in life. Third, they used categories and models from the curriculum to identify him. In their discussion of the *Upanishads*, for example, William was identified as "out of control," as unable to select "worthy" goals. In their discussion of *The Pearl*, he was identified as "content" with his low station and unwilling to "work" to improve it. Participant examples facilitated this use of curricular categories and models to identify William. Discussion of William as a character in the examples became tacit commentary on William himself. By using William as a participant example, they cast him as "undiscriminating" and "out of control," "strong," not brainy and "content" with his low station in life. The teachers probably used at least some of these participant examples in order to involve William in class, and they clearly intended to offer examples that might help students understand the curriculum. As we have seen, however, the participant examples also had the unintended consequence of contributing to William's identity as an unpromising student.

William's trajectory of identification did not involve sharp shifts in identity across the year. For the first month or two, neither William's identity nor the emerging local model of promising girls and unpromising boys had thickened. If he and others had behaved differently early in the year, his local identity could have developed differently. But by the time the class discussed William as out of control on November 30, the locally circulating model of unpromising boys and William's identity as the prototypical boy were becoming more firmly established. Each of these models contributed to the formation of the other. Having William emerging as a prototypical unpromising boy helped Mrs. Bailey and the girls establish the model of promising girls and unpromising boys, though other students were also identified using this model. And having the emerging local metapragmatic model of unpromising boys helped teachers and students identify William. These two models were different – one was a local metapragmatic model that characterized boys and girls in general and that was shared across teachers and students, while the other applied to William as an individual – but they emerged jointly and contributed to each other. As the academic year went on, these two local models became more commonly and more easily presupposed.

William's identity as an unpromising boy was not only established at the local timescale, however. As described above, metapragmatic models of boys as more likely to resist school and less academically promising circulate more widely in contemporary U.S. society. The local model of promising girls and unpromising boys could not have been established as easily if the sociohistorical model had not been available. Nonetheless, many other gendered sociohistorical models of identity circulate at least as widely and could have become salient in Mrs. Bailey and Mr. Smith's classroom. These teachers and students consistently drew on the "promising girls, unpromising boys" model in particular as they identified each other, and in doing so they established a more dense local circulation of this model than one would find in the larger society. As teachers and students used the model to identify William across many events, they simultaneously helped establish the robust circulation of the model in the classroom and gave empirical reality to the model by identifying William as the prototypical unpromising boy. A full account of William's social identification in this classroom, then, must refer both to publicly circulating sociohistorical models and to locally emerging models of gender and school success.

Although they are both crucial, the sociohistorical and the local timescale are not by themselves sufficient to create a plausible explanation of how teachers and students socially identified William across the year. Neither the local nor the sociohistorical model determined particular events of identification. As shown by the case of "William the slave," William's social identity was established in contingent events, and in any event teachers and students could draw on both expected and unexpected metapragmatic models to identify him. When they discussed slavery on January 18, William was not primarily an unpromising boy but a fellow African American. On other occasions the teachers treated him as a reserved student whom they were trying to support, instead of as an unpromising boy. But in most events where William's identity was at issue, teachers and students did treat him as the prototypical unpromising boy. Each event might have turned out differently, as the class on slavery did, but in fact most other events coalesced into instances of William as unpromising. Thus the social identification of William over the year depended on a configuration of various resources, including sociohistorical models of boys and girls' differential attitudes and success in school, the local model of promising girls and unpromising boys, and the creation of interactional positions for William in particular events across the year. Metapragmatic models emerged contingently at each of these timescales, and the resulting indeterminacy in social identification was only overcome as emerging resources from each timescale came together in a robust configuration that established a clear identity for William in the classroom.

It has been important to introduce the local model of promising girls and unpromising boys because this model provides important background against which Tyisha gets identified and serves as an important resource for Maurice's emerging identity. As shown in Chapters 4 and 5, Tyisha and Maurice have more complex trajectories of identification than Erika and William – both because their identities change more than once across the year and because they are exceptions to the local model of promising girls and unpromising boys. Because of the dense circulation of this local model in the classroom, teachers and students had to take it into account as they identified Tyisha and Maurice. But they had to do more work to adapt this model for these two exceptional cases. Before moving to the analyses of Tyisha and Maurice, Chapter 3 explores in more detail the process of learning the curriculum and the ways in which students' identities can facilitate learning. Now that we have seen the central role that local metapragmatic models can play in social identification, we can go on to explore how local metapragmatic models can systematically overlap with local cognitive models to create local power/knowledge or self/knowledge interconnections.

3

Academic Learning and Local Cognitive Models

Chapter 2 has shown that individual students become socially identified across trajectories, as metapragmatic models of identity come consistently to apply to them both within and across events. Individuals' identities seem natural not only because of sociohistorically developing models like those described by Hacking (1990) and others, but also because of locally developing models like those that emerge in a classroom over a year, and because of the work participants do within events to make sociohistorical and local models fit individuals. This chapter sketches an account of academic learning that reveals important similarities between academic learning and social identification. Academic learning also occurs across trajectories as students draw on and construct cognitive models that help them make sense of curricular content. Like metapragmatic models, these cognitive models develop and circulate both sociohistorically and locally. An adequate account of academic learning must describe resources from different timescales, like the sociohistorical and the local, and explain how various resources work together to constitute academic learning.

The first part of this chapter presents an account of academic learning, describing how such learning depends on locally developing cognitive models. The second part of the chapter illustrates this account by analyzing how students in Mrs. Bailey and Mr. Smith's classroom learned about two central themes from the curriculum. The last part of the chapter describes how social identification and academic learning can overlap with and facilitate each other. Local cognitive models of curricular themes, which facilitate students' academic learning, can contain categories that teachers and students use to identify each other. And the local metapragmatic models that teachers and students use to identify each other can become resources for students learning the curriculum. This meshing of local cognitive and metapragmatic models is a type of power/knowledge or self/knowledge relation that develops at a shorter timescale than the one described by Foucault (1975/1977). Chapters 4 and 5 analyze in detail how local cognitive and metapragmatic models overlapped across Tyisha and Maurice's trajectories in the classroom.

THE PROCESS OF ACADEMIC LEARNING

Events of Cognition

All learning manifests in events of cognition. We know that someone has learned, and the learning has an effect, only because people make sense of something in an actual event. I will use "cognition" to describe the process of making sense of experience at the timescale of specific events, reserving "learning" for a longer timescale process that takes place across events. Much research in cognitive science focuses on events of cognition – often problem solving of various sorts – as a window into learning (following, for example, Newell and Simon, 1972). Despite the fact that behaviorists also focus on events, cognitive scientists go beyond a behaviorist focus on simply getting the right answer. Since the work of Piaget (e.g., Piaget and Inhelder, 1969), Bruner (Bruner, Goodnow and Austin, 1956) and other cognitive pioneers, cognitive science has been interested in conceptual insight – in how people go beyond the right answer and develop deeper conceptualizations that endure over longer timescales. Learning involves the development of a tacit or explicit understanding of some topic or situation, across time, such that one can appropriately react or explicitly represent subsequent instances in productive, insightful ways.

As an example of academic cognition, consider the following segment. This occurred early in the January 24 discussion of Aristotle's *Politics*. Mrs. Bailey and Mr. Smith have been defending Aristotle's claim that the state is prior to the individual because the whole is prior to the part.

> **ERK:** how could it be that the state is prior to the
> individual if it takes the individuals to make the
> state? (4.0)
> 110 **NAT:** I agree with her.
> **FST:** me too.
> **FST:** me three.
> **T/B:** so you mean to say Aristotle's making no
> sense at all?
> 115 **ERK:** maybe he saying that-
> **T/B:** okay, go ahead.
> **ERK:** maybe he's saying that no one comes before
> anybody- anybody else I guess.
> **T/B:** which does Aristotle think is more
> 120 important? [the state or the individual?
> **CAN:**   [the state

FST: the state.
CAN: the state
MRC: the state.
125   **CAN:** the state has to rule over the people (1.0)
CAS: maybe he's [s-
CAN: [to give the laws.
CAS: maybe he's saying that as a whole we're
important but by our<u>selves</u> [we're=
130   **FST:**   [yeah
CAS: =just like, like we cut off our <u>hand</u>, if
we cut off our <u>arm</u>, we don't have much <u>use</u>, will
we? °we won't have much use for it.°

In line 107, Erika asks an important question, one that has engaged politicians and intellectuals for centuries. Being a contemporary American who has not yet learned many alternative conceptualizations of society, she assumes that any state is composed of individuals whose rights as individuals are prior to the collective. Given this assumption, Erika asks how Aristotle can say that the state is prior to the individual. This question fits well with the teachers' agenda for the discussion. They realize that Aristotle's conception of the individual/society relation is counterintuitive to contemporary Americans, and they want the students to explore the alternative assumptions underlying Aristotle's claim. Thus Mrs. Bailey asks at line 113 whether Aristotle is making sense – implicitly suggesting that the students should explore what Aristotle's reasoning might be.

Erika's first response, at line 117, is to claim that Aristotle's emphasis on the collective means that no individual should be treated better than any other. Erika seems to be envisioning a democratic state in which individuals are equal. Although this is a reasonable response for a contemporary American high school student, this interpretation fails to appreciate how deeply Aristotle's account differs from the modern assumption that individuals are prior to the collective. So Mrs. Bailey asks at line 119 whether the state or the individual is more important. Aristotle did not think that a state was composed of people who individually possessed inalienable rights and then agreed to live together. He had a fundamentally different conception of the relation between individuals and society, one in which the society was preeminent and the individual was not fully human outside of a collective. The teachers want students to grasp this more fundamental difference between Aristotle and modern views.

At lines 128–133, Cassandra moves toward understanding Aristotle's view. She borrows an analogy Aristotle makes between a body and the state: Just as individual pieces of a body would not function apart from the whole, individual citizens cannot function apart from society. Using this analogy, Cassandra argues that Aristotle could answer Erika's question.

Even though individuals make up the state in one sense, the whole can be more than the sum of the parts. If we think of individuals not as autonomous beings endowed with rights and capacities prior to their participation in the collective, but instead as pieces whose function is determined and made possible by their position in a larger whole, we come closer to understanding Aristotle's position. Cassandra's brief statement by itself does not necessarily establish or indicate deep understanding on her part, and other students may or may not understand her idea. But if the students use this analogy to explore Aristotle's account of the individual/society relation, Cassandra's comment could be the beginning of genuine cognitive insight.

How is such insight possible, however? Cassandra has borrowed an analogy between the body and the state from Aristotle, and she construes Aristotle's account of the individual/society relation in terms of the body part/whole body relation. As Holyoak, Gentner and Kokinov (2001) point out, such analogical reasoning depends on context-specific inferences. The two elements of an analogy (the state and the body, in this case) have an indeterminate number of aspects that might be crucial to the analogy. How do people know which aspects to reason from in any given case? For instance, Cassandra would be mistaken about Aristotle if she used a model of the body in which the central nervous system controls various parts of the body, with the body parts as subservient tools. This hierarchical conceptualization of body part relations does not capture Aristotle's point, although it accurately describes the human body in some respects. Only some of the ways in which the *body : body parts :: state : individual* analogy could be construed would be accurate and useful. To gain an insight that may help them understand Aristotle, the students need to know which of the many possible analogical relations between body and state capture the point.

This turns out to be a general problem for all theories of cognition. In both routine and extraordinary insights, people cannot simply be grasping the correct general concept given the event that they are trying to understand or the problem that they are trying to solve. Like Cassandra's analogy at lines 128–133, any object or event can be interpreted in many potentially relevant ways. In practice, people often understand analogies and other problems as they were intended, and they often gain productive insights into the objects and events they are trying to understand. However, such success cannot be explained simply by cognitive rules that unproblematically connect an object or event like Cassandra's analogy to a fuller conceptualization of the issue, like Aristotle's more sociocentric conception of the relation between individuals and society (Christensen, 2004; O'Connor and Glenberg, 2003). Instead, people seem to depend on other things they know. They must make inferences from background knowledge and relevant context in order to interpret the focal event productively. In Cassandra's case, students must know that a hierarchical conception of body part relations, though accurate in some contexts, will not be productive for interpreting Aristotle's analogy between the state and the body.

This raises a problem for theories of cognition: How do people know which aspects of the context are relevant, in such a way that they can interpret an object or event productively? This is an important philosophical problem that has been addressed in contemporary terms for at least half a century (Dreyfus, 1979; Goodman, 1955; Wittgenstein, 1953). Cognitive solutions to this problem typically involve background knowledge of one sort or another, knowledge that comes in "mental models," "background theories" or "frames" (e.g., Johnson-Laird, 1983; Murphy and Medin, 1985; Searle, 1983; Trabasso, et al., 1984). According to these theories, people often reach productive insights because they use relevant background knowledge to infer which of various possible conceptualizations are most plausible. In Cassandra's case, she and other students might have read that Aristotle believed in democracy (at least democracy among citizens). From this background knowledge, they might have inferred that he would not consider some individuals to be mere tools for those in power to manipulate. Using this background knowledge, they might have rejected the potential analogy between central nervous system control of the body and an authoritarian state where some individuals control others. This would have led them to search for other ways to understand the analogy between the body and the state, and perhaps they would have focused on the interdependence of body parts and the fact that a whole body is an entity different from the sum of its parts. If so, they would have been more likely to understand Aristotle.

Just like social identification, then, academic cognition confronts the indeterminacy of relevant context. Signs, statements, problems or events can be understood in multiple ways, depending on which aspects of the context are taken as relevant. Successful accounts of both social identification and academic cognition must explain how relevant context is limited in practice. The most widely accepted solution to the cognitive problem is similar to the account given in the last chapter. People must attend to indexical signs in the problem or situation and infer that certain aspects of the context are relevant. Then they must draw on preexisting models of relevant context and infer productive conceptualizations of the problem or event at hand (Bateson, 1972; Sperber and Wilson, 1986). As described in Chapter 2, such models constrain the possible meanings of particular signs or events and allow people to infer an appropriate conceptualization.

There remains the problem of how one accesses relevant background knowledge, as opposed to the other cognitive models that must be in the background to facilitate all the other inferences one might make. Even if one assumes elaborate innate cognitive models, which rule out many potential incorrect inferences (as proposed by, for example, Keil, 1989 and Astuti, Solomon and Carey, 2004), there must be some process through which the correct cognitive model is selected in practice. Just as in the process of social identification, relevant cognitive models must be selected and inferred from so that a particular insight emerges in context. For instance, in order for Cassandra and other students to interpret the *body : body parts :: state : individual* analogy in a way that illuminates Aristotle, they must infer that the dependence of body parts on the body is a key feature of the analogy. They would be able to do this by drawing on a cognitive model of the body that presents the whole as more than the sum of the parts. But how can they know that this is the right way to interpret the analogy, as opposed to using other potentially relevant cognitive models that might also fit the analogy (like the "central nervous system controlling body parts" model)? No fully adequate solution to this problem has been developed in cognitive science, although some have developed pragmatic rules of inference that claim to describe how people access relevant background information in context (e.g., Sperber and Wilson, 1986).

As is true of social identification, successful academic cognition cannot be understood simply at the timescale of events. In order to explain how people solve problems and gain productive insight in context, we must posit cognitive models that allow them to infer the concepts appropriate to understanding a particular instance. Cognition cannot simply be bottom-up, because particular objects and events can be productively interpreted only with respect to cognitive models that persist over longer timescales. At the same time, however, concepts and models have cognitive use only as they are contextualized in events (Cole, 1996; Hedegaard, 2002). A cognitive model may have to be altered, or may prove inappropriate, given the particular context of a problem. Cognitive models must be tailored to particular problems or events to allow inferences appropriate to those problems, and thus cognition cannot simply be the top-down imposition of preexisting cognitive models.

Many have proposed a "dialectic" between top-down and bottom-up processes. Piaget (e.g., Piaget and Inhelder, 1969), for instance, described the importance of both enduring cognitive models and specific events in his dialectic between "assimilation" and "accommodation." Piaget's account contains the important insight that even event-based cognition depends on relations across timescales and cannot be explained either by event-bound cognition or by enduring cognitive models alone. Nonetheless, Piaget and subsequent cognitive scientists have been unable to explain successfully how top-down and bottom-up processes interrelate to allow successful cognition and development (Christensen, 2004; Gergen, 1982; Haroutunian-Gordon, 1983).

Artifacts and Activity Systems

Cognitive scientists have still not developed a complete account of how relevant context gets structured in practice so that individuals productively and often effortlessly understand their world (Christensen, 2004; O'Connor and Glenberg, 2003). This may simply reflect the difficulty of the problem, and cognitive scientists are still working to specify types of background knowledge and processes for accessing that knowledge. Others have argued, however, that cognitive science by itself cannot solve this problem (e.g., Bickhard, 1980, 1993; Coulter, 1989; Gergen, 1982). These critiques identify at least two fundamental assumptions made by contemporary cognitive science that block an adequate solution.

Bickhard (1980; 1993) has developed a critique of what he calls "encodingism," the assumption that cognition involves mental representations that symbolically encode the world. He shows that encodingist cognitive accounts cannot explain cognitive errors or genuine learning, handle skeptical challenges or explain the ultimate ground for their encodings. Against encodingist accounts, Bickhard (1993; Christensen and Bickhard, 2002) argues that cognition is not separate from activity in the world – as if one must first build a representation of an activity and only subsequently participate in it. Cognition emerges out of action, not out of cognitive mirroring of the world. The world is best conceived not as a set of objects that exist independent of people and that people cognitively represent from a distance. Instead, cognition involves integrating oneself further into and transforming person-related processes in the world. Thus the appropriate unit of analysis for cognition is not the individual mind, separate from and encoding representations of the world, but instead processes that connect people to aspects of the world through practical activities.

Dreier (2003), Lave (1988), Rogoff, Baker-Sennett, Lacasa and Goldberg (1995) and others offer a second, related critique of contemporary cognitive science. They argue that cognition does not involve the transmission, internalization, transfer and then application of mental representations located inside the individual. Unlike Bickhard, who still reserves a central place in cognition for the individual organism, advocates of this second critique argue that cognition is not primarily a property of the individual. Instead, cognition depends on representations, tools and processes drawn from the individual, the setting and the activity. As Putnam (1998), Williams (1999), Wittgenstein (1953) and other philosophers have argued, cognition depends on supra-individual objects and processes like language and shared judgments.

If we assume that cognition primarily involves the development of representations inside an individual, it is hard to explain how people select a productive cognitive model from among many potentially relevant ones available to understand any given case. Cognitive scientists have had to propose increasingly elaborate innate models and constraints in their efforts to solve this problem (e.g., Keil, 1989; Astuti, Solomon and Carey, 2004). But if we argue that cognition involves more than individual mental representations – that it emerges through action, with essential contributions from other people, organized practices, and both physical and symbolic tools – we have sources of constraint other than elaborate innate cognitive models. An adequate account of how top-down and bottom-up cognitive processes interact will most likely come from an action-based, sociocentric approach to cognition that acknowledges the essential role of resources beyond the individual.

I am arguing that an adequate account of cognition will use a unit of analysis larger than the individual mind. The unit of analysis, as described by Vygotsky (1934/1987), is the smallest unit that preserves the properties of the whole. Analyzing water by studying the behavior of hydrogen and oxygen atoms in isolation would not allow us to understand all the properties of water. Similarly, studying individual minds – although minds certainly exist and play a role in cognition – provides a misleading picture of cognition and learning. People gain cognitive insight not just because of what happens inside their minds, but also because of larger systems that include interrelations among minds, other people, settings and activities (Bateson, 1972; Engeström, 1993; Lave, 1993).

Vygotsky's (1934/1987) seminal insight about cognitive mediation through artifacts shows how the units of analysis for cognitive science must extend beyond the individual mind. Vygotsky describes cognition as a process in which people use artifacts – like mnemonic devices, diagrams and words – to organize their activity and achieve cognitive insight. Artifacts are incorporated into activity such that the relevant unit for understanding cognitive activity is an amalgam of the person and artifact. Vygotsky's account of artifact-mediated cognition can help solve the problem of selecting among many potentially relevant aspects of the context and many potentially relevant cognitive models because artifacts provide structure that constrains inferences. When struggling to make sense of a problem or event, people do not face an indeterminate number of inferences if they can draw on an artifact that limits the cognitive models potentially relevant to the problem.

This Vygotskian insight has been elaborated in various traditions, from "activity theory" (Leont'ev, 1978) to "ecological psychology" (Bronfenbrenner, 1979) to "situated cognition" (Kirshner and Whitson, 1997) to "sociocultural" accounts of development (Rogoff, 2003; Wertsch, 1998) to work on "communities of practice" (Lave and Wenger, 1991). These accounts borrow Vygotsky's concept of mediation to propose systems of cognitive resources that include minds, artifacts, settings and other participants. Bateson, for instance, describes the activity of chopping down a tree as involving a system of "tree-eyes-brain-muscles-axe-stroke-tree" (1972: p. 317). He argues that it makes no sense to propose the individual as a privileged unit of analysis for understanding this system. Instead, the activity depends on interrelations among components that cross the boundaries of the body, the mind and the physical context. An analysis limited to attributes of the individual would not account successfully for the activity, just as an account of hydrogen atoms or hydrogen molecules would not suffice to understand water. Many others have argued that cognition depends on systems that include tools and artifacts, the physical layout of settings, the distribution of knowledge among people and other components (e.g., Goodwin, 1995; Greeno, 1997; Hutchins, 1995; Lemke, 2000).

If productive cognition depends on constraints beyond the individual mind, then it depends on resources from several timescales. As Cole puts it, "human cognition [is] the emergent outcome of transformations within and among several developmental domains: phylogenetic history, cultural history, ontogeny and microgenesis" 1996: p. 147). Goodwin (1995), Hutchins (1995) and others describe how cognitive tools and the physical layout of task settings can facilitate productive cognition. Such tools develop historically, emerging from sociocultural processes that take place over a timescale of decades and centuries (Bowker and Star, 1999; Latour, 1999; Wertsch, 2001). Hutchins (1995), Rogoff (1990) and others describe how individuals are apprenticed to activities and how teams of individuals collectively represent a body of knowledge that no individual necessarily represents alone. Such apprenticeship and team building takes place over a timescale of months and years. Goodwin (1995), Wortham (2001b) and others describe how cognitive problems often emerge or get transformed at the level of events, over seconds and hours, in a particular context to which people must adapt.

In solving a cognitive problem, then, people bring to bear various components of a cognitive system to design a solution in context, thus creating interrelations across several timescales. When Hutchins (1995) describes the cognitive task of navigating a battleship, for instance, he describes cognitive tools like maps and devices for taking bearings. Decades of technological innovation are required to create the structure inherent in such tools. He also describes how the team responsible for navigation has worked together for months in order to develop the complementary thoughts and actions required for successful navigation. Finally, he describes how participants organize the events of taking a bearing, communicating, and calculating positions in a productive way, over a timescale of minutes. Collectively, the various components of such a system constrain the potentially relevant cognitive models enough so that people find a productive solution to their problem. As Knorr-Cetina (1999) shows, different fields and different types of problems habitually require different configurations of resources. No one set of resources or timescales can explain all instances of cognition.

Individuals do represent partial or complete cognitive models, and people do often infer appropriate understandings using such models. But these models generally circulate publicly instead of being individual constructions or possessions. Furthermore, sociohistorical artifacts like the physical configuration of task spaces and cognitive tools like maps also facilitate successful cognition and provide essential supplements to relevant cognitive models. A full account of cognition would describe how configurations of resources at several timescales work together to facilitate cognition in particular cases. The term "cognitive system" usefully summarizes the heterogeneous, cross-timescale character of successful cognition, but a full account would more specifically describe how heterogeneous resources work together in various types of cases. Such a comprehensive account of cognition is beyond the scope of this book. In examining the relationship between academic learning and social identification, however, it is important to see that both processes draw on resources from several timescales. In Mrs. Bailey and Mr. Smith's classroom, as we will see, local cognitive and metapragmatic models played an important role in both processes.

Cognition in a classroom will be constrained in part by resources specific to classrooms. In some ways, classrooms are impoverished cognitive environments. As many have pointed out, schools decontextualize knowledge from practical contexts and activities (Heath and McLaughlin, 1993; Lave, 1988; McDermott, 1997; Rogoff, 2003) and often remove artifacts, teamwork, "genuine" objectives and other components of "real world" cognitive systems. Nonetheless, cognition does occur in school, and it depends on systems of resources (Hedegaard, 2002). The school curriculum is not simply composed of decontextualized knowledge that is learned in the abstract. Successful academic cognition is woven into complex sociocultural practices (Falmagne, 2001; Luke and Freebody, 1997). Schools use cognitive artifacts like computer software and group activities to mediate academic cognition (Lensmire, 1994). They use textbooks and curriculum guides to organize and constrain knowledge (Apple, 1986). Students and teachers establish local practices for organizing discussions and framing problems in classrooms, they establish divisions of labor in which different students are responsible for different aspects of tasks, and they bring together curricular constraints, instructional materials and activities as they solve particular problems (Cohen, Raudenbush and Ball, 2001; O'Connor, 2001).

Cassandra's insight, for instance, would develop into a deeper understanding only if components from various timescales were to come together. Erika's question about the relation between individuals and society has been discussed, and provisional answers and arguments have been developed, over centuries and millennia. These questions, answers and arguments entered the classroom through the textbooks and the teachers, both of which brought particular versions of sociohistorically circulating ideas. The textbooks favored certain positions because of the cultural and institutional contexts in which they were written. The teachers favored certain positions because of their own intellectual histories and points of view. The students had also been exposed to views about the relation between the individual and society outside the classroom, from their families and from popular culture. So before the students engaged with the issue in the classroom at all, various models of the individual/society relation were available to shape their view of the curricular issue. Over the academic year, as shown in detail later in this chapter, these teachers and students discussed questions about the appropriate relation between individuals and society and developed local agreements about reasonable positions on the issue. That is, they developed local cognitive models about curricular concepts, models that had been shaped by but could not be reduced to more widely circulating ones. There were other important local constraints as well. For instance, Erika and Cassandra were generally identified as serious students, and these identities facilitated an academic discussion. Mrs. Bailey had established a good working relationship in the classroom, with students generally asking questions of each other and exploring positions constructively. The teachers and students also encountered Cassandra's comment within a particular event, in which familiar ideas came together in a unique way.

We cannot analyze Cassandra's insight simply by abstracting out the conceptual issue – Aristotle's view of part-whole relations and the nature of society – and examining whether students' comments counted as instances of that concept. We must, instead, examine the constraints and affordances from various timescales that might have been relevant to cognitive insight in this case. Any cognitive insight will depend on a larger system of heterogeneous resources that come together in context. As was the case in analyzing social identification, in this book I cannot analyze all the components relevant to the cognitive insights gained by teachers and students in this classroom. I will focus on the local versions of curricular topics that teachers and students developed over the academic year. This will show how academic cognition can rely on resources in addition to those in individual minds and those in widely circulating cognitive models, and it will show how academic cognition depends on configurations of heterogeneous resources from several timescales. I also focus on local cognitive models because this timescale is crucial to the systematic overlap between social identification and academic learning that the book explores.

Because I focus on cognitive models local to the classroom, I pay less attention to constraints and affordances from other timescales that may have been relevant to academic learning and social identification in this case. For instance, I will not focus on personal habits and personal models that individuals develop and that can contribute to learning in context. Others have described the development of such personal constraints and affordances, and how they interrelate with longer timescale processes (e.g., Hedegaard, 2002; Rogoff, 2003; Wertsch, 1998). I do not ignore these because they are irrelevant in this case. In fact, local cognitive models only facilitate academic learning in combination with resources from other timescales. I focus on local models for two reasons: to show how this often-ignored resource can play a central role in both social identification and academic learning; and to show how this timescale can be key to power/knowledge or self/knowledge, to the meshing of social identification and academic learning.

Learning across Trajectories

Having presented multi-timescale systems as essential to cognition, we must move beyond a focus on isolated cognitive problems. Most work in "situated cognition" relies on multi-timescale systems, but uses these to understand how individuals or groups solve problems at the timescale of events. As Engeström (1999), Hedegaard (2002) and others have pointed out, this focus on face-to-face event-level cognition leads us to ignore longer timescale processes like the social distribution of cognitive artifacts. Instead of focusing on problem solving at the timescale of events, one might focus on longer-timescale processes like the ontogenetic question of how individuals develop into functioning members of society (Rogoff, 2003), or the phylogenetic and ontogenetic question of how infants can develop uniquely human capacities (Tomasello, 1999). Such analyses explore cognitive success in particular events, but only as these event level analyses contribute to understanding learning and development at longer timescales. Analysis of academic learning requires such a shift in focus to other timescales beyond particular events.

I have been using "cognition" to describe reasoning about problems at the timescale of events. I will use "learning," following Dreier (2003), to refer to a process that only occurs across events. Dreier argues that we must not imagine learning as occurring and being completed in a single event. People do not generally construct or internalize cognitive models in single events, then transfer these to solve problems in new contexts (cf. also Lave, 1988, 1993). As Cole (1996) and Rogoff (1998) put it, an event is not a self-contained task for the use of established knowledge. Productive cognition in any event depends on a heterogeneous set of resources drawn from different timescales. As people move from one event to another, they are constrained by and adopt different sets of resources in new settings. There are consistencies in the cognitive resources used from one event to the next, however. Most importantly, people can systematically change the cognitive tools they use and how they react to affordances across events. Instead of being the one-time construction of a full-blown internal representation or capacity, then, learning occurs across events as people deploy cognitive resources in changing ways. Learning is "change in the relations between persons and their situation in a way that allows for the accomplishment of new activities" (McDermott, 1997: p. 127).

To study learning in this sense, we must study a "trajectory of participation" (Dreier, 2003), examining the cross-context connections and changes that people make. If we follow people across contexts, we sometimes see them realizing and pursuing new possibilities in other contexts, taking what Dreier (2000) calls "new angles." When people pursue new angles, we should not immediately posit individual skills or representations as the primary source of the change. Instead, we must explore what resources are present in events along the trajectory, how the configurations of resources change from event to event, and whether some cross-timescale configurations change or recur so as to facilitate the new angles people adopt. We cannot generally explain learning by proposing a fully formed representation that individuals transfer from one context to the next, but neither is every cognitive accomplishment situation-specific (Dreier, 2003). Instead, we must work to describe the changing configurations of resources across contexts that facilitate learning. These resources will often include representations and skills that individuals develop and bring with them, but these generally constitute only some of the resources through which people learn.

So even if we knew more about how other students reacted to Cassandra's analogy between the body and the state, this event by itself could not be an example of academic learning. In order to examine whether and how Cassandra and other students might be learning in this classroom, we would have to examine events before and after this one, and we would have to identify the various resources that students bring to bear in understanding Aristotle – the themes and texts in the curriculum, the teachers' prestructuring of questions and possible answers, the teachers and students' emerging local cognitive models of the curricular themes and so on. If Cassandra's comment represented the first use of a new type of resource like the analogy between the body and the state, or if it represented a change in local understandings, then it might be an important moment in students' emerging trajectory of learning.

In fact, in January the students did start to develop a new locally circulating cognitive model in which they argued that the collective was in some sense more important than the individual. They articulated this position with specific reference to state welfare programs, arguing that a society owes support to vulnerable members. So, while Cassandra's example itself was not the one catalytic event, it contributed to the development of a classroom-specific position on the individual/society relation. Across several events in January and February, students developed a "new angle" on the question about appropriate relations between an individual and society. Having initially been unable to imagine how society could be more than a collection of individuals, some students came to see how the society can be more than the sum of its parts – at least insofar as the collective should take responsibility for underprivileged individuals. This emerging local cognitive model did not mature into deep understanding of Aristotle and the curricular theme. But, especially given that these were ninth grade students, it represented significant academic learning.

The empirical analyses in the next section of this chapter illustrate how this local cognitive model of the individual/society curricular theme developed across many weeks in Mrs. Bailey and Mr. Smith's classroom. Students drew on the texts, their own and the teachers' comments, cognitive models that circulate outside school and other resources as they developed their argument and applied it in specific events of cognition. The empirical analyses in this chapter show how students created and deployed this local cognitive model to address specific topics in class discussion. Chapters 4 and 5 show how metapragmatic models that teachers and students used to identify Tyisha and Maurice also became important resources as students built their arguments about the individual/society relation. The last section in this chapter gives a theoretical account of how resources used for social identification contributed to academic learning and vice versa.

The most comprehensive framework for conceptualizing academic learning across events comes from "cultural-historical activity theory" (e.g., Cole, 1996; Engeström, 1999; Leont'ev, 1978). This tradition, which draws on and expands Vygotsky's work, attends to phylogenetic, sociohistorical, cultural and situational resources for and constraints on learning. Like Geertz (1973), Tomasello (1999) and others, activity theorists study how humans have evolved to be as dependent on sociohistorical artifacts like symbolic tools and cultural models as on neuropsychological and other physiological capabilities. Humans differ from animals because human evolution can proceed very rapidly through socially acquired artifacts and ideas that extend our phylogenetically evolved capacities – without having to wait for genetic change to establish new ways of acting or thinking. Activity theorists thus broaden Vygotsky's original account of the cognizing subject, the mediating artifact and the object of cognition, to include the situation, the type of recurring sociocultural activity, the relevant communities and their rules, plus the division of labor through which artifacts are distributed and societies are partly organized (Engeström, 1999).

The resources that facilitate learning come from this large set of phylogenetically evolving structures and processes, ontogenetically developing mental representations and capacities, sociohistorically developing artifacts and activities, locally developing situational patterns and constraints and so on. Activity theory is particularly useful for analyzing the cognitive trajectories described by Dreier (2003) in three respects: its emphasis on change at all relevant timescales, emphasizing processes instead of static structures; its expansive list of resources for learning at many potentially relevant timescales; and its insistence that any given phenomenon must be explained with reference to a system of heterogeneous resources at multiple timescales. Applied to a classroom, this means that academic learning occurs as teachers and students adapt changing sets of resources to approach academic problems across events. In Mrs. Bailey and Mr. Smith's class, one important resource was an emerging local cognitive model of the individual/society relation. As described below, students also learned to participate in the somewhat unusual interpersonal activity of Paideia discussion, and this facilitated their academic learning as well.

In his account of resources for learning, Engeström (1987, 1999) develops a concept particularly useful to those of us interested in locally circulating resources. He points out that Vygotsky (1924/1971) described not only the use of preexisting artifacts in cognition ("internalization"), but also the creation of artifacts that could subsequently be used ("externalization"). In a cognitive activity, across days, months or years, participants sometimes create artifacts and practices through which the activity undergoes an "expansive cycle." Activities are often repetitive, with participants acting in similar ways and using habitual resources from one event to the next. Classroom life notoriously involves repetitive activities. Sometimes, however, activities "expand" when people develop new tools and ways of acting. The inclusion of such innovations in the systems that facilitate learning can allow individuals or groups to think more effectively. When students and teachers built a new local model of individual/society relations and applied it to new texts, they entered an expansive cycle.

This emerging local cognitive model, together with other cognitive tools and the new ways of relating to each other that students were learning, allowed them to solve the problem of indeterminate relevant context in this case. Cassandra gave the analogy between the state and the body at a point in the semester where students and teachers were developing their local cognitive model of relations between the individual and the collective. By the time of Cassandra's analogy, they had provisionally established a few features of this model: They were searching for a way to value some aspects of the collective over the individual because this idea appealed to many of them; the example of social welfare programs seemed to support this idea because it involves individuals sacrificing for others; they were firmly committed to what Pole (1992) calls "equality of esteem," equality in the sense that no one is better than anyone else. So when Cassandra gave her analogy, students and teachers who already presupposed the rudiments of this local model would have tended to rule out the hierarchical, central nervous system-driven model of the body that might, in other contexts, have been a reasonable interpretation of the analogy between the state and the body. The local model was one constraint that limited relevant context and directed teachers and students toward a "whole is more than the sum of the parts" interpretation of Cassandra's analogy and of Aristotle.

I am not arguing that all students unproblematically adopted the same account of the individual/society curricular theme. As Engeström (1999) and Packer and Goicoechea (2000) argue, calling the set of resources that contribute to cognition and learning a "system" should not imply that the various resources move unproblematically in the same direction. Instead, there can be tensions between resources, and both among and within people, tensions that can either disrupt cognition or lead to innovation. Chapters 4 and 5 describe struggles that happened in Mrs. Bailey and Mr. Smith's classroom, as teachers and students struggled over which models and arti-facts to use and struggled over their own social identities.

I will show local cognitive models of more widely circulating curricular themes became important to students' academic learning in Mrs. Bailey and Mr. Smith's classroom – and also how these local cognitive models became important to the social identification of some students. But such year-long, classroom-specific models do not always play a central role in shaping academic learning. For different instances of cognition and learn-ing, different resources from different timescales will play central roles. Like social identification, then, learning depends on different heteroge-neous sets of resources in different cases. We cannot tell exactly which timescales and sets of resources will be relevant to understanding cogni-tion or academic learning in any given case. In a limited set of cases, even behaviorist accounts of learning can describe the central processes and con-straints on academic and other learning (Schwartz, 1986; Wortham, 2003). Instead of universal theories restricted to the same set of resources in every case, and instead of vague appeals to a "dialectic" among different types of cognitive resources, we must empirically investigate how different con-figurations of resources actually make cognition and learning possible in various cases.

LEARNING CURRICULAR THEMES IN A PAIDEIA CLASSROOM

Students learn academically when they use new combinations of resources to represent or react productively to subject matter across events. Relevant resources can include new ways of drawing on what others know, new symbolic tools such as maps or diagrams, new cognitive models drawn from texts or others' comments and so on. In Mrs. Bailey and Mr. Smith's classroom, teachers and students developed at least three important cogni-tive resources over the academic year. First, students learned to participate in Paideia "seminars" (Adler, 1982), which involve a distinctive way of dis-cussing subject matter. Second, the teachers built a curriculum organized into themes, in which series of assigned readings developed contrasting positions on central questions. Third, teachers and students developed local cognitive models of their favored positions on two central curricular themes. This section describes these three resources and presents evidence that students used these resources to learn academically throughout the year. Other cognitive resources were relevant to students' academic learn-ing, and I note some of these during the empirical analyses, but I focus on these three cognitive resources that developed at the local timescale.

The Activity of Paideia Discussion

According to Adler (1982), Paideia instruction involves three modes. First, teachers use didactic instruction to communicate essential information to students. Mrs. Bailey and Mr. Smith each ran separate 40-minute classes three days a week in which they did didactic instruction that included worksheets, tests, known-answer questions and other familiar classroom activities. Second, teachers use coaching, or one-on-one guidance, to tailor instruction to the needs of individual students. Mrs. Bailey and Mr. Smith sometimes coached individual students during their didactic lessons, and they also did so through feedback on written assignments.

"Seminar" is the third and most distinctive of Adler's three modes. The history of this pedagogical practice goes back to Socrates in some respects, and in other respects goes back to decades-old educational models and institutions like Adler's Paideia Group (Adler, 1982) and the Great Books Foundation (1991). In seminar, teachers and students engage with "essentially contestable" questions and with texts rich enough to support more than one interpretation. In such discussions, teachers ideally do not offer their own opinions and do not give answers. Instead, teachers open class with a genuine question, one which they cannot definitively answer themselves and one which might be answered in at least two different ways given the evidence in the text. Teachers then guide students as they offer provisional answers and supporting arguments, with teachers pointing out inconsistencies, arguing the opposite point of view and pointing to specific evidence in the text (cf. Haroutunian-Gordon, 1991, and Weltman, 2002, for more extensive descriptions of this type of discussion). Mrs. Bailey and Mr. Smith ran joint seminar discussions with their students two days a week in a combined 80-minute block.

Adler's (1982) Paideia philosophy, at least as adopted by Mrs. Bailey and Mr. Smith, presupposes a Western conception of universal human commonality – assuming that we all struggle with basic questions about the significance of life, the best organization for human societies, the causes and legitimacy of hierarchical relations and similar issues (Weltman, 2002). Young people and all future generations will struggle with similar questions, although they may develop new answers. Different cultural traditions have provided us valuable resources by identifying basic questions, articulating provisional answers to these questions and providing arguments to support these answers. Educational institutions should expose young people to this legacy of questions, answers and arguments so that they have the resources to struggle with basic questions in a productive way and so that they can participate fully in society.

Despite their regular use of didactic instruction, Mrs. Bailey and Mr. Smith built their curriculum with the seminar in mind. They wanted students to learn facts about literature and history, but their primary goal was for students to engage with essentially contestable questions. They coordinated their English and history curricula, both by having students read texts from the same historical period at similar times during the year and by assigning sets of English and history texts that addressed several essentially contestable questions in turn (for example, the question of whether the individual or the society should be preeminent). Because they built the curriculum around such questions, even their didactic lessons were less teacher-centered than in the typical U.S. high school class. The teachers did give tests and expect students to know certain facts but they were more concerned that students recognize basic questions about human experience, that they recognize typical answers to these questions and that they learn to formulate and defend their own answers to these questions. Because these ninth grade students were in their first year of the Paideia program, Mrs. Bailey and Mr. Smith saw themselves as beginning the students' apprenticeship into the central Paideia activities of recognizing essential questions, formulating arguments and offering evidence. They expected students to develop more fully as they moved through the four-year program.

By using a Paideia curriculum in an urban school, Mrs. Bailey and Mr. Smith were following Adler's social agenda (Adler, 1982; Weltman, 2002). *The Paideia Proposal* explicitly intended to accomplish an educationally "classless society" and educational "equality of treatment" for all children. Adler and his colleagues intended the Paideia curriculum to overcome the unequal intellectual experiences children had outside of school by providing all students with high-quality curriculum, exposure to the common intellectual heritage of humankind and the ability to cultivate and communicate their own ideas. Haroutunian-Gordon (1991) and Wheelock (2000) provide evidence that a Paideia approach can work with underprivileged students in urban schools.

In this section, I will focus on three aspects of Mrs. Bailey and Mr. Smith's Paideia approach: their emphasis on understanding multiple perspectives instead of finding the one right answer, their insistence that students argue from textual evidence and their use of analogies between the students' experience and curricular topics. One might focus on different aspects of the pedagogical approach – see Criscoula (1994), Haroutunian-Gordon (1991), Muldoon (1991), Billings and Fitzgerald (2002), Weltman (2002) and Wheelock (2000) for somewhat different analyses of Paideia and Great Books teaching. I focus on these three aspects of Paideia discussion both to communicate the feel of Mrs. Bailey and Mr. Smith's Paideia approach and because these three aspects contributed to students' academic learning and to their social identification. The analogies between students' own experiences and curricular topics, in particular, became important resources that facilitated both academic learning and social identification.

To some extent, the teachers' emphases on promoting multiple perspectives, arguing from textual evidence and creating analogies with students' experience are not specific to Paideia teaching. Teachers often try to engage students with contestable questions and set up arguments between proponents of different positions – for example, in the "position-driven" science and mathematics discussions described by Hatano and Inagaki (1991), Michaels and Sohmer (2001) and O'Connor (2001). Teachers of history and literature often try to engage students with multiple perspectives and draw analogies to students' own experience. Lensmire (2000), for instance, advocates English instruction that keeps open multiple interpretive possibilities as students engage with texts. Wineburg (2001) describes good history instruction as guiding students to appreciate multiple perspectives on historical events so that students develop the judgment required to balance competing opinions and formulate more complex historical accounts. Wineburg also describes how good history instruction gets students to see similarities between past actors and themselves – by using strategies like analogies between historical events and students' personal experience – as well as getting them to see genuine differences between others and themselves. The learning that students did in Mrs. Bailey and Mr. Smith's classroom, then, was afforded not only by Paideia techniques that involve multiple perspectives and analogies, but also by more widely circulating techniques that these teachers adopted in their Paideia classroom. As I argue in Chapter 6, this means that the patterns I describe in Mrs. Bailey and Mr. Smith's classroom probably occur in other sorts of classrooms as well. Nonetheless, the teachers implemented these more widely circulating strategies within their Paideia approach, so I describe them in that context.

Mrs. Bailey and Mr. Smith explicitly instructed students in the three skills of considering multiple perspectives, arguing from evidence and drawing analogies to their own experience. On October 9, for instance, they were discussing creation myths from around the world, and Mrs. Bailey argued that they all address the basic question of "why am I here?" In the following segment, she tells the students that cultural traditions have developed different answers to this question.

> **T/B:**   different people
>   have asked, where did I come from? and we see: that when
> 375   they ask this they don't just mean, where did I come from-
>   directly, as far as, who are my parents? or what act
>   produced me? there seems to be some implication here that
>   they're really asking why I am here? what is my
>   relationship to the rest of creation? we look at the insect in
> 380   Pampu, we can see that the Chinese have an answer to that
>   question that might be different than our answer.
>   . . .
>   Why I am here
> 395   changes from group to group based on how they choose to
>   answer that question. and based to some extent on their
>   experiences and their imagination.

Mrs. Bailey regularly told students that basic questions have multiple plausible answers. She wanted them to go beyond the typical student stance – which she believed students had been forced into during their previous eight years of schooling – a stance in which they expect their teachers to know the one right answer to every question. In seminar, students should listen to others and explore new evidence from the text, and this will often lead them to consider different arguments. These teachers did want students to develop and defend their own positions, but they also wanted students to acknowledge that fundamental questions often have multiple plausible answers.

As the year progressed, students became more comfortable with the idea of essentially contestable questions and multiple plausible answers, and the teachers continued to encourage students to appreciate different perspectives. At the beginning of class on December 17, for instance, Mrs. Bailey gave students instructions for how to discuss "The Cemetery Path," a text that they had begun discussing earlier. This time, she says, students must adopt a different position. They are discussing the question of whether a character ("Ivan") was courageous.

10 **T/B:**   the only twist this time
     was I said argue the opposite. if you're listening to other
     people in the seminar, you are picking up their arguments.
     so if you thought Ivan was not courageous then your task
     was to find those things that would [allow=
15 **FST:**   [that he was
     T/B: =you to argue he was courageous. if you said
     Ivan was not courageous then your task was to argue the
     opposite. now what I'd like you to do is I'd like you to
     listen to the arguments that your classmates give. and
20 many of you are so focused on your own arguments, or
     your own ideas, that you don't hear your classmates. so,
     you know which students within the room felt the opposite
     of what you do- that you did, and therefore you should
     have- if you couldn't remember their argument you should
25 have [3 unintelligible syllables]
     FST: you want us to be open minded.
     T/B: I want you to be open minded. most issues should be
     argued from both sides.

A student and Mrs. Bailey both use "open minded" here to describe a disposition possessed by the successful Paideia student. By December, students understood that they should consider multiple points of view.

Whether students were seeking to interpret another's point of view or to articulate their own position on a question, the teachers also insisted that they provide evidence by referring to specific passages in the text. On January 18, for instance, the class was discussing Aristotle's *Politics*, and two students had a heated side conversation about the text. Mrs. Bailey did not discipline them, probably because she valued students' deep engagement with curricular issues. Instead, she encouraged Martha and Jasmine to share their dispute with the class. The specific topic involved Aristotle's view of obedience, as in a woman's duty to obey her husband.

> **T/B:** okay. uh, Martha. I'm kind of interested. you were very animated. what were you talking about?
> **MAR:** no, she say obeyed, like you know, when you, when
> 30   you say obey over here, and when you make your vows when you get married, that's two different kind of obeys. that's what I was trying to explain to her. when you get married, that's more like you and your husband, you and your husband
> 35   **JAS:** listen to each other.
> **FST:** right, you know, listen to each other's problems.
> (10.0)
> **JAS:** she said she's not supposed to obey nobody in her family, and I said to her
> 40   **T/B:** okay, what line are you bouncing off of from the text?

Mrs. Bailey tries to capture the students' enthusiasm, but she also asks for evidence from the text at line 40.

On February 22, while discussing Pericles' *Funeral Oration*, Mr. Smith encouraged other students to provide specific evidence that a comment by Tyisha was wrong. Tyisha had claimed that the Athenians would kill her, a dark-skinned person, if she visited their city.

> **TYI:** they'd think, they would kill me because I came. I'm different probably and they don't want no one to be different than them.
> **T/S:** whoa.
> 810   **TYI:** they'd be curious.
> **T/B:** she's saying something that contradicts the reading.
> **T/S:** yeah.
> **T/B:** find it and help her understand it. this is where your responsibility as students comes in. when somebody says,
> 815   hey, if I go into Athens and I'm, I'm from Africa, I'm going to be killed. find something that says that she's wrong.

A few lines later, in a segment presented in Chapter 2, Mrs. Bailey says, "Erika's got it; where we read before," and Erika proceeds to read lines from the text that disprove Tyisha's claim. Because Tyisha was not making an argument about an essentially contestable question, but was offering an incorrect interpretation of a minor point, the teachers could simply have said that she was wrong. But Mr. Smith's comments illustrate how the teachers regularly asked students for specific evidence from the text.

Because the Paideia approach assumes that fundamental, contestable questions are universal, the questions must apply to students' own lives too. In fact, this is the major value of teaching students about basic questions and classic answers – so that they will have intellectual resources to help them struggle with these questions in their own lives. The questions that a well-designed Paideia curriculum addresses are so fundamental that students will recognize them, and the teachers regularly ask students to explore questions by analogy with their own experiences. The teachers expect these analogies to make sense because they assume (often correctly) that fundamental issues from the curriculum apply to students' lives too.

In the discussion of creation myths on October 9, for instance, while discussing the question "where do I come from" addressed by many myths, Mrs. Bailey asks, "Martha, how do you answer that question? If I asked you where you came from, what would you say?" Martha answers, "from my parents." This is somewhat amusing, of course, because it is not the kind of answer Mrs. Bailey was looking for and because it may lead students to imagine what her parents did to produce her. But the discussion remains focused on the academic substance. The class discusses how Martha knows that she came from her parents, and Mrs. Bailey asks Martha another question.

> **T/B:** why do, you
> know, at this point, you challenge your mother on
> 165 everything. why do you, believe, that your mother is telling
> the truth when she says, your father and I had you. we
> didn't find you under a cabbage tree?
> **STS:** [laughter]
> **MAR:** [4 unintelligible syllables] I mean, you know, they
> 170 was crazy, so.
> **STS:** [laughter]
> **T/B:** okay, you've seen a pregnant woman, right?
> **FST:** yeah.
> **T/B:** and pregnant women have?
> 175 **FSTs:** babies.
> **T/B:** babies, okay? so okay. so, what we've got here, what
> we've got here is Martha's experience. she answers that
> (2.0) that question through experience. go back to ancient
> man or earlier civilizations, other than ours. why don't they
> 180 just say, two people come together and have a baby? why
> do they ask the question, where did I come from, meaning
> more than just, you know, who were my parents? what acts
> produced me? why did they ask that question? why aren't
> they just happy with Martha's answer my mom and dad got
> 185 together and here I am.

After students laugh at her joke at line 168, Mrs. Bailey takes control of the discussion. She develops an analogy between Martha and humans who lived long ago. Both Martha and ancient humans ask, "where do I come from?" Martha knows from experience that babies come from their mothers. Mrs. Bailey then turns to the other side of the analogy, saying, "go back to ancient man" (lines 178–179). "Go back to..." is a typical locution for these teachers, moving students from a discussion of their own experience, as the source of the analogy, back to the curricular issue that is the target of the analogy. This discussion takes place early in the year, and the analogy does not advance the discussion much, but the teacher is introducing a common pedagogical and cognitive device in this Paideia classroom – an analogy between students' experience and curricular topics.

On November 2, they discussed Hammurabi's code, an early Babylonian legal code. The code contains laws like this: "If the robber is not captured, the man who has been robbed shall, in the presence of God, make an itemized statement of his loss, and the city and the governor in whose province and jurisdiction the robbery was committed shall compensate him for whatever was lost." The teachers encouraged students to discuss this text with reference to their own experiences of crime and justice. Tyisha gives an example, saying that things have been stolen from her at Colleoni High. Mrs. Bailey responds by asking how Hammurabi would have dealt with the situation.

20   **T/B:** okay, but the person hasn't been <u>caught</u>, right? hasn't
      been penalized? okay, so she lost <u>two</u> hundred dollars
      worth of stuff. (3.0) <u>nobody</u> has had to <u>pay</u> for taking her
      stuff. she <u>lost</u> it at school, if this school operated
      according, according to the code of Hammu<u>rabi</u>, what
25   would happen?

This is the first instance in my data of an analogy between the school or the class itself and a text from the curriculum. In January and February, analogies like this became more common. Teachers and students compared their own classroom to a society, and explored curricular questions about social relations by examining their own relations in the classroom. As we will see, these analogies played a central role in the meshing of social identification and academic learning that took place.

The last several paragraphs have shown how Mrs. Bailey and Mr. Smith explicitly coached the students to consider multiple perspectives, to offer textual evidence to support their arguments and to develop analogies between curricular topics and their own experience. As the year progressed, many of the students improved at these three tasks. As apprentices in the activity of Paideia discussion, they learned how to do these three things with less and less scaffolding by the teachers. They did not become fully competent participants in the activity. Given that they were only ninth-grade students who were exposed to it twice a week over an academic year, however, many of them did make significant progress toward more competent participation.

In the following discussion from December 14, for instance, Maurice and Candace argue about whether a character was courageous.

> **T/B:** okay. <u>one</u> conversation at a time, ex<u>cuse</u> me. we're trying to- to ex<u>plore</u> this to<u>gether</u> and <u>not</u> in groups. go ahead.
>
> 75 **MRC:** <u>Can</u>dace.
> **CAN:** mm hmm.
> **MRC:** would you say this man is <u>not</u> courageous?
> **CAN:** he's <u>wasn't</u>.
> **MRC:** =how do you know he wasn't trying to <u>prove</u> it to
> 80 himself? and <u>not</u> trying to prove it to <u>others</u>?
> **CAN:** no.
> **MST:** shut up.
> **STS:** [3 seconds of laughter]
> **MRC:** he went in the cemetery when it was <u>dark</u>. maybe
> 85 he was trying to prove it to himself.
> **CAN:** no he was not. he was trying to <u>prove</u> it to other people.
> **MRC:** no. maybe he was trying to prove it to him<u>self</u>.
> **CAN:** no. he wasn't. I doubt it.
> 90 **STS:** [2 seconds of overlapping chatter]
> **T/B:** do you see these ha[nds?
> **STS:**   [3 seconds of overlapping chatter]
> **T/B:** they keep their <u>mouths</u> shut because they put their
> 95 hands up.
> **MRC:** but I'm saying he <u>wanted</u> to do something-
> **T/B:** shh. okay. uh. Cassandra.
> **CAS:** Maurice. why would you <u>think</u> or where would you <u>find</u> that he i:s courageous?
> 100 **MRC:** would you <u>go</u>, into a cemetery, while it was <u>dark</u>, to stick a <u>sword</u> in the <u>middle</u>=
> **CAS:** that's foolish
> **STS:** [students, including one male student, repeatedly echo Cassandra in saying "that's foolish"]
> 105 **T/B:** °let's uh, one at a time°
> **MRC:** might be foolish to <u>you</u> but it might not have been foolish to <u>them</u>. he was overcoming his <u>fear</u>.
> **CAN:** but I think he was still scared when he was running through the cemetery-

110   **MRC:** but he did [it=
       CAN: [he's definitely scared
       MRC: =so that's courage.
       CAN: wait a minute.
       MRC: you say he was <u>scared</u>, right? he was scared, it was
115   fear and he was overcoming his fear, isn't it?

Despite potentially distracting comments by other students (at lines 82–83, 90–93, 103–104), Maurice and Candace persist in their discussion of whether the character was courageous. They state their positions, provide some supporting evidence and assess the other's position, as the teachers have taught them. Note also Cassandra's question, "where would you find that he is courageous" (lines 98–99), which echoes the teachers' demands for textual evidence. This was not an ideal seminar discussion, but the students were clearly learning some crucial seminar skills.

Students themselves also learned to give analogies to their own experience, following the teachers' lead. In the following segment from February 22, for instance, Jasmine creates a participant example that she and Martha connect to the text. The class is discussing Pericles' claim that Athenian soldiers, although not trained as incessantly as Spartans, nonetheless had confidence.

330   **MAR:** yeah, wait. <u>you're</u> comparing, you're comparing
       <u>Sparta</u> to <u>A</u>thens. now, <u>they</u> telling <u>me</u>, just because they
       get, they have <u>confidence</u>, all this=
       MRC: a lot of work
       MAR: yeah, going into a <u>war</u>, they going to face <u>people</u>
335   whose experience in war, I mean, <u>think</u>, <u>eat</u>, feel <u>nothing</u>
       but military training-
       T/S: what <u>you're</u> doing is calling Pericles a <u>liar</u> here.
       T/B: (hh)
       T/S: okay, we've got four hands at once. I don't know who's
340   first.
       FST: Jasmine.
       T/S: Jasmine? okay.
       JAS: now, Martha.
       FSTs: (hh)
345   **JAS:** if you was about to fight <u>William</u>, <u>he's</u> <u>bigger</u>, <u>he's</u>
       <u>taller</u> than you, don't you think he'll beat you up?
       MAR: cause he got the-
       JAS: wait, wait a minute. <u>don't</u> you think he can beat you?
       yes or no?
350   **MAR:** but not [10 unintelligible syllables]
       JAS: I'm <u>sure</u> that he could beat you. he's got more
       <u>training</u> than you.

[bell rings (3.0)]
FSTs: [5 seconds of yelling back and forth about William
355   fighting Martha]
MAR: but then I just have to keep fighting, right?
FST: that's what they're doing.
MAR: they just keep fighting, but they would <u>never</u> beat
Sparta.

Jasmine helps Martha explore her argument by introducing a participant example at lines 345–346. Jasmine creates an analogy between students' own experience with physical force and the conflict between Athens and Sparta. She has learned that this sort of analogy is appropriate for seminar discussion. They go on to act like good Paideia students at lines 357–359 when they begin to connect the participant example back to the curricular issue. (As discussed in Chapter 2, this example also contributes to identifying William as brawny and potentially violent. While identifying William, however, the example also addresses the curriculum and illustrates how students are learning to make analogies between the text and their own experiences.)

The analyses of curricular themes in the next section provide further evidence that many students in Mrs. Bailey and Mr. Smith's class did in fact learn to consider multiple perspectives, to provide evidence for their arguments and to reason by analogy with their own experience. Their successful apprenticeship in the activity of Paideia discussion facilitated their academic learning because Paideia strategies organized their cognitive activities and made certain sorts of insights more likely. For instance, some specific analogies between the curriculum and students' own experiences developed into locally circulating analogies that organized students' and teachers' thinking across weeks and months. The Paideia strategy of building analogies with students' own experience did not by itself determine the academic understanding that students developed. But some analogies combined with other cognitive resources to facilitate academic learning.

Local Versions of Curricular Themes

Over the year in Mrs. Bailey and Mr. Smith's classroom, most students participated more and more competently in the activity of Paideia discussion. At the same time, two other year-long processes were occurring. First, the teachers organized their curriculum around questions of enduring concern by assigning both history and literature texts that took conflicting positions on common questions. In doing this they focused students' attention on a different enduring question in each of several two- to three-month periods, and they encouraged students to engage with a few classic answers to each question. Second, while students and teachers discussed these enduring questions they developed local versions of and answers to them, answers that were in some ways specific to this classroom. These emerging local cognitive models became available for individual students' reasoning and in classroom discussions. This chapter introduces two curricular themes that became important, not only to students' academic learning but also to the social identification of Tyisha and Maurice, and it provides evidence that students learned something about these themes. Chapters 4 and 5 show how local versions of these themes, together with analogies between students' own experience and the curriculum, facilitated systematic overlap between social identification and academic learning in this classroom.

I use "curricular theme" to mean a widely circulating question plus well-known answers to the question. The first curricular theme, introduced above, involves the appropriate relation between an individual and society. This theme was the focus of seminar discussions during January and February. On January 24, Mrs. Bailey explicitly mentioned the theme during their discussion of Aristotle's *Politics*.

> **T/B:** and the principle that I find extremely interesting in here is this idea that the state is prior
> 30 to the individual. the state is prior to the individual. uh, if you would take a look on the second page, the first column. (6.0) the beginning of the second paragraph. further, the state is by nature clearly prior to the family and to the individual, since the
> 35 whole is of necessity prior to the part. and I am asking- my question here is, do you agree that the state is prior to the individual, or do you even know what that means maybe?

The teachers arranged their curriculum to include multiple perspectives on this question, from the extreme collectivist position of Lycurgus in ancient Sparta to the extreme individualism of Ayn Rand, with Athenian democracy in between the two extremes. They guided students to recognize these well-known positions and to develop their own positions, always with reference to evidence that might support their arguments.

As students and teachers discussed the individual/society curricular theme, they drew heavily on students' own experiences. The teachers repeatedly used examples that construed the theme in terms of some student's own experience, or in terms of a contemporary phenomenon students were familiar with, and they explicitly intended for these examples to help students learn about the theme. Teachers and students would sometimes refer back to these examples in subsequent classes, using the example to stand for a recognizable local argument about the theme. The examples, given over the two months in which they intensively discussed the individual/society theme, primarily drew on two issues the students were familiar with: the welfare system in the contemporary United States, which served as an example of how society should be responsible for helping the disadvantaged; and their own relationships in the classroom, which involved students' individual freedom to develop their own opinions and their collective responsibility to nurture the group discussion.

Thus two analogies developed in the classroom across several discussions. When students and teachers considered an argument for individualism, they would often support or critique it in terms of its implications for the U.S. welfare system – claiming, for example, that extreme individualism cannot be right because it would allow welfare recipients to suffer. When they considered an argument for collectivism, they would often support or critique it in terms of its implications for their own classroom "society" – arguing, for example, that collectivism must be right in some respects because students in a classroom must cooperate in order to have coherent group discussion. As they discussed this curricular theme during January and February, the teachers and most students came to favor a moderate position: A society should be sufficiently individualist to allow freedom but sufficiently collectivist to ensure coherence and support the disadvantaged. The teachers and sometimes the students presented their Paideia classroom itself as analogous to an ideal society – one that found the golden mean between excessive individualism and excessive collectivism.

So students learned about the individual/society theme in part through analogies between concepts from the curriculum and their own experience, analogies that emerged over many weeks. The Paideia emphasis on analogies between the students' own experiences and the curriculum led teachers and students to create their analogies. Some of these analogies were incorporated into local cognitive models. Over weeks and months they developed local models that responded to the enduring curricular question, models that centrally included concepts from their understanding of the U.S. welfare system and their own classroom relationships. These local cognitive models became one important resource that helped shape students' emerging understandings of the curricular theme. As discussed more extensively at the end of this chapter, some of these models also included categories that students used to identify each other. In Tyisha's case, for instance, the same categories that came to identify her as an outcast in the classroom also contributed to the emerging local cognitive models that students used to make sense of "beasts" (in Aristotle's sense of the word) who ignore the common good. Students came to understand the limits of individualism in part by discussing people like Tyisha who disrupt society while pursuing their own interests. Tyisha was thus identified at the same time and through some of the same categories that students used to understand academic arguments against individualism. The following sections trace the emergence of this and related local cognitive models that teachers and students developed while learning about the individual/society curricular theme.

Equality 7-2521 and Lycurgus

In developing their curriculum for January and February, the teachers selected texts that argue for one position or another on the question of whether the individual or the society should have precedence. For instance, they assigned Ayn Rand's *Anthem*, which argues for extreme individualism, Plutarch's *Life of Lycurgus*, which articulates Lycurgus' arguments for extreme collectivism, and Pericles' *Funeral Oration* (as well as Aristotle's *Politics*), which argue for a moderate Athenian democracy with both individualist and collectivist elements. The teachers deliberately juxtaposed these positions, both to expose students to well-known arguments about the appropriate relation between the individual and society and to show students that there are multiple plausible answers to the enduring question.

The class discussed Rand's novel *Anthem* on January 25. The character named Equality 7-2521 describes a society in which there is no "we," only "I," in which "we do not owe anything to our brothers." This society rejects altruism, holding that each individual should pursue his or her own self-interest. Mrs. Bailey opens the discussion by asking whether it is possible to live without owing anything to others.

> **T/B:** is it, is it possible to live in a group, a society,
> 235 a state, and not owe people?
> **FST:** no.
> **FST:** possible to what?
> **T/B:** to live in a society or a state and not owe
> people?
> 240 **FST:** no.
> **T/B:** I mean, do you in here owe people?
> **FST:** yeah.
> **T/B:** identify some of the places you owe people.
> **FST:** my mother.
> 245 **T/B:** okay, you owe your parents.
> **FST:** friends.

She seems to set up the question for a negative answer, by asking "is it possible" at line 234, and at line 245 she accepts the students' response that one always owes others. Then she and the students spend several minutes describing why individuals always owe others. Note that Mrs. Bailey is personalizing the discussion, connecting the subject matter with the students by talking about "you in here" at line 241 and subsequently.

After Mrs. Bailey and the students establish that we owe things to others, which seems to oppose Rand's argument, she adopts one of her common pedagogical techniques. She switches her position and begins to argue that Rand was at least partly correct. Although we might owe something to others, in many cases society should not take things from one person and give them to another. With this argument she apparently hopes to convince students that Rand's position has some strength and hopes to provoke students into defending their anti-individualist arguments. To make her case, Mrs. Bailey gives a participant example about Brenna the welfare mother.

Mrs. Bailey imagines that Brenna – an extremely quiet white student who participates only when asked – becomes a widow with two young children. She asks how Brenna is going to support herself, and whether society owes her anything.

> **T/B:** she's got, shhh, she's got two little <u>kids</u> <u>who</u>
> 515 are in <u>diapers</u> yet, how can she go out and get a job?
> **FST:** she's gotta do <u>something</u>.
> **TYI:** go to the um, go to the <u>wel</u>fare people.
> **T/B:** ahhh. o<u>kay</u>, she's going to go to the <u>wel</u>fare
> people. who, where does the <u>wel</u>fare get their
> 520 money from?
> **FST:** the government.
> **MRC:** they got their <u>money</u> from the <u>gov</u>ernment.
> **STS:** the taxes.
> **T/B:** okay, so you're <u>saying</u> <u>tha:t</u> <u>I</u> have <u>to,</u> °because
> 525 I'm working°, <u>I</u> have to give <u>money</u> so that <u>Brenna</u>'s
> kids and she [bell rings] don't <u>starve</u>. does that
> sound fair?
> **CAN:** yeah, that seems reasonable because there's
> not a lot of people, that's nice to other people.
> 530 **T/B:** I have to be nice to other people.
> **CAN:** you don't <u>have</u> to, but.
> **FST:** yeah
> **T/B:** well, what does it say here? I owe <u>no</u>thing to
> my brothers. and now you're <u>tell</u>ing me I have to be
> 535 <u>nice</u> to <u>her</u>. I mean, I'm all <u>sor</u>ry about your
> husband <u>dy</u>ing, leaving you with these two <u>kids</u>, but
> I don't see why my <u>hard</u>-earned money should go to
> take care of your little two <u>rug</u>rats there.
> **STS:** [1 second of laughter]
> 540 **TYI:** especially if you, you know you're <u>tied</u> up for
> money for yourself to eat.

Tyisha introduces the topic of welfare at line 517. The class has discussed this topic before, and they discuss it several times more during January and February. Mrs. Bailey accepts welfare as a topic at lines 518ff. and incorporates it into her argument for Rand's individualism.

Welfare was a topic familiar to many of these students through direct experience as recipients or as acquaintances of recipients. The debate between critics and supporters of welfare programs was also contentious and familiar to many people living in America in the 1990s, because the U.S. government was scaling back its social welfare system. Mrs. Bailey uses this familiarity to help them understand Rand's position on the individual/society question. She points out at lines 524–527 that support from social welfare programs means that working people like her have to pay for people like Brenna the hypothetical widow. Taking Rand's side, she presents this as unjust. Why should she have to use her hard-earned money to support someone else? This mobilizes models of identity from contemporary U.S. society and from some students' own neighborhoods in order to help students understand the curriculum. People like the teacher have to pay for welfare recipients like Brenna the hypothetical widow because our society is not as individualistic as Rand's.

More than once in January and February, Mrs. Bailey argued for individualism by arguing that social welfare programs are unjust. A society in which we do not owe anything to our brothers, as Rand puts it, makes some sense if one believes that people should not be forced to support others. As Mrs. Bailey says later during this discussion on January 25, still playing devil's advocate, "maybe we're the fools here" – those of us who work and support others. By connecting the curricular theme to contemporary U.S. society in this way, Mrs. Bailey both illustrates its continuing relevance and helps students understand it. As a result, in this and other class discussions, students often formulated their arguments about individualism and collectivism in terms of welfare and their understandings of people like the teachers who pay taxes that support welfare benefits. Thus they developed a local cognitive model focused on welfare, which they used to make sense of texts like Rand's and to develop their own arguments about individualism and collectivism.

The class discussed another participant example that involved welfare on February 7 while they were talking about the extreme collectivism presented in Plutarch's *Life of Lycurgus*. Like the example of Brenna the welfare mother, this participant example used models from students' own experience to facilitate their emerging understanding of the curriculum. Lycurgus was a Spartan political leader who helped govern a highly collectivist city-state. In order to combat the evils of private wealth, he ordered that all currency be made out of heavy iron so that it would be impractical to amass it and carry it around. He also supported the practice of bringing a newborn baby before the ruling council of elders and judging it for its potential contributions to the society. If it was sickly they could order it left outside to die of exposure because the good of the future society was more important than the rights of the individual baby and its parents.

The class discussion of Lycurgus resembled the earlier discussion of Rand in some respects. The students strongly opposed Lycurgus' position. The teachers defended Lycurgus, both to help students understand his position and to force students to defend their own positions. While making their arguments, teachers and students refer to a participant example given by Jasmine.

> **T/S:** and if you bring someone in[=
> **JAS:** [[3
> unintelligible syllables]
> 275 **T/S:** =there that isn't going to do their share as the
> wall of Sparta. you're giving that- that person,
> something that could be used better bu- by someone
> else. I- I sort of think that's perfectly right[=
> **JAS:** [that's
> 280 not-
> **T/S:** =if a baby can't hack it you get rid of it. that's
> going to be a problem in the future.
> **JAS:** they- they not equal if- if she had a baby and
> hers lived and I had a baby and mine didn't. we not
> 285 equal.
> **T/B:** yeah you're right. you didn't produce a
> healthy baby.
> **T/S:** that's [right
> **JAS:** [how do you know that. they just say
> 290 that one ain't healthy. and then lookit. mine
> probably grew up to be taller and [stronger
> **T/S:** [because they're
> the Spartan Ephors[=
> **JAS:** [and [5 unintelligible
> 295 syllables]
> **T/S:** =who make a decision. the Ephors know what
> makes a good Spartan because they're sixty years
> old and they've seen an awful lot. and they know
> what makes a good soldier. they've been in it from
> 300 the time they were seven.

In lines 272–282, Mr. Smith defends Lycurgus' collectivist position on infanticide: The good of the society outweighs the rights of the sickly child, so it should be killed. Jasmine responds with a participant example. She argues that, although her baby might seem sickly, it might contribute to society later on.

As the discussion of this example continues, the teachers vigorously defend Lycurgus' position – imagining that Jasmine's baby would turn into an "unhealthy runt" and would "lie around, drinking beer" while being supported by others. Jasmine and other students respond that the teachers are defending a "totalitarian" Spartan system. At this point Mrs. Bailey explicitly connects this debate between collectivism and individualism to the welfare debate.

395   **T/B:** I mean- what is the <u>problem</u> with this Jasmine.
       we're- what do we do. let anybody mate with
       everybody else in our society. we've got all of
       these <u>crack</u> babies. and all of these- you know
       babies that are born to <u>twelve</u> year olds and ar- are
400   premature and therefore have all these problems.
       we have mental incompetents mating with mental
       incompetents producing children. and going back
       to our discussions on the [2 unintelligible syllables]
       and- and Aristotle's *Politics*, I'm <u>tired</u> of footing the
405   bill for these people. if you can have a <u>healthy</u> baby
       <u>fine</u>. but why should <u>I</u> have to contribute to the
       support of <u>your</u> retarded kids and you just keep
       producing them.
       FST: go:d.
410   **T/B:** they're not going to contribute to me in my
       old <u>age</u> and I have to contribute to them now.

Here the discussion about Jasmine's hypothetical Spartan baby becomes a discussion about contemporary "crack babies" (line 398) and a welfare system that forces people like Mrs. Bailey to support such babies. Mrs. Bailey shifts from defending Spartan collectivism to defending her own right not to support others. To defend collectivism, she would have had to argue that the society, not herself, should be spared the burden of supporting Jasmine's baby. Mrs. Bailey may be revealing something about her own politics here by identifying with taxpayers and against welfare recipients. In any case, Mrs. Bailey's analogy – between contemporary debates about welfare and the cases of individualism and collectivism described by Rand and Lycurgus – may help students understand the curriculum and may also motivate them to defend their own position.

Mrs. Bailey's analogy between contemporary debates over welfare and ancient Sparta also continues to build the local cognitive model that construes the individual/society curricular theme in terms of welfare debates. While building this local model, Mrs. Bailey argues that societies like ours should not necessarily support "freeloaders." In making this argument she herself sides with what Rand might call "productive" members of the society, such as those forced to pay taxes that support social welfare programs. The students take the opposite side, however, that of the "freeloaders." As shown by one student's "god" at line 409, and by comments later in the discussion in which they accuse the teachers of heartless and immoral disregard for the needy, the students side with those who receive welfare instead of those who pay for it. Thus Mrs. Bailey's discussion of Jasmine's example highlights a difference between the identities of the teachers and the students. The teachers are white, middle-aged, employed taxpayers. The students who speak in this discussion are urban black adolescents, some of whose parents rely on welfare. In accord with the teachers' pedagogical goals, teachers and students use their own experiences to build cognitive models of the curricular theme. Students understand Rand and Lycurgus in part by building a local model of individual rights and collective responsibilities that takes the U.S. social welfare system as a good thing. As explained more extensively below, such local cognitive models are not exclusively cognitive. They can also mobilize and influence teachers and students' own social identities.

As they continued discussing Jasmine's example, the teachers made an argument that recurs several times during January and February. They claimed that contemporary American society achieves a golden mean between individualism and collectivism. In applying this argument to Jasmine's example, the teachers admitted that they do not in fact want our society to kill unhealthy babies, and they accepted the students' claim that every child has a right to survive. But they insisted that Lycurgus had one thing right. A good society expects individuals to contribute to the common good and it makes individuals "productive."

755 **T/B:** when- when I- we want a society of
productive individuals but we also say anyone that's
born has a right to survive. (1.0) kay- now what do
we do with all these surviving individuals. what's
in the best interest in our society?
780 **CAS:** use them.
T/B: to use them to make them productive. which
means we might have to do a few things in between
right? we might have to give them an education. we
might have to also what? (3.0) job training. create
785 jo: b programs.
T/S: make them healthy.
T/B: give pre-natal care.
T/S: make certain they have homes.
FST: no
790 **STS:** [hahahahaha   haha
T/B: [talk about sex education in- in- in- in classes
so that kids are not producing children at an- at too
early an age. (1.0)
CAS: talk about diseases
795 **T/B:** talk about diseases. set up health plans. you
see we're about the same thing as the Spartans are

about in some ways. except we started with a
different sense of who should live. we're trying to
make people productive too.

800   **JAS:** we- we like- we like them a little little bit.
        T/B: just a little bit.

Here the teachers present contemporary American society as an ideal. Like
Lycurgus, we are concerned that individuals contribute to the society. In
places like Colleoni High, for instance, we educate children (line 783) and
advise them not to have babies when they are too young (lines 791–793).
By raising individuals who have the right to think and act for themselves,
but who also want to act for the common good, contemporary America
achieves the best of both individualism and collectivism. The teachers only
begin to make this argument here. But in discussions about Athens over
the following two weeks, they argued more extensively that Athens and
contemporary America represent an ideal balance between individualism
and collectivism.

While discussing Jasmine's hypothetical baby, the students argued that
society should help needy people like welfare recipients. The teachers
agreed, but argued that this should be done by institutions like schools
that help people become socially productive. This represented an important shift in the emerging local model of the individual/society theme.
From this point on, teachers and students used not only welfare but also
education as an example of the relations between individuals and society.
In discussing individualism and collectivism after February 7, teachers and
students often used their own identities and their own classroom "society"
as favored participant examples while discussing the curricular theme. The
teachers and some students argued that the class itself represented a golden
mean between the extremes of Rand's individualism and Lycurgus' collectivism. This emerging local cognitive model facilitated and constrained
students' learning about the first curricular theme.

Pericles and the Analogy Between Athens and the Classroom

In addition to highly individualistic positions like Rand's and highly collectivist ones like Lycurgus', the teachers assigned texts that defended intermediate positions. They contrasted Spartan collectivism with the Athenian
system, particularly as Pericles describes it in his *Funeral Oration*. As shown
at the end of the February 7 class on Lycurgus, the teachers themselves
advocated an intermediate position on the individual/society theme. Being
Paideia teachers, they did not advocate this position continuously. They
asked genuine questions in seminar and pursued students' ideas most
of the time. But sometimes they also advocated the following position:
Individuals should have freedom to think and act and they should take
responsibility for themselves, but they should also sacrifice for the common good. As the class developed its own local model of and position on

the individual/society theme, the teachers and many students presented Athenian democracy as a third alternative that combined the best of the extreme positions.

In Athens, as Pericles and the teachers presented it, individuals advanced "not as a matter of privilege, but as the reward of merit." This contrasted with Sparta, where most citizens were forced to adopt the same aspirations and values. Mrs. Bailey opened the discussion of merit on February 21 by asking about the students' aspirations. As she had done throughout the year, she explored the students' own experiences in order to help them understand the differences between Spartan collectivism and moderate Athenian democracy. Cordell responds to Mrs. Bailey's question by saying that she wants to be a pediatrician. Mrs. Bailey asks whether Cordell's own hard work would suffice for her to attain this, and the students agree that it would not.

> **T/B:** is there anybody in your family that was ever a
> doctor?
> **COR:** °no°
> **T/B:** no. in fact if we go back a hundred and thirty or forty
> 160   years, we find that all of the people in your family were
> slaves, weren't they.
> **STS:** [1 second of laughter]
> **T/B:** at least a lot of them. okay. now how is it that she's
> able to go that far? (4.0) is it just Cordell and the fact she
> 165   works hard and is smart?
> **TYI:** no because she- she- she got the- she can do it. I
> mean back then, they- they couldn't do it. and now she
> equal, and everybody got a chance at being something they
> want to be.
> 170   **T/B:** so we created what?
> **TYI:** an equal?
> **T/B:** come on, somebody give me the word, we're playing
> fill in the blank with Mrs. Bailey. an equal what?
> **FST:** society.
> 175   **T/B:** society, or state, or whatever we want to call it.

Cordell works hard and is smart, as Mrs. Bailey says at line 165, but she points out that this in itself will not allow Cordell to become a pediatrician. If Cordell had been born a slave, she would not have had the opportunity. In addition to her own hard work, the society must be organized to provide opportunities and reward merit.

Both teachers and students are discussing Athens in this segment, but the discussion consistently links to what "we" (line 170) do "now" (line 167), making an analogy between moderate Athenian democracy and contemporary America. Our society provides opportunities, both because it recognizes merit and because it provides schools and similar institutions to help people develop talent. Thus our society combines good aspects of individualism (e.g., rewarding merit) with good aspects of collectivism (e.g., helping the disadvantaged develop their abilities). The teachers and students are building a local cognitive model that presents Athenian democracy and contemporary American society as examples of a golden mean between individualism and collectivism.

As teachers and students continue discussing Pericles' text, they continue to develop this analogy between Athens and the contemporary United States. In the following segment, for instance, Mr. Smith talks about "us" who recognize and reward others' merit. "He" in line 187 refers to Pericles.

> T/S: in other words, he's <u>not</u> only <u>praising</u> the <u>per</u>son who
> <u>ha:s</u> the ability and <u>li:ves</u> in a society that says Cor<u>dell</u>, you
> have the ability to be a <u>pedia</u>trician, and <u>therefore</u> you <u>will</u>
> 190   be. he's <u>also</u> praising the <u>rest</u> of us who <u>recognize</u>, Cor<u>dell</u>,
> says I, you <u>have</u> the ability to be a <u>pedia</u>trician. and <u>when</u>
> you <u>are</u>, I'll let you treat my children because I be<u>lieve</u> in you.

The participant example of Cordell the aspiring pediatrician leads teachers and students to talk not only about Athens but also about contemporary America and our similar belief that merit should be rewarded. The students' emerging local cognitive model of Athens thus includes categories from their own experience in contemporary U.S. society.

This emerging model of Athenian democracy, as a golden mean between Rand's individualism and Lycurgus' collectivism, involves more than contemporary American society in general. In addition, they discuss the classroom itself as analogous to moderate Athenian democracy. Mrs. Bailey, Mr. Smith and other teachers reward students for being smart and hardworking. The teachers praise Athenian democracy for being individualist in a similar way. Like the teachers themselves, Athenians rewarded individual merit. In order to understand where Pericles stands on the individual/society issue – and in order to understand what an ideal society should be like given that the teachers and some students treat Athenian democracy as the golden mean between individualism and collectivism – the students explore how their own society and their own teachers reward merit.

But Athens was also collectivist in important respects. Citizens had many freedoms, but they were also constrained by a collective vision of the social good. Mr. Smith gives another participant example to illustrate this point.

> 555   T/S: <u>o</u>kay, let's take an example. uhh, does anyone, <u>o</u>kay.
> does anyone really tell you how to <u>dress</u>?
> TYI: no.
> T/S: does anyone [say
> TYI: [well yes, <u>some</u>times.

560 **T/S:** sometimes, but not <u>all</u> the time. does- does someone
    tell you <u>when</u> and when you cannot speak <u>e</u>very <u>mi</u>nute of
    the <u>day</u>?
    MRC: you and Mrs. [Bailey.
    TYI: [no. some[times.
565 **T/S:**   [a:nd, does anyone tell you,
    uhh, what you <u>must</u> and must <u>not</u> do and- a:nd what you
    <u>can</u>'t do <u>all</u> the time?
    FST: no.
    TYI: somebody tell me what I <u>can</u> do?
570 **T/S:** <u>and</u> can<u>not</u> do <u>all</u> the time.
    TYI: yeah.
    T/S: <u>all</u> the time? you have <u>no</u> free choice.
    TYI: oh, no, not <u>all</u> the time.
    T/S: o<u>kay</u>. does anyone, <u>uhh</u>, isn't this how you live your
575 life?
    TYI: yeah, it <u>is</u>.
    T/S: you have some <u>free</u>dom?
    TYI: yeah.
    T/S: okay. did the <u>A</u>thenians <u>have free</u>dom?
580 **STS:** yes.
    T/S: to do <u>what</u>?
    TYI: to do what they <u>wanted</u> just like <u>I</u> can do what I
    want.
    T/S: could they do everything- <u>any</u>thing?
585 **TYI:** no, not anything. they couldn't break the <u>la:ws</u>, but.

By talking about the students in lines 555–556, in order to explore Pericles' description of Athenian freedoms, Mr. Smith seems to be claiming
that the students' freedoms are analogous to the Athenians'. He makes the
analogy explicit at line 579, when he moves from discussing the students'
freedoms to the Athenians'. As with the earlier discussion about merit, in
their conversation about freedom they use categories from the students'
experience to develop their understanding of Athens. Like Athenian citizens, contemporary Americans like the students have freedom to pursue
their own desires (lines 572, 577).

But when Tyisha takes the point too far, claiming at lines 582–583
that they could "do what they wanted just like I can do what I want,"
Mr. Smith makes her qualify this. Just like in the contemporary United
States, Athenians had to obey laws and act in some cases to support the
public good. The same is also true of the classroom itself. As Mr. Smith and
Mrs. Bailey regularly remind the students, they must accept agreed-upon
definitions and follow norms of classroom participation in order for the
class to achieve their goal of productive inquiry into the subject matter.
As we will see in Chapter 4, Tyisha sometimes acts in the classroom as if

she can do whatever she wants, but the teachers make clear that this is not acceptable behavior if the classroom "society" is to flourish. The class is individualist in rewarding merit and encouraging students to make their own arguments, but collectivist in insisting on participation that facilitates the common good.

In another segment during their discussion on February 21, Mrs. Bailey and the students explicitly contrast Athenian democracy with Spartan collectivism, and they make the analogy between themselves and Athens particularly clear.

> **T/B:**　　　　　　　　　　　　　　　　　okay, so here we
> are, we're in- we're in Sparta, and everybody gets to be
> 805　equal, but they get to be equal without- because nobody
> gets anything, is basically how it comes out. but in Athens,
> what do we do? (4.0) are you all dressed alike in this room?
> **STS:** no
> **MST:** [2 unintelligible syllables]
> 810　**T/B:** did you- did you wear what you wore today because
> it's the only thing you own to wear?
> **STS:** no. [2 seconds of laughter]
> **T/B:** (hh) you gotta do your laundry, Ivory?
> **T/S:** we'll ask Ivory that question.
> 815　**T/B:** okay, so- so, basically you have more things you
> could wear if you got caught up, right?
> **IVR:** yeah
> **T/B:** okay. (1.0) does that make you bad?
> **FST:** no
> 820　**T/B:** does that lea:d to all kinds of awful things?
> **FST:** no.
> **T/B:** it could or it could not. depends upon on whether
> you're a Spartan or you're Athenian. the Athenian is
> agreeing with you, he's saying what?
> 825　**FST:** that you can wear what you want.

In Sparta, as they learned two weeks before, women had only one standardized garment that made them look like everyone else. Several students were horrified by this idea. At lines 806–807, Mrs. Bailey makes clear that in the students' world, and by analogy in Athens, they are not so constrained by collectivist rules. In Sparta, dressing in your own individual way would be considered bad (line 818) and a precursor to awful things (line 820), but the Athenians and the students themselves value sartorial freedom.

In this segment, teachers and students even more strongly presuppose the analogy between Athens and the classroom. In lines 806–807, Mrs. Bailey says, "In Athens what do we do?" The first-person pronoun here presupposes that the class is analogous to Athenian society. In lines

823–824, she says that "the Athenian is agreeing with you," thus presupposing the convergence between Athenian and the students' own perspectives. Ivory, the student that the teachers joke about at lines 813–814, is a student known for her distinctive outfits. In Athens, as in their classroom, Ivory's distinctive clothing is tolerated and even valued. In overly collectivist societies like Sparta it would be condemned.

As they discuss the individual/society theme, especially during February, teachers and students developed a local cognitive model in which Athenian democracy occupied the golden mean between individualistic societies like Rand's and collectivist ones like Sparta. They developed this local model in part through participant examples that presented Athenian democracy as analogous to contemporary American society and as analogous to the social organization of the classroom itself. Students thus came to understand the individual/society theme through categories that they also used to understand U.S. society and their own classroom relationships. Teachers and students' cognitive models of the classroom – as a miniature "society" in which individuals explore their own ideas in such a way that everyone contributes to the consideration of a common question – became resources for understanding individualist and collectivist visions of society.

Tyisha, for instance, as someone who (by January) was identified as an outcast disrupting the common good of the classroom, exemplified the dangers of unfettered individualism. We have seen in the January 24 discussion of Tyisha the beast that she did serve as a participant example, illustrating the drawbacks of extreme individualism. Late in the class on January 24, for instance, Mrs. Bailey referred back to the "Tyisha the beast" example.

```
905    T/B: okay i- if- if- if we use (2.0)
       MRC: (hh)
       T/B: this idea of- of beast and see the beginning of
       it with Tyisha. she can act as her cat eating and
       sleeping when she wants to to some extent in the
910    summertime because she doesn't have the school
       society to deal with. what other kinds of behaviors
       might you engage in if you were outside a society?
```

In this segment Mrs. Bailey returns to Aristotle's concept of a "beast" and its implications for Aristotle's position on the individual/society question. At lines 907–911 she refers back to the example of Tyisha the beast, because they have used this example to develop their understanding of Aristotle's concept. Aristotle argues that people who live outside society are "beasts" and are not fully human. On January 24, students' emerging understanding of that argument is indexed by and partly dependent on the Tyisha example. As the analogy between the classroom and an ideal "society" develops, across many classes including January 24, Tyisha's identity as a disruptive outcast helps students build a local cognitive model of what it means to be an individualist who refuses to sacrifice for the good of the group. Chapter 4 describes in detail how Tyisha's emerging identity came to play an important role in this emerging local cognitive model.

Of course, students' use of categories from their own experience may or may not help them accurately understand the curriculum. There are significant differences between the collectivism found in the classroom and that found in Athens. The teachers may have relied too heavily on the analogy between the classroom and Athens, and as a result students may not have developed adequate understandings of ancient Athens. I do not fault them for this, however. Ninth grade students do not normally read Aristotle, Pericles, Plutarch and similar texts. These fourteen-year-olds developed some understanding of rich, important, complex texts and of enduring questions about individuals and societies. They left Mrs. Bailey and Mr. Smith's class in good position to deepen this understanding later in high school and beyond.

The students learned, for example, about Aristotle's concept of a "beast." Initially, they believed that an individual living in the woods would nonetheless be essentially similar to other human beings, even if a bit unusual. As they discussed Rand's *Anthem* and the example of welfare, many students began to see how unfettered individualism can undercut social cohesion and hurt the disadvantaged. They began to see how individuals should and do depend on society in difficult times. As they discussed Athenian democracy and their own classroom society, many students came to see that productive group discussion relies on individuals who control their own desires for the good of the group. Thus they built a local model of classroom "beasts" – people who refuse to sacrifice for the good of the group, like libertarian taxpayers and disruptive students.

By emphasizing the analogies between contemporary America and Athens, the teachers and many students built a local cognitive model that was both limiting and illuminating. Disruptive students are not a perfect example of Aristotle's "beasts," but they are not a bad start. This local model provided one resource through which students came to understand the individual/society curricular theme. Other resources included more widely circulating sociohistorical models of the individual and society, the Paideia emphasis on applying enduring questions to students' own experience, the teachers' choice of texts that included individualist, collectivist and intermediate positions on the individual/society theme, the teachers' personal beliefs as well as other resources. Students were able to learn something about the curriculum – despite the fact that any comment, example or fact could have been interpreted in many different ways – in part because of the emerging local cognitive model traced above.

An Example of Student Learning

This section provides an extended example of how many students did in fact learn academically as they discussed the individual/society curricular theme. Students learned in several senses. First, they developed their Paideia skills, learning to consider multiple perspectives, to provide arguments and evidence, and to develop analogies between the curriculum and their own experiences. Second, they learned to recognize curricular themes. When given a new text like Rand's *Anthem,* many students could identify the individual/society curricular theme as central to the text and locate the author's argument with respect to other well-known positions on the theme. Third, students learned how to develop their own positions and how to defend these positions with evidence. Finally, students learned to use their own experiences in order to interpret others' ideas and develop their own. The students did not make as much progress as the teachers might have hoped, but many students made some progress in each of these four ways.

In several classes during January and February, the students asked incisive questions and formulated arguments about the individual/society theme. The discussion on January 25 about Rand's *Anthem* provides several examples. In this discussion students developed their own moderate position on the individual/society question, a few weeks before the teachers did the same thing during the discussion of Lycurgus. In *Anthem,* as described above, the narrator advocates an individualistic society in which people do not have to contribute to the common good, in which we "do not owe anything to our brothers." Students object to this, supporting collective responsibility for the disadvantaged.

> **T/B:** okay, so, so we se:e, if- if I'm hearing you correctly, we're seeing that by: helping, by paying this money, in taxes or whatever, you're making a better community, whatever. does that mean, then,
> 715 tha:t (3.0) °I guess, I'm I'm trying to figure out how to phrase this° does that mean then- tha:t we do owe something to our brothers?
> . . .
> **KTN:** that's what I said, I think they have differences, of our society and the Anthem society.
> 740 **T/B:** okay, the society he's creating is going to be different than our society.=
> **FST:** =from ours.
> **T/B:** okay, and it's going to be different in what ways do you see.
> 745 **KTN:** well, if we do, if we do [1 unintelligible syllable] our brothers and stuff, things would

probably be different. they probably don't have to
do that if they don't want to.
FST: what?

750   **T/B:** okay, they don't have to do that if they don't
want to, they don't have to pay taxes and things like
that.
TYI: they don't have to do nothing if they don't
want to do it.

755   **T/B:** okay.
FST: then he won't take them.
MRC: if they didn't, they would have a poor
society. all these bu:ms on the street, people that
can't afford to feed their babies and people dying

760   constantly.
FST: right.
T/B: okay, so he's creating a society that you don't
think is going to be a good society[=
MRC: [right.

765   **T/B:** =because you need to, have it built in that you
help people.
MRC: right
T/B: okay, everyone can't take care of themselves,
is that what you're telling me?

770   **CAN:** right, you gonna need somebody to do
different things. you can't do everything all by
yourself.
MRC: right.
FST: just like farming. we don't know how to

775   farm, so other people farm for us and then we- we
pay for them to bring food, to bring the food over.
some people know how to umm, you know, make
money. we don't know how to make money.
T/B: well, take the farmers. the farmers aren't

780   doing a real efficient jo:b, and as a result we have
all these farm subsidies. we give farmers money to
keep them operating. is that what we should do?
CAN: yeah, it's helping us eat.
T/B: it's helping us eat, so we're doing something

785   even though they're not doing, perhaps some would
say not a very good job? therefore
CAN: I think in order to be a farmer, that's kind of
dangerous job for the people to do. other people,
they live by themselves, other people. they have to

790   have survival and-
FST: Mrs. Bailey

T/B: yes?
FST: also our taxes help us to have <u>funds</u> and
<u>scho</u>larships for people who can't go to school, that
795   can't afford it for <u>free</u> clinics for people that's poor
and need a <u>checkup</u>.

In this passage, students display understanding of Rand's text and begin to develop an argument about the individual/society theme. Their comments at lines 738–739, 745–748 and 753–754 and the fact that they mount a well-reasoned counterargument show that at least some of the students understand Rand's claim that individuals should pursue their own self-interest.

Students also engage in the kind of Paideia seminar discussion that the teachers hope for. In this passage, students connect their reading of Rand to earlier discussions about individualism and collectivism, articulate their own position on the curricular theme and defend that position by citing examples from their own experience. As illustrated earlier, on several other days the teachers and students have discussed the relative merits of individualism and collectivism in terms of taxes and the welfare system in the contemporary United States – asking whether "productive" members of a society should have to support "unproductive" ones through welfare and other social programs. When Mrs. Bailey asks her question at lines 711–717, and when she mentions "taxes" again at line 751, she is indexing earlier discussions in which the topics of taxes and welfare helped students make sense of the individual/society theme. She helps students formulate their understanding of Rand's individualism by analogy with their own experiences with welfare and taxes. The students then use their understandings of taxes and welfare to develop an argument against Rand's individualism.

At lines 757–760, Maurice begins a counterargument to Rand, pointing out that a society where individuals only look out for themselves would fail to care for the needy. He implies that this would degrade the quality of life for others, because there would be "bums on the street." And he implies that it would be wrong to have a society in which some people "can't afford to feed their babies." Candace extends Maurice's argument at lines 770–772, claiming that people cannot be self-sufficient. Maurice and Candace are beginning to formulate their own position against Rand's extreme individualism.

At lines 774–778, another student takes Candace's point in a different direction. The student seems to be arguing for a division of labor, in which different members of society contribute different things. This has the potential to undermine Maurice and Candace's emerging counterargument because Rand defended a capitalist system that could involve such a division of labor. The teacher notices this opening and defends Rand's position at lines 779–786. Her complaint about farm subsidies echoes earlier discussions of welfare, when she argued that "productive" individuals should not be forced to support unproductive people through welfare programs. Despite Maurice and Candace's promising beginning, the teacher continues to play devil's advocate and defend Rand's individualism.

But the students rise to the challenge, at line 793, by expanding the argument that Maurice and Candace began earlier. This student argues against Mrs. Bailey and Rand that more fortunate members of society should support medical care and education for the less fortunate. This is exactly what the teachers want: for students to defend themselves when their arguments are challenged. The student's argument would of course need further development to be fully convincing. But in this discussion the students challenge the author, articulate an alternative position and defend it against Rand and the teacher. They thus demonstrate their developing Paideia skills. And they continue to develop a local cognitive model about the relation between individuals and society, a model that will facilitate cognitive insights in future discussions of the curricular theme.

In developing this local cognitive model on January 25, students present "our" society – see the first-person pronouns at lines 739, 745, 774, 783 and 793 – as a more desirable alternative to Rand's individualist society. We in the United States fund scholarships and (sometimes) provide medical care, and in doing so we support a more collectivist society than Rand's. As opposed to us, "they" who follow Rand's ideas (lines 738, 747–748, 750, 753, 757) create social problems and behave immorally. In setting up this opposition between Rand's individualism and the contemporary United States, the students are beginning to build the local cognitive model that the teachers elaborated on February 7 – the model in which Athenian democracy and contemporary American society occupy the golden mean between individualism and collectivism. Thus the January 25 discussion lies earlier along the trajectory across which teachers and students developed this local cognitive model.

The following excerpt from later in the January 25 discussion of _Anthem_ illustrates how students refer back to earlier discussions of the individual/society curricular theme, thereby continuing to establish their local cognitive model of that theme. When she refers to an "equality society" in the following segment Mrs. Bailey means the individualist one described by Rand.

1145 **T/B:** Katie you got out on there on a limb (hh) by
your (hh) self? why is it that you would not want to
live in that soci- why it- why is it that you would
like to live in equality society?
FST: °I told you°
1150 **T/B:** pardon?
KAT: °you don't have to do anything you don't
want to?°

T/B: you don't have to do anything you don't want
to. °okay.°
1155 **MRC:** °so she wouldn't have to come to school?°
T/B: what happens in a society where you don't
have to do anything you don't want to.
FST: (hh)
MRC: you[become beasts.
1160 **FST:**   [°you become a cartoon°
CAN: I mean, who gonna help you when you
become=
FST: [°yeah°
CAN: [=poor ho:meless[=
1165 **FST:**   [yeah, who gonna help
you?
CAN: =you be by yourself. you'll die girl. (hh)
[laughter from a few female students]
CAN: you get lonely.
1170 **FST:** (hh)
CAN: you'll get lo:nely, we're human beings, human beings
get lo:nely, hu:ngry.

As Mrs. Bailey did earlier, Katie has defended Rand's ideal society, in which each individual looks out for himself or herself. Maurice begins a counter-argument by referring back to the previous day's discussion of "beasts" at line 1159. By using the word "beast" in an appropriate context, he indexes Aristotle's argument that individuals who only look out for themselves are not fully human. This in itself shows that Maurice recognizes the larger theme and can connect the discussions of Rand and Aristotle. Candace and another student support his position at lines 1161–1172, arguing that Katie herself might need others and arguing that humans depend on others. Maurice, Candace and other students thus continue to develop their argument for a moderate collectivism, against Rand, Katie and Mrs. Bailey.

Maurice and Candace's argument further illustrates their emerging local model of the curricular theme. By January 25 the teachers had exposed students to both Aristotle's moderate collectivism and Rand's extreme individualism. Students engaged with these positions around the more concrete question – drawn from their own society and in some cases their own experience – of whether a society should have social welfare programs. The teachers and many students liked Aristotle, at least insofar as he emphasized cooperation within a collective as opposed to "beasts" who reject the collective. While discussing Rand's *Anthem* they began to include Aristotle's idea of a "beast," which they had learned the day before, in order to criticize Rand's extreme individualism. A fully individualistic society, they argued, would encourage people to act like beasts, and their discussion of Aristotle showed how that would go against human nature. On

February 7, when they read Lycurgus, the local cognitive model became more complex. As described above, they added an extreme collectivism to their repertoire of possible positions. For the rest of February, as they continued to discuss the individual/society theme, the students and eventually also the teachers continued to argue against both of the extremes and for a moderate Athenian democracy.

This emerging local cognitive model shaped their understanding of the theme and thus helped them learn about an important piece of the curriculum. The texts that they read from Aristotle, Plutarch, Rand and others contain many interesting arguments and could have been interpreted in different ways. There was indeterminacy at several timescales – in how these texts will be interpreted over historical time, in how these teachers and students might have come to understand the texts, in how any given discussion would turn out. The students' learned academically as many of these indeterminacies were overcome, if only provisionally. In particular events, comments and passages from the text came to have more definite meaning for the students as the cognitive structure of the event solidified and people came to agree on what things meant. Over a trajectory of many such events, local cognitive models of the curricular theme solidfied, and these in turn constrained the interpretations that could emerge in particular events. Over the academic year, students increasingly mastered Paideia skills like considering multiple points of view and building analogies with their own experience, and their resulting behavior further constrained the types of interpretations that students were likely to develop. Over time, then, a configuration of resources from various timescales contributed to many students' increasingly solid understandings of individualism and collectivism.

The Second Curricular Theme: The Legitimacy of Resistance

Beginning in late February, and running intermittently into May, the teachers shifted their curricular focus away from the theme of individuals and society toward another theme. This second theme built on the first one because it also considered the obligations of an individual within a society. However, this time the teachers presupposed that the society was hierarchical and probably unjust. The questions became: What makes power legitimate? Should a common person resist illegitimate power? Several of the texts relevant to this theme focused on ancient Rome, as it is described by Cicero, Shakespeare and others. But they also read texts from various traditions and time periods that engaged with the questions, often texts that discussed the exploitation of one racial or economic group by another.

Like the individual/society theme, questions about loyalty and resistance have been raised in many traditions across many centuries. These questions are also essentially contestable – that is, reasonable people can differ in their answers. Authors and characters in the assigned texts advocated at least three positions. Some, like an oppressed Native American in Steinbeck's story *The Pearl*, advocate resisting those in power. Some, like Antony in *Julius Caesar*, advocate supporting the powerful. And some, like Cicero in his "Letter to Atticus," advocate keeping one's head down and avoiding a decision. Teachers and students debated and advocated all three of these positions across their discussions from February to May.

The teachers successfully engaged students in discussions of this theme. While discussing *The Pearl* on April 12, for instance, Germaine and Erika argued that Quino (the Native American who gets exploited) should resist this exploitation. Mrs. Bailey helped them connect their arguments about Quino to the larger question of resistance against exploitation.

> **T/B:** that's not the immediate dangers. but you're telling me that he should change the situation, right? isn't that what you just all agreed? how's he going to change the
> 555 situation between himself and the Europeans?
> **FST:** by not going along with them?
> **T/B:** by not going alo:ng with them. defying the social structure? okay, that's part of it, but isn't there more to it?
>
> . . .
>
> **T/B:**   but then you're also telling me he should sell the pearl for a thousand pesos.
> 625 **FST:** I wouldn't cause
> **FST:** say it again?
> **T/B:** well you're saying to me that that he should change the situation. he, representing the Indian community . . .

As this discussion proceeded, students reflected on the difficulties that oppressed people like Quino face. Chapters 4 and 5 show in more detail how the teachers and students energetically discussed the question of when the oppressed should resist, both on April 12 and on other days.

In the classes I observed, the students did not develop one shared local position on this second curricular theme in the same way as they did for the first. During January and February, as shown above, the teachers and most of the vocal students agreed that a moderate Athenian democracy was a good model for the relation between individuals and society. This emerging local cognitive model, together with the analogies between Athens and contemporary U.S. society, helped students understand the first theme. While discussing the loyalty/resistance theme, in contrast, students took strong stands supporting each of the three positions – resist oppression, support the powerful and stay neutral – in different discussions across three months. Because they lacked one consistent position on the theme, students and teachers developed several more fragmented local cognitive models that helped them understand the question and the various arguments. Perhaps because of this fragmentation, I do not have data showing students developing deep understandings of the second theme.

Some students did nonetheless develop smaller scale local cognitive models that represented various aspects of the loyalty/resistance theme. One such model involved an analogy between the classroom itself and a hierarchical society. On one side of this analogy, teachers and students noted that teachers have power in the classroom and that students are subject to that power. On several occasions, the teachers imagined that they themselves were despotic and abused their power, and they asked whether the students should resist them or not. In the April 12 discussion of *The Pearl*, for instance, Mrs. Bailey volunteered herself as a despot who wants to exploit the students by taking their jewelry and paying them only a fraction of its worth. This participant example was analogous to the text, in which European dealers try to exploit Quino by buying his valuable pearl for much less than its true value.

300   **BRE:** well, he can <u>choose</u> what he wants to. maybe he
        could have gotten more money for the pearl.
        T/B: how much do you think this pearl is <u>worth</u>?
        BRE: maybe five thousand pesos.
        T/B: five <u>thousand</u>? there's another figure in the book
305   fifteen thousand. it certainly <u>seems</u> to be worth more than
        one thousand pesos. does he <u>have</u> to take the price?
        FST: no, he don't have to. that's his choice, if he wanted
        to.
        T/B: okay, everyone in here has a piece of jewelry on
310   today, except maybe the guys. you guys don't have
        jewelry?
        STS: [2 seconds of laughter]
        T/B: okay, I offer you, one-<u>tenth</u> the value of whatever the
        piece of jewelry you have on is. you gonna take it?
315   **FST:** no, I paid good money for it. because I know what
        it's worth.
        FSTs: [1 second of laughter]
        T/B: you're not gonna take it?
        FST: because I know how much it's <u>worth</u>, really. you
320   wanna, you wanna give me something much lower than
        that.
        T/B: but I'm going to give you <u>grades</u> on Tuesday.
        FST: yeah, so?
        FSTs: [2 seconds of laughter]
325   **FST:** I don't think it's got anything to do with you buying
        what I got.

T/B: you don't think it has anything to do with me <u>buy</u>ing what you've got?
FST: no,
330 **FST:** if you have good <u>grades</u>.
STS: [1 second of chatter]
FST: it shouldn't.
FST: it could help my <u>grade</u>, cause she- I would have sold it to her.
335 **FST:** it shouldn't have anything.
T/B: it <u>should</u>n't have anything to do. (3.0) but might it?
FST: yeah, depending on the way you gonna think.
FST: [2 seconds of laughter]
T/B: well what if I <u>think</u>, that because I give you a <u>grade</u>, I
340 can also tell you to do <u>any</u>thing <u>else</u> that I want to tell you.

Mrs. Bailey introduces the participant example at line 309, and she introduces herself as a hypothetical despot at line 313. Then at line 322, she makes clear that she has power over the students because she gives them grades.

This analogy between the classroom and the text has cognitive potential. Some aspects of the teachers' relationship with the students are analogous to Quino's relationship with the Europeans, and the students might gain insight into Quino's predicament and into the larger curricular theme by exploring the analogy. At line 333, for instance, a student notes that the oppressed can often benefit, if in small ways, from being loyal to those in power. Both *The Pearl* and other assigned texts illustrated this fact: Loyalty to the powerful can pay and is generally much easier in the short run, while resistance often has serious costs. So the example may have helped the student understand one aspect of the larger curricular theme, and in fact students re-articulated this particular understanding in subsequent discussions. The analogy between the classroom and hierarchical societies thus facilitated a local cognitive model. Chapter 5 provides more extended examples of how this cognitive model recurred in other class discussions. Although I do not have extensive evidence of this, some students seemed to use this local model to understand the second curricular theme – in the same way that the local model of moderate Athenian democracy helped them understand the individualism/collectivism theme.

However much they may have learned from this local analogy between hierarchical societies described in the loyalty/resistance theme and the hierarchical organization of the classroom itself, this local cognitive model also drew on metapragmatic models that they used to identify each other. Participant examples like the one about Mrs. Bailey buying their jewelry, and the emerging local analogy between the classroom and a hierarchical society, worked cognitively because teachers and students used metapragmatic models in which teachers have power to evaluate students and in which students respond to power in different ways. Students knew that teachers have the power to assign grades and they knew that bad grades can lead to unpleasant consequences – including angry parents and even dropping out of school. Their own experiences with hierarchy in schools helped them understand Quino's situation, as they borrowed categories of identity from metapragmatic models of teachers and students to construe the curricular theme. The next section shows how this sort of overlap between cognitive and metapragmatic models allowed social identification and academic learning to facilitate each other.

On April 12, Mrs. Bailey hastened to make clear that teachers vary in how they use their power.

350   **FST:** I know some teachers who would do that.
       T/B: but I'm not that kind of teacher. yeah, you don't
       know?
       FST: how we supposed to know?
       T/B: how are you supposed to know? how would you
355   know if I were that kind of teacher?
       FST: [4 unintelligible syllables]
       FST: I guess you would've already done that.
       STS: [1 second of laughter]
       T/B: is that s-, is that what has happened to Quino's people?
360   **FST:** yeah
       T/B: has that already happened to them?
       FST: that's why he's being very precautious about,
       precautious.
       T/B: they take advantage of him.
365   **FST:** they were used to it and he defied them by not doing
       it.
       T/B: uh huh.
       FST: yeah
       T/B: oh yeah?
370   **FST:** yeah.
       T/B: was he right to defy them?
       FST: yes. he was right to defy them.
       FST: it was right
       FST: it was wrong, but in that case he should've did it. I
375   think.

At lines 353–358, the students briefly tease Mrs. Bailey about whether she is in fact the kind of teacher who would abuse her power. I infer that they are teasing, based on their laughter at line 358 and the fact that Mrs. Bailey does not take offense. The students know that Mrs. Bailey is not that kind of teacher. She is well respected by both teachers and students, who know that she would not use her power to extort money from them. At line 359, Mrs. Bailey shifts the topic from the classroom analogy back to Quino, and they proceed to discuss Quino's defiance of the Europeans. Mrs. Bailey raises the question of whether such defiance is right at line 371. The students take different positions on this question, and the discussion continues.

Chapter 5 analyzes the April 12 class in more detail, as well as other class discussions of the loyalty/resistance theme. The analyses in Chapters 4 and 5 will show how this theme played a minor role in Tyisha's identity development and a major role in Maurice's. The analogy between hierarchical relations in the classroom and the hierarchical social relations involved in the loyalty/resistance theme helped students develop a local cognitive model that seemed to illuminate the curriculum for some students some of the time. With respect to the second curricular theme, I do not claim that these students learned the curriculum as accurately or extensively as they might have. They had some productive seminar discussions, but they did not develop robust local cognitive models as they did for the first theme. But Mrs. Bailey and Mr. Smith were exposing young students to more complex Paideia-inspired ways of reading and arguing for the first time, and they did not expect students to grasp the nuances of everything they read. They hoped to teach students some basic facts about history and literature, expose them to a few essentially contestable questions and help them learn to develop arguments and engage in Paideia discussions. Although the students did not fully understand all the texts they read, the teachers succeeded in these broader goals with many of the students.

The Overlap of Academic Learning and Social Identification

Having developed conceptual accounts of social identification and academic learning, and having given brief empirical illustrations of how these processes occurred in Mrs. Bailey and Mr. Smith's classroom, we are now in a position to analyze more precisely how social identification and academic learning can mesh with and facilitate each other. Several have recently argued for what Packer (2001) calls an "ontological" approach to learning (cf. also Dreier, 2003; Wenger, 1998). According to an ontological approach, learning changes not just what and how the learner knows (which would be simply "epistemological") but also who the learner is. To learn is to take up a new practice, to change one's position in a community, and thus it changes the self. According to an ontological account, learning by definition overlaps with social identification. "Because learning transforms who we are and what we can do, it is an experience of identity" (Wenger, 1998: p. 215). My argument fits under the umbrella of ontological approaches to learning because I am also arguing that social identification and academic learning mesh with and cannot be extricated from each other.

The interdependence of social identification and academic learning has become a popular topic recently, and various mechanisms have been proposed to explain how the two processes connect. First, some describe how students develop types of identities that are tied to curricular content, such that a student can become a type of math student, for example (Greeno et al., 1998; Walkerdine, 1988; Zack and Graves, 2001). Thinking of oneself as a "good" or "bad" math student is certainly an aspect of identity, and developing this aspect of identity may well influence how much a student learns. Identifying himself or herself as a good math student, for instance, may encourage a student to work harder and do better. Second, some describe how identity-driven interactional patterns can shape opportunities for students in classroom activities, and how access to such activities can then influence how much students learn. Gender, for instance, sometimes influences the course of classroom interactions (Brickhouse, 2001), and the way a teacher deals with gender can influence the subject matter that students learn (O'Connor, 2001). To use a stark example, if boys refuse to let girls talk in science class, then the girls might not develop certain skills in science. Finally, some describe how types of curricular content are correlated with types of identity (Lemke, 1990; Luke and Freebody, 1997). Successful science students are often considered "nerds," for example, and this identity can influence both their social and academic lives.

It would take more extensive arguments, but all three of these mechanisms that describe interconnections between identity and learning (and likely other such mechanisms) can be plausibly defended. All three fall under the broad umbrella of ontological approaches to learning, describing how academic learning and social identity are inextricable. I am proposing a mechanism that is parallel to these three, in that it also describes one way that social identification and academic learning can overlap. But my mechanism is different because it describes how *specific contents* of the curriculum mesh with and facilitate social identification. Each of the other three mechanisms involves curriculum only in a broad sense. In contrast, I describe how specific themes and categories from the curriculum themselves become resources for identifying students, and how categories for identifying students become resources for learning the curriculum.

This chapter has shown how, in classrooms, local cognitive models of curricular topics can develop over the academic year. These local models borrow from and contextualize more widely circulating cognitive models that enter the classroom through textbooks, other media and individuals' prior knowledge. Along with other cognitive resources, these local models can contribute to the systems of constraints and affordances that facilitate academic learning. Students learn about the curriculum in part because their inferences are guided by locally circulating models that they and others develop across events. For example, Mrs. Bailey and Mr. Smith's students learned about Rand, Lycurgus and Aristotle in part as they developed a local model of how extreme individualism undermines both social welfare programs and productive classroom discussion.

When the curriculum involves people as part of the subject matter, as in literature, history, social studies and similar content areas, the local cognitive models that teachers and students develop to help them understand the curriculum inevitably include metapragmatic models. Any representation of human subject matter, whether it comes from a locally developed or more widely circulating cognitive model, a textbook or another source, will represent humans using metapragmatic models. Historical or philosophical discussion of the relation between the individual and society, for instance, could make available various categories of identity – dutiful citizens, emasculated sycophants, loyal opposition, scathing critics, refusenik hermits and many others – depending on the texts read and the arguments introduced. In any classroom discussion of this topic, students and teachers will use some such categories of identity and not others.

This book describes overlap between the local cognitive models teachers and students develop as they learn the curriculum and the local metapragmatic models that teachers and students develop as they socially identify one another. The curriculum becomes a resource for social identification as students and teachers borrow categories of identity from their local cognitive models and use them in the local metapragmatic models they use to identify each other socially. This happens, for instance, when teachers and students used the curricular concept of "beast" or outcast to identify Tyisha. And the social identities of students become a resource for learning the curriculum as students and teachers borrow categories of identity from local metapragmatic models and use these categories in the local cognitive models that facilitate their understanding of the curriculum. This happens, for instance, when teachers and students used Tyisha's identity as a disruptive outcast to help them learn about the dangers of extreme individualism.

Preceding sections have described a local cognitive model that Mrs. Bailey and Mr. Smith's students developed in the middle of the year. In this model the vocal students presented the collective as preeminent over the individual, insofar as everyone should contribute to those in need and support productive joint activities. The students opposed individualist claims that everyone should take what they can while ignoring others' needs, and they insisted that no citizen should feel superior to others. This local model contained both explicit and tacit categories of identity, plus what Bakhtin would call "ventriloquation" or evaluation of people who inhabit those categories (Bakhtin, 1935/1981; Wortham, 2001a). For instance, with respect to this model, an individual who refuses to value the collective over the group and thinks he or she is better than others would likely be identified as inappropriately self-centered and disruptive. As shown in Chapter 4, a category of identity like this became part of the metapragmatic model that teachers and students developed to identify Tyisha, at the same time as the local cognitive model of self-centered "beasts" was emerging in the classroom.

But the local cognitive model, and the students' understanding of the curricular theme, was not first established as a purely cognitive entity, then transferred full-formed to the social domain as a resource for identifying Tyisha. The local cognitive model was still emerging when Tyisha herself began to be identified as a "beast." The cognitive model had space for a category of identity like what I will call in Chapter 4 the "disruptive outcast." But this category was not explicitly formulated as part of the local cognitive model before Tyisha's identity became relevant both to social identification and academic learning during January discussions of the first curricular theme. Teachers and students had been developing a local metapragmatic model through which they could identify Tyisha in November and December, before they began to engage the curricular theme of the proper relation between an individual and society. The fact that they were formulating this local metapragmatic model, and that this model included an identity that resembled a disruptive outcast, facilitated the development of this category in the emerging local cognitive model. The process of socially identifying Tyisha thus helped them develop a local cognitive model that students could draw upon to learn about the first curricular theme, because the cognitive model was not fully specified in advance of them identifying Tyisha as a disruptive outcast. The resulting cognitive model then afforded students' learning. Development of this local cognitive model also facilitated a more precise metapragmatic model for identifying Tyisha, because the curricular concept of "beast" or "outcast" became available to identify her. The local metapragmatic and cognitive models thus co-developed.

For analytic purposes, it can make sense to treat social identification and academic learning as separate processes, but in the world these processes are not discrete. They overlap and mesh with each other. I have been distinguishing between "metapragmatic" and "cognitive" models in order to give clear accounts of social identification and academic learning. But in fact these are often not different entities. Human activity in the world is not divided into two discrete types – identity-related ones, in which we develop metapragmatic models to do identity work, and cognition-related ones, in which we develop cognitive models to learn academic content. Models of identity can simultaneously help us learn academically about the social world and identify people in it. In Mrs. Bailey and Mr. Smith's classroom, teachers and students developed local models that functioned in significant part as both metapragmatic and cognitive models. Chapters 4 and 5 illustrate in detail how this overlapping of local metapragmatic and cognitive models occurred. Chapter 6 returns to the theoretical question of how best to conceptualize social identification and academic learning as part of larger heterogeneous processes.

The joint development of local metapragmatic and cognitive models in the classroom was greatly facilitated by *experience-near teaching*. When Mrs. Bailey and Mr. Smith developed analogies between the students' own experiences and the curricular themes, and when they used participant examples to explore these analogies, they facilitated overlap between metapragmatic and cognitive models. A participant example presupposes both metapragmatic and cognitive models. In order to gauge the example's implications for participants' identities, students and teachers must draw on metapragmatic models. In order to understand the conceptual point being made with the example, students and teachers must draw on cognitive models. As I have described elsewhere (Wortham, 1994, 2001b), the simultaneous use of both metapragmatic and cognitive models through participant examples means that categories and evaluations from one type of model can easily be used in the other. Students can be identified using categories from the curriculum or curricular topics can be conceptualized using categories from models of identity. When students and teachers use themselves as a resource for understanding the curriculum, in participant examples and other forms of experience-near teaching, they often blend metapragmatic and cognitive models.

In earlier work I have explained this mutual constitution of social identification and academic learning only at the timescale of particular events. In contrast, this book studies trajectories of identification and trajectories of learning across months. By studying trajectories, we can see how participant examples can also facilitate more robust interdependence between social identification and academic learning across a year, as local metapragmatic and cognitive models emerge and overlap across many events. Chapters 4 and 5 describe two trajectories across which students and teachers were identified and curricular themes were explored – and across which these processes of social identification and academic learning meshed. The chapters analyze series of participant examples across which Tyisha and Maurice were consistently used as characters in examples which the class used to discuss the curricular themes. These series of participant examples facilitated the joint development of local metapragmatic/cognitive models. Students and teachers built the local model they used to identify Tyisha, for instance, partly by using categories drawn from their emerging understandings of the curricular theme about individuals and society. And they built the local model they used to understand this theme partly by using categories drawn from their emerging model of Tyisha's identity. The local model became a joint product of and resource for both social identification and academic learning.

Participant examples depended upon and facilitated the interdependence of social identification and academic learning particularly well in this case, because the two series of participant examples contributed to two different *analogies* between the social organization of the classroom and the two curricular themes. Much experience-near teaching takes this form, in which teachers help students understand subject matter by developing analogies between students' own experiences and curricular topics. As described earlier in this chapter, and in both Chapters 4 and 5, the series of participant examples that involved Tyisha and Maurice built upon analogies between some aspect of the curriculum and some aspect of students' experience. For instance, the teachers drew an analogy between Athenian democracy, an allegedly ideal balance between individualism and collectivism, and the classroom itself. Just as Athenian democracy both empowered the individual and insisted on the primacy of the group, Paideia classrooms urge students to express their own arguments but insist that they conform to the collective purpose of advancing group understanding of the text. Students and teachers used this analogy to explore Athenian democracy, by examining whether and how their classroom organization accorded with texts from Aristotle and Pericles. The analogy between classroom and society became part of a local cognitive model students used to think about the curriculum.

Because the analogy was established and explored in substantial part through participant examples that involved students like Tyisha, the analogy also presupposed a metapragmatic model that identified "beasts" like Tyisha and more cooperative students like Erika and several of the other girls. Thus the analogy played a central role in the locally circulating metapragmatic/cognitive model that was developed as they learned about the curriculum and as Tyisha was socially identified. While discussing the examples, and at other times, students and teachers represented their classroom as a society that balanced individual desires and the collective needs. They accomplished this representation in part by describing Tyisha as a disruptive outcast whom one would not want to have in a society. The analogy, and the participant examples it depended on, facilitated the local metapragmatic/cognitive model that students and teachers relied on for both social identification and academic learning.

Chapters 4 and 5 trace how social identification and academic learning meshed with and facilitated each other in Mrs. Bailey and Mr. Smith's classroom through jointly emerging and overlapping local metapragmatic and cognitive models. I am not claiming that this is the only potential mechanism through which social identification and academic learning overlap and facilitate each other. The two processes often depend on interrelated resources from various timescales, including but not limited to the local timescale. In different cases, different configurations of these resources will be relevant to understanding the two processes and their overlap. For instance, social identification and academic learning sometimes jointly use sociohistorical resources. Bowker and Star (2000) and Foucault (1966/1971) describe cases in which sociohistorical systems of classification provide the essential mechanism through which social identification and academic learning overlap. In these cases, locally emerging models may not be important to explaining the overlap. In the case examined in this book, however, the overlap between social identification and academic learning happened most saliently at the timescale of weeks and months, as local cognitive and metapragmatic models emerged and meshed. Both social identification and academic learning relied on *and jointly helped constitute* locally circulating metapragmatic/cognitive models that included categories like "disruptive outcast." Thus I am describing local power/knowledge or self/knowledge. But I do not claim that social identification and academic learning always overlap in the same way. It is an empirical project to discover which resources social identification and academic learning jointly use in any particular case.

4

Tyisha Becoming an Outcast

In Mrs. Bailey and Mr. Smith's class, teachers and students developed two sets of overlapping metapragmatic/cognitive models during the year. Each involved an analogy between the classroom and one of the curricular themes, plus a series of participant examples that became important resources through which the analogy was established. Across each series of examples, together with other events, teachers and students developed metapragmatic/cognitive models that they used both to identify particular students and learn about a curricular theme. The metapragmatic and cognitive models were distinct in some respects, but they co-developed and came to overlap significantly as teachers and students used the same categories to identify students and to construe the curriculum.

The first such overlapping, local metapragmatic/cognitive model has already been introduced. The curricular theme involved the appropriate relation between an individual and society, with an analogy between society in general and the social organization of the classroom itself. The most salient category of identity in this model became the "disruptive outcast" category that was inhabited by Tyisha. This chapter traces in detail how Tyisha came to be a disruptive outcast and how a local cognitive model contributed to her emerging identity. The second model involved the curricular question of when an individual should accept the authority of those in power and when he or she should resist. Teachers and students developed an analogy between power relations in society and those in the classroom. In the classroom "society," the teachers have power and the students must either join or resist them. The most salient category of identity in this model became a person caught in the middle between those in power and those resisting power. Chapter 5 will show how Maurice came to inhabit this category.

Neither Tyisha nor Maurice had a simple or predictable social identity. Their identities emerged across months-long trajectories of events, in ways that borrowed from but did not simply replicate local or sociohistorical models. Chapter 2 described the salient local contrast between promising girls and unpromising boys that became important to both sets of over-lapping local metapragmatic/cognitive models. With respect to the first curricular theme, as the teachers and students developed their model of individuals who refuse to cooperate with society, the boys (prototypically William) were often identified as people who refused to participate pro-ductively in the classroom "society." This role made sense for the boys, given their local identities as "unpromising." But Tyisha became an excep-tion to local gender expectations when she was increasingly identified as a disruptive outcast, despite being a girl who talked a lot in class. With respect to the second curricular theme, the boys were often identified as resistant because they did not conform to the teachers' agenda for the classroom "society." Maurice, because of his position as the only boy who participated constructively in class, was caught in the middle between the girls who conformed and the boys who resisted. Tyisha, then, was a highly visible unpromising girl, and Maurice was sometimes the one promising boy. But their identities were not mirror images of each other. This chapter and the next trace the unexpected shifts in their distinctive trajectories of identification across the academic year.

OVERVIEW OF TYISHA'S LOCAL IDENTITY DEVELOPMENT

This chapter traces Tyisha's identity development over the academic year. It analyzes a series of participant examples that included her as a char-acter, many explicit statements that students and teachers made about her identity, and the implicit interactional positions that she willingly or unwillingly occupied in the classroom. Tyisha's behavior remained stable over the year in important respects. She spoke often, did not hesitate to disagree with the teachers and emphasized her own opinions and experiences – as opposed to discussing others' opinions or points made in the texts. In September and October the teachers identified her as a cooper-ative student because they wanted students to present their own positions on curricular themes and to defend those positions with reference to their own experience. While most other students were still trying to figure out what the teachers wanted to hear, Tyisha was articulating and defending her own opinions. In December, however, teachers and students began to identify Tyisha as disruptive. By then many other students were offering their own arguments, as the teachers wanted, and the teachers began to label Tyisha's insistence on her own opinions as a refusal to conform to classroom norms.

Tyisha was identified in four different ways across the year. First, from September into November she was just another promising female student. Second, from November to January teachers and students began to object to Tyisha's emphasis on her own opinions and experiences. Before they began discussing the first curricular theme, teachers and students began to identify Tyisha as a problematic student. In this phase, they some-times opportunistically used categories from the curriculum to identify Tyisha's undesirable characteristics, but there was no systematic overlap between cognitive models of curricular themes and metapragmatic models of Tyisha's social identity. If they had never discussed the first curricular theme, Tyisha might have been identified as "self-centered" or as "needing attention," or with some related category. But she probably would not have inhabited the particular category of "disruptive outcast."

Third, from late January into February, they drew systematically on emerging cognitive models of the first curricular theme to identify Tyisha as a disruptive outcast from the classroom "society." Teachers and students moved from the more vague sense of Tyisha as self-centered and problem-atic to identifying her more specifically as a disruptive outcast. This iden-tity developed, in significant part, as teachers and students used categories from the curriculum to build the local metapragmatic/cognitive model of a social outcast. The development of Tyisha's identity as an outcast solid-ified as teachers and students discussed the appropriate relation between individuals and society, and as they drew curricular categories into the emerging metapragmatic model that they used to identify Tyisha. When the class discussed how societies generally ask individuals to sacrifice for the good of the whole, and how individuals who refuse to conform cause problems, they developed a local cognitive model that described appropri-ate social behavior. Someone who pursues his or her own desires without regard for the group's needs, for example, is a "beast" who should be cast out. As discussed in Chapter 3, teachers and students developed an anal-ogy between some aspects of the curricular theme and their own classroom relationships: If students pursued their own ideas and desires in class with-out following the group's norms, the class would face the serious problems foreseen by critics of individualism; however, if students did not express any ideas of their own, at least in this sort of Paideia class, the discussion would grind to a halt. Ideally, their class should include both conformity to group norms and the opportunity for individuals to develop their own arguments. Teachers and students developed this analogy between their class and "society" in part through a series of participant examples that used students' classroom behavior to illustrate the various possible rela-tionships between individuals and society. In several of these examples, Tyisha was cast as an extreme individualist, a person who disrupts and is excluded from the group. Her transition from "good student" to "disrup-tive outcast" solidified as teachers and students developed the category of social outcast as a central overlapping category in their emerging cognitive and metapragmatic models.

Fourth, and finally, from late February into May teachers and students used categories from the second curricular theme – the question of loyalty to and resistance against those in power – to shift Tyisha's identity again. During the spring Tyisha sometimes remained an outcast, but at other times teachers and students identified her as an outcast legitimately resisting authority, a dissenter who enriched group discussion by defending alternative positions.

At the same time as emerging local cognitive models of the individual/ society relation helped to establish Tyisha's social identity in the classroom, students also learned about the curricular theme in part as they drew on the metapragmatic model of Tyisha as an outcast. There was in fact one complex metapragmatic/cognitive model that developed as they identified Tyisha and construed the curriculum through the same classroom events. In addition to helping them identify Tyisha, this metapragmatic/cognitive model became a resource that they used to understand the dangers of individualism. Teachers and students made sense of Aristotle's and other arguments against individualism by building local models of how individuals should relate to society. As discussed earlier, they understood these curricular topics in part by analogy with individual/group relations in the classroom. Tyisha's emerging identity as a disruptive outcast co-developed with and contributed to these emerging cognitive models – especially when Tyisha became a participant example analogous to "beasts" or other outcasts discussed in the curriculum. Students understood the dangers of individualism in part by discussing Tyisha and her disruptive classroom behavior. The following analyses show how these metapragmatic and cognitive models co-developed and jointly facilitated social identification and academic learning.

STARTING AS A REGULAR STUDENT

Tyisha was a fourteen-year-old African American girl who was enrolled in Mrs. Bailey and Mr. Smith's class for the entire academic year. Partly because this was her first year in high school, the teachers had limited information about her. Her scores on the citywide exam for eighth grade students placed her in the third quartile among students taking the test – about average for Mrs. Bailey and Mr. Smith's ninth grade class, although somewhat below average for all students in the Paideia program at Colleoni High. As described in Chapter 3, Tyisha and her classmates had been admitted to a special program available to students from across the city. This meant that she and her parents had taken the time to gather information about school choice options and that they had successfully navigated the bureaucracy to have her enrolled in the Colleoni Paideia program. Tyisha regularly interacted with her peers, often teasing and joking with them both in and out of class, but she did not seem to have any close friends in the class. This may have been because she commuted from a different part of the city and did not live close to other students.

Anyone observing Mrs. Bailey and Mr. Smith's class for the first time would probably have noticed Tyisha. She drew attention to herself both verbally and nonverbally. On most days she participated regularly in class discussion, answering teachers' questions and offering opinions of her own. One or two other students spoke as often as she did, but she called attention to herself by speaking loudly and colorfully and by referring often to her own opinions and experiences. After getting accustomed to a typical day in this classroom, one would notice when Tyisha was absent – in fact, teachers and students remarked on a few such occasions that it was quieter than usual without her. Tyisha also exhibited unusual physical energy by moving around in her seat more than most students, both when she was raising her hand and at other times. I observed her inadvertently create a commotion several times when she dropped something on the floor during class – often her entire pile of readings, handouts and notes, which fell out of her folder and cascaded across the floor.

Despite drawing attention to herself in these ways, Tyisha was not officially classified as a problem student. She was not diagnosed with any disorder, nor was she identified as having special needs. She finished the year in this class, received a passing grade and planned to return for her sophomore year. Based on the fifty hours I spent observing this classroom over the year, I believe that she was probably more intelligent than the average American ninth grader. She had attended elementary and middle schools that had fewer resources and had not been able to prepare her as well as the average American ninth grader. But she was more quick-thinking and verbally skilled than her average peer.

Tyisha's behavior was not labeled as inappropriate during the first two or three months of the year. The teachers treated Tyisha the same as, and occasionally as more promising than, other girls who participated in class. As I argued above, this was probably because her focus on her own opinions and experiences fit the teachers' pedagogical strategy, which encouraged students to develop their own arguments instead of relying on teachers' interpretations. We can see this in their discussion on October 9, about a month into the academic year. On this day the class discussed origin myths from various cultures around the world. Mrs. Bailey argued that, despite their apparent strangeness, these myths attempt to explain universal human mysteries like the creation of life and the meaning of death. Characteristically, Tyisha participated actively in this discussion. The teachers took her comments in various ways – some as wrong or misguided, some as correct or helpful, and one as taking the class off-topic. She was treated like the other students who participated, as someone who had both good and bad ideas and was trying to contribute to the discussion. In contrast to their reactions later in the year, the teachers did not criticize Tyisha's incorrect answers or her off-topic comments.

Sometimes Tyisha gave an answer the teachers did not want to pursue, as she and another student do in the following segment. At this point in the discussion Mrs. Bailey has argued that myths sometimes explain where life comes from. Students have objected that parents' "getting together" provides a perfectly good explanation.

> **T/B:** why aren't
> they just happy with Martha's answer, my mom and dad
> 185 got together and here I am.
> **TYI:** because somebody [had to create
> **CAN:** [because
> **T/B:** shhh. think about it for a second. (2.0) when
> somebody says, where did man come from they mean more
> 190 than where did I come from? so, why would they
> ask that question? (11.0) why did they ask that question?
> Candace?

At lines 186–187, Tyisha and Candace both begin to answer Mrs. Bailey's question, but she tells them to "think about it" and directs them toward another point. Mrs. Bailey does not accept Tyisha's comment here, but neither does she single out Tyisha for criticism. This is not remarkable teacher behavior, but it contrasts with how the teachers responded to Tyisha later in the year.

In the following segment, Tyisha again gives an answer that the teacher does not accept. Mrs. Bailey is continuing to explore how creation myths explain the creation of the race or the group, in addition to the creation of individual life.

> **T/B:** is it just curiosity about our origins that does that?
> **TYI:** I think so.
> 195 **T/B:** just curiosity about our origin. Natasha, my Genesis
> book.
> [slight laughter from a few female students]
> **T/B:** Natasha, do you read Genesis just to find out where
> you came from?

Tyisha acts cooperatively here, in answering Mrs. Bailey's question at line 194. But Mrs. Bailey's response, especially the "just" at line 195, indicates that she was not looking for this answer. The teacher goes on to give an example that helps students articulate a different answer, without any further remarks about Tyisha's comment.

Note that Tyisha refers to herself explicitly in her answer at line 194. Most other students would have said "yes" or answered in another way, without referring explicitly to themselves. Such explicit reference to herself was typical for Tyisha. Here is another example, from earlier in the discussion.

T/B: okay, we've got women having ba:bies. how does
that relate to having women goddesses?
40   **TYI:** it doesn't, to me.
T/B: it doesn't to you. how about you?
FST: maybe they think that that's supernatural.
T/B: that that's supernatural? having a baby is
supernatural.

At line 40, Tyisha emphasizes her opinion by adding the phrase "to me."
Mrs. Bailey seems to encourage this, by repeating Tyisha's utterance and
by going on to ask for another student's opinion at line 41. Mrs. Bailey
often asked several students, in turn, for their opinions. Tyisha habitually
cast her comments as her own opinions, and this fit with the teachers' hope
that students would make their own arguments instead of repeating what
the teachers or the textbook said. Mrs. Bailey reacted positively to Tyisha's
offering her own opinions, early in the year, because she wanted other
students to do the same.

In none of the three excerpts so far did Tyisha give an adequate answer,
from the teacher's point of view. But in each case, Mrs. Bailey responded
as if Tyisha had made a legitimate attempt to contribute to the class. Even
though Tyisha may have been wrong, the teacher did not treat her as being
disruptive, off-topic or unintelligent. Such behavior may not seem remarkable against the background of classroom behavior in general. When a
typical student offers an incorrect answer, after all, teachers often appreciate the attempt and try to help the student work toward the right answer. As
illustrated in the next section, however, by January the teachers no longer
treated Tyisha as a typical student. At that point they regularly responded
to Tyisha's off-topic or incorrect comments by explicitly disciplining her or
by implicitly positioning her as a student prone to disrupt class discussion.

In the October 9 discussion of creation myths, Tyisha also makes helpful
contributions that the teacher ratifies as correct. In the following segment,
for instance, they are discussing bees in order to understand a Chinese
myth that compares humans to insects. Tyisha points out that some bees
die after stinging once.

T/B: how long do insects live?
CAN: maybe ten days, about [a week
320   **MRC:**   [a week.
T/B: a day, a couple of months, alright.
TYI: some of them a day because you know, if they bite
you, they die.
T/B: okay some of them as soon- as soon as they, they, they
325   put their stinger in it, they're dead. okay, now put that back
to Pampu. why might the Chinese believe or feel that ma:n
comes from the earth as an insect. that ma:n is similar to
an insect?

At lines 324–325, Mrs. Bailey ratifies Tyisha's comment as a useful contribution, one which allows the teacher to go on to her analogy between the mortality of bees and the idea of humans as insects.

Once, in the October 9 class, Tyisha says something deliberately off-topic, apparently intended as a joke. Before Tyisha made her constructive comment about bees' mortality, she responded less constructively to another question.

> **T/B:** bees do what?
> **TYI:** kill.
> [laughter]
> **MRC:** some bee pollen, they raise[pollen
> 295 **T/B:** [they fertilize=
> **FST:** flowers.
> **T/B:** what do spiders do? they fertilize plants. bees are
> people who, are insects who ahh, Cassandra?

At line 293, several students laugh at Tyisha's comment and thus treat it as a joke. It was a small joke, but apparently successful. The teachers do not discipline Tyisha for this. Mrs. Bailey simply ignores Tyisha's comment and continues with the discussion.

So in the first two or three months of the year Tyisha was treated in two ways. Occasionally the teachers treated her opinions and her references to personal experience as model behaviors for a Paideia student. Most of the time, however, Tyisha was treated like any other cooperative and promising female student. She made both useful and off-target comments in class, and the teachers responded as if she was trying to make constructive contributions. When she got the answer wrong, and even when she made a distracting joke, the teachers did not belittle or discipline her. At this point in the year, they used the same metapragmatic model to interpret Tyisha's and the other promising girls' behavior. They were all generally cooperative students who contributed regularly.

FROM REGULAR STUDENT TO OUTCAST

From November into early January, however, teachers and students began to interpret Tyisha's behavior differently. Instead of treating her contributions as well intentioned, they started to interpret many of her comments as both wrong and disruptive. They began to apply a different metapragmatic model to frame Tyisha's behavior: She was no longer a typical promising girl, but instead a disruptive student. Several types of evidence support this claim. First, teachers began to make explicit comments about Tyisha and her behavior, comments that labeled her as badly off-base and disruptive. These comments began sporadically in December, and then became regular in January and thereafter. Second, from December through February they discussed several participant examples in which Tyisha appeared as a character, and the discussions of Tyisha's characters within the examples identified her as a disruptive outcast. Third, teachers and students often positioned Tyisha interactionally as an outcast. She was excluded from the core group of teachers and girls who dominated classroom discussions. All three of these discursive mechanisms contributed to Tyisha's descent from promising girl to disruptive outcast.

Tyisha as Explicitly a Problem

Teachers often make evaluative comments that follow up and characterize students' contributions (Mehan, 1979; Sinclair and Coulthard, 1975). As illustrated in the last section, during the first few months of the year Mrs. Bailey and Mr. Smith evaluated Tyisha's comments the same way they did other students' – as sometimes right and sometimes wrong, but well intentioned. As the year progressed, however, the teachers began to evaluate Tyisha's comments differently. At first, they used slightly more explicit negative comments when they characterized Tyisha's contributions as wrong or inappropriate. The following segment is the first instance in my data in which a teacher reacted somewhat harshly to Tyisha. On November 2, Tyisha objected that a text is misogynistic even though it claims to describe rights for both men and women.

> **TYI:** but- it shouldn't be the rights of men and women
> 370   because the only people that got <u>rights</u> in here is the <u>men</u> or
> the <u>husband</u>.
> **T/S:** whoa, whoa, the only one who has rights in
> here are <u>men</u>. could you give me some concrete examples,
> from this. well no, all of them, you know, just sort of being
> 375   vague. we want be specific to show us that you've actually
> <u>read</u> it.

At line 374, Mr. Smith puts words into Tyisha's mouth. He acts as if "well, no, all of them, you know" is something Tyisha would characteristically say, and he labels such comments as "vague" – despite the fact that her comment in this case seems to have merit. At lines 375–376, he also suggests that Tyisha did not do the reading and implies that her claim was not "specific."

As the year proceeded, the teachers made increasingly blunt evaluations of Tyisha's comments that did not resemble evaluations they made of other students. Right before the following segment (from January 18), Mrs. Bailey had just given an interpretation of Aristotle's text. Aristotle was not saying that women are slaves to men, Mrs. Bailey argues, only that the relationship between a man and woman is in some ways analogous to the relationship between a master and a slave.

TYI: okay, when- um Sylvia was talking about the slave
and the <u>ma:ster</u>, the <u>master</u>, okay, the <u>slave</u>, he uses
his hands and stuff but- they won't give him a chance to use
his- to teach him to read and stuff and the master know
435   how, so he using his <u>mind</u>. why does he [[4 unintelligible
syllables]
     T/B: [okay, didn't- <u>you</u>
<u>just missed</u> the con<u>nection</u>, the con- the thing is that-
do <u>not</u> look at this as <u>saying</u> that <u>slaves</u> are manual <u>workers</u>,
440   slaves- women are <u>slaves</u>. look at these as four dis<u>tinct</u>
re<u>lationships</u>.

Tyisha's reasoning wanders from lines 431–436, but she seems to be struggling with issues relevant to the text. Mrs. Bailey, nonetheless, interrupts to tell her, "you just missed the connection."

This incident alone might have been momentary impatience on the teacher's part, but the following evaluation comes soon thereafter.

     T/B: and in Greeks- in <u>Greece</u>, there <u>certainly</u> were
<u>slaves</u> that used their <u>mind</u>. yeah?
     FST: I'm talking about going back to what <u>Tyisha</u> said
450   about how slaves that- <u>well</u>- if, okay if a master didn't teach
the slaves how to read, how did <u>they</u> learn <u>how</u> to read?
how did we know how to <u>read</u> and <u>talk</u> ourselves?
     T/B: o[kay, you just <u>missed</u>-
     TYI: [<u>right</u>, <u>thank</u> you.
455   **T/B:** you <u>just missed</u> the point.
     JAS: you <u>missed</u> the point. we're not compari[ng them.
     TYI: [I know,
but I'm talking about-
     T/B: okay, look at this again, <u>mental</u>, <u>manual</u> workers,
460   are mental workers

At line 449, a student refers back to the previous comment by Tyisha, building on Tyisha's point in order to ask a question. These teachers normally encourage students to refer to each other's comments because they want the group to develop more complex arguments together. And at line 454, Tyisha explicitly thanks the other student for referring to her point. But Mrs. Bailey immediately jumps in (at lines 453–455) and returns to her earlier evaluation of Tyisha's point, with similar phrasing: "you just missed the point." The speed of Mrs. Bailey's intervention and her blunt characterization of Tyisha's (and the other student's) point is unusual for this class. These teachers wanted students to develop their own arguments, and they generally helped students who were struggling to articulate a point. But Mrs. Bailey's impatience with Tyisha suggests that, by January, the teachers had started to interpret Tyisha's comments as disruptive and not substantive. Note that another student (Jasmine) echoes Mrs. Bailey's evaluation of Tyisha, at line 456. Other students are also coming to interpret Tyisha's comments as off-topic and disruptive.

These explicit comments by teachers and students provide one source of evidence that teachers and students were starting to identify Tyisha differently from November through January than they had earlier in the academic year. From November through January, teachers and students began to interpret Tyisha's behavior with reference to several categories of identity that coalesced into a distinctive local metapragmatic model: She interjects her own opinions without attending to others' contributions and the flow of the discussion; she often refuses to give evidence from the text, expecting that her opinion is sufficient; she often gives wrong or unproductive answers; and she consistently disrupts teachers and students' attempts to build coherent discussions. It will take substantially more evidence – from other explicit comments, from participant examples and from tacit interactional positioning – to show how this metapragmatic model emerged and was consistently used to identify Tyisha. But we can already see hints of the model in the few explicit comments reviewed thus far.

As January wore on, Tyisha increasingly became identified as a disruptive student who made intellectually unproductive comments. The following segment, for instance, comes from January 25.

> **T/B:** okay. well I think that he's talking more not
> about <u>not</u> being with people, but that <u>he</u>: will <u>not</u>
> have to have <u>people</u> bail him out at any point. he
> 1215 can make it on his own.
> **TYI:** so you gonna be the only person living
> there?
> **T/B:** <u>no</u>. that's <u>not</u> what he's <u>saying</u>, <u>Tyisha</u>.
> **CAN:** he's saying that he can live with<u>out</u> people
> 1220 helping him.

At lines 1212–1215, Mrs. Bailey summarizes her interpretation of a point. Tyisha asks a question at lines 1216–1217, a question which misstates Mrs. Bailey's point. The teacher reacts immediately by telling Tyisha that she is wrong. This quick and blunt response contrasts with the teachers' habitual reaction to other students, and to Tyisha earlier in the year, when they would have explored her point or been gentler in evaluating her response. Another student gives a more accurate gloss at lines 1219–1220, and the class goes on to discuss the point without Tyisha.

The following segment makes more explicit the teachers' emerging characterization of Tyisha as a disruptive student. This segment comes from the January 24 discussion of Tyisha and Maurice as "beasts in the woods" – an example that was introduced in Chapter 1 and is more fully analyzed later in this chapter. After initially valuing Tyisha's contribution to the discussion, Mrs. Bailey has asked her to cooperate several times.

T/B: okay, uh, kay, important point. and this- we
keep on having a problem with you Tyisha, and this
830 has been ta:lked about and ta:lked about. people
cannot communicate in this kind of conversation
unless they agree on using certain terms, a certain
way, agree on definitions.
TYI: but [I
835 T/B: [and if you don't want to agree on the
definition then- I think you remove yourself from
the conversation for a while, and see where it goes.
because we- we are using Aristotle's definitions
here, and Sheneather was right and that's- (1.0) the
840 issue that we constantly have with you is that you
want to come up with a different definition. and
that's not what we're about. we're trying to have a
discussion based on definitions we've agreed on or
come from the piece.

As Mrs. Bailey says at line 829, the class has now explicitly talked about Tyisha's "problem" several times now. In order to have coherent Paideia seminar discussions the class must adhere to certain norms, including common definitions. Tyisha has repeatedly violated these norms, and has thereby excluded herself from the group discussion (line 836). Everyone else apparently adheres to the norms, but Tyisha insists on generating her own definitions (lines 840–841), and "that's not what we're about" (line 842). *We* – that is, all the other students and teachers except Tyisha – are trying to have productive discussions that *you*, Tyisha, are disrupting.

By late January and early February, both Mrs. Bailey and Mr. Smith often reacted quickly to Tyisha, assuming that she was a disruptive student. In the following segment, from February 11, Mr. Smith explicitly characterizes Tyisha as a bad student who does not listen.

50   T/S: I will do a spot check, spot check your notebook.
the notebook, and you better listen Tyisha, because you
have a habit of never listening to me. °Tyisha°
TYI: I know what you're talking about=
T/S: =no.
55   TYI: you're talking about[the notebook
T/S: [°your ears are unfortunately
closed sometimes.°
. . .

T/S: number five. who made the laws?

65   **FST:** the assembly.
        T/S: okay [what page?
        TYI: [°the king°
        T/S: <u>no</u>. you're <u>wrong</u>. because you're <u>guessing</u> without
        <u>looking</u>. and that is[=
70   **TYI:**   [no way.
        T/S: =exa<u>ct</u>ly what you <u>do</u> as a <u>bad</u>[student.=
        TYI: [no <u>I</u> wasn't
        T/S: =halt.

At line 52, Mr. Smith says that Tyisha never listens to him. And at line 71, he calls her a bad student. Mr. Smith sometimes made comments like this about other students too. But Tyisha was much more likely to be the target because her identity as a disruptive student had emerged and solidified by February.

My data contain at least a dozen other instances, from December through May, of teachers and students explicitly identifying Tyisha as disruptive. They accused her of not listening, being factually wrong and making comments that led discussion off-track. Any one or two of these events could be interpreted in different ways – as teasing, momentary impatience or attempts to involve Tyisha constructively in discussion. But, taken together, these evaluations of Tyisha show that the teachers and students had begun to identify her differently than they had earlier in the year. Instead of taking time to explore the reasoning behind her comments – and, it must be said, there was only sometimes defensible reasoning discernible in them – by January the teachers and other students quickly dismissed Tyisha and moved back to their own discussion. She had moved along a trajectory from being just another good student, to being a student overly focused on her own ideas, to being a disruptive student.

Tyisha was not simply the passive recipient of this shifting identity. She managed her own presentation of self, and she reacted to others' characterizations of her. As illustrated in detail below, she often embraced her new identity as a disruptive student and reveled in her ability to derail discussions. She regularly created disruptions and made off-the-wall comments, such that she would have been a difficult student for any teacher to handle. Thus Tyisha shared responsibility with the teachers and other students for her emerging identity in the classroom. The teachers did make harsh judgments about Tyisha, especially in January and February, perhaps out of frustration and impatience at Tyisha's genuinely disruptive behavior. We should not excuse these harsh judgments or the teachers' inappropriate comments about Tyisha, and Chapter 6 returns to examine the teachers' responsibility. But, before judging the teachers, we need to examine in more detail how Tyisha's own acts combined with others' and with more widely circulating resources to create Tyisha's emerging social identity.

The impulse to blame the teachers for inappropriately identifying Tyisha comes in part from the racial stereotyping apparently involved in this identity. In labeling Tyisha a "disruptive student" just for enthusiastically defending her own opinions, the teachers seem to be inappropriately stereotyping her as a "loud black girl" – as this racial stereotype has been described by Fordham (1996) and others. This sociohistorical category did likely facilitate Tyisha's emerging identity. If she had been East Asian, for instance, it would have been harder (though not impossible) for the teachers and students to identify her as a disruptive student. As I argued in Chapter 2, however, sociohistorical categories only identify people as those categories are mediated through local metapragmatic models and the contingent processes of identification in any given event. In this classroom, Tyisha was not just the typical "loud black girl." Her emerging local identify as a "disruptive outcast" drew on but significantly modified this sociohistorical category. It is also important to note that there were many other black girls in this class, some of them quite vocal, who were not labeled as loud and disruptive. In this classroom, teachers and students drew on and modified sociohistorical presuppositions about race, gender and other categories to create a distinctive local identity for Tyisha. Only by tracing the emergence of this identity across events can we understand how sociohistorical categories combined with other resources to construct the local identities that were actually lived.

Tyisha as "Conceited"

Tyisha's developing social identity as a disruptive student emerged not only through teachers and students' explicit reactions to her comments, as these were summarized in the last section. An explicit comment about someone's identity – like Mr. Smith's description of Tyisha as a "bad student" on February 11 or Mrs. Bailey's description of her as disruptive and uncooperative on January 24 – is rarely the first time a model of identity has been applied to an individual. For a teacher to call someone a "bad student" out of the blue, without any prior indications that the student was having problems, would generally seem abrupt and inappropriate. As is typical, by the time Mrs. Bailey and Mr. Smith made blunt explicit descriptions of Tyisha's identity as a disruptive outcast, they and others had tacitly positioned Tyisha this way many times. The excerpt from November 2 presented above, in which Mr. Smith implies that Tyisha has not done the reading, was the first instance of such tacit positioning in my data.

As teachers and students – including Tyisha herself – tacitly positioned her as disruptive, as a weak student, and as an outcast from the class, her emerging identity "thickened." It eventually became so solid that teachers could make blunt explicit comments about her in late January and February without these comments seeming remarkable. The rest of this chapter traces the thickening of Tyisha's identity as it was accomplished through tacit interactional positioning that others did to her and that she did herself. Tacit positioning happens when participants treat an individual as if she were a recognizable type of person, as if some metapragmatic model applies to her. Tacit positioning is enacted and not necessarily represented by participants – so it involves what people do as much as what they know. Evidence of tacit positioning comes from a series of signs that index a particular metapragmatic model.

My analyses of the tacit positioning done by and to Tyisha focus on participant examples that included her as a character. I also attend to tacit interactional positioning not accomplished through participant examples in several analyses. But, as described in Chapter 1, participant examples can be a powerful mechanism for social identification. Discussion of participants' characters within the example can presuppose that the student herself is being identified in the same way as her character. In the following example, for instance, Tyisha's character in the example was "conceited" and looked down upon by others. Teachers and students also presupposed that Tyisha herself, while perhaps not conceited in the same way, was self-involved such that she was not worthy of membership in their group. In participant examples like this, similar models are applied both to the curricular topic and the participant's own social identity. The example thus allowed categories of identity to be drawn from emerging cognitive models of curricular topics and incorporated into the metapragmatic models they used to interpret Tyisha's identity in the classroom. In this first example, teachers and students opportunistically seized on the curricular category of "conceited" to identify traits of Tyisha's that they do not like. They had not begun to discuss the curricular theme of individuals and society, and there was not yet any systematic overlap between cognitive and metapragmatic models. They were still establishing that Tyisha was a problematic student who should be cast out of their group, and the participant example of Tyisha as conceited became another event that tacitly positioned Tyisha in this way.

This example was discussed on December 17. The class had read "The Necklace," de Maupassant's short story about a woman who is very proud of her beautiful necklace. She loses the necklace, but she continues to be "conceited." Mrs. Bailey made Tyisha's own behavior in the class an example of conceit, as if Tyisha valued her own opinions in class as much as the woman valued her necklace. This is the first extended segment in my data in which Tyisha was identified as a deficient and marginal member of the classroom community. So this discussion was an early step in Tyisha's transformation from typical girl to disruptive student.

As described earlier, by December other students had begun to offer arguments in the preferred Paideia format. Tyisha began to look worse by comparison because offering an opinion was no longer sufficient to win the teachers' praise. At this point in the year the teachers were ratcheting up their expectations of students. They had so far been satisfied with students giving and defending their own opinions, but by December they also wanted students to recognize others' arguments and to be able to give evidence even for arguments that contradicted their own. In order to participate in a good seminar discussion, the teachers said, students must engage with others' arguments. Mrs. Bailey said on December 17, in a segment quoted in Chapter 3, that she worried some students were not making this transition to recognizing others' arguments, that they were "so focused on your own arguments" that they did not consider others'. Given Tyisha's typical behavior, this comment might indicate that Tyisha was one of the problems. It may not be an accident, then, that Mrs. Bailey nominated Tyisha as an example of a student "conceited" about her own ideas.

Paideia seminars traditionally center around a question about the text, a question prepared by the leader and written on the board before discussion starts. In this class, Mrs. Bailey begins their discussion of "The Necklace" by developing such a question together with the students. Tyisha contributes productively to framing the question.

125   **T/B:** what does, what does the writer (1.0) what does the
        writer do by giving us that <u>end</u>ing?
        TYI: °showed us that people don't always <u>learn</u> their
        lesson.°
        T/B: Tyisha, I can't <u>hear</u> you.
130   **TYI:** shows us that people don't always <u>learn</u> their <u>les</u>son.
        T/B: o<u>kay</u>.

Mrs. Bailey then formulates the final question, which she writes on the board: "Is it possible for someone who's conceited [like the main character in the story] to not remain conceited even when what they're conceited about [the necklace] has been taken away?" At lines 125–126, Mrs. Bailey indicates that she wants to focus on the ending of the story, on the character's continuing conceit even after her necklace is gone. At lines 127–128, Tyisha appears to understand at least part of the central point when she talks about people not "learning their lesson." It will turn out to be ironic that Tyisha contributes to framing the question here at the beginning of the discussion, when she is about to become an example of someone who has not learned her lesson about how to behave in class.

Immediately after Mrs. Bailey writes the question on the board, students offer both positive and negative answers: yes, it is possible for someone to remain conceited even after losing a necklace or something similar, but it is also possible that people would learn their lesson and behave differently than the story's main character. Mrs. Bailey then nominates Tyisha as an example of someone conceited.

T/B: how many of you can <u>think</u> of an example for
Tyisha, of maybe someone who was conceited about
<u>one</u> thing and now is conceited about something <u>else,</u>
155 having had the first thing taken away from them.
FST: well, you take something away from her and she
says, so.
T/B: you take something away from Tyisha. she says <u>so</u>.
[4 seconds of students and T/B laughing]
160 **T/B:** is that an example, Cas<u>san</u>dra?
CAS: no.
FST: it sort of is.
JAS: °in this case of somebody, they don't care.°

"An example for Tyisha," at lines 152–153, is ambiguous. It might be an example to discuss with Tyisha, as she was the one to talk about people not "learning their lesson." As it turns out, however, it comes to mean an example from Tyisha's own experience, with Tyisha as the main character, illustrating how she herself might be conceited. There is no apparent reason in the transcript or the text for why Mrs. Bailey would select Tyisha as opposed to another student here. One plausible explanation is that Tyisha's own behavior fits in some respects with "conceit" as it is illustrated in the text. As the rest of this chapter will show, Tyisha gets chosen many times as an example when the relevant character in the text is disruptive or a social outcast. This may be an early instance of Tyisha being chosen as an example because her own emerging classroom identity fits with a category of identity illustrated in the text. Another possible explanation – not mutually exclusive – is that Mrs. Bailey is getting increasingly frustrated with Tyisha and so had Tyisha's behavior on her mind while she was looking for an example.

At lines 156–157, a student begins to elaborate on the analogy between the story and the new example, imagining that when you take something away from "her," the conceited person, she says "so" – apparently meaning that she does not care and does not change her conceit. At line 158, Mrs. Bailey makes clear that they are discussing an example with Tyisha as the main character, and then she substitutes Tyisha into the student's formulation of the analogy. Teachers and students laugh at this, perhaps because they already think of Tyisha as stubborn and not likely to change her behavior, or perhaps simply because they are teasing her.

Note that teachers and students' use of pronouns in this segment excludes Tyisha from their conversation. From her introduction of Tyisha as an example in lines 152–153, Mrs. Bailey consistently calls her "Tyisha," "them" or "she," and another student uses "her." Even though Tyisha is sitting right there and just participated in the conversation a few seconds ago, they do not address her with "you" – and thus they exclude her while they talk about her as an example. This positioning of Tyisha outside the core group of vocal students was repeated many times during the year, and it helped establish Tyisha as a marginal member of the classroom community.

At line 160, Mrs. Bailey asks Cassandra whether "that" is in fact an example. It is so far an odd example because the analogy between Tyisha and the character in the story is unclear. Mrs. Bailey gets a negative response from Cassandra, then one "sort of" and one potentially positive response from other students. She goes on to elaborate the example, and Jasmine helps her.

> **T/B:** you think that we can <u>beat</u> Tyisha into submission?
> 165 make her <u>hum</u>ble?
> **JAS:** you take something like her keys away, like <u>now</u>
> when we <u>ar</u>guing with her, she just says she don't <u>care</u>,
> but if we wasn't talking about this and I just went over and took
> her <u>keys</u>, she'd have a <u>fit</u>.
> 170 **STS:** [3 seconds of laughter]
> **T/B:** well, what if we took away her, her, her <u>pre</u>tense or
> her, her <u>claim</u>, which is her pretense, her <u>claim</u> to be a
> <u>thinking</u> individual whose <u>ideas</u> have merit?
> **STS:** [2 seconds of laughter]

Mrs. Bailey's question at line 164 can be understood in terms of an analogy between Tyisha and the conceited character in the story, but it is a stretch. If Tyisha is stubborn in retaining her conceit, the class might (hypothetically, within the example) have to "beat" her "into submission" and "humble" her. This is not fully analogous to the story because no one beats the woman's conceit out of her. Mrs. Bailey and the students struggle to make Tyisha work as an example here, but they persist. Perhaps they sense something appropriate about the example because they consider Tyisha herself to be conceited just like the main character.

Why would Mrs. Bailey talk about beating Tyisha at line 164 if there is no basis for this in the story? As I have argued, comments about characters within a participant example often have implications for the participants themselves. Perhaps the teacher feels that there is something that needs to be beaten out of Tyisha herself. Tyisha did have some undesirable characteristics that exasperated the teachers. She often expressed her own opinions and overrode or ignored others', and her comments did sometimes lead the class off-track. As the discussion of this example continues, Tyisha's emerging identity as a disruptive student does become relevant. Line 167 begins to suggest how. Jasmine says that "we" (the rest of the class, including the teachers) are often "arguing with her" (Tyisha), because Tyisha disagrees often and focuses on her own claims. It was this sort of behavior that exasperated the teachers.

Jasmine also develops the analogy between Tyisha's own local identity and the story more explicitly at lines 166–169. If someone were to take Tyisha's keys, "she'd have a fit." This characterizes Tyisha as touchy and explosive. Perhaps she is like the woman in the story in that she would not change her ways easily. This characterization of Tyisha elicits laughter from other students, perhaps because they recognize that she is prone to outbursts or simply because they consider her fair game for being teased. They may no longer be talking only about an example in order to explore the story here. They may also be talking about Tyisha herself in order to tease or criticize her. The real Tyisha says "so" and does not care about others' opinions, and perhaps she needs to be humbled. Thus the characterizations that teacher and students are making of Tyisha within the example may have implications for Tyisha's real identity in the classroom.

At this early point in the interaction, however, we do not yet know for sure what models will emerge as the most relevant for identifying Tyisha herself in this instance. If Tyisha had joined in at this point, with productive contributions that generated a good discussion of the text, these early comments by teacher and students could have been forgotten, as incidental teasing, and she could have been identified over the course of this interaction as another promising student. Although only a few well-placed academic contributions might have shifted the emerging organization of the discussion in this way on December 17, it would have taken other similar events to reverse Tyisha's trajectory from good to disruptive student. In December, however, she was not too far down the path from good student to disruptive outcast, and her trajectory of identification could have shifted if she, other students and the teachers had behaved differently. In fact, however, both in the December 17 discussion and in her larger trajectory, Tyisha was increasingly identified as disruptive and as an outcast.

In the segment above, Mrs. Bailey focuses more clearly on Tyisha's tendency to push her own opinions at lines 171–173, when she replaces Tyisha's keys with her "claim to be a thinking individual whose ideas have merit." This elaboration of the example is pivotal because it focuses the discussion on Tyisha's own vigorous defense of her ideas. If they had pursued the example of Tyisha's keys, the example might have had very different implications for Tyisha's identity. The woman in the story was proud of her necklace and retained her conceit even when she lost the necklace. In Mrs. Bailey's version of the example, Tyisha is proud of her ideas, but she may lose her claim that they are legitimate ideas. The academic point of this example is clear: Tyisha could have the same relation with her ideas that the woman has with her necklace. But with respect to the social identities at issue, this is a risky example. It would be risky for any teacher to state, even hypothetically, that a student's ideas had no merit – although it is possible to imagine cases where this could work as an example if handled delicately. It is particularly risky here because the example now obviously describes Tyisha herself. Tyisha does in fact take pride in her contributions, regularly putting forth and defending her ideas. And the teachers are getting sick of her disruptive comments and might want to undermine Tyisha's pride. This hypothetical example raises non-hypothetical questions about Tyisha's own identity and standing in the classroom.

At this point, Mrs. Bailey turns directly to Tyisha and makes clear that her contributions to class are, in the example, analogous to the necklace.

175　**T/B:** do you, do you think your ideas are <u>worth</u> <u>some</u>thing?
　　　TYI: <u>yeah</u> I do.
　　　T/B: okay, do we all <u>know</u> she thinks that?
　　　FST: yep
　　　FST: (hhhh)
180　**T/B:** how can we <u>know</u> that she thinks <u>that</u>.
　　　TYI: cause I <u>tell</u> you.
　　　STS: [4 seconds of overlapping talk]
　　　T/B: <u>o</u>kay, what happens if- what happens when people
　　　say <u>hey</u> but that's <u>wrong</u>?

Just as the woman in the story takes pride in her necklace, Tyisha takes pride in her ideas. Mrs. Bailey gets both Tyisha and other students to agree that Tyisha is proud of her ideas. Tyisha characteristically, and admirably, sticks up for herself at lines 176 and 181. Then Mrs. Bailey goes on at lines 183–184 to extend the analogy between Tyisha's pride in her ideas and the woman's pride in her necklace, imagining that unidentified "people" might show that Tyisha's ideas have no merit in the same way that the woman lost her necklace.

In this segment, in addition to extending the analogy between Tyisha and the woman in the story, and in addition to highlighting Tyisha's habit of defending her ideas vigorously, the teacher and students also continue to position Tyisha outside their own interaction. At line 175, Mrs. Bailey addresses Tyisha as "you" for the first time since the beginning of the participant example. Briefly, Tyisha is a participant in the discussion together with Mrs. Bailey and the other students. In her next comment (at line 177), however, Mrs. Bailey switches back to calling Tyisha "she," excluding her from the conversation again. The teacher and students enact an interactional division between Tyisha on the margins and the rest of the class. Both Tyisha and the teacher presuppose this split. At line 177, Mrs. Bailey opposes "we" (referring to the teachers and students other than Tyisha) and "she" (Tyisha). At line 181, Tyisha herself uses "I" and "you" (referring to the rest of the class and the teachers), thus presupposing the same interactional split. While they discuss this example that identifies potentially anti-social and inappropriate aspects of Tyisha's classroom behavior – her tendency to emphasize her own ideas while ignoring others' – teachers and students push her to the margins of the classroom interaction.

Perhaps they interactionally marginalize Tyisha in this way because of her "conceited," inappropriate behavior. She takes unjustifiable pride in her own ideas, not recognizing the merit of others'.

185   **FST:** she gets stubborn.
      STS: [overlapping chatter and laughter]
      FST: she gets an attitude.
      T/B: she gets an attitude? okay.
      STS: [5 seconds of laughter]
190   **T/B:** some of us are out to lunch okay?
      STS: [3 seconds of laughter]
      T/B: okay. so, so what we see in the end is
      that there is a general idea here about, you know, what
      happens if we take one thing away from a person that
195   makes- you have this part of them that makes them feel
      they are entitled to certain things and do they then not
      substitute something else. okay, uhh how about war?

Instead of losing her unjustified pride when she loses her necklace, the woman in the story continues to be conceited. Similarly, Mrs. Bailey and the students suggest, Tyisha continues to defend her ideas even when they are shown to be lacking. She gets "stubborn" and she gets an "attitude" (lines 185–188). The students may laugh at this because of the doubling of roles facilitated by the participant example. They have been discussing an example in order to illuminate the text, yet they have simultaneously managed to characterize some of Tyisha's own classroom behaviors in terms of categories drawn from the text.

Mrs. Bailey wraps up the discussion of "conceit" at lines 192–197, trying to summarize the general point that underlies both the text and the example of Tyisha. Her conclusion is not very convincing, however. It is not clear what she means by "substitute" at line 197, and the analogy between Tyisha and the woman was not articulated convincingly. We will see examples below in which the social identification of students helps teachers and students make substantive arguments about the curriculum. But this example does not seem to contribute much to academic learning. Perhaps Mrs. Bailey and the students pursued the example less as a device for learning the curriculum and more as a device for identifying Tyisha.

By December 17, teachers and students had begun to notice Tyisha's vigorous defense of her own ideas. This behavior could be interpreted many ways – earlier in the year it had been interpreted by the teachers as good Paideia student behavior. The example of Tyisha as conceited, however, began to provide a different metapragmatic model for framing this behavior, one that identified it as inappropriate and disruptive. On December 17 this model was still provisional, in two ways. First, it was a contingent accomplishment to identify Tyisha as inappropriate and disruptive in this event on December 17. If they had discussed Tyisha's keys and not her ideas, she would likely have been identified differently. Second, the model of Tyisha as inappropriate and disruptive that was established on December 17 did not necessarily apply to Tyisha across events. This event might have been an aberration.

However, in subsequent classes the metapragmatic model was refined and reinforced, such that Tyisha's identity as an outcast and as a disruptive student thickened. Through other participant examples like this one, through the type of interactional marginalization illustrated in this case, and through explicit evaluations like those summarized in the last section, teachers and students increasingly acted as if Tyisha was disorganized, prone to offer comments that took the class off-topic and concerned with her own ideas more than with contributing to coherent discussion. As this model was used to identify Tyisha across more events, it took less work within an event to identify Tyisha this way. Thus her trajectory of identification became more rigid. Tyisha was becoming an exception to the local metapragmatic model of promising girls and unpromising boys. She was becoming a girl who was not a good student and was not cooperative.

Tyisha the Courageous Liar

After the example of Tyisha as conceited, Tyisha was more likely to be identified as self-centered and disruptive. But this metapragmatic model could have been ignored or changed if teachers and students had not continued to use it. They could have gone back to treating her as another promising girl, or they could have developed another metapragmatic model to characterize her. Both teachers and students had some power in determining which way Tyisha's identity would develop. In the example from December 17, Mrs. Bailey was primarily responsible for identifying Tyisha as overly fond of her own ideas and for positioning Tyisha as marginal in the classroom interaction. Mrs. Bailey may have focused on Tyisha because she thought Tyisha was tough and could take it, or she may have been frustrated with Tyisha's refusal to curb her opinions in class. But in any case the teacher, supported by a few students, was mostly responsible for identifying Tyisha on December 17.

Tyisha did not become a disruptive outcast only through the teachers' initiative, however. Tyisha herself often embraced an oppositional identity. Sometimes she did this in ways that the teachers identified as productive, when she challenged others' arguments and forced teachers and students to reason more clearly. Sometimes, however, the teachers felt that she pushed arguments too far and wasted class time while refusing to admit a mistake.

She also made jokes and interrupted the teachers in apparently deliberate attempts to antagonize them. By acting in these ways, Tyisha sometimes embraced her identity as disruptive. She was not fully responsible for her emerging identity. The teachers and other students partly imposed it on her. But Tyisha was not a passive victim either.

The following example illustrates how Tyisha behaved in ways that irritated the teachers. This example also illustrates how Tyisha herself sometimes embraced her identity as disruptive and marginal. By energetically and vividly embracing her identity as disruptive at this pivotal point in her trajectory of identification, when that trajectory had shifted toward her identity as a disruptive outcast but had not yet become rigid, Tyisha made an important contribution to the thickening of her own identity. This discussion occurred on January 18 while the class was exploring Aristotle's definition of courage as articulated in his *Politics*. During this discussion, Mrs. Bailey asked whether a person can courageously obey as well as courageously resist. She went on to suggest that one can in fact obey courageously, and she offered the example of overcoming anxiety to give a presentation in class. Tyisha then volunteered her own participant example, apparently to support Mrs. Bailey's point, saying, "Mrs. Bailey, I think I have one."

As it turns out, however, Tyisha's example does not illustrate Mrs. Bailey's point and it leads the class in a direction that the teachers find unproductive. Given that Tyisha laughs several times while giving the example, and that she defends her example with increasingly outrageous claims, I argue that she willingly turned her example into a joke and took the class off-topic. She did similar things at other times during the year. We will see another extended instance of this behavior in the full analysis of the January 24 "Tyisha the beast" example. Like that January 24 discussion, Tyisha's example on January 18 also allows categories of identity from the curriculum to be used in identifying her – but in this case Tyisha instigates it herself.

Tyisha introduces her example as follows.

280   **TYI:** okay, I(hhh)- I had a <u>friend</u>. and she was like,
      sneaking out with a <u>boy</u>, and she lied and said that she was
      going with her <u>friends</u>. (hh) a(h)nd she told <u>me</u>, if my
      mother call, to tell her she was at the <u>zoo</u> with her friend
      <u>Stacey</u>. now that took her <u>courage</u> to te(h)<u>ll</u> me.
285   **FST:** (hh[h)
      TYI: [and it took c(hh)oura(h)ge for <u>me</u> to tell her
      <u>mother</u> that.
      FST: °mhm°
      T/B: did it take courage for [her to tell her mother tha[t?
290   **FST:**   [no   [I
      don't think so

T/B: why would th[at
TYI: [yeah it took <u>courage</u> to tell my friend's
mother
295 **FST:** [3 unintelligible syllables]
MRC: I don't think it took courage.

Tyisha gives her example at lines 280–284, and then at lines 286–287 she claims that it took courage for her to lie to her friend's mother. Because they are discussing Aristotle's definition of courage, this might be a relevant example to explore. Tyisha's example does not, however, illustrate the concept of "courage through obedience" that Mrs. Bailey had asked for. It seems to illustrate courage through disobedience instead.

The example presents interactional problems for the teachers, which may be why Tyisha laughs throughout her description of the example. Because the example involves immoral behavior (at least from a typical adult's point of view), if Tyisha's behavior was in fact courageous then the teachers would have to acknowledge her courage while condemning her behavior. Tyisha may be using categories from the curriculum to put the teachers in an awkward position here – forcing them either to condone her illicit behavior as courageous or to argue that her apparently courageous behavior was in fact not. At the very least, she is skillfully slipping illicit topics into legitimate academic discussion in such a way that she cannot be punished for it. She is reveling in an oppositional identity, as an adolescent who helps her friend get away with illicit dates, and she is also managing to talk about her inappropriate behavior in an academic discussion – perhaps even in such a way that her oppositional behavior gets identified as courageous. Thus she both describes and enacts an oppositional position. She helped her friend evade her mother's authority and she herself acts oppositional in the class by describing her inappropriate behavior as an example. By acting oppositional in this way, Tyisha voluntarily positions herself as an outcast of sorts – not a disruptive, inappropriate one but a cool one who might be admired by her peers.

The laughter of Tyisha and another student (at lines 280–286) supports this interpretation of her example as partly a joke and perhaps also as an attempt to force the teachers into condoning her inappropriate behavior. At line 289, Mrs. Bailey implies that Tyisha's behavior was not courageous, and a student agrees with her at lines 290–291. Tyisha interrupts Mrs. Bailey's next comment to restate that it did in fact take courage on her part. Maurice then sides with the teacher at line 296, denying that Tyisha's lie took courage. The teachers' first response to Tyisha's challenge, then, is to deny that Tyisha was courageous.

Mr. Smith, however, gives Tyisha another opportunity to make her case. He interrupts Mrs. Bailey's subsequent attempt to change the topic, saying, "let her finish." Then he asks:

    T/S: then, which is <u>courage</u>?
    T/B: shhh
310 **FST:** [so you gonna sit there and <u>lie</u> to[her face
    T/S: [lying   [to <u>lie:</u> or to tell the
    truth be[cause you=
    FST: [°to tell the truth°
    T/S: =knew that she was wrong.
315 **CAN:** °cause it's wrong°
    FST: tell the <u>truth</u>. tell the <u>truth</u>
    TYI: <u>both</u> of them=
    JAS: both of them take courage [to me
    TYI: [=both of them take
320 cou[rage, you all wrong
    T/S: [explai:n how both.

Mr. Smith asks Tyisha to elaborate on her example, perhaps hoping that she will provide further material for interpreting Aristotle's account of courage. At lines 308 and 311–312, he asks whether it was really courageous to lie or whether it would in fact have been more courageous to tell her friend's mother the truth. Other students then side with Mr. Smith, claiming that lying is wrong and that telling the truth would have been more courageous. But at line 317, Tyisha claims that both lying and telling the truth could have been courageous, and at line 318 Jasmine agrees with her. Tyisha's academic argument seems plausible here because her lie required some disposition that at least resembled courage. From Tyisha and Jasmine's perspective, then, the teachers owe a further account of how Tyisha's lie was not courageous.

Before the teachers get to this, however, Tyisha punctuates her argument with a characteristic utterance at line 320: "you all wrong." With this utterance she separates herself off from the rest of the class, except perhaps from Jasmine. "You all" refers to the teachers and the students who are on the teachers' side. Tyisha happily separates herself from these people and defends an unpopular position. This separation is both *enacted* in her argument against the teachers and some other students in the classroom, and also presupposed in the *content* of the example. By describing herself as someone who breaks moral rules to which the teachers and many of the students adhere, Tyisha willingly separates herself from most others in the classroom.

Mr. Smith then asks Tyisha to explain how both lying and telling the truth could be courageous, so she continues.

    TYI: because (hhhh[h)
    FST: [because
    T/S: let her

325 **TYI:** if I lyin'- If I'm sittin' here lying in another person
     <u>mo</u>ther <u>face</u>, that took courag(h)e. [and if I'm=
     T/S: [why?
     TYI: =telling her be<u>cause</u> you don't-
     FST: lies.
330 **T/S:** have you never <u>lied</u> to your mother?
     FST: °hnuh°
     TYI: no- not- not to no one <u>else</u>'s momma, <u>no</u>.
     T/S: have you ever <u>lied</u> to a <u>tea</u>cher who is a mother?
     FST: uh(hhh)
335 **TYI:** that's <u>dif</u>ferent.
     FST: aw <u>man</u>.
     STS: [2 seconds of laughter]
     TYI: that's <u>very</u> different um- I mean that's <u>dif</u>ferent. I'm
     always over there visiting this <u>friend</u> and her mother, might
340 have had trus- trust in me and I come over and tell her this
     big, <u>bo:ld</u> faced lie.

From lines 322–328, Tyisha reiterates her claim that lying to her friend's
mother took courage. She is continuing to make a plausible argument that
the teachers have not refuted. Mr. Smith seems to be making a counterargument at lines 330 and 333, although it is not clear how Tyisha's earlier
truthfulness would make this lie any less courageous. Tyisha herself points
this out at lines 339–341.

But in fact Mr. Smith's question at line 333 makes interactional sense,
even if it does not make a convincing academic argument. His question
makes the example even more relevant to students and teachers' own identities in the classroom because he mentions "a teacher who is a mother."
Everyone knows that Mrs. Bailey is a mother – in fact, the mother of a
teenage girl. So Mr. Smith's question highlights the interactional tension
that Tyisha's example raises. Tyisha is clearly proud of the fact that she
lied to her friend's mother. But everyone in the classroom knows that
Mrs. Bailey would undoubtedly empathize with the friend's mother and
consider Tyisha to be wrong. By making Mrs. Bailey's own identity as a
mother relevant in this way, Mr. Smith makes clear that Tyisha is opposing
herself to Mrs. Bailey and people like her.

Tyisha revels in this oppositional identity, as illustrated in the sequence
of increasingly colorful terms that she uses to describe her lie. She initially
used the verb "tell" to describe what she said to her friend's mother (at line
283). Mr. Smith reframed this as a "lie" at line 301, and opposed such lying
to "telling the truth" (line 311). Another student spiced this up a bit: "so
you gonna sit there and lie to her face" (line 310). Tyisha herself embraced
this characterization of her act at lines 325–326: "I'm sitting here lying in
another person mother face." Then she produces an even more colorful

formulation: "Her mother might have had trust in me and I come over and tell her this big bold-faced lie" (lines 339–341). Far from euphemizing or downplaying what she did, Tyisha embraces the inappropriateness of her action and flaunts social norms. This clearly opposes her to Mrs. Bailey, who might well be worrying about her own daughter's friends doing the same thing to her.

In addition to embracing an oppositional identity in this way, Tyisha also skillfully embeds her oppositional identity within their academic discussion of Aristotle's concept of courage. This hijacking of the discussion itself constitutes another oppositional act. Tyisha did something wrong by lying to her friend's mother. She proudly discusses it in class. And she gets away with it by framing it as a legitimate discussion of the curriculum – which it is. Mr. Smith acknowledges Tyisha's legitimate argument by pursuing the academic merit of the example. His pursuing the example allows Tyisha to continue to revel in her oppositional behavior in the classroom interaction, and it allows her to pursue what seems a plausible academic argument.

> **T/S:** did you feel courage or did you feel guilt?
> **TYI:** I felt both of them   °[2 unintelligible syllables]°
> **T/S:** courage to be guilty? [quizzical intonation
> 345   contour]
> **TYI:** (hhh) nah, but it took courage to do [that.
> **JAS:**   [it do take
> courage to be guilty.
> **FST:** [1 second of laughter]
> 350   **TYI:** I know. like we goin' to [steal something. it took=
> **T/S:**   [you should be guilty
> **TYI:** =courage for me to go sneakin out of the store, right?
> **FST:** hahaha
> **T/S:** courage to be guilty.
> 355   **JAS:** you thief.
> **STS:** [1 second of laughter]
> **JAS:** cause- and you- okay, you go in the store. and you steal
> something, I mean [that take courage=
> **TYI:**   [it took courage to do it
> 360   **JAS:** =to steal something, and then you gonna be guilty
> afterward, right? right?
> **TYI:** s- say it. go ahead.
> **STS:** [2 seconds of laughter]

At line 342, Mr. Smith returns to the question of whether Tyisha felt courage or guilt while lying. Tyisha claims she felt both. Mr. Smith then seems to make fun of her argument by asking quizzically whether it can take courage to be guilty. After Tyisha reiterates that her lie was courageous at line 346,

Jasmine may be making fun of Tyisha at lines 347–348, saying "it do take courage to be guilty," and students laugh.

At this moment it is not clear whether the other students are laughing at Tyisha or with Tyisha. If my reading has been correct, Tyisha has all along intended for her example to be provocative. So it may be that she has succeeded in getting other students to laugh with her. Jasmine's comment at lines 347–348, however, seems to follow up on Mr. Smith's quizzical comment and to make fun of Tyisha. Tyisha responds with a second example, one involving the more serious transgression of robbery, at lines 350–352. This example also has academic merit, because they could discuss whether the immoral act of stealing requires courage. But by escalating the immoral act from lying to stealing, Tyisha may also be trying to build on the success of her first example, in which she managed to admit and condone apparently immoral behavior while at the same time making a valid academic argument. But Mr. Smith's immediate response at line 354 echoes Jasmine's teasing, and then Jasmine herself laughingly calls Tyisha a thief. At line 356, then, the students seem to be laughing at Tyisha.

But then the interactional tables turn. Jasmine sides with Tyisha at lines 357–361. She agrees with Tyisha that moral transgressions like stealing take courage. Tyisha echoes this at line 359, and the two of them together get other students laughing. It is relevant here that Jasmine is the most verbally skilled of the students. She won the schoolwide student talent competition that year, and she regularly had the class rolling with laughter. Her comments here contribute to the academic argument, but they are also funny and delivered skillfully. At line 363, then, the students are laughing with Tyisha.

At this point, in several lines not included here, a student objects that stealing is wrong. Tyisha and Jasmine then defend their claim that stealing can be both courageous and guilt inducing. Another student brings the discussion back to the concept of courage.

        LIN: I don't think that's <u>c</u>ourage to go and steal a <u>c</u>andy bar
               [because <u>c</u>ourage- right=
        MST: [it's stupid
395   **LIN:** =cause courage, the virtue of courage, what we read
        of courage was to <u>do</u> something- something <u>goo:d</u>, not to
        do <u>some</u>thing and go and do <u>some</u>thing [evil.
        TYI: [that's <u>not</u>
        true
400   **FST:**   [yeah that's
        right
        TYI: <u>c</u>ourage is not just doing something <u>goo:d</u>.
        [students talking at once]
        TYI: if I go [shoot you in the <u>head</u>

405   **T/B:**   [shhhhhh
       [students arguing]
       T/B: ahh, if we can- if we can talk about courage as being
       something good, the virtue of courage, and go back to that
       definition, and I know you never bought into it, but the rest
410   of us seem to be, using this as a definition, so therefore,
       we'd ask you to kind of go along with it.
       FST: okay.
       T/B: the idea of courage, was not just doing things you're
       afraid to do, but doing things that- overcoming your fear
415   for a good reason. Linda?
       LIN: I was saying what Tyisha said, if you go shoot
       somebody in the head, you gonna call that courage? or you
       is gonna call that stupid?

During Linda's argument that stealing does not require courage (from lines 392–397), one of the male students slips in a characterization of stealing: "it's stupid" (line 394). One might infer that people like Tyisha who defend such behavior are also stupid. Linda then gives an even more marked evaluation of stealing: It is "evil" (line 397). This casts Tyisha and Jasmine as defending something totally wrong.

Tyisha continues to argue that one can courageously commit immoral acts. On the face of it, this seems a reasonable academic argument. But at line 404, she chooses an example that does not seem appropriate in an academic discussion. "If I go shoot you in the head" is provocative because of the second-person pronoun and because shooting is more unethical than either stealing or lying. By escalating the immorality of the topic, Tyisha seems to be pushing the discussion toward what Goffman (1974) called "flooding out" – bursting out of its character as an academic discussion and becoming simply an occasion for laughter or confrontation. Tyisha seems to have made a choice here. She is not content merely to pursue an academic argument with Jasmine against other students and the teachers. She chooses at line 404 to push the discussion toward a non-academic type of interaction.

Because her argument has academic merit, up until line 405 the teachers had tolerated Tyisha's provocative discussion of her own unethical behavior. But once Tyisha escalates by imagining shooting "you" in the head at line 404, they discipline her. At lines 407–411, Mrs. Bailey reacts to Tyisha's example of shooting as if she had been trying to disrupt classroom discussion (which may have been Tyisha's intention). Mrs. Bailey could have said, "That's an interesting argument Tyisha, but how can an act be both virtuous and immoral at once? Would Aristotle have agreed with that?" Instead, she skillfully frames Tyisha's comment as moving against the will of the rest of the class, without baldly asserting her own authority as a teacher.

She starts by establishing her own version of the contested issue as a "definition," at lines 407–410. Tyisha has argued that immoral acts can require courage, but Mrs. Bailey asserts that courage is by definition something good. Tyisha and Jasmine "never bought into" this definition, "but the rest of us" did. Mrs. Bailey thus positions Tyisha and Jasmine as marginal to the core classroom group, as people who insist on idiosyncratic definitions and thereby hinder seminar discussion. Mrs. Bailey then acknowledges their dissent and asks them to go along with the larger group. It would violate her pedagogical philosophy to tell students what to think, so she does not force them. The teacher skillfully shifts the metapragmatic model organizing their classroom identities and relationships. Tyisha is not a clever student who manages to tweak the teachers to the delight of fellow students while making plausible academic arguments. Mrs. Bailey has instead characterized Tyisha and Jasmine not only as marginal, but also as the sort of people who refuse to accept agreed-upon definitions and who disrupt the productive work being done by the rest of the class.

In this discussion of lying, stealing and shooting, Tyisha both embraces an oppositional identity and also skillfully inserts these illicit topics into legitimate academic discussion of the curriculum. The teachers and most other students respond by identifying her as morally suspect. They marginalize Tyisha, pushing her away from the core group of teachers and other vocal students in two ways. First, Tyisha gets willingly characterized as the sort of unethical person who would boldly lie to a friend's mother, unlike other students who condemn this behavior. Second, she positions herself and gets positioned in the classroom interaction as a student who makes jokes, takes the class off-topic and refuses to accept generally agreed-upon definitions. The participant example facilitates both a denotationally explicit characterization of Tyisha as morally suspect and interactional positioning of her as marginal to the core group of teachers and students. At her own initiative, then, Tyisha's identity as a disruptive student gets further solidified.

By embracing an oppositional identity while discussing this example of herself as a courageous liar, Tyisha responded to teachers and students' earlier characterization of her as disruptive. The "Tyisha as conceited" example illustrated how, in December and January, teachers and other students began to identify Tyisha as disruptive and position her outside the core group of teachers and students. No clear metapragmatic model had emerged yet to identify Tyisha, but her vigorous defense of her own opinions was beginning to seem more negative than positive. The example of "Tyisha the courageous liar" shows that Tyisha responded by continuing to defend her ideas vigorously and by embracing an identity as marginal in the classroom. By reacting this way, Tyisha made it more difficult for herself to return to her earlier identity as just another promising girl.

It was not yet clear, however, which metapragmatic model would emerge as the habitual one for making sense of Tyisha's outspoken classroom behavior. The teachers were inclined to identify Tyisha as disruptive and to marginalize her, although Mrs. Bailey might have hoped that she would "go along" with Paideia classroom norms and return to being a cooperative student. Some students also objected to Tyisha's arguments, and they might have adopted Mrs. Bailey's characterization of Tyisha as disruptive. But Jasmine and perhaps other students seemed to value Tyisha's presentation of herself as someone who defends unpopular positions and successfully makes provocative arguments within seminar discussion. Either of these models, and perhaps others, might have become the ones teachers and students habitually used to identify Tyisha. On January 18, it was still too early to tell which way Tyisha's trajectory of identification would go.

CURRICULAR THEMES AS A RESOURCE FOR IDENTIFYING TYISHA

After January 18, Tyisha could have become a class jester, valued by other students for defending unpopular positions and tweaking the teachers. She could have become a productive dissenter, valued by teachers and students for raising questions about apparently settled conclusions. But in fact she became habitually identified by both teachers and students as a disruptive student who refused to cooperate with others in seminar discussion and who became an outcast from the core group of teachers and students. This thickening local identity depended on resources from various timescales – sociohistorical models of appropriate classroom and Paideia behavior, sociohistorical models of "loud black girls" and other students who might challenge teacher authority, emerging local models of typical female student behavior, contingent events like the examples discussed on December 17 and January 18, Tyisha's own active embrace of her emerging outcast identity and so on.

These various resources came together to constitute the robust local metapragmatic model of a disruptive outcast, a model that was habitually applied to Tyisha by the end of January. This model solidified in significant part because of one catalyst: the emerging local cognitive model of the individual/society curricular theme. This cognitive model by itself could never have accomplished the social identification that happened to Tyisha. But it was emerging at the right time, in such a way that it catalyzed the thickening of a "disruptive outcast" identity for Tyisha. In late January, the emerging metapragmatic model of Tyisha as disruptive and marginal and the emerging cognitive model of an individual who refuses to sacrifice for the good of society overlapped and co-developed. This overlap allowed teachers and students to develop a robust metapragmatic model of Tyisha as a disruptive outcast. Without the intervention of the curricular theme,

Tyisha might have been identified as disruptive and marginalized in classroom discussions. But these identities probably would not have become as robust as they did, and her trajectory of identification may have shifted in a different direction. In fact, however, an emerging local cognitive model of the curricular theme became analogous to Tyisha's emerging identity, and this allowed the processes of social identification and academic learning to mesh with and reinforce each other.

The examples of Tyisha as conceited and as a courageous liar did allow teachers and students to use isolated categories from the curriculum to identify Tyisha. Her transformation from good to disruptive student was facilitated in part through the use of curricular categories like "conceited" and "[not] courageous," as teachers, other students and Tyisha herself used these categories (among other resources) to identify her as overly focused on her own opinions and as disruptive. But these examples from December 17 and January 18 merely involved the opportunistic use of isolated curricular categories like "conceited" to identify Tyisha. Complex models of the curriculum did not become resources for socially identifying Tyisha until later in January.

The overlap between the curriculum and Tyisha's emerging identity became more systematic as the class engaged the first curricular theme. As discussed in Chapter 3, the teachers assigned several texts that explored whether individuals should sacrifice for the good of the society or whether the society should be organized to maximize individual autonomy. Students came to recognize arguments for both collectivist and individualist positions, and many students defended a position of their own on this question – that a good society should facilitate individual autonomy, but that the group should also work together to help the underprivileged. As they articulated their position, teachers and students developed an analogy between their own class and the societies they were reading about. They cast their own classroom as analogous to moderate Athenian democracy, which facilitated both the rights of the individual and the needs of the group – as opposed to overly collectivist Sparta and Rand's overly individualist ideal. From this perspective, the students concluded that individuals who exclusively pursue their own interests are inappropriately selfish and disruptive. By analogy, students who pursue their own interests at the expense of the group act inappropriately and might be labeled as disruptive in the classroom.

Tyisha's transformation into a disruptive outcast solidified as the class discussed the curricular theme of collectivism and individualism. Tyisha became the favored example when a text included an outcast – someone who acts for his or her own good without considering the good of the society. Students learned about this curricular issue in part by discussing Tyisha's position as an outcast, through several examples and the analogy between the class and a society. At the same time, Tyisha's identity as a disruptive outcast thickened. The analogy between the classroom "society" and the curricular theme of collectivism and individualism thus became central to Tyisha's identity development and to students' learning about that curricular theme. What had been separate but vague metapragmatic and cognitive models became a more precise, co-developing, overlapping metapragmatic/cognitive model.

Tyisha the Beast

The example of Tyisha as a "beast," introduced in Chapter 1, was crucial in creating systematic overlap between the emerging metapragmatic model of Tyisha as a disruptive outcast and the emerging cognitive model of the individual/society curricular theme. If Tyisha's identity in this contingent event had not emerged as it did, her trajectory of identification might have been different. But this one event did not suffice to create her identity. Her overall trajectory of identification depended on the various heterogeneous resources I have been describing.

This class occurred on January 24 when Tyisha's transformation into a disruptive student was well underway. On this day students had read selections from Aristotle's *Politics* in which he argues that "the state is by nature clearly prior to the individual since the whole is of necessity prior to the part." Aristotle also says that "he who is unable to live in society, or who has no need because he is sufficient for himself, must be beast or god" (Book I, Chapter 2, 1253a: 19–20, 27–29). Aristotle argues for a more collectivist position than the one commonly found in the contemporary West. As the teachers try to help students understand his position, they focus on the character of a "beast," a person who refuses to make the sacrifices necessary to live as part of society. Near the end of the discussion Mrs. Bailey summarizes their discussion of the curricular concept "beast":

> **T/B:** okay so a <u>man</u> who lives out<u>side</u> of society we
> can understand has this <u>beast</u> quality to him because
> he's going to do what
> 1170 **FST:** °he wants to do°
> **T/B:** he wants to do <u>when</u> he wants to do it <u>as</u> he
> wants to do it, with no <u>checks</u>, and no <u>chance</u> to
> lea:rn what is just or unjust, what is fair or right, to
> take into account anything beyond what <u>he: wants</u>
> 1175 to <u>do</u>.

Earlier in the discussion, Mrs. Bailey and some students distinguish between such a "beast" and a human being. They explore Aristotle's claim that one who does not live in society is not fully human by discussing what humans have that animals do not. They develop a tentative answer:

Humans have goals while animals do not. Tyisha objects to this distinction in the following passage:

> **TYI:** Mrs. Bailey? I- I have to disagre:e.
> [class laughter]
> 660 **T/B:** can I- can I finish this before you disagree,
> okay. the idea that he's putting out here is that
> they- they have goals, and that they can in
> discussion decide the best way to accomplish their
> goal. now, Tyisha what's your disagreement?
> 665 **TYI:** becau(hh)- because if a- like- if my- okay,
> if my cat want to- um you know to get to the top of
> something, you know, he might sit there and be
> [three unintelligible syllables] and he'll sit there and
> try everyday. and then finally he will do it, that was
> 670 the goal to try and get up there. he had a goal.
> **T/B:** okay (1.0) he's got a [goal but
> **FST:**   [was his goal really
> necessary? [laughter from class]
> **T/B:** let's- let's- let's take what- (3.0) let's take
> 675 what your cat's doing that every day he sees that-
> counter that he wants to get on, and every day when
> he passes that counter he tries to get up there. that's
> a goal. okay
> **FST:** yeah.
> 680 **T/B:** how is that different than your goal, the goal
> that you might have had last night when you had
> this reading, or [some chattering]
> **TYI:** °I don't know°

Tyisha offers a good argument here: The teacher and other students have claimed that "goals" distinguish humans from beasts, but Tyisha points out at lines 665–670 that her cat has goals too. Mrs. Bailey accepts Tyisha's objection at line 671 and at lines 674–678, granting that Tyisha's cat has goals. She then begins to distinguish between the types of goals Aristotle claimed were uniquely human and the types of goals that beasts also have.

Thus Tyisha's argument forces the teacher to formulate her interpretation of Aristotle's text more precisely, and the whole class benefits as they go on to define uniquely human goals. Tyisha demonstrates her intelligence here, and that she is closely following the academic discussion. Her argument also illustrates how she and many other students have learned to make arguments as these Paideia teachers wanted. She articulates and defends her own position, and she does so with reference to her own experience.

Despite her academic contribution here, however, there are already indications that other students do not identify Tyisha as a serious student. At line 659, students laugh after Tyisha's first utterance. They probably laugh because Tyisha's description of her own action – "to disagree" – fits well with the model they are developing of her identity, as a student who often interrupts class by disagreeing and offering off-topic opinions. Tyisha's comment at line 658 contains very little information. It is only together with her presupposed disruptiveness that Tyisha's use of "disagree" becomes something to laugh at. At lines 672–673, another student tries to defeat Tyisha's argument with a brief, unconvincing counterargument. Other students' subsequent laughter seems to indicate that, because of Tyisha's tendency to give off-topic and faulty arguments, her argument can be easily defeated. As I will discuss below, however, there is another possible interpretation of the laughter at lines 665 and 673.

Despite these students' apparent lack of respect for Tyisha, Mrs. Bailey recognizes the strength of Tyisha's argument. She uses Tyisha's example of her cat to pursue an academic topic relevant to Aristotle: How are humans different from beasts if beasts have goals just like us? To continue the discussion, Mrs. Bailey adopts Tyisha's example at lines 674–682. She turns it into a participant example. Both Tyisha and her cat become characters in the example, and the class explores how Tyisha's goals might differ from her cat's. Tyisha thus becomes an example of a generic human being, and the class discusses her and her cat in order to understand the difference between humans and beasts. This role as a generic human does not initially seem to have any negative implications for Tyisha herself.

Figure 4.1 represents the example at this point. The embedded rectangle in the figure represents the denoted content of the example, in which Tyisha has described her cat's goal of jumping on the counter and Mrs. Bailey has introduced Tyisha's goal of doing her homework. Mrs. Bailey distinguishes between Tyisha and her cat in order to illustrate how humans' goals can differ from beasts'. The vertical line between Tyisha and her cat represents this distinction between humans and animals. The outer rectangle in Figure 4.1 represents the interaction among teachers and students. At lines 672–673, other students try to exclude Tyisha by ridiculing her argument, but Mrs. Bailey accepts her argument and treats her as a productive member of the class. Thus the figure represents Tyisha inside the class.

In the next segment, teachers and students continue to discuss Tyisha's example in order to understand how humans differ from beasts.

> **FST:** humans can do more things than cats can do,
> like they can build
> **TYI:** no that's not- just a goal. my goal is to win
> in Nintendo and
> 695 [laughter by a few girls in the class]
> **FST:** that's your goal?

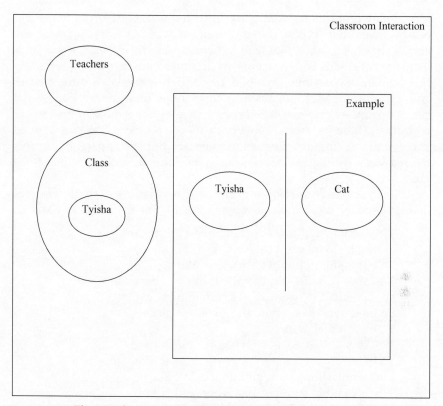

FIGURE 4.1. The initial example of Tyisha and her cat.

TYI: it's a go:al, so
T/B: okay maybe winning at Nintendo is like your cat's goal of getting on top of the-
700　**TYI:** right
T/B: the- the counter. but aren't- don't we have more [long=
FST: [better
T/B: =ranged goals than your cat getting on
705　top of the counter, or you winning Nintendo?
TYI: but I'm just saying they're goals. you said animals can't have goals or something, so I just told ya I disagree.
T/B: okay, but can we- can we qualify that then.
710　**TYI:** yeah.
T/B: can we qualify that and say that man (2.0) doesn't just have immediate goals, but also has- long- range goals.
T/S: umm, consider your cat. [Tyisha giggles a bit]
715　your cat gets sleepy. what does your cat do?

Mrs. Bailey and other students try to distinguish between humans and beasts' goals, but Tyisha resists the distinction. At lines 693–694, she argues that her goals – like winning Nintendo video games – are similar to her cat's. Mrs. Bailey accepts her argument at lines 698–699, granting that humans have some goals that are similar to beasts'. But the teacher goes on to argue that humans also have "more long-ranged goals" that beasts do not. At lines 706–708, Tyisha reiterates her claim that the teacher and other students should have been more specific when they argued that "goals" distinguish humans from beasts. But she apparently accepts the teacher's distinction between uniquely human and more beast-like goals.

At line 714, Mr. Smith begins to elaborate on Tyisha's example. He goes on to pursue the distinction between uniquely human and other goals.

     T/S: what <u>goal</u> did you have in mind this morning,
     even when you went to sleep.
     TYI: [laughing] I didn't h(h)ave o(h)ne.
     T/S: sure you did. didn't you- didn't you have the
730   goal you had to wake up at a certain <u>time</u>, get
     <u>dressed</u> in a- by a certain <u>time</u>, <u>get</u> to a place
     TYI: yeah that's true.
     T/S: so <u>you</u> had goals even before you s[tarted
     TYI: [but not in
735   the summertime. I just got up, see, just like
     T/S: <u>ah</u>, and in summertime when you got up
     because you <u>didn't</u> have to come to school what was your
     goal or was it to sleep until three in the after<u>noon</u>?
     or to get up and play with your friends?
740   **TYI:** the same goal my cat had, to go to <u>sleep</u>,
     and get up and <u>eat</u>.
     T/B: ahhh, isn't that interes[ting? [increase in pitch,
     'mocking' effect]
     T/S: [ahhhh

At lines 728 and 732, Mr. Smith gets Tyisha to contribute information about the content of the example, which he uses to argue that Tyisha has uniquely human goals. But at lines 734–735 and 740–741, Tyisha returns to her earlier argument: She has some goals that are qualitatively similar to her cat's, and therefore the teachers' attempt to distinguish humans from beasts based on goals cannot work. Mrs. Bailey has already granted that Tyisha and other humans do have beast-like goals, but she has gone on to argue that we also have uniquely human goals. Tyisha nonetheless continues to make her old argument, that humans like her have beast-like goals too.

Tyisha may be arguing that all human goals are beast-like – an argument that would be supported by behaviorists, microeconomists and others. But her persistence in returning to her old argument also indicates that there have been two possible ways of construing the interaction since her initial comment at line 658. Each of these represents a different metapragmatic model of the classroom, a different set of social identities for teachers and students. First, Tyisha may have been making an argument that contributes to the academic substance of the discussion. On this model of the interaction, teachers and students would be on the same side, collaboratively participating in seminar discussion. Tyisha contributed to the discussion by making a useful counterargument at lines 665–670, but her continued objections would make her an increasingly disruptive student who blocks further productive discussion of the topic – unless she could more convincingly argue that all human goals are in fact beast-like.

Second, Tyisha may have been using her example as an opportunity to make jokes, as she did on January 18 when discussing courage, by referring to aspects of everyday life that students would not normally be able to discuss in the classroom. The laughter at lines 665 and 673 would in this case reflect Tyisha's skillful manipulation of an academic discussion to introduce normally inappropriate topics. In this case, Tyisha would be a "clown," making other students laugh, and she might gain status by successfully bending the teachers' rules about what can legitimately be discussed. We have already seen an example of similar behavior on January 18, and she behaved this way on other occasions as well. This second model of the interaction would place teachers and students on opposite sides, with teachers as guardians of classroom order and students as restively subject to the teachers' rules.

Both of these models of the interaction could reasonably be used to interpret behavior from lines 658–741 (by us as analysts and by the participants themselves). The teachers try to frame Tyisha's example as a contribution to academic discussion, and they initially succeed. Tyisha did make a good point, and Mrs. Bailey both acknowledged this and helped her draw it out. But the "joking" model remains potentially relevant up through line 741. A few students laugh at line 695, perhaps because the topic of playing Nintendo is not one normally discussed in school, or perhaps because Tyisha represents herself as playing video games – an activity teachers often condemn, but also one that Tyisha has managed to get away with mentioning. After Mrs. Bailey accepts Tyisha's argument at line 709 and goes on to pursue the distinction between uniquely human and more beast-like goals, Tyisha laughs at lines 714 and 728. She may be trying to turn the example into a joke at this point because she has lost control of it. She is no longer making an argument and simultaneously introducing taboo topics. The teachers have taken control of her example, making it part of an academic argument, and Mr. Smith is now controlling the content that Tyisha contributes to the example.

From the teachers' point of view, they are simply returning to normal classroom business. Tyisha made both an argument and a joke with the same example, and now that she has made a substantive point and had her fun, they take control of the example to pursue the argument. Tyisha, however, does not cooperate. She reverts to the same old argument. From the teachers' point of view – using the first interpretation of the classroom interaction as an academic discussion – this old argument is now an inappropriate disruption. When Tyisha's claim was both a new, substantive argument and also a joke, they tolerated the joke for the sake of the argument. But Tyisha's old point no longer contributes to the argument. Thus the teachers may be getting frustrated. I suspect that other students pick up on this because no one laughs at Tyisha's descriptions of her indolence at lines 734–735 and 740–741. At this point, however, a third potential model of the interaction emerges. It includes a third possible social identity for Tyisha. At line 742, Mrs. Bailey reacts to Tyisha in a way that presupposes that Tyisha is neither a student making an argument nor a student making a joke. Mrs. Bailey's mocking tone suggests that Tyisha is the butt of a joke. In this third possible model of the interaction, the joke is on Tyisha.

Tyisha's strategy – to resist the distinction between uniquely human and beast-like goals, and perhaps to joke with other students by introducing her indolence and video gaming – led her to emphasize her own beast-like tendencies. This gives teachers and other students an opportunity to position her as in fact beast-like. They take advantage of this opportunity as the discussion proceeds.

745   **T/B:** same goals as her (1.0)[cat=
       FST: [cat had
       T/B: =had. wow.
       FST: so you are like an animal.
       T/B: so you are like an animal.
750   **TYI:** I'm not saying, I just don't have
       somewheres to be at.
       T/B: okay, but that's not- don't confuse the issue.
       one point at a time, Tyisha. you throw out seventeen
       things and then- nobody can even begin to address
755   any of these things.
       MST: tss [hissing laughter]

At line 748, a female student makes explicit the teachers' interactional move here, calling Tyisha an animal, and Mrs. Bailey echoes her comment. This is not part of the argument that teachers and students have been developing to understand Aristotle. Nor is it part of Tyisha's joking around by introducing taboo topics and opposing the teachers' agenda. It is a third model of the interaction, in which teachers and students single out Tyisha and laugh at her instead of with her. This third model presupposes different social identities: The teachers and all students except Tyisha are on one side, participating in academic discussion and also using that discussion to tease Tyisha; Tyisha is on the other side, as someone who disrupts the academic discussion and as the object of their teasing.

At line 750, Tyisha, probably recognizing the risk that comes with emphasizing her own indolence, backs off. She had succeeded in joking and arguing at the same time, but now she sees that she has taken it too far – she was outdone in her joking by Mrs. Bailey, who has managed to stay within the frame of discussing the example while teasing Tyisha. Once Tyisha breaks off the example at line 750, Mrs. Bailey creates a fourth model for the interaction when she switches from teasing Tyisha to disciplining her. Speaking in her role as teacher and disciplinarian, Mrs. Bailey explicitly characterizes Tyisha as a disruptive student who does not follow the norms of seminar discussion. This fourth model for the classroom interaction, of course, borrows from and reinforces the emerging local metapragmatic model of Tyisha as disruptive.

After this disciplinary interlude, the class continues to discuss Aristotle's idea of a "beast" and his argument that someone living outside of society is not fully human. Mrs. Bailey returns to Tyisha's example a few minutes later.

> **FST:** a beast- a beast is someone who roams around
> 805   earth.
> **T/B:** a beast is someone who what.
> **FST:** °roams around the earth.° I mean [overlapping chatter]
> **T/B:** you were seeing the connection with Ty-
> 810   Tyisha's behavior in the summer with being a beast.
> what's the connection?
> **TYI:** I'm not a beast, and my cat is not a be[ast.
> **FST:**   [you
> are a beast.
> 815   [students laugh]
> **T/S:** by your definition, you're telling us- by your
> definition, you're telling us because you have no
> society, to which you belong in summer by the
> definition of Aristotle, and your own words, you=
> 820   **TYI:** [but-
> **T/S:** =[become a beast in summer [=
> **TYI:**   [because-
> **T/S:** =like your pet.
> **TYI:** that definition is not the real definition

825   that's in the dictionaries.
        [students shouting and laughing, overlapping with
        T/S and T/B]
        T/B: okay, uh, kay, im<u>port</u>ant point. and this- we
        keep on having a problem with you Tyisha, and this
830   has been <u>ta:lked</u> a<u>bout</u> and <u>ta:lked</u> a<u>bout</u>. people
        can<u>not</u> communicate in <u>this</u> kind of conversation
        unless they a<u>gree</u> on using certain terms, a certain
        way, agree on definitions.
        TYI: but I=
835   **T/B:** <u>and</u> if you don't want to agree on the
        definition then- I <u>think</u> you remove yourself from
        the conversation for a while, and see where it goes.
        because we- we are using <u>A</u>ristotle's definitions
        here, and Sheneather was right and that's- (1.0) the
840   issue that we constantly have with <u>you</u> is that <u>you</u>
        want to come up with a <u>diff</u>erent definition. and
        that's <u>not</u> what we're about. we're trying to have a
        discussion based on definitions we've a<u>greed</u> on or
        come from the piece.

At line 809, Mrs. Bailey returns to Tyisha's example, apparently hoping
to explore Aristotle's argument further. Tyisha, however, takes this as a
return to teasing, and she objects at line 812. Then other students join in at
lines 813–815 as if Mrs. Bailey had been teasing.

Mr. Smith's comments at lines 816–823 could support either an "academic discussion" (the first) or a "teasing Tyisha" (the third) model of the
interaction. His tone is matter of fact, and he might be using the example to continue interpreting Aristotle. But the content of his comments,
in which he claims that Tyisha has "no society" like a beast, might continue the teasing. His emphatic stress at lines 817–823 also supports this
second interpretation. The students' laughter and comments at line 826
presuppose that Mr. Smith has indeed been teasing Tyisha here.

Mrs. Bailey responds to the students' spirited teasing and off-topic
comments by speaking again as a disciplinarian, starting at line 828. She
returns to the fourth model of the interaction at lines 828–844, explicitly
identifying Tyisha as a disruptive student who does not participate cooperatively in seminar discussion. She marginalizes Tyisha interactionally,
continuing the personal pronoun opposition between "you" and "us."
"*We*'re trying to have a discussion" and "*we* keep on having a problem
with *you*." In order for students to have the opportunity to voice their
opinions in class, everyone must follow the group rules. But Tyisha does
not follow these rules, and thus she removes herself from the classroom
community.

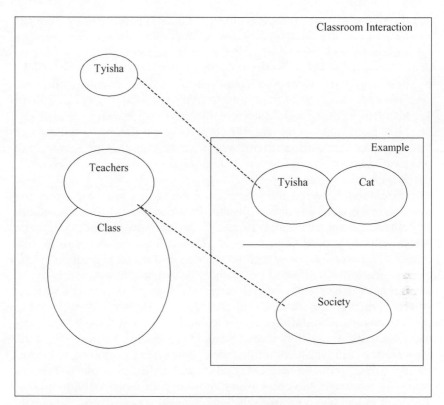

FIGURE 4.2. The example at the end of the discussion.

Figure 4.2 represents the classroom discussion at this point. The over-lapping ovals for Tyisha and her cat indicate their essential similarity. The horizontal line between Tyisha and society represents a fundamental division between Tyisha and human society. In the classroom interaction, the horizontal line represents how Tyisha has been positioned as an out-cast who does not cooperate with and is not welcome in the classroom "society." Within the example, Tyisha has argued and the teachers have accepted that she is essentially like her cat. Neither Tyisha nor her cat pur-sues uniquely human goals, and they are therefore removed from human society as Aristotle conceives it. In the classroom itself, a parallel organi-zation has emerged. This parallel is represented by the dotted lines in the figure. Because Tyisha does not obey the rules of the classroom "society," she has been excluded. The teachers and other students have agreed on certain rules, and by following them they belong to the classroom society and act in uniquely human ways. According to Aristotle, after all, ratio-nal deliberation in society was essential to being human. But Tyisha has refused to follow the rules, so she is an outcast from the society, a "beast in the woods."

Like all participant examples, the example of Tyisha the beast doubled Tyisha's roles in the classroom. She was both described as a beast like her cat and was treated like an outcast in the classroom interaction. In some participant examples, including this one, participants' two roles run parallel – in other words, the focal participant *enacts* a role analogous to the role *described* as the content of the example (Wortham, 1994). The example of Tyisha the beast described Tyisha as someone who acts like an animal and does not participate in society. While participating in the discussion of this example, Tyisha the student herself enacted an analogous role: Like Aristotle's "beast," she refused to follow classroom norms, and as a result she was excluded from the social group.

This parallel between the referential content of the example and the interactional positioning accomplished while discussing the example both facilitated and relied upon systematic overlap between metapragmatic and cognitive models. Categories of identity from the curriculum, like Aristotle's concept of a beast, helped teachers and students position Tyisha as an outcast and reinforced her identity as a disruptive student. At the same time, Tyisha's emerging identity as a disruptive outcast and their emerging metapragmatic model of classroom relationships contributed to the local cognitive model about what Aristotle means by "beast." The local metapragmatic model they were developing to identify Tyisha's role in the classroom and the local cognitive model they were developing to understand the first curricular theme started to mesh in this example, as Tyisha's beast-like characteristics became an important component of both models. This joint model was a type of self/knowledge, because it simultaneously contributed to Tyisha's social identity and the students' academic learning.

Through this co-development of social identification and academic learning, in which curricular categories and local categories of identity meshed, Tyisha's identity as a disruptive outcast solidified. Aristotle argues that society cannot include people who, like "beasts in the woods," focus on their own desires and disregard the needs of the group. By analogy, classroom "society" cannot function if someone consistently pursues his or her own interests at the expense of the group. For more than a month as we have seen, Tyisha had been increasingly identified as inappropriately self-centered and disruptive. Thus she was the perfect example of a beast, and the example of her as a beast cemented her marginal position in the classroom. Furthermore, as Mrs. Bailey said at the end of the discussion, Tyisha had "removed herself" from the classroom interaction with her disruptive behavior, and so was herself responsible for her newly thickened identity as a disruptive outcast.

Tyisha Continuing as a Beast

Before the January 24 example, the teachers had begun to identify Tyisha as disruptive and to marginalize her in the classroom, and Tyisha had embraced an oppositional identity. Across a trajectory of events from November into January, Tyisha had shifted from being identified as another promising girl to being identified as a disruptive student who pushed her own opinions to the detriment of the class. But no one metapragmatic model had emerged that could be routinely and unproblematically used to identify Tyisha. The example of Tyisha as a beast on January 24 helped teachers and students use curricular categories to create a local model that was then routinely available to identify Tyisha. By including the curricular concept of "beast" – or self-centered outcast who pursues his or her own needs and ignores the group's – and by incorporating this category of identity into the already-emerging metapragmatic model of Tyisha as a disruptive outcast, teachers and students left the January 24 discussion with a more robust category of disruptive outcast that anchored Tyisha's identity.

If January 24 had been an isolated occurrence of the curricular topics of individuals, society and "beasts," the overlap between local cognitive and metapragmatic models might not have had much effect. But in fact the category of disruptive outcast recurred often because, as described in Chapter 3, teachers and students read and discussed several texts in January and February that addressed the individual/society curricular theme. Discussions of this theme consistently included categories like "beast," "outcast" or person unwilling to sacrifice for the good of the group. Once this category of identity had begun to get incorporated into the metapragmatic model used to identify Tyisha, as happened on January 24, the recurrence of the category in the curriculum over the next several weeks provided repeated opportunities for teachers and students to apply it to Tyisha. If the category of beast or outcast had not been part of a curricular theme – perhaps like the category "conceited" discussed on December 17 – teachers and students would have had to work much harder to identify Tyisha as a disruptive outcast, and her trajectory of identification might have been somewhat different.

Instead, from January 24 through the end of February they discussed various positions on the curricular theme, ranging from Rand's individualism through Sparta's collectivism, and they ended up construing Athenian democracy as the golden mean. They also developed a local analogy between the curricular concept of "society" and the social organization of their classroom. Using this analogy they built local cognitive models of individualist classroom "societies" in which people consider only themselves and cannot sustain collective discussion, collectivist ones in which individuality is flattened by coercive policies, and the golden mean (like their own Paideia classroom) in which students and teachers work together so that individuals can express and collectively examine their own arguments in productive group discussions. On January 24, Tyisha's emerging social identity started both to draw on and contribute to this local cognitive model. Now they could understand Aristotle, Rand and other texts by considering Tyisha's own position in the classroom. And they could more routinely identify Tyisha by drawing on categories like "beast" from their emerging cognitive model.

As teachers and students continued to discuss this curricular theme over the weeks following January 24, they continued to use the category of disruptive outcast both to identify Tyisha and build their cognitive model of the curriculum. Some evidence for this has been presented earlier in this chapter in the discussions of explicit comments about Tyisha's identity – such as the example of Mr. Smith calling her a bad student on February 11. As teachers and students increasingly presupposed Tyisha's identity as a disruptive outcast, she was even characterized as disruptive when she was absent. In the following segment, for instance (from February 7) Brenna is summarizing the Spartan practice of infanticide.

> **BRE:** they just put them out an- as a test. if it lives
> then it's strong. and if it dies then it dies.
> **T/B:** I'm going to play Tyisha. that's not right
> **STS:** hahahahaha
> 250 **T/B:** these people are stupid. that's not right
> we're[missing=
> **STS:** [hnh   haha
> **T/B:** =her today.
> **STS:** [7 seconds comments and laughter]
> 255 **T/B:** she- you know that's what she'd say? what
> is your response to that?
> **STS:** [unintelligible response] hahahahaha
> **T/B:** you'd never say that when she's in the room.

When Mrs. Bailey imitates Tyisha at lines 248–250, she portrays Tyisha as opinionated and judgmental. In the teacher's rendition, Tyisha objects to the practice described in the text without giving much of an argument. She just voices her opinion and calls the practice "stupid." At line 258, the teacher also suggests that Tyisha dominates classroom discussion, when she says that other students would not dare dismiss her comments in person. Even when she is absent, then, teachers and students reinforce Tyisha's local identity.

While discussing the curricular theme in January and February, Tyisha also continued to position herself as marginal by adopting more extreme individualist positions than others. During the January 25 discussion of Rand's individualist society, for instance, she says a bit wistfully, "They don't have to do nothing if they don't want to do it" (lines 753–754). During the February 21 discussion of Pericles, she vigorously defends individual freedom and she stresses that in her life, "I can do what I want" (lines 582–583). Given the analogy between the curricular theme and the classroom "society," Tyisha's spirited defense of individualism fit with her identity as the disruptive individualist in the classroom. As illustrated above, teachers and students pointed this out by identifying her as a bad student and a disruptive outcast.

By February, then, Tyisha had shifted from being another promising girl, to being poorly behaved and marginalized, to being identified with the much more specific and robust model of a disruptive outcast. Teachers, other students and Tyisha herself accomplished this contingent trajectory of identification by drawing on resources at several timescales. Pivotal events like the participant examples on January 18 and 24 could have happened differently. In both the "Tyisha the courageous liar" and the "Tyisha the beast" discussions, there were moments where teachers and students could have moved away from the joking aspects of Tyisha's comments and toward a more straightforward academic discussion. If this had happened, Tyisha might have been identified as an occasional jester instead of a regularly disruptive outcast, and the curricular theme might never have become a resource for identifying Tyisha. Sociohistorical and local models of identity only live in actual events, and participants can always construe such models and categories unexpectedly in any given event. Like all social identities, Tyisha's identity as a disruptive outcast depended on the contingent emergence of that social identity within various events of identification.

As I have argued elsewhere (Wortham, 2005), the emergence of an identity across a trajectory of events involves similar contingency. Having been identified in one event as a disruptive outcast, teachers and students might have never used this metapragmatic model to identify Tyisha again. Or they might have transformed it in subsequent events, making her (for example) a heroic individualist instead of a disruptive outcast. For a metapragmatic model to emerge and allow an individual's social identity to thicken, that model must recur across several events in a trajectory. If it does not, that individual travels along a different trajectory of identification. So for Tyisha to become a disruptive outcast, both contingent events and contingent trajectories of identification had to take shape as they did, when it could easily have been otherwise.

I have argued that the emergence of a joint metapragmatic/cognitive model of classroom relationships and of the individual/society curricular theme played an important role in stabilizing Tyisha's trajectory of identification as a disruptive outcast. The students were learning academic concepts at the same time as Tyisha's social identity was emerging, and some of these concepts were incorporated into the metapragmatic model they used to identify Tyisha. This systematic overlap between cognitive and metapragmatic models helped keep Tyisha on her trajectory toward becoming a robust disruptive outcast at a time when Tyisha's identity both within and across events could have emerged differently. I am not arguing that the curricular theme and the local cognitive model were the only or even the predominant factors in Tyisha's shift from good student to disruptive outcast. Resources from several other timescales played a crucial role, but the emerging local cognitive model was nonetheless an important component.

THE OUTCAST RESISTING AUTHORITY

Tyisha's local identity shifted once more after the class stopped discussing the first curricular theme. This final shift also illustrates how local cognitive models can be important resources for students' identity development. As the year progressed, another local metapragmatic model used to identify Tyisha's identity overlapped to a lesser extent with the second curricular theme – the question of whether a citizen should be loyal to or resist exploitive rulers. As the class began to discuss the loyalty/resistance theme, starting late in February, the curricular category of legitimate resistance helped provide an opening that was not available to Tyisha earlier in the year. On January 18 and on other occasions, she had tried to position herself as opposed to the teachers and perhaps allied with other students in subverting or resisting the teachers' authority. But the teachers labeled her behavior as disruptive, and this identity stuck. Once the category of legitimate resistance appeared in the curriculum, however, Tyisha's "disruptions" could more easily be identified as reasoned resistance. In late February and beyond, Tyisha, other students and the teachers did sometimes reframe her vigorous counterarguments as legitimate resistance.

The analogy between the classroom itself and "society" was central to the emerging, local version of this second curricular theme. As shown in the February 7 discussion of Lycurgus, discussed in Chapter 3, teachers and students sometimes construed power relationships in the classroom as analogous to power relationships in the larger society. They developed a local cognitive model that presented teachers as powerful, like exploitative rulers, and students as subject to that power. As they developed this model to understand legitimate and illegitimate resistance, it also became available to characterize teachers and students' own identities. This happened, for instance, on February 21, when teachers and students reinforced the analogy between power in the classroom and power in society while discussing Pericles' *Funeral Oration*.

> **T/B:** who are many here that he's talking about versus who
>   are the few? when he's talking democracy what's the
45   difference. many or few. how does that relate? (2.0)
>   **EUG:** the rich are rulers
>   **T/B:** pardon?
>   **EUG:** the rich- rich people are the rulers
>   **T/B:** rich people have the rule? okay. as opposed to what?

50   what is a democracy out here?
      FST: every- everyone votes.
      T/B: everyone, everyone votes. we all have equal say in
      things. so is this room a democracy or is this room being
      ruled by the few?
55   **FST:** is this what?
      T/B: is this room a democracy or is this room ru:led by
      the few?
      MRC: ruled by the few.
      EUG: ruled by the few.
60   **T/B:** Eugene is right on target these last ten minutes here.
      T/S: oh yeah.
      T/B: this is not a democracy. [2 unintelligible syllables]
      (hh) you don't get to vote (hh) about whether, whether
      you're going to do an assignment or not.
65   **T/S:** it makes for benevolent despotism.

As they continued to pursue this analogy between the classroom and society while discussing the loyalty/resistance theme in the spring, teachers and students both explicitly referred to and implicitly presupposed the hierarchical relationship between teachers and students. The second curricular theme thus provided new categories that became available to identify students and teachers. The analogy between power relations in society and hierarchical relations in the classroom allowed overlap between emerging models of the curriculum and emerging metapragmatic models used to identify students.

As analyzed in Chapter 5, Maurice's identity was most heavily influenced by categories drawn from the second curricular theme. His identity as both a boy and a good student allowed him to be an example of the tensions between resistance against and loyalty to the teachers. But Tyisha's identity also intersected with the second curricular theme to some extent. Like someone who resists authority, Tyisha sometimes tried to undermine the teachers' agenda for the classroom. While discussing the analogy between resistant students in the class and legitimate resistance in society, teachers and students occasionally discussed whether Tyisha should have resisted authority as she did. Sometimes, they identified Tyisha as a legitimate dissenter. Thus her local identity shifted again, away from being a disruptive outcast.

From Disruptive to Skeptical

The classroom "society" that Mrs. Bailey and Mr. Smith hoped to create was one that encouraged reasoned dissent. They believed that students should actively formulate and defend their own arguments, and they often acted on these beliefs by giving Tyisha and others significant freedom to disagree. They gave Tyisha more latitude to express her opinions than most teachers would have. But in January and February, when her identity as a disruptive outcast thickened, the teachers often anticipated that her comments would be disruptive and quickly closed off her contributions. In the spring, however, as Tyisha's identity began to shift again, the teachers sometimes evaluated Tyisha's vigorous defense of her own position as legitimate resistance to authority. She did not lose her identity as a disruptive student. Teachers and students still identified her this way some of the time. But Tyisha developed another local identity as a student who sometimes offered reasoned dissent.

This new local identity emerged most vividly in two participant examples. The first was discussed on February 22, during the class' second seminar on Pericles' *Funeral Oration*. Pericles eulogizes Athenians who have been killed in battle with the Spartans, praising them for defending the democratic Athenian system against the repressive Spartans. Unlike the Athenians, Spartan citizens were raised to be warriors, and their individual freedoms were severely limited so that their city could be powerful. At age seven, for instance, they moved to group dormitories and began their military training. While discussing Pericles' text, the teachers and some students construe the Spartans as a powerful oppressive force moving toward the Athenians, whom they present as victims.

The teachers' initial question on February 22 was why an Athenian citizen would agree to fight against such an overwhelming enemy as Sparta. In order to address this question, Mrs. Bailey gives a participant example that includes both Tyisha and herself.

75   **T/B:** let, let, let me toss out just an example to see where
         we get with it. um, Tyisha, you've got a pen in your hand,
         right? okay, I come up to you with a gun and say give me
         your pen. what are you going to do?
         TYI: give it to you.
80   **T/B:** okay. I come up to you with a gun and you are, you
         are at home with your family and your baby sister, and all
         of that kind of stuff and I'm standing outside your door with
         a gun. do you open it and say, come on in. take my,
         take my family, kill us, if you will?
85   **TYI:** no, I leave you out there.
         T/B: okay. now, what- what's the difference between not
         wanting to fight about your pen and maybe being willing to
         take action against someone who wants to come in and kill
         your family? (3.0) what's the difference?
90   **FST:** [4 unintelligible syllables]

TYI: I don't have a choice when you came to me with the gun, sticking it right up to my head. I mean, my life is more important than a little pen.

T/B: okay. your life is more important than a pen. is your

95   life more important than your family?

TYI: myself. I would give up my life for my family, yeah, but.

T/B: why?

TYI: because I love 'em. not all of my family, but some of

100   'em.

STS: [2 seconds of laughter]

Mrs. Bailey introduces an example at lines 75–78, casting herself as a robber and Tyisha as her victim. Tyisha is analogous to an Athenian: just as Sparta attacked Athens, Mrs. Bailey is hypothetically attacking Tyisha. Mrs. Bailey elaborates the example at lines 80–84. Tyisha then says that she would defend things she really valued – thus behaving as many Athenians did.

    A few moments later in the discussion, Tyisha returns briefly to this example.

155   **TYI:** I was saying if you love, I mean, I feel he's saying that if you really keep what you have, your privileges that the Spartans do not have, then fight for 'em. at least that's what I think he's saying. if you want to keep 'em, you should fight for it. just like if I want to keep my

160   family, I'd die for 'em, so, if they want to keep their privileges, for other people like their kids then maybe they had to go die and fight for it.

By returning to the example and connecting it to the text, Tyisha makes clear that she understands the point.

    This brief participant example, and the picture of Athenian citizens that Mrs. Bailey paints in surrounding discussion, continues the consistently positive evaluation of Athens that was described in Chapter 3. Athenian citizens valiantly defended their city because it was a model society. But why did Mrs. Bailey choose Tyisha for her participant example here? Are there any categories that can be used to describe Tyisha's own identity that also apply to the hypothetical Athenians? As the discussion proceeds, it becomes clear that there are. Like her character in this brief participant example, Tyisha sees herself as a victim. In the classroom she gets singled out and becomes a victim of the teachers, and she resists this treatment. As they continue discussing Pericles' text, this other potential identity becomes available for Tyisha.

    Tyisha's identification of herself as a victim becomes clearer in a second participant example given on February 22. The topic has shifted to other virtues of the Athenian system. Several students, including Tyisha, claim that Athenians treated their slaves more humanely than the Spartans did. Because many of these students associate slavery with the experiences of their African American ancestors, and because of the analogy teachers and students have been building between the United States and Athens, several students make inferences about Athenian slavery with respect to American slavery. I explore this in some detail, for two reasons. First, this discussion of slavery leads into the subsequent discussion on February 22, in which Tyisha is identified as a legitimate dissenter for the first time. Second, students' identities as the descendants of slaves become important to classroom discussion of the second curricular theme, and the analysis here provides important background for Chapter 5.

700   **TYI:** that um, I got something about their <u>slaves</u>. they gave
       them a <u>chance</u> to be citizens.
       MRC: who?
       CAN: the Athenians did, not the Spartans.
       T/B: [5 unintelligible syllables] the Spartans [6
705   unintelligible syllables]
       T/S: okay.
       NAT: and another one is that, like, if they saw that you
       were like, had some kind of a <u>talent</u>, at being excellent at
       something, you were <u>recognized</u> in Athens. but in, but in
710   Sparta, like, when slaves, if they, if they were smart or
       something, they could kill 'em or something, but Athens
       they used them, you know-
       TYI: so they noticed their [1 unintelligible syllable]
       CAN: right. where the Spartans would just kill 'em.
715   **T/S:** didn't the Athenians <u>mistreat</u> their slaves?
       FST: what?
       FST: no.
       FST: say it again.
       NAT: all they <u>did</u> was they <u>just</u> had their <u>labor</u>. just let
720   them work.
       FST: I really didn't hear him.
       T/S: if I made you work in the <u>silver</u> mines from <u>morning</u>
       until <u>night</u>, wouldn't you be <u>worse</u> treated than if I made
       you serve my <u>tea</u> and <u>crumpets</u> (1.0) during the day?

Tyisha, Candace and Natasha argue that Athenians were humane to their slaves. At lines 700–701, Tyisha claims that they allowed slaves to become citizens. She may be inferring from the analogy between the contemporary United States and Athens. In the United States, African American slaves were eventually freed and made citizens who were able to participate in civic life. If Athens is like the United States, then they may have freed

slaves too. Although this may have been a sensible inference, given the
analogy, her claim is false. Athenian slaves might have been treated better
than slaves in Sparta, but they remained enslaved.

The teachers face a pedagogical challenge here. They want to correct students' misunderstanding, but they also want to sustain students' interest
in this topic. Mr. Smith tries to capture students' interest by following up
the implicit analogy between the students' own experiences in the United
States and slaves' experiences in Athens. At line 722, he begins another participant example that connects students themselves to the curricular topic.
He imagines that he is a slave owner and that some unnamed student(s)
are slaves. They continue to discuss this example, and eventually Tyisha
nominates herself as a hypothetical slave. Right before the following segment, Ivory has said that she would not want to live in Sparta because of
the military discipline.

> T/B: okay. she's saying she wouldn't want to live in a
> society where at seven they take you away and make you a
> 745   soldier, okay. and, but, what's wrong with Athens, though?
> they've got all these luxuries, and they've got all these neat
> things, and they've got a democracy. and.
> T/S: they appreciate beauty and jewelry and ornamentation,
> clothing, and things like that.
> 750   FST: only if you're a white girl.
> FST: material things.
> . . .
>
> T/B: okay, but what else? what's wrong with Athens?
> 770   IVR: they had slaves.
> FST: doesn't every place have slaves?
> T/B: does that bother you, Ivory- this idea that you'd own
> slaves or maybe be one?
> FST: yeah, it should bother you.
> 775   TYI: if I was a slave, I would rather go to [2 unintelligible
> syllables] before I would go work for the Dorians.
> T/B: we can't hear you.
> TYI: I'd rather go here than to Sparta because at least I got
> a chance to work and maybe have some kind of,
> 780   freedom.

At lines 745–749, the teachers continue to characterize Athens positively,
as teachers and students have been doing for several classes. But at line 750
a student disagrees, apparently claiming that only whites would enjoy the
benefits of Athenian society. This student's point presupposes the emerging analogy between Athens and the United States. In America, resources
and status are disproportionately allocated: African Americans used to be
enslaved, and white people continue to receive more than their fair share

of resources. By analogy, the student seems to be arguing at line 750 that perhaps only certain kinds of people in Athens had access to the benefits of the society. This was of course the case. Athenian slaves and women, for example, did not enjoy the benefits of citizenship.

Mrs. Bailey follows up at line 769, asking what was wrong with Athens and Ivory responds that they had slaves, making the assumption that any society with slaves is undesirable. Mrs. Bailey then asks whether that would bother her, and the teacher brings the Athenian situation closer to Ivory herself by saying, "This idea that you'd own slaves or maybe be one" (lines 771–772). As everyone in the class knows, many of Ivory's ancestors – as well as ancestors of most of the students in the room – were slaves in the United States. So, because of the developing analogy between Athens and the United States, and because teachers and students are using categories from students' own experience to build cognitive models of the subject matter, Mrs. Bailey has made the students' own racial identities salient in the discussion of Athens. Are these black students analogous to Athenian slaves in any way? What implications might that have for understanding Athens and for students' own identities in the classroom?

At line 775, Tyisha offers herself as an example through which these questions might be addressed. Note that she uses the proximal deictic "here" in line 778 to describe Athens – by using this word she acts as if Athens and its more desirable political system are closer to the United States and to the classroom itself. At this point Mr. Smith recognizes the analogy that students are using, and he responds by criticizing them for assuming that all slaves are black.

> T/S: can I ask a strange question? I think it comes up again
> in many other readings. do you assume that the minute the
> word slave is written, it means only blacks?
> STS: no.
785 ERK: I mean, it's like, I don't think.
> T/S: huh?
> ERK: weren't there black people back then?
> T/S: yeah, well suppose you visited Athens. what might
> you visit Athens other than being, let's say an African,
790 which would be the only black state.
> FST: I thought that Athens was [2 unintelligible syllables]
> T/S: could you be a visitor? could you be a visitor from a
> far off land?
> STS: yeah.
795 T/S: what would happen to you as a- as a black visitor?
> you'd be
> JAS: in where?
> T/S: made a- in Athens, or in Sparta.

JAS: they would consider everybody else [4 unintelligible syllables]

800 **TYI:** they'd think, they would kill me because I came. I'm different probably and they don't want no one to be different than them.

T/S: whoa.

TYI: they'd be curious.

805 **T/B:** she's saying something that contradicts the reading.

T/S: yeah.

T/B: find it and help her understand it. this is where your responsibility as students comes in. when somebody says, hey, if I go into Athens and I'm, I'm from Africa, I'm

810 going to be killed. find something that says that she's wrong.

Mr. Smith prefaces his question at line 781 by calling it "strange." The question is not academically strange or irrelevant because he makes clear that he believes the students are misunderstanding Athenian slavery. It might be "strange" interactionally, with Mr. Smith recognizing that race is an awkward topic in mixed-race conversations like this one.

At line 788, Mr. Smith gives a participant example, imagining that one or more black students were visiting Athens. Although this shifts the students from being hypothetical Athenian slaves to hypothetical African visitors, it continues to make their identity as African Americans relevant. Mr. Smith's point here is to show the limitations of students' U.S.-based conception of race. Despite the American linkage between slavery and race, at other places and times black people have been honored visitors and white people have been enslaved. However, despite his explicit point about Athens being different from the United States, his participant example continues to presuppose categories from students' experience. The students experience an unjust distribution of rights and resources as African Americans in the contemporary United States. By singling them out as black people in the participant example, he makes this aspect of their identity salient. And students' identities as African Americans continue to be relevant in what follows.

Tyisha steps into the participant example at lines 800–802 and claims that the Athenians did not like people different from them and would kill her because of her black skin. She is probably inferring from her knowledge about Americans' maintenance of racial boundaries. Earlier, the analogy between Athens and the United States led students to infer positive things about Athenian society. But here the analogy leads Tyisha to infer something negative: Americans are often racist, and if Athens is like America then Athenians might have been racist too. The teachers respond by interactionally turning away from Tyisha, making her an object of discussion by calling her "she" and "somebody" (at lines 805–811). They characterize her as lacking understanding, failing to read carefully and needing help from other students. This echoes the identity they have attributed Tyisha over the past two months, as a student who is often wrong and may be disrupting the class.

Tyisha's claim about Athens is wrong, of course. Athenians did not summarily kill African visitors, but in a deeper sense she has a point. If we read her objection not as a claim about how Athenians treated Africans in particular but as a claim about the analogy between Athens and the United States, it may make sense. The teachers and some students have claimed (on February 7, as described in Chapter 3, and in other classes) that Athens represents a golden mean between the extremes of Rand's individualism and Spartan socialism, and that contemporary U.S. society is itself close to this golden mean. Without articulating it clearly, Tyisha may be pointing out that neither Athens nor the contemporary United States is an ideal society. In both places, certain groups of people do not have access to resources. If she were making this point, Tyisha would be using the analogy between Athens and the United States as the teachers intended. She would be using her own experience with inequality in America to speculate about inequality in Athens.

As described above, teachers and students sometimes went beyond an analogy between Athens and the United States to presuppose an analogy between Athens and the classroom itself. As in Athens, the classroom both allowed individual freedom of opinion and demanded that students sacrifice for the common good. If Tyisha's new version of the analogy were to hold, then there should be differential access to resources in the classroom itself. There were in fact at least two salient ways in which people in the classroom did experience social hierarchy. The teachers had power over the students. And, with respect to schooling and other opportunities, the African American students suffered discrimination because of their race.

Although teachers and students had not explicitly discussed racial inequalities in the United States, their discussion of slavery primed them to be sensitive to issues of race and inequality. The "William the slave" example analyzed in Chapter 2 showed that students' identities as African Americans sometimes became salient and influenced classroom interactions. In that case, despite William's well-established identity as an unpromising boy, African American students refused to go along with the teachers' example of him as a slave. For legitimate reasons, slavery was a sensitive topic for them, and they would not accept the teachers' example of William as a slave. Something similar may be happening on February 22. Tyisha leads the criticism of Athenian slavery. In the process she gets her historical facts wrong. Given her established identity as a disruptive outcast, we would expect teachers and students to criticize and dismiss her. Mr. Smith does this, but we will see that the students do not let him organize the interaction as just another criticism of Tyisha.

As the discussion proceeds, Mr. Smith continues his criticism of "some" students who assume that all slaves are black. In doing so he continues to make the African Americans' shared racial identity salient. And he also positions himself as a knowledgeable teacher who will correct the students' misperceptions. At the beginning of this next segment Erika reads the passage that Mr. Smith has asked for, which shows that Tyisha's claim was wrong.

> **ERK:** it says, our city is thrown open to the world and we never expel a foreigner or prevent him from seeing or
> 830 learning anything of which the secret if revealed to an enemy might profit. that's why I was saying that I don't think just because they would be black they would be slaves.
> **T/S:** yeah, I, I have found this come up Mrs. Bailey, a
> 835 couple of times when we've covered slaves. some of you are carrying your own luggage (hh) into the reading. you say, you think to yourself, I'm black. I'm an African American. I'm descendents of slaves, therefore, any time the word slave is mentioned, it has to be black.
> 840 **FST:** no. I don't think that. [echoed by other students]
> **T/S:** but you're doing that, but you're doing that.
> **CAN:** let me talk, but, Africa, Africa had slaves=
> **T/S:**   [go:od.
> **CAN:** =[I mean of their own kind. I know that already.
> 845 **TYI:** I know we had slaves too.
> **CAN:** I mean, a long time ago they used to have servants and peasants and slaves. I know all that.
> **T/S:** okay, I know. numbers of you have been doing this. this isn't the first time. that maybe as you read the word
> 850 slave, you somehow think they're talking about you a:nd remember, like you said, you did it, you pointed to that board and said, see, they're all white. they're not black. blacks must be slaves.
> **TYI:** no, I didn't say that.
> 855 **T/S:** but that's what you did.
> **TYI:** no I did not. and why you putting words in my mouth?
> **T/S:** okay, okay, I apologize. but I did want you to understand that when you talked about the word slave
> 860 doesn't mean it's always black people.

At lines 828–833, Erika reads the passage she has found in response to Mr. Smith's request for evidence that contradicts Tyisha's claim about Athenians killing African visitors. Then at lines 834–839, Mr. Smith reiterates his claim that the students assume all slaves are black. He does so by speaking directly to Mrs. Bailey and contrasting the teachers' "we" to the mistaken students "you." He explicitly describes these mistaken students as African American. Furthermore, he says that these black students are carrying "luggage" (line 836). This is apparently a variant of the idiom "carrying baggage," which is often used to describe people who manifest past trauma by bringing their own issues into other settings. The black students, he implies, make the mistake of assuming all slaves are black because they are bringing their own people's history into other contexts. In addition to telling them they are wrong, then, Mr. Smith also positions them as African Americans who are fixated too much on their own history.

Not surprisingly, several black students react angrily. Candace, who is vocal but normally polite, says, "let me talk" at line 842. Several other students say that they know perfectly well that slaves can be white and slave owners can be black. Tyisha concurs, referring to people of African descent as "we" at line 845. By using "we," Tyisha adopts the same distinction that Mr. Smith has used, identifying herself as an African American separate from whites like the teachers. Note how this shifts the interactional terrain. Mr. Smith might have been identifying Tyisha as the familiar hasty, disruptive student who has done it again by making things up about Athens. This would have established a familiar interactional organization for the classroom, with Tyisha as an outcast separated from the teachers and the cooperative, promising students. But by discussing slavery and making the students' race salient, Mr. Smith activates a more powerful metapragmatic model. The vocal African American students align themselves with Tyisha and against the white teacher.

As the conversation proceeds, Mr. Smith reinforces this interactional division between himself and the students. He continues to call the students mistaken at lines 848–853 and 855. Then at lines 856–857, Tyisha accuses him of "putting words in my mouth." In the face of the students' anger and legitimate objections, Mr. Smith apologizes at line 858 before going on to presuppose at lines 858–860 that he has nonetheless been right and the students have been wrong.

At this point, Mrs. Bailey steps in and tries to defuse the issue.

> **FST:** how many black people in here.
> **T/B:** I think the problem is that, that, that, with some
> miscommuni<u>ca</u>tion, be<u>cause</u> and I'<u>m</u> guilty of it as <u>you</u> are,
> that when we think of <u>slaves</u>, not that, you know, we
> 865 certainly know and I know you know that blacks were not
> the only slaves that ever were et cetera, but the <u>on</u>ly thing

that we really know a whole lot about slaves is from our
American experience. and so: we tend to try to put that
into place. so that might lead Mr. Smith to think that you
870 didn't know what you know.
FST: I read that book.
T/B: I know that you know that only blacks weren't slaves.
but somehow the institution of slavery and the way it was
carried out in other cultures, and at other times, we're not
875 that- that well versed in it. I mean, I don't know a lot about
it which would lead me to suspect that you probably don't
know a whole lot about it either and so we go back to
our American lives sometimes.

At line 864 Mrs. Bailey uses "we" to refer to herself and the students
together, and at lines 867–868 she refers to "our American experience,"
one presumably shared by whites and blacks alike. She also acknowledges
that she too makes mistakes. Thus she tries to overcome the interactional
split between teachers and students, and between black people and white
people, that Mr. Smith has established in this discussion.

Mrs. Bailey's comments placate the students somewhat. But the discussion of slavery has nonetheless opened up another possible identity for
Tyisha. As she has consistently done over the year, she actively contests
the teachers' opinions on February 22 – she defends unpopular positions
and readily identifies herself with slaves and other marginal people. Mr.
Smith reacts to her as the teachers have reacted since December, identifying
her as a student who is getting the wrong answer and disrupting the class.
But then a new curricular topic complicates the classroom interaction. In
Athens, it turns out, there were slaves – a group of people who did not
enjoy the benefits of the society and who thus might have had grounds
to resist authority. In the classroom, Mr. Smith's comments make salient
two types of disempowered people who might be analogous to Athenian
slaves: students who must obey the teacher and African Americans who
still suffer discrimination. This opens up a possible alternative identity for
Tyisha. Instead of being a disruptive outcast, perhaps she speaks up for the
unjustly disempowered and resists illegitimate authority in the classroom.

At this point in the discussion on February 22, of course, Tyisha is only
potentially a legitimate dissenter. Because of students' reaction to Mr. Smith
and the topic of slavery, Tyisha has at least for the moment been interactionally realigned – as a member of the students' group, opposed to Mr. Smith.
This makes possible the more robust re-identification of Tyisha later in the
class session. As discussion proceeds, Mrs. Bailey goes on to characterize
Tyisha, not as a disruptive outcast, but as a valued skeptic.

Throughout this class, and several others later in the year, Tyisha often
argues that people are "being tricked." Athenians, she had argued at the

beginning of this discussion on February 22, were tricked into becoming soldiers: "I just think that they're fooling them in some kind of way" (lines 49–50). Immediately following the discussion of slavery, she argues that the students themselves have been tricked by the teachers and the assigned texts, which are probably false. Thus she positions herself as a skeptic who will defend other students against the teachers' misinformation.

890 **TYI:** all this stuff is probably phony.
    T/B: all of this stuff is phony. you've been in a class now for the last seven months where you've been receiving phony information.
    TYI: and nobody cannot tell me, prove it to me that this.
895 is true. so I just listen and talk, just like I believe it.
    T/B: well, you know, I think that's a good point. I think that you should question. what would be the evidence that this might be true?
    TYI: that it's just in Greece.
900 **T/B:** you don't think there was a Greece?
    TYI: yeah, I do believe that. we found it on the map, but when we go there we gonna see different, totally different stuff. I don't know, I just don't believe it.
    T/B: okay, you don't think there are any documents from
905 the period? you don't think there are any things that- that have been left around from like when Athens was in its glory?
    TYI: some people probably went to Athens and made up the story.

At line 890, Tyisha claims that the information in the curriculum is "probably phony." She refuses to believe it, although she pretends that she does in order to get by in class. Given the teachers' reactions to Tyisha over the past two months, we might expect that Tyisha's challenge would generate a hostile or dismissive response. But, after initially being sarcastic at lines 891–893, Mrs. Bailey praises Tyisha for "questioning" at lines 896–897. This is one of the highest values in the teachers' pedagogical philosophy. One must continually question, as Socrates did. So Mrs. Bailey's comment seems to be uncharacteristic praise for Tyisha. Just this one segment by itself did not change Tyisha's habitual identity. We will need evidence from later in this discussion and subsequent classes in order to assess the significance of Mrs. Bailey's comments. But February 22 may be a turning point in Tyisha's trajectory of identification, if she shifts from disruptive outcast to reasonable skeptic.

    Mrs. Bailey follows up Tyisha's challenge with a discussion of evidence and skepticism in history. The teachers have students look through another text they have just read for evidence that might contradict Pericles' description of Athens. In this way they model historians' methods for the students. They also show how Tyisha's position as a skeptic is integral to the practice of historical interpretation. Mrs. Bailey then summarizes their discussion.

> **T/B:** . . . and, certainly, in your class, you've gone back
> five thousand years ago. where are these documents? how
> 1070 do we know that they're real, and they just weren't made up
> by somebody who wanted to lie? and those are questions
> that historians deal with? and you know what a cynic Mr.
> Smith is and can you imagine an enti:re community full of
> Mr. Smiths who are going around trying to make a name
> 1075 for themselves by saying this is false. okay, people like you
> that go, I don't believe this. I'm going to go and find out
> that it was false and spend the rest of my life proving this
> wasn't false. and there have been millions of people,
> thousands of people, certainly hundreds of thousands of
> 1080 people, that have engaged in that kind of inquiry. so I, I
> appreciate your skepticism. I think, I think it's right. I think
> that you need to sometimes say, where is this information
> coming from? but I'd also like you to recognize that you're
> not the first person to have those questions and that there are
> 1085 people who have devoted their lives to authenticating, to
> saying this is really real or did somebody make it up? okay.
> is it time to go yet? you want to pull this together wherever
> you are at the moment. I really like this question. it's very
> good.

At lines 1069–1071, Mrs. Bailey echoes Tyisha's question, and at lines 1071–1072 she makes clear that professional historians ask questions similar to Tyisha's. There is an interlude from lines 1072–1078 where she paints a somewhat unflattering picture of Mr. Smith. But at line 1081, she "appreciates" Tyisha's "skepticism," and at lines 1088–1089 she again praises Tyisha's question. Mrs. Bailey thus identifies Tyisha as an independent thinker and a valued dissenter. People need someone to dissent on their behalf, and Tyisha willingly adopts that role. In this discussion on February 22, then, Tyisha may be changing from a disruptive outcast into a reasoned skeptic.

This new social identity for Tyisha, which did recur in subsequent classes, was made possible by a new metapragmatic model of the classroom itself. In their discussions of the first curricular theme, the teachers favored a metapragmatic model of the classroom that involved a golden mean between individual freedom and sacrifice for the common good. As in an idealized Athenian democracy, teachers and students agreed to focus on common topics and follow classroom rules for the good of the group. But they also allowed individuals to develop their own opinions within this framework. In this model of the classroom, Tyisha's rigorous defense of her own opinions left her as a disruptive outcast. But their February 22 discussion of race and slavery made another metapragmatic model of the classroom salient – the powerful white teachers were in some way opposed to the black students. This made another category available for identifying Tyisha. For the first time on February 22, teachers characterized Tyisha's identity as a dissenter positively, identifying her as a reasoned skeptic. At this point Tyisha's new identity was only provisional and might not have been presupposed by teachers in subsequent classes. As the spring went on, however, legitimate resistance to authority became a central topic in the curriculum. So the new metapragmatic model that identified Tyisha as a legitimate dissenter became more robust as the class developed an overlapping cognitive model that included the category of legitimate resistance to authority. This metapragmatic/cognitive model of Tyisha as a legitimate dissenter did take hold in some classes, even though it was never established as firmly as her disruptive outcast identity. In the spring she sometimes continued to be a disruptive outcast as well.

Resisting Exploitation

Tyisha's dissent was also framed as legitimate resistance on April 12, when teachers and students juxtaposed Tyisha's identity as a dissenter with a protagonist who analogously refused to go along with authority. The class had read a story, John Steinbeck's "The Pearl," in which a poor Native American named Quino finds a pearl. He brings it to the Europeans who dominate the local town and they offer him 1,000 pesos for it. Because he knows that the pearl is worth much more, and because Europeans have often cheated the Indians, Quino refuses their offer and makes a perilous journey to get a fair price. Given the theme of loyalty and resistance that the students and teachers have been discussing, students take Quino to represent people who have been exploited and the Europeans to represent unjust rulers. The central question for the seminar is whether Quino should have sold the pearl to the Europeans. Should he have been content with his station in life, or should he have resisted the Europeans' attempt to exploit him?

Early in the discussion, Tyisha and Maurice both enter the class late. Mrs. Bailey greets them as follows.

> **T/B:** okay, ahh, for the benefit of Tyisha and Maurice, so
> we don't shh, so we don't have to cover all the same
> 1015   ground since they came in late. we have already
> established the fact that there is a history of being cheated.

Mrs. Bailey says in line 1013 that she is acting for Tyisha and Maurice's "benefit." In lines 1014–1015 she points out that she is also acting on behalf of the whole class. But she opposes the rest of the class, which she refers to as "we," to Tyisha and Maurice ("they") who came in late and disrupted the class. Our two "beasts," then, start this class as outcasts.

Tyisha continues in this marginal position later in the discussion when she offers an example. A student has asked how Quino knows his pearl is worth more than 1,000 pesos. Tyisha responds with an unclear analogy to Nike Air Jordan basketball shoes.

> **TYI:** it's just like these <u>Nike</u>'s that out- that's out. <u>people</u>
> want it <u>now</u> cause they <u>think</u> they <u>J</u>ordan.
> 1075 **MRC:** (hh)
> **TYI:** but when he got on tv, and <u>said</u>, they not <u>real</u>. they
> got mad, you know they <u>not</u> real, but you know he's like
> they not bad. <u>people</u> <u>stop</u> <u>buy</u>ing them.
> ...
> 1090 **T/B:** whoa, whoa, whoa, I, I, I <u>lost</u> the con<u>nec</u>tion to the
> <u>pearl</u> here.
> **STS:** (hhh)
> **T/B:** per<u>haps</u> you could make the con<u>nec</u>tion be<u>tween</u>-
> **TYI:** just like people see this <u>pearl</u> and they think it's
> 1095 <u>real</u> so they willing to spend <u>money</u> on it.
> **FST:** yeah, like the [<u>gym</u> shoes.
> **JAS:**   [yeah, like my shoes.
> **T/B:** oh, so you're making the con<u>nec</u>tion, your con<u>nec</u>tion
> here is a repercussion to what Ger<u>maine</u> said. that
> 1100 Ger<u>maine</u> was saying, <u>hey</u>, he knows it's <u>worth</u> something
> because everybody <u>else</u> seems to think it's <u>worth</u>
> something[and=
> **TYI:**   [right
> **T/B:** =you're saying <u>people</u> can <u>ha:ve</u>, <u>all</u> be
> 1105 deceived. is that what I'm hearing Tyisha?
> **TYI:** yeah sure.
> **FST:** (hh)
> **T/B:** so you're re<u>scind</u>ing what Ger<u>maine</u> said.
> **TYI:** no I'm agreeing with her.
> 1110 **T/B:** <u>no</u>. you're dis<u>agree</u>ing with Germaine.
> **TYI:** what'd she say?
> **FST:** the opposite of what <u>she's</u> saying.
> **TYI:** oh, my <u>fault</u>. I'm disagreeing with her.
> **STS:** [3 seconds of laughter]
> 1115 **T/B:** you have to start relating your points di<u>rect</u>ly so we
> all follow your <u>think</u>ing.

The analogy between Tyisha's account of fake Jordan shoes (at lines 1073–1078) and Quino's pearl is not clear, as Mrs. Bailey points out at lines 1090–1091. Tyisha tries to clarify at lines 1094–1095. But because Quino's pearl was real, the analogy apparently does not hold.

Mrs. Bailey tries to articulate Tyisha's point such that it makes some sense at lines 1098–1105. But Tyisha's response at line 1106 sounds sarcastic – as if she does not really care what she was trying to say. The student laughter at line 1107 seems to support this interpretation of Tyisha's comment. At line 1111, Tyisha then acknowledges that she was not following the earlier discussion. And at line 1113 she makes a joke, seeming to indicate again that she does not really care about the topic. Mrs. Bailey responds to this oppositional behavior with a comment at lines 1115–1116 that echoes other characterizations she has made about Tyisha's disruptive comments. Mrs. Bailey distinguishes between Tyisha ("you") and the rest of the class ("we"). Tyisha is again a disruptive student who does not care enough to contribute constructively to class discussion.

As the class proceeds, however, they discuss the curricular theme of resistance against authority by talking about African Americans' experience with Jim Crow laws. As it did on February 22, the topic of race again opens up the identity of legitimate dissenter for Tyisha. As this part of the discussion begins, Tyisha argues vigorously that Quino should not have sold the pearl to the Europeans, while several other students argue that he should have sold it and not been greedy. Because she habitually defends the disempowered, it makes sense that Tyisha would take this side. Mrs. Bailey makes the argument more relevant to students' own identities by giving a participant example. She imagines that the students are facing oppression like Quino, and she asks whether they would resist it. The specific topic concerns education. In the story, Quino wants to get more money for the pearl in order to buy medicine for his child. In the example, African American students must decide whether to tolerate a "separate but equal" Jim Crow education or whether to demand a more adequate education.

>   **T/B:** okay, I, I, ex<u>cuse</u> me, I'm a <u>southern</u> state. a:nd uh,
> 1180 I'll give you an <u>e</u>ducation <u>J</u>asmine. I'll give you an
>   education in that building over <u>there</u>, with all these kids
>   <u>crammed</u> in, with textbooks that are fifty years <u>old</u>. o:r
>   (1.0) you can take a chance. and you can stand <u>up</u> to the
>   power <u>structure</u>. and maybe even pull your kids out of
> 1185 school and <u>boycott</u> <u>schools</u> for a <u>while</u>. and maybe not get
>   any education at all for a while because you want a <u>real</u>
>   education and not this Jim <u>Crow</u> education.
>   **FST:** right.
>   **T/B:** what do you do?
> 1190 **FST:** you stand <u>up</u> for what you be<u>lieve</u> in.

T/B: you <u>take</u> what you can g<u>et</u>? <u>or</u> do you go after what
is <u>really</u> what you <u>want</u>?
STS: [3 seconds of chatter]
TYI: because, if he had been <u>poor</u> for this <u>long</u>, and he had
1195   a chance to be <u>happy</u> with his <u>life</u>, why don't <u>give</u> it to
someone you know that's not gonna be satisfied as you?
JAS: but, but in, in the long run, wait a minute, in the long
run you <u>might</u> not even get <u>no</u>thing, so you <u>just</u> gonna <u>sit</u>
there.
1200   **TYI:** I'd <u>ra</u>ther go try, then just sit there and say this is
about sitting down. I- I think I could have got <u>more</u> than
<u>that</u>. I'm not gonna sit there <u>no</u> longer, I'm gonna go out
and <u>search</u> for some <u>mo</u>ney. <u>I</u>'m not gonna <u>be</u> like that.
. . .

1230   **T/B:**   . . . for it is said that
humans are <u>never</u> satisfied, that you <u>give</u> them <u>one</u> thing
and they <u>want</u> something <u>more</u>. and this is said in
dis<u>pa</u>ragement? °that means <u>put</u> down, kind of [5
unintelligible syllables]° <u>whereas</u> it is one of the greatest
1235   talents the species <u>has</u> and one that made it <u>superior</u> to the
<u>a</u>nimals that are satisfied with what they have. that <u>Ja</u>smine
who's telling us should be <u>satisfied</u> with what you <u>have</u>,
we've got <u>Ty</u>isha <u>say</u>ing <u>hey</u>, go for <u>it</u>. <u>now</u>. <u>this</u> a<u>gain</u>
we're <u>circling</u> around, do <u>we</u>? are we to be <u>content</u> with
1240   what we have or should we go <u>af</u>ter other <u>things</u>?

At lines 1200–1203, Tyisha argues that Quino should not have been satisfied
with the Europeans' offer. She imagines herself in such a situation, using
"I," and says that she would not cooperate with the Europeans' attempt
at exploitation. At line 1238, Mrs. Bailey summarizes Tyisha's position as
"go for it." And she uses Tyisha's argument to restate the larger question
about whether people should resist exploitation.

This participant example sets up an analogy between students' identities as African Americans – who have been and in many cases continue to
be denied adequate public education – and Quino's identity as a Native
American exploited by Europeans. Mrs. Bailey clearly makes race relevant at line 1187 when she mentions "Jim Crow." This analogy between
the African American students and Quino participates in a broader analogy, developed over many classes, between the students as disempowered
black people and the "citizens" of the second curricular theme who must
decide whether to remain loyal or resist authority. As we saw in the February 22 discussion of Pericles, this analogy opens up a new metapragmatic
model of the classroom – one in which Tyisha is a full member and a
defender of the African American students' group.

As shown above, analogies like this one can mediate both social identification and academic learning. Teachers and students constructed local
cognitive models to understand the curricular topic of legitimate resistance. Chapter 5 describes these models in more detail, but they included
people in power, the citizenry that is oppressed by those rulers and members of resistance groups who oppose the rulers. In developing this local
cognitive model, teachers and students used categories of identity from
their own experience – like the legitimate resistance to Jim Crow segre-
gation that some of the students' ancestors may have engaged in. Categories of identity from these cognitive models then became available to
amend or construct metapragmatic models they used to identify each other
socially. When participant examples brought the analogy into the classroom and applied cognitive categories to students themselves, the curriculum became a resource for identifying students like Tyisha. At the
same time, students' metapragmatic models of hierarchy and racial identity became a resource that helped them learn the curriculum.

On April 12, this happens when the students think about Quino and
his dilemma, and by extension about the larger curricular theme, with reference to African Americans' struggle for equality. The analogy between
Quino and African Americans facilitates Tyisha's new emerging identity
as a reasoned dissenter and a defender of the disempowered. Those who
worked for equal education during the Civil Rights Movement pursued
a just cause. If Quino is like them, then he should resist exploitation and
stick up for himself. By analogy, in the classroom, Tyisha's regular dissent
against the teachers could also be framed as legitimate resistance. And in
fact, in the discussion on April 12, Mrs. Bailey does end up positioning
Tyisha this way. Earlier in the discussion Tyisha had been labeled as disruptive, but by line 1238, Mrs. Bailey has begun to identify Tyisha as a
student who contributes to the conversation by defending an alternative
point of view.

In lines 1200–1203, Tyisha both articulates and enacts a position of
opposition or resistance. She argues that marginalized people like Quino
should oppose the majority and stand up for themselves. She also defends
her opinion against several others in the class. As we have seen, she
habitually opposes herself to the teachers and other vocal students by
defending unpopular positions. So in this discussion Tyisha enacts what
she recommends that marginalized people should be doing. People like
Quino who stick up for themselves are not greedy, but are justifiably
defending their interests against others who take advantage of them.
Mrs. Bailey's favorable response to Tyisha here endorses Tyisha's position. The teachers value students who vigorously defend themselves with
reasoned arguments, just as Tyisha values Quino's decision to stick up for
himself.

At the end of the seminar on "The Pearl," Erika gives an example that further develops the analogy between students' own racial and socioeconomic positions and the loyalty/resistance theme. She compares Quino's desire to get a fair price to an urban resident's desire to get out of the projects. Here the students continue to develop a local cognitive model of the curricular theme, drawing on their knowledge of and experience as urban residents. By discussing this example intelligently, the students show that they are engaging with the curricular theme and that the analogy between their own experience and the curriculum facilitates their reasoning.

> **JAS:** okay, if he wasn't greedy, then he would of. okay.
> like at the beginning of the book he was happy and
> whatever without the money, and if he wasn't greedy he
> would've remai:ned the sa:me as he was in the beginning of
> 1475 the book.
> **ERK:** if you were a:ll in the projects, and you had the
> chance to get out, you would not just settle for that.
> **STS:** [2 seconds of yelling]
> **T/B:** okay, Erika. let Erika explore this point a bit.
> 1480 go on and say, everybody listen, Germaine, shh.
> **ERK:** if you're in the projects you know you gonna try
> and get out, nobody [wants to live.
> **JAS:**   [maybe he likes it in the projects, girl.
> **ERK:** nothing's wrong with having the chance to get out
> 1485 to make a better life for yourself and your family, you
> should do whatever it takes to get out of the projects.

Erika begins her example at line 1476. People living in urban housing projects often experience unpleasant conditions and must decide whether to fight to get out, just as Quino had to decide whether to fight for a fair price for his pearl.

This example makes available concepts from the students' own experience to understand the text. Just as many people living in the projects have been victimized by an unjust society in the United States, Quino has been victimized by the Europeans. Should they be content with what they have, or should they resist? With this example, Erika draws on categories students use to conceptualize disadvantage in their own lives – like poverty and perhaps race – in order to understand the curriculum. Their discussion of "The Pearl" ends soon afterwards. In subsequent discussions of the second curricular theme, teachers and students elaborated the analogy between students' own identities as disadvantaged people and they developed their understanding of the loyalty/resistance curricular theme. Chapter 5 describes more fully how teachers and students developed this analogy between their own experience and the second curricular theme, while tracing how discussion of that theme facilitated Maurice's identity development.

At the end of the school year, then, Tyisha was sometimes positioned as a legitimate dissenter – as someone who expressed reasonable doubts about majority opinions and stuck up for her point of view. But at other times teachers and students continued to position her as a disruptive outcast. The shift in curricular theme, from individual/society to loyalty/resistance, facilitated the emergence of her new dissenter identity. The second curricular theme was not the only resource that facilitated Tyisha's shift from disruptive outcast to legitimate dissenter. Longer timescale models and the emergent structure of particular events also contributed. Nonetheless, the curricular theme made available the model of legitimate resistance, and as they discussed resistance with respect to students' own experience they developed an overlapping metapragmatic/cognitive model that they sometimes applied to Tyisha and other students' own identities. Tyisha's identity was not, however, central to the class' work on the loyalty/resistance theme. More often, Maurice was the student whose identity meshed with this second theme. Students and teachers used Maurice's experience, drawing especially on metapragmatic models of gender and race relations in the classroom, in order to develop more robust local cognitive models of the second curricular theme.

CONCLUSIONS

Over the academic year Tyisha went from being another promising female student, to being a marginalized and problematic student, to being a disruptive outcast, to sometimes being a reasoned dissenter and sometimes being a disruptive outcast. These shifts in classroom social identity happened despite the fact that her behavior remained relatively consistent across the year – she focused on her own opinions and vigorously defended them. In December, teachers and students began to identify Tyisha's vigorous defense of her own opinions as inappropriate. In January, categories from the first curricular theme helped her identity as a "disruptive outcast" thicken. Tyisha's identity development was accomplished – by her, the teachers and other students – partly using categories made available through the curriculum. As they built local cognitive models of the first curricular theme, these models overlapped systematically with the local metapragmatic models they constructed to identify Tyisha. Then, in the spring, the category of "reasoned dissenter" became available to identify Tyisha when the class started discussing the loyalty/resistance theme.

These categories of disruptive outcast and reasoned dissenter came to identify Tyisha, especially as they were used in participant examples that drew on Tyisha's own experience to illustrate topics from the curriculum.

Participant examples were crucial to the developing analogies between students' experiences and the curriculum. While discussing the first curricular theme, students and teachers increasingly used their own experience with welfare, and then their own classroom interactions, as the source of an analogy with "society." While discussing the second curricular theme, students and teachers used the students' experiences as disempowered African Americans as the source of an analogy with citizens who must choose between loyalty and resistance. Because teachers and students used these analogies both to develop local cognitive models of the curriculum and to develop local metapragmatic models of Tyisha's identity, the participant examples and analogies facilitated systematic overlap between local cognitive and metapragmatic models. Drawing on these joint models, teachers and students first identified Tyisha as a disruptive outcast and months later as a reasoned dissenter. At the same time, students also learned to make arguments about the curricular themes using categories of identity drawn from their own experience. In fact, at least with respect to the first curricular theme and Tyisha's "disruptive outcast" identity, these models co-developed and became joint local metapragmatic/cognitive models.

Teachers and students did not accomplish social identification solely or even primarily through the intervention of local cognitive models, however. Tyisha did not change from normal girl to disruptive outcast just because the curricular category of an outcast became available. Teachers and students drew on many other resources as they identified each other socially. Similarly, teachers and students drew on other resources besides metapragmatic models as they learned the curriculum. As explained in Chapters 2 and 3, social identification and academic learning involve complex interrelations among resources from several timescales. Tyisha's trajectory of identification occurred as it did because of the affordances of the Paideia teaching approach, because of her own ontogenetically developed tendencies to speak out, because of sociohistorically entrenched models of gender and race, and because of other relevant processes. I claim merely that local cognitive models can also play an important role in social identification, and I hope to have shown how metapragmatic/cognitive overlap can happen at the local timescale.

I also hope to have shown how both social identification and academic learning must be studied in context. Sociohistorical categories only take hold in particular contexts. Tyisha, for instance, was not simply a generic "loud black girl." Her identity in this classroom drew on but was not reducible to such stereotypes. Instead it was mediated through local categories of identity that solidified over weeks and months in this classroom and through the emergent organization of particular events. Her identity in this case depended on contingent, emergent actions, models and other resources from several timescales. Similarly, the students' academic learning about collectivism and individualism did not simply involve the internalization of abstract sociohistorical models. Their academic learning only took hold as mediated through local models of curricular themes. In cases like this one, where social identification and academic learning overlap at the local level, analysts must take both processes into account and must not limit themselves to sociohistorical or event-level categories.

5

Maurice in the Middle

This chapter traces Maurice's emerging social identity across the academic year in Mrs. Bailey and Mr. Smith's classroom. Maurice's trajectory of identification resembled Tyisha's in three important ways. First, Maurice's classroom identity also emerged against the background of the local metapragmatic model of promising girls and unpromising boys. Maurice was the only atypical boy with respect to this model. The other boys rarely contributed to class discussion, but Maurice participated actively and successfully throughout the year. Second, despite his gender, Maurice also began the year being treated by teachers and students as a typical promising student. In the first two or three months of the academic year, the teachers and many female students accepted and even praised his regular contributions to class discussion. After a few months, however, the vocal female students and sometimes the teachers began to identify him in a less flattering way – not as the same sort of disruptive outcast that Tyisha became, but as an outcast nevertheless. Third, the local metapragmatic models teachers and students used to identify Maurice also overlapped with their emerging local cognitive models of the two curricular themes. As they did with Tyisha, teachers and students incorporated categories from the curriculum into the local metapragmatic models they used to identify Maurice. Categories from the second curricular theme were more important to Maurice's emerging identity.

In two crucial respects, teachers and students identified Maurice differently than Tyisha. First, his classroom behavior fit with the teachers' expectations for "promising" students: He almost always answered questions willingly, articulated his own arguments about the subject matter and engaged in constructive discussion with the teachers and other students. Because of his constructive behavior and intelligent contributions throughout the year, the teachers did not criticize him as they did Tyisha – although, as described in detail below, they did occasionally force him into uncomfortable interactional positions. Second, Maurice was male.

This mattered in two ways. He could not be just another of the promising vocal students, because all the others were female and gender mattered in this classroom. Maurice's relationship with the vocal girls became increasingly contentious over the year, as both he and they struggled with his locally atypical identity as a promising boy. Maurice's relationship with the other boys was also complex. Especially toward the end of the year, Maurice worked hard to identify himself as masculine while maintaining his status as a good student. Thus Maurice's trajectory of identification was neither exactly like nor diametrically opposed to Tyisha's. Their emerging identities involved some similar shifts and relied on some similar resources, but each trajectory was unique.

After having been treated as just another good student by the teachers and the girls over the first few months, Maurice began to struggle with the vocal girls. In December, the girls began to contradict Maurice and tease him during class discussion. In some cases they treated Maurice in the same way that they treated William – as a typical unpromising male student. Unlike William, however, Maurice fought back vigorously, and he was often supported by the teachers. When the class began discussing the curricular theme of collectivism and individualism in January, Mrs. Bailey and the girls sometimes used curricular categories to identify Maurice. They treated Maurice as an "outcast," and Maurice willingly positioned himself as an individualist – as someone outside the girls' group who nonetheless articulated his own arguments. This involved a partial analogy between the social organization of the classroom and the academic subject matter: The girls were like a society and Maurice was like an outcast from that society. But the analogy between Maurice's emerging social identity and the first curricular theme did not hold in crucial respects. Unlike Tyisha, Maurice was not a disruptive outcast. The teachers welcomed Maurice's contributions and did not identify him as a bad student, although Mrs. Bailey did sometimes join the girls in teasing him. So he was excluded from the girls' group because they sometimes successfully identified him as an unpromising boy. But the teachers, despite their occasional teasing, generally included him in the classroom community. Thus Maurice was not marginalized in the classroom as often or as dramatically as Tyisha was.

When the class began discussing the loyalty/resistance curricular theme, classroom life became more difficult for Maurice. This theme afforded a different analogy between the curriculum and the social organization of the classroom. In several participant examples, teachers and students began to act as if the boys who resisted participating in class were like the political resistance described in the curriculum. In such examples the girls sometimes acted as if they were political loyalists who joined the teachers' side. Maurice fell awkwardly in the middle. He did not want to be one of the girls, and he worked hard to maintain a masculine identity.

But he also wanted to join the teachers and the girls by contributing constructively to classroom discussion. The teachers and the vocal girls made it difficult for Maurice to maintain both of these aspects of his identity. The analyses in this chapter show how this tension in Maurice's local identity emerged and how teachers and students used categories from the curriculum to increase the tension. At the same time, Maurice's predicament became a cognitive resource that students used to reflect on the second curricular theme. His example provided categories that helped them model the theme of loyalty and resistance, as the emerging local metapragmatic model of Maurice's identity overlapped with the emerging local cognitive model of the curriculum.

JUST ANOTHER GOOD STUDENT

Maurice was a fourteen-year-old African American boy who entered Mrs. Bailey and Mr. Smith's class at the beginning of ninth grade and remained throughout the academic year. Like most of his fellow students, Maurice had scored in the third quartile on the citywide test for eighth graders. Like Tyisha and many of his peers, he was verbally skilled and seemed more intelligent than his test scores indicated. Maurice was relatively popular with his fellow students and had a few close friends in the class. He joked and wrestled playfully with his male friends before and after class. He also tried to sit near at least one of the other boys, and he would sometimes talk to them surreptitiously during class. Maurice was physically larger than average, and like William he played on the football team. He was also attractive, and many of the girls flirted with him throughout the year. He was interested in the girls as well, and he flirted, teased, and occasionally fought with them both during and outside of class.

Maurice participated actively in class discussions all year. He was routinely one of the half dozen students most actively contributing to seminar discussions, and he made thoughtful contributions to most classes. For the first three months of the year, both teachers and students identified Maurice as a valued participant. Neither the girls nor the teachers treated him much differently than they did the "promising" vocal female students. In the discussion of creation myths on October 9, for instance, Maurice contributed actively.

> **T/B:** if I asked you where you came from what would you say?
> **MAR:** from my parents.
> 150 **T/B:** from your <u>parents</u>. <u>why</u> would you say from your parents?
> **MAR:** because I know [4 unintelligible syllables]
> **T/B:** because you <u>know</u> something. <u>how</u> does she <u>know</u> that?

155   **FST:** because she learned it.
       T/B: she's <u>learned</u> it. how did she <u>learn</u> it?
       MRC: someone taught her.
       CAN: someone had to <u>teach</u> her.

At line 157, Maurice volunteers an answer, one that elaborates the response given by a female student at line 155. He does not position himself against the girls, as he will do later in the year. And the girls treat Maurice as a valid participant, as illustrated by Candace's echoing of his comment at line 158. Characteristically, Maurice contributes to this discussion along with the girls and they jointly develop answers to the teachers' questions.

As he did all year, on October 9 Maurice also willingly discussed topics that the teachers introduced. The teachers ratified his contributions and treated him as a good student. In the following segment they are discussing why a creation myth compares humans to insects.

280   **T/B:** okay, so in the <u>a</u>nimal kingdom, where do insects <u>fall</u>?
       FST: nowhere.
       MRC: the lowest, the lowest.
       T/B: they're the lowest <u>form</u>, or pretty close to what we
285   would call the lowest <u>form</u>. they're <u>v</u>ery unimportant, aren't
       they? or are they?
       MRC: they aren't.
       T/B: they <u>aren't</u>?
       JAS: some.
290   **MRC:** oh yeah some of the <u>bees</u> are important.
       T/B: bees do what?
       TYI: kill.
       [laughter]
       MRC: some bee pollen, they raise [pollen
295   **T/B:**   [they fertilize

Maurice answers the teacher's questions at lines 282, 287, 290 and 294. And at lines 284–286 and 295, the teacher ratifies Maurice's answers as correct. Note also how Maurice echoes Jasmine's contribution at line 290, supporting and elaborating her point. He and the girls build on each other's points here, as they did in the prior segment, without any hint of opposition between boys and girls.

In the following segment Maurice makes a more complex point in response to the teacher's question.

       T/B: <u>why</u> <u>might</u> the <u>C</u>hinese be<u>lieve</u> or <u>feel</u> that ma:n
       comes from the earth as an insect. that <u>ma:n</u> is <u>s</u>imilar to
       an <u>i</u>nsect?
       CAS: cause we crawl on the earth.

330   **T/B:** pardon?
      CAS: we <u>crawl</u> on the earth like insects.
      T/B: we <u>crawl</u> on the earth like insects.
      MRC: maybe cause um
      FST: [1 unintelligible syllable]
335   **T/B:** shh
      MRC: people, maybe cause um, people, we're <u>born</u>, we
      <u>live</u>, we get <u>old</u>, and then we <u>die</u>.
      T/B: okay, we go through <u>stages</u>, like many insects do. the
      larva stage, the pupa stage, and all of that. it's been a while
340   since I've had biology. o<u>kay</u>, well what else?

After the teacher quiets other students in order to allow him to speak at
line 335, Maurice describes how humans are analogous to insects in at
least one respect. Mrs. Bailey had been pushing for students to offer more
metaphorical interpretations of the myth, and Maurice responds successfully. At lines 338–340, Mrs. Bailey evaluates Maurice's answer positively,
saying "okay" twice and expanding what he said. I am not claiming that
Maurice's argument here is unusually compelling. But these brief examples illustrate how, early in the year, he acted in concert with the girls while
contributing to classroom discussion, and how the girls and the teachers
accepted him as another good student.

Like most students, Maurice also wanted to be acknowledged for his
contributions. On November 2, for instance, Maurice complained "that's
what I said" after someone else repeated a point he had made. This was the
first of several times he made such complaints. In the following segment
they discuss the rights of women as defined by the ancient legal system
described in Hammurabi's Code.

1060 **T/S:** so, in other words, she seems to have the right to
      <u>property</u>, but <u>only</u> when?
      COR: only when her husband [3 unintelligible syllables]
      T/S: so, she has rights, but it's de<u>pend</u>ent on <u>some</u>
      condition, just like the <u>child</u>ren. (7.0)
1065 **FST:** what'd you say, Maurice?
      MRC: [3 unintelligible syllables]
      T/B: okay, the <u>death</u> of her <u>hus</u>band.
      T/S: the <u>death</u> doesn't give her rights.
      MRC: that's what <u>I</u> sa:id.
1070 **T/S:** read it a<u>gain</u>.

Maurice apparently feels that he himself made the point that Mr. Smith
makes at line 1068, and at line 1069 he claims that his authorship of the
point should have been acknowledged.

Something similar happened on February 7 in their discussion of Lycurgus. Because the students do not answer his question in the way he wants, Mr. Smith accuses them of not doing the reading.

> **T/S:** Maurice[what did the Spartans ne[ed.
> **MRC:**   [mmm.   [I don't know.
> **T/S:** didn't you read it?
> 45   **MRC:** yeah
> **T/S:** did they need <u>food</u> [<u>did</u> they need <u>food</u>.
> **STS:**   [yeah yeah
> **FST:** to eat? [9 unintelligible syllables]
> **T/S:** I have a feeling they didn't <u>read</u> this Mrs.
> 50   Bailey.
> **STS:** hahaha I read it. [background [comments]
> **GAR:**   [I- I have a question.
> **T/S:** Gary.
> 55   **GAR:** Maurice- Maurice was <u>right</u> when he said
>   that they had to keep their money at home? cause in
>   the <u>last</u> sentence it says the rich were on the same
>   footing with other people as they could not spend
>   their <u>money</u> but were forced to keep it idle
> 60   [mispronounced, with short i] at home.
> **T/S:** idle. right. I <u>told</u> you °you could find it.°
> **MRC:** I read that a long <u>time</u> ago. but you all were
>   talking about something else.
> **T/D:** oh I'm- I a<u>pol</u>ogize Maurice. you should
> 65   have inte<u>rrup</u>ted us
> **GAR:** see
> **T/S:** okay

Mr. Smith complains about the students at lines 49–50, but Gary comes to Maurice's defense at lines 55–60. Mr. Smith's comment at line 61 indicates that this was the answer he was looking for, and then Maurice claims that he had in fact given this answer "a long time ago" (lines 62–63). As in the previous segment, Maurice makes clear that he wants to be acknowledged for his contributions to class. Mr. Smith gives him such an acknowledgement by apologizing at line 64, although he claims that Maurice should have been more aggressive in making his point.

Despite his desire to participate, and the girls and teachers' acceptance of him early in the year, there was one point in the October 9 conversation that foreshadowed the gendered difficulties Maurice faced later on. The following exchange occurred while they discussed a creation myth in which the original life-giver is female.

CAS: maybe, I don't know, she starts a new generation.
T/B: she starts the new generation. who's respon- who's
110 the life giver?
FST: wome[n
MRC: [man.
T/B: the woman seems to be the life giver.

In lines 108 and 109, both Cassandra and Mrs. Bailey use "she," following the text in assuming that the life-giver is female. At line 111, a female student continues to assume that the life-giver is female. But at line 112, Maurice proposes that the life-giver is a man. Mrs. Bailey ignores his comment and ratifies the opposite point of view in line 113. This brief disagreement passes without further comment. It shows Maurice sticking up for his gender against Mrs. Bailey and the girls, however, something that became much more common as the year continued.

GENDERED TENSIONS

Early in the academic year, then, Maurice behaved and was treated as just another good student. After a few months, however, the vocal girls began to challenge Maurice's opinions and exclude him from their classroom conversations. Mrs. Bailey had by now both described and enacted her stereotype of promising girls and unpromising boys, as described in Chapter 2. This reinforced the tensions between boys and girls that often exist in early adolescence and that are carried by widespread sociohistorical models of identity portraying girls and boys in conflict. These boys and girls engaged in playful shoving matches and gendered teasing outside of class. As winter came, the split between boys and girls also became salient in classroom discussions. Chapter 2 described how Mrs. Bailey and the girls sometimes teased William during class. As the only boy who spoke extensively, Maurice also became a target. The girls could not tease him as effectively as they could William because Maurice fought back verbally and made substantive academic contributions. The girls nonetheless often objected to Maurice's contributions and tried to exclude him from classroom conversations.

The Girls Against Maurice

In my data, the first extended example of the vocal girls ganging up on Maurice occurs on December 17. They are discussing "The Sniper" by Liam O'Flaherty, a short story in which a soldier for the Republican side unwittingly shoots his brother during the Irish Civil War. In the following segment they define "civil war," and the girls jump in quickly when it looks as if Maurice is about to make a mistake.

T/B: what kind of <u>war</u> do you get <u>f</u>amily on opposite
sides? (2.0) <u>c</u>ivil war. what's a <u>c</u>ivil war?
FST: °a wa[r°
FST: [a war
40   **MRC:**   [a war against- one country against-
FST: <u>no</u>:
FST: no
FSTs: [2 seconds of overlapping chatter]
T/B: okay, a <u>war</u> with<u>in</u> the <u>count</u>ry. a war with- shhh
45   **FST:** [6 unintelligible syllables]
T/B: a <u>wa:r</u> with<u>in</u> the country. so <u>brother</u> fights against
<u>brother</u>. <u>neigh</u>bor fights against <u>neigh</u>bor. is there any
<u>out</u>side in<u>va</u>sion going on here, am I pro<u>tec</u>ting my home
against a bunch of <u>for</u>eigners?
50   **MRC:** <u>no</u>
FST: <u>no</u>:
FST: no

At line 41, a female student says "no" with noticeable stress (it may be the
same intonation contour as one would find with "duh," meaning, 'How
could you be so stupid as to say that?'). Another student repeats "no" at
line 42. Maurice had only begun to make an error, but the girls quickly
jump on him. At line 50, Maurice says "no" himself, perhaps attempting
to preempt the girls' criticism. But the girls repeat "no" at lines 51 and 52,
with the same intonation contour at line 51, probably to remind Maurice
and everyone else of his earlier mistake.

As the conversation proceeds, the girls continue to object to Maurice's
comments. This illustrates an interactional pattern that recurred from
December through the end of the year: Several girls tease or disagree with
Maurice and the teachers do not intervene. In the following segment, the
class continues to discuss civil war.

T/B: you don't know who you're fighting a<u>gainst</u>? you <u>do</u>
know who [3 unintelligible syllables] you're fighting
90   a<u>gainst</u>, don't you?
FST: right=
FST: yeah
T/B: who's that?
FST: [4 unintelligible syllables]
95   **MRC:** same people in the=
FST: <u>no</u>
T/B: the <u>peo</u>ple that are <u>like</u> you. people in your <u>count</u>ry.

At line 95, Maurice begins to answer Mrs. Bailey's question. His truncated
response may well have been correct, but at line 96 a female student cuts

him off with another "no." The teacher steps in immediately and gives the correct answer, without commenting on whether Maurice might have been correct and without intervening in the developing conflict between Maurice and the girls.

After being treated like this several times during the December 17 class, Maurice began to withdraw from the conversation. Before doing so, he makes one disgruntled comment. Right before the following segment, Mrs. Bailey has asked whether a civil war can ever be justified, given the many things that compatriots have in common.

> **T/B:**   it seems to <u>me</u> that when
> you get down to these <u>ideas</u> that- that your ideas that you
> could <u>play</u> with in your <u>head</u>, what <u>caused</u> you to want to
> <u>play</u> with that idea in your head? (2.0)
> 105   **MRC:** °you asked <u>us</u> the question°
> **T/B:** I mean <u>really</u>. when you're <u>reading</u> that story and you
> read it a <u>lo:t</u> and you get to that <u>end</u> and you discover that
> you [5 unintelligible syllables] what was your reaction.
> **FST:** that he was <u>stupid</u>.
> 110   **T/B:** that he was <u>stupid</u>.

Mrs. Bailey is trying to engage students with one of the deeper questions raised by the story – why people kill each other in wars despite their commonalities. On other occasions, Maurice contributes productively at moments like this. But at line 105 he responds with "you asked us the question" – implying that he himself has no particular interest in the issue. Note that his utterance opposes "you" (the teacher) to "us" (the students), presupposing that Maurice and at least some other students are aligned in their opposition to the teacher. Neither Mrs. Bailey nor the female students ratify this alignment, however. The teacher continues at lines 106–108 by repeating her question, and several female students go on to offer various answers. Despite Maurice's desire to participate constructively in class discussion, then, and despite his general success at doing so, on December 17 the girls' ostracism apparently drives him to an uncharacteristically oppositional stance. The teacher does not remark on or discipline Maurice for this comment, as she might have if Tyisha had been the speaker. But the girls' treatment of him apparently leads him to withdraw from this classroom conversation.

This one experience did not change Maurice's behavior in general. He continued to participate in other classes throughout the year. Nonetheless, the girls continued to ostracize him, from December through the rest of the year, and with Mrs. Bailey's occasional support this treatment began to change Maurice's identity in the classroom. He was no longer just another good student. He was also the only male student struggling against the vocal girls to contribute in class. This aspect of Maurice's emerging identity first developed as the girls teased and marginalized him in classroom interactions. This social identification drew on more widely circulating metapragmatic models, from the playground as well as the classroom, in which a group of girls tease and exclude a boy. As the year went on, teachers and students developed a local version of this metapragmatic model and used it to identify Maurice as an unusual male student who wanted to participate in class. His identity as a boy became consistently relevant in classroom interactions – as opposed to other aspects of this identity that might have become relevant (as an African American, as a football player, etc.). The vocal girls consistently tried to position him as an unpromising boy, using the emerging local metapragmatic model that they were applying to William and others. Even when they failed to make this identity stick to Maurice, they were nonetheless identifying him as the lone vocal boy and challenging his claim to be a promising student.

Gender as a Curricular Concept

In developing this gendered local model of Maurice's identity, teachers and students sometimes used categories from the curriculum. The subject matter that Maurice helped discuss on December 17, about the definition of a civil war, did not connect directly to the first curricular theme. Interactionally, however, the girls were beginning to position Maurice as an outcast from the core group of vocal students in the classroom. He consistently tried to participate in the "society" of girls and teachers who dominated classroom discussion. Beginning in December, however, the vocal girls often objected to his comments and ostracized him. He was thus *potentially* an example of the curricular category "outcast" on December 17 and thereafter. He did not explicitly become an example of this category until the January 24 "beast" class that was introduced in Chapter 1. On January 24, as we will see later in this chapter, the local metapragmatic model used to identify Maurice overlapped more systematically with the first curricular theme.

Maurice was socially identified, in part, as teachers and students developed and used the local metapragmatic model that sharply distinguished between the promising girls and the unpromising boys. This metapragmatic model overlapped with the curriculum not only in participant examples like "Maurice the beast" on January 24 but also when gender itself became a curricular concept and an explicit focus of classroom discussion. Both history and literature involve gender in various ways, and Mrs. Bailey and Mr. Smith's curriculum included various works that touched on gender – although gender did not figure prominently in any curricular theme. By the time gender became an explicit curricular topic, the interactional split between boys and girls in the classroom had long been in place, William had been identified as the stereotypical unpromising boy and Maurice had been identified as the atypical male who participated in class. When gender occasionally became an explicit topic in the curriculum, the class could use the metapragmatic model of their own gendered classroom positions as a resource for understanding the topic – although they did not always do this, and they need not have done it at all.

Teachers and students might have created full-blown participant examples involving Maurice and his gender. Such examples might have opportunistically used gender and related categories from the curriculum to help develop Maurice's emerging identity – in the same way as teachers and students used the curricular category of "conceit" as they began to identify Tyisha as an atypical, disruptive girl. But in fact Maurice did not become the subject of a full-blown example explicitly involving gender until February 18. When the topic of gender was discussed earlier in the year, it did not overlap systematically with students' identities and relationships in the classroom. Before February 18, Maurice was in fact positioned as an outcast because of his gender, as not belonging to the group of vocal girls who dominated class discussion. At the same time, various texts in the curriculum discussed the differences between men and women. But these two (identity-related and curricular) patterns did not converge. The curriculum did not become a resource for building metapragmatic models of gender until later in the year. This illustrates how many potential resources for social identification are not in fact used in any given case.

Before February 18 the curricular concept of gender did nonetheless seem to motivate Mrs. Bailey and the girls to participate energetically in class discussion – especially when they focused on a misogynistic text – and Maurice sometimes became the target of such energetic discussion. The topic on January 18, for instance, was Aristotle's *Politics*, specifically his account of the natural relations between men and women, masters and slaves, and mental and manual workers. Aristotle privileges the first group in each of these oppositions, and the class was trying to figure out what made men, masters and mental workers superior. At one point, the girls and Mrs. Bailey rejected a point made by Maurice. They did not foreground Maurice's own gender, but they did attack his position on gender. This fits with how they had by that point come habitually to position him in classroom interaction.

Before the following segment, they had been discussing Aristotle's claim that a woman can be courageous by being obedient. Mrs. Bailey asked for an interpretation of a difficult passage from Aristotle's text, and Maurice offered a gloss.

> **MRC:** it's just saying that the woman should <u>not</u> have
> 75 <u>cour</u>age in telling the man that she's <u>not</u> going to do what
> he <u>tells</u> her?
> **T/B:** well, I don't know.

JAS: that's what it's saying.
T/B: it's saying what?
80 JAS: it's saying that she don't have courage if she don't
obey.
T/B: okay, does it take courage to obey?
JAS: no
FST: no
85 JAS: I told him, I told him-
MRC: it's saying she shouldn't=
JAS: that's not courage
MRC: she shouldn't have courage, enough courage, to
tell him, if he tells her to do something, she should not have
90 enough courage to tell him she's not going to do it.
JAS: right
FST: right
T/B: so it's saying that women should not have courage,
should not have the courage of telling a man that they're not
95 going to do what they're being told.
MRC: right.

Maurice gives his interpretation at lines 74–76: According to Aristotle, a woman should not perform the courageous act of disobeying a man. Mrs. Bailey disagrees at line 77, then Jasmine agrees with Maurice at line 78. But when Jasmine gives her own gloss at lines 80–81, it turns out that Jasmine's interpretation is different from Maurice's. She is saying that, according to Aristotle, a woman does not have courage if she does not obey. Mrs. Bailey reacts at line 82 as if Jasmine had claimed something different than Maurice. But Maurice then repeats at lines 87–90 what he said before. Mrs. Bailey repeats his point at lines 93–95, and Maurice acts as if the matter is settled at line 96.

The teacher and the girls do not let the matter rest, however. Maurice has acted at lines 86–90 and 96 as if he and Jasmine gave the same answer and as if others have accepted this interpretation. But Jasmine's position was in fact different from his, and Mrs. Bailey and the girls do not accept Maurice's interpretation.

T/B: then why? okay, that's what it's saying?
JAS: say what?
T/B: Maurice is saying it's saying she should not have the
100 courage to say I'm not going to do what you tell me. is that
what it's saying?
FST: [well=
T/B: [explain
FST: =she said not
105 MRC: I'm not saying, Tyisha was saying.

T/B: okay, but your interpretation of Aristotle is saying women shouldn't have the courage to say no to men.
ERK: that's not what it says.
T/B: okay, Erika.
110 **ERK:** it says the courage of a man is in- okay, wait. is shown in commanding. and the lady, if she shows courage, she is obeying what he said.
T/B: so it's not that she shouldn't have courage or should not be courageous.
[brief interruption by the intercom from the school office]
. . .
T/B: okay, uh, Erika, I'm sorry. where were you when you said?
ERK: no, I was just saying that he's saying that when a woman shows courage, she's obeying her husband's
130 command, or the man, the man that's commanding her. she's obeying what he says to do.
T/B: how can that be conceived as courage, gentlemen? we've dealt with courage. ladies. we've dealt with courage.

At lines 99–101, Mrs. Bailey restates Maurice's interpretation, labeling it explicitly as Maurice's and asking explicitly whether Maurice's interpretation is correct. This apparently communicates to Maurice that the teacher disagrees with his interpretation. He backs off at line 105 and tries to attribute the interpretation to Tyisha. At lines 106–107, the teacher does not let him shift responsibility. And at line 108, Erika takes the opportunity offered by Mrs. Bailey and claims Maurice is wrong. Erika goes on to quote the text to support her interpretation: According to Aristotle, courage for a woman is to obey a man.

Mrs. Bailey has arranged the discussion such that Erika – who was, as described in Chapter 2, the stereotypical promising girl – can criticize Maurice's answer as wrong. Mrs. Bailey makes a reasonable pedagogical move here because Maurice's interpretation of Aristotle does in fact seem to have been wrong. But it represents another instance of Mrs. Bailey and the girls separating themselves from Maurice and casting his contributions as mistaken. He tried to contribute to the discussion, but the teacher and the girls point out how his answer was wrong. The girls do not treat him as harshly here as they did on December 17, when they did not even let him finish his sentences, but this incident also illustrates how the vocal girls are ready to point out Maurice's mistakes.

The very end of this segment also offers some evidence that the students' own gendered identities are relevant to the discussion. At lines 132–133, Mrs. Bailey uses the terms "gentlemen" and "ladies." These are vocatives here, asking students to answer her question about how Aristotle can say female obedience is "courage." But these particular terms explicitly indicate that there are two genders present in the classroom. They are also terms that Mrs. Bailey often used to begin disciplinary interludes, identifying what the "gentlemen" (and less often the "ladies") were doing wrong. In line 132 Mrs. Bailey could have said, "How can that be conceived as courage, everybody," or she could have used other formulations unrelated to gender. But the gender of the students was salient for her at that moment, perhaps because of Aristotle's apparently misogynist claim. In this discussion on January 18, then, the curricular topic of gender and the interactional fact of gender in the classroom coexisted, but they did not yet overlap systematically.

As discussion continued on January 18, Maurice contributed several more times. He did make one more mistake, which was pointed out by a girl.

> **T/B:** where does he use the word superior? take a look.
> **FST:** oh, by nature.
> 755 **T/B:** by nature.
> **MRC:** oh, okay I see it now.
> **T/B:** what's by nature mean, Maurice?
> **MRC:** that man was here first?
> **CAN:** no:. that man is stronger.
> 760 **MRC:** doesn't it mean that? never mind.
> **FST:** that a man is stronger than a woman.

At line 760, Maurice realizes his mistake and withdraws his claim by saying, "never mind." Neither the teacher nor the girls pursue the issue, however, and for the rest of the discussion Maurice participates constructively and without opposition. He has apparently been forgiven for his incorrect answers and his gender, at least for the rest of this day.

At one point later in the discussion, on January 18, he even joined together with some of the girls to articulate an egalitarian position on the curricular topic of gender. In the following segment they are discussing how differences in human nature might justify differences in power among groups.

> **JAS:** yeah, they can be different by nature, but still how-
> are they going to?
> 865 **FST:** yeah, that men are born, are they smarter, stronger?
> **T/B:** Maurice?
> **MRC:** yeah everybody is different by nature, but uh,
> nobody is superior over anybody by nature.
> **FST:** right.
> 870 **JAS:** yeah, where they get that idea from? just cause you
> all a little bit different?

At lines 867–868, Maurice nicely summarizes a position contrary to Aristotle's but in line with what several girls and the teachers have been proposing. Jasmine then agrees with Maurice's point. She treats him as a fellow student making a good point. This illustrates how Maurice was not always a target of objections, teasing and ostracism. Throughout the year, even as the tension between him and the girls increased, the teachers routinely and the girls occasionally treated him as a good student and a full-fledged member of the core group that dominated class discussions. Maurice's emerging identity in December and January, as an outcast from the vocal girls' group, was not as robust as Tyisha's emerging identity as a disruptive student. Despite his emerging identity as the lone vocal boy and the girls' attempt to identify him as academically unpromising, within specific events, Maurice could still be identified relatively easily as another good student.

MAURICE THE OUTCAST

By the middle of January, the girls and occasionally Mrs. Bailey sometimes marginalized Maurice. They did not explicitly call him an outcast, and the teachers and occasionally the girls treated him as just another good student. But the vocal girls were helping Mrs. Bailey develop the local metapragmatic model of promising girls and unpromising boys, and they sometimes tried to identify Maurice as an unpromising boy. The teachers did not ratify these attempts, but the girls' regular attempts to marginalize him did successfully build another metapragmatic model of habitual classroom relations in which Maurice was the lone boy trying to contribute to discussions dominated by the teachers and the vocal girls. And the girls sometimes made him an outcast by contesting his points or by teasing him.

Maurice's emerging identity as an outcast depended on resources from various timescales: sociohistorical models that increasingly portray boys as less likely to succeed in school; sociohistorical models that portray black boys as particularly likely to reject school; the characteristic antagonism between these early adolescent boys and girls; the robust local metapragmatic model of promising girls and unpromising boys that was developing in this classroom; and contingent events in which Maurice was identified as an atypical boy. When the class started discussing the first curricular theme, cognitive models of the curriculum became available as another resource for identifying Maurice as an outcast.

On January 24, Maurice's identity was both similar to and different from Tyisha's. Like Tyisha, he was often treated as an outcast by the female students. Unlike Tyisha, he was not normally identified as an outcast by the teachers because he continued to make productive contributions to classroom discussion. Like Tyisha, Maurice embraced his identity as an outcast from the vocal girls' group. Unlike Tyisha, however, this did not lead Maurice to behave disruptively. He adopted the identity of an individualist, one who defended opinions different from the vocal girls in the class, but he was not a subversive individualist who disrupted the teachers' agenda for the class. He continued to present his opinions as contributions to the discussion, and the teachers generally treated them as such.

As we saw with Tyisha, Maurice's identity as an outcast solidified further in late January, when curricular categories from the first theme became available as resources to identify Maurice as an outcast from the vocal girls' group. As described in Chapters 3 and 4, in January the class began discussing the curricular theme of collectivism and individualism. Students and teachers began to construct local cognitive models of this theme, and they began to incorporate curricular categories like "outcast" into their local metapragmatic model of Tyisha. This curricular theme also became a resource for reinforcing Maurice's marginal interactional position and developing his local identity as an outcast. Both the vocal girls and the teachers used Aristotle's concept of "beast" to construct a more specific metapragmatic model of Maurice as being excluded from the group of girls who dominated classroom discussion. Unlike Tyisha, however, the teachers did not consistently identify Maurice as an outcast from the classroom community – apart from a few discussions where they joined the girls in teasing him. Thus the analogy between Maurice's identity in the classroom and the individual/society theme held with respect to the girls as a "society," but not with respect to the teachers and the whole class as a "society."

Maurice the Beast

On January 24, as we have seen in Chapters 1 and 4, the class discussed selections from Aristotle's *Politics* in which he argues that "the state is by nature clearly prior to the individual since the whole is of necessity prior to the part" and that "he who is unable to live in society, or who has no need because he is sufficient for himself, must be beast or god." Discussion focused on the character of a "beast in the woods," a person who refuses to make the sacrifices necessary to live in society. Long before discussion of the participant example that includes Tyisha and her cat, Mrs. Bailey nominated Maurice as a hypothetical beast in the woods.

315   **T/B:**   I mean think of what- he's saying
        there. he's saying if Maurice went <u>out</u> and lived in
        the <u>wo:ods</u> (4.0) [some laughter]
        FST: °they're talking about you°
        T/B: and <u>never</u> had any <u>contact</u> with the <u>rest</u> of us,
320   he would be- uh- like an <u>animal</u>.

This example might allow curricular concepts to be drawn into the gendered metapragmatic model they are developing to identify girls and boys in the classroom. The social organization of the classroom included the girls and teachers as a kind of "society" and the boys as outcasts or "beasts" of sorts who refuse to participate. For at least a month the vocal girls had been trying to push Maurice out of their group, toward the interactional position of an outcast. Aristotle's text thus contains concepts that could have been used to identify Maurice in the classroom and the participant example begins to facilitate the analogical use of those concepts to identify him.

The example of Maurice the beast was dropped relatively quickly at this point in the discussion, although they returned to it later in the class. But the brief early discussion foreshadowed something important about Maurice's response to this example and his response to the role of an outcast more generally.

```
        FST: yep.
        T/B: [yep?=
        FST: [but
        T/B: =why.
325     FST: °I don't know°
        TYI: animals, I mean, you know.
        CAN: animals can have other people with them. yeah, animals don't
        they need other people?
        MRC: no.
330     CAN: yes they [do.
        TYI:          [they by themselves.
        FST: they what?
        MRC: [not if they're a beast
        CAN: [I said animals need other people too, don't
335     they?
        TYI: okay now
        T/B: okay what do animals [need=
        CAN:                       [yes they do
        MRC:                       [no they don't
340     T/B: =other animals for?
        MRC: to eat?
        FST: sex. (hh)
```

At line 321, a female student endorses the idea of Maurice as an animal, but the subsequent discussion does not focus on Maurice as an example. Instead, they discuss animals' nature. At line 327, Candace suggests that animals are not necessarily all alone, without any society. This is relevant to the curricular issue because Aristotle used the term "beast" to describe people outside of society. Note that Maurice argues against Candace that animals are not social at lines 329, 333 and 339. And when Mrs. Bailey presupposes at lines 337–340 that animals do need others, he suggests that they need other animals only "to eat." We will need more evidence, but this is an early instance of Maurice valorizing the beast or outcast role. Later in this class, and in subsequent discussions, Maurice presents the outcast as a positive figure. We will also see that, at the same time as he evaluates "outcasts" or "beasts" positively, Maurice also embraces the interactional position of an outcast defending himself against the girls in the classroom.

Much later in the conversation, a few minutes after the discussion of Tyisha and her cat, Mrs. Bailey returns to the participant example of Maurice as a beast.

	T/B: now we put Maurice out in the woods. Maurice, when would you get up? and go to bed.
915	**MRC:** <u>when</u> I was ready to.
	T/B: when you were ready to. Maurice, if you had your <u>dru</u>thers what would you be eating all day long, [liver=
	MRC: [whatever I want.
920	**T/B:** =or ice cream? you going to eat liver? or are you going to eat ice cream.
	STS: ice cream.
	MRC: with what?
	FST: I eat liver.
925	**STS:** <u>ice</u> cream. [students echo ice cream and chatter about the choice of ice cream or liver]
	MST: druthers
	T/B: you have a choice.
	FST: °every day°
930	**MRC:** ice cream.
	T/B: ice cream. ummm.
	FST: °be healthier if you ate the liver°
	T/B: shhh. (2.0) the- the water where you <u>are</u> is very, very <u>cold</u>. and it's [not very warm outside.=
935	**MRC:** [[3 unintelligible syllables]
	T/B: =how often are you going to- to- to clean yourself off? [laughter]
	FST: Right Guard
940	**MRC:** depends when we're talking about.
	T/B: okay, so you might go the <u>whole</u> winter and well into the <u>summer</u>, right? without ever getting <u>clean</u>.

By singling out Maurice at line 913, Mrs. Bailey potentially puts his social identity in play. Teachers and students may infer something about Maurice himself from their discussion of him as a hypothetical beast in the woods.

Could Mrs. Bailey be implying that there is something beast-like about Maurice?

There is some evidence that this example does help identify Maurice himself as an outcast in the classroom. In this passage Mrs. Bailey is clearly joking with Maurice, as well as pursuing the curricular topic. She describes the hypothetical Maurice not eating liver (line 918) and not bathing (line 937). By choosing topics that are likely to elicit laughter from teenagers, she is probably joking as well as pursuing the academic discussion. Other students also act as if they and the teacher have in fact been joking with Maurice, when they laugh at line 938 and a student makes a joke at line 939. But the characteristics that Mrs. Bailey attributes to Maurice the hypothetical beast are not only funny. They also describe typical behaviors of "irresponsible" or "difficult" children. Such children stereotypically want to eat only ice cream, refuse to eat healthy food (lines 917–921), resist bathing (lines 933–937) and refuse to go to bed on time (line 914). We have seen that Mrs. Bailey identifies male students as difficult, and in this example she is offering Maurice a hypothetical identity as a beast that does not follow social norms. At lines 915, 919 and 930, Maurice readily makes the appropriate choices and takes on the role of a beast. He is playing the role of a cooperative student here, but he may also be expressing an affinity for the role of an outcast.

At this point in the discussion on January 24, Maurice the beast is in a position that resembles Tyisha the beast in some respects. Like Tyisha, there is an emerging metapragmatic model that identifies him as outcast from the core group that dominates class discussions – although Tyisha is increasingly being excluded by the teachers while Maurice is not. We will see more evidence below that, like Tyisha, Maurice also sometimes embraces the role of outcast by vigorously defending positions that diverge from the vocal girls'. Furthermore, Mrs. Bailey selects both Tyisha and Maurice as examples of beasts in a way that allows curricular categories to help identify these two students themselves. Note also the similarity, in the following segment, between the tone of questions Mr. Smith directs toward Maurice and those that he asked Tyisha just a few minutes earlier (at lines 726–739 – see the discussion in Chapter 4).

1025 **T/S:** Maurice, when you woke up this morning.
      what time?
      MRC: nine o clock.
      T/S: you sleepy?
      MRC: °yeah°
1030 **FST:** [4 unintelligible syllables]
      T/S: why didn't you stay asleep? you're sleepy,
      sleep.
      MRC: because I had to get up and come to school.

By choosing Maurice as an example of a beast, and by questioning him in this way, the teachers open up the possibility that he is becoming a beast just like Tyisha. In both cases the curriculum served as a resource for social identification, providing the category of "outcast" that might have been incorporated into emerging local metapragmatic models of the students' identity.

But Maurice himself was less of an outcast in the classroom than Tyisha, at least during their discussions of the first curricular theme. Tyisha was excluded from the classroom by both the teachers and the students. She more fully *enacted* the participant example of "Tyisha the beast," when she became both an example of a beast and a student who was getting interactionally excluded from the classroom "society" of teachers and students. Maurice only partly enacted his example. He was both a hypothetical beast and an outcast from the group of vocal girls, but he was not treated as an outcast by the teachers. So the curricular concepts of "society" and "outcast" characterized Maurice's own identity in one respect, but not in another.

The non-outcast side of Maurice's local identity becomes more salient as the discussion continues.

990   **T/B:** what's- what's the difference between the <u>two</u>
       aspects. Mau<u>rice</u> in the forest and the Mau<u>rice</u> that
       <u>we</u> know in this classroom, who <u>doesn</u>'t scratch
       when he itches.
       FST: he's <u>ci</u>vilized.
995   **MRC:** <u>that's</u> what I said.
       T/B: umm, he's <u>ci</u>vilized. what did you say
       Maurice?
       MRC: <u>that's</u> what <u>I</u> said.
       T/B: you're <u>ci</u>vilized. what does it <u>mean</u>?
1000   **MRC:** it means- uh (4.0) if <u>you</u> civilized, it means
       you going to do things like- (1.0) I don't know.
       T/S: Maurice
       MRC: if you civilized you do- do things like the
       <u>rest</u> of the people do, but if you uncivilized just-
1005   like- like you said, in the forest living by yourself,
       doing <u>what</u>ever <u>you</u> want to do.
       T/B: doing what<u>ev</u>er you want to do, and what-
       what controls what <u>you</u> want to do?
       FST: °so<u>ci</u>ety°
1010   **MRC:** °society°
       T/B: no- you're in a- in a forest=
       MRC: oh, in the woods. <u>I</u> con<u>trol</u> what I
       want to do.

At lines 990–993, Mrs. Bailey distinguishes between Maurice "in the forest" and Maurice "in this classroom." Unlike the Tyisha case, in which the boundary between Tyisha the beast and Tyisha the student blurred, here Mrs. Bailey explicitly separates Maurice the hypothetical beast from Maurice the real student. Maurice himself also behaves like a cooperative student in this section, answering the teacher's questions at lines 1000, 1003, 1010 and 1012. And at lines 995 and 998 he also shows that he is concerned to get credit for his contributions. This contrasts with Tyisha's behavior a few minutes earlier, in which she opposed the teachers' arguments to the point of disrupting the class. This event could have gone differently, if Maurice had vigorously enacted the role of beast in the same way as Tyisha did – by pushing his own point of view, making jokes and disrupting the teachers' agenda. If he had embraced such a disruptive outcast identity in this event, and had this continued across future events, this might have changed his trajectory of identification to look more like Tyisha's. But in fact he did not act like Tyisha, and the teachers continued to identify him mostly as a good student.

Although Mrs. Bailey generally positioned Maurice as a good student during the discussion of Maurice the beast, she nonetheless made life difficult for him in two ways. First, she picked him as an example. A "beast" is not a flattering role, and she could have picked any of the other students. I have been arguing that it was no accident that Tyisha and Maurice were the two students singled out as beasts on January 24. Their identities in the classroom lent themselves to this role because they were both becoming marginal in the classroom itself. The teachers perhaps unwittingly took advantage of these analogies between the students' own identities and the curriculum, using Tyisha's and Maurice's identities as resources for helping students learn the curriculum.

Mrs. Bailey also makes Maurice's life difficult when she changes the example at the end of the class. She starts by summarizing their discussion of beasts as people who act only for their own immediate self-interest.

        T/B: but, if you don't ha:ve a:ny
                checks on you, no laws, no need to be civilized,
   1060 don't you tend to do what makes you feel good. that
                you control.=
                FST: °yeah°
                T/B: =I want to eat now.[=
                FST: [[laughs]
   1065 **T/B:** =I want to eat ice cream. I want to scratch,
                °okay°, where it itches. I want- you know just like
                the- animals you have at home, right?
                MRC: °right°
                T/B: or the animals that you see in- in wild

1070 <u>king</u>dom movies. they <u>do</u> things (2.0) be<u>cause</u> <u>it</u>
       gives them <u>pleasure</u>, <u>satis</u>faction, <u>fits</u> an im<u>med</u>iate
       goal, as opposed to a long- term goal.

Teachers and students used this account of animals to characterize Tyisha as someone who says whatever comes into her head and pushes her own point of view without considering the rest of the class. This description does not fit Maurice as well as Tyisha, but Mrs. Bailey did select him as the other example of a beast, so a question remains about whether Maurice is beast-like in any way.

   Mrs. Bailey goes on to characterize Maurice as perhaps even more dangerous than a beast when she tries to explain another of Aristotle's points. Aristotle says:

       T/B: for <u>man</u>, when perfected,
       is the <u>best</u> of animals, but when <u>sep</u>arated from <u>law</u>
1145 and justice, he is the <u>worst</u> of all, since <u>armed</u>
       injustice is the <u>more</u> dangerous. and he is <u>equipped</u>
       at birth with <u>arms</u> meant to be used by intelligence
       and virtue, which he may <u>use</u> for the w- worst ends.
       wherefore if he have not <u>virtue</u>, he is the most
1150 un<u>holy</u> and most <u>savage</u> of animals and the most
       <u>full</u> of <u>lust</u> and <u>glut</u>tony. but justice is the <u>bond</u> of
       men and states.

For Aristotle, then, an anti-social, self-centered human can be even more dangerous than a beast. Mrs. Bailey illustrates this point with reference to Maurice.

       T/B: what
       happens if you <u>take</u> someone like Maurice out in the
1105 forest is doing what <u>he</u> wants to do, for the
       im<u>med</u>iate pleasure of what <u>he</u> wants to do and then
       you <u>add</u> on to it the component that he can <u>also</u>
       think about <u>future</u> pleasures, doing what he <u>wants</u> to
       do. and he can have some <u>planning</u> mechanism
1110 there, to think in terms of the things in the <u>future</u>
       that he can <u>plan</u> to do that will make him feel good.
       <u>what</u> happens to him? a <u>lion</u> is dangerous, but what
       about a <u>Maurice</u>?

This new hypothetical Maurice is a beast in some ways but not in others. The stereotypical beast, perhaps like Tyisha, is self-interested but unable to reason in complex ways. But the new hypothetical Maurice is self-interested and highly intelligent.

The students do not immediately understand this idea, so Mrs. Bailey elaborates.

> **T/B:** okay, a lion is dangerous when you see it,
> 1120 right?
> **FST:** yeah, he want to kill me.
> **T/B:** because if a lion is hungry, he is going to?
> **FST:** get you.
> **T/B:** get you, as I understand it. °I'm not an expert
> 1125 on lions° but Maurice is somebody maybe you
> don't even see and you know, he can be doing
> what?
> **FST:** [2 unintelligible syllables]
> **T/B:** the lion you see, you know he's dangerous.
> 1130 Maurice you can see- °let me put it this way°
> Maurice you can see now (1.0) and don't perceive
> him as being dangerous, but what else could be
> happening?
> **FST:** he could be sneaky.
> 1135 **T/B:** he could be plannin' how to get somethin' or
> do somethin' that makes him feel good in two years,
> two weeks, two hours. °right.° do- do, am I getting
> this totally muddled or are you following what I am
> saying?

Mrs. Bailey presents the hypothetical Maurice here as "dangerous," as out to "get you" and as sneaking around unseen in a menacing way. He is intelligent, but he pursues what makes him "feel good." After this new variation on the "Maurice the beast" example, Maurice himself stays silent for the rest of the class.

This was only a brief episode, but it does show a pattern that recurred at least twice more during the spring (we will see another instance on May 10). Mrs. Bailey occasionally presented Maurice not only as an outcast, but also as a dangerous outcast. This does not seem parallel to Maurice's own position in the classroom. He was not dangerous to the girls, except perhaps when he wrestled with them outside of class. They were more dangerous to him, ostracizing him as they did. Nor did Maurice act dangerously toward the teachers. Mrs. Bailey's characterization of the hypothetical Maurice here may be related to her metapragmatic model of males as difficult and potentially disruptive. If so, her final twist on the example of Maurice as a beast might position him as like the non-participating boys. This would be an early instance of a pattern that occurred more robustly during the discussion of the second curricular theme, when the teachers and the girls forced Maurice to choose between his identity as a male and his identity as a good student.

Maurice was in any case a fair example of a "beast" in the sense of 'social outcast' because he was often marginalized in the classroom by the vocal girls. The analogy between Maurice's own emerging identity and the curricular theme did not bite as deeply as it did for Tyisha, however, because the teachers treated Maurice as a promising, non-disruptive student. Despite the potential link that this participant example made between curricular categories like "outcast" and emerging local metapragmatic models of Maurice's own identity, Maurice was not forced into the role of outcast as Tyisha was. It was only when the class began discussing the second curricular theme that the teachers and the girls used curricular categories more extensively and effectively to identify Maurice himself.

Embracing Individualism

Maurice's classroom identity developed through three phases over the academic year. Initially, as we have seen, Maurice was just another good student. During the second and third phases, the girls and the teachers placed increasing pressure on him. In the second phase he became an outcast from the girls' group. The girls, and occasionally Mrs. Bailey, challenged his opinions and excluded him from their group. In the third phase, as we will see below, the teachers and girls increased the pressure on Maurice by forcing him to choose between being one of the boys and being a good student. Each of the two curricular themes facilitated Maurice's emerging social identity. The first theme provided the curricular category of "outcast" that teachers and students used to identify him during the second phase of his identity development. The second curricular theme provided the category of "resistance" that teachers and students used to identify Maurice and the other boys during the third phase of his identity development. It was only during discussion of this second curricular theme that the emerging metapragmatic model of Maurice's identity overlapped systematically with local cognitive models of the curriculum.

Before turning to the second curricular theme, however, we need to examine how Maurice himself contributed to his own social identification. Like Tyisha, he actively embraced and resisted aspects of his emerging classroom identities. We have seen brief instances of how Maurice responded to the girls' attempts to exclude him from their group. In part, he kept contributing to discussions like a good student, and the teachers continued to identify him as such. But he also embraced some things about the outcast role – both in the academic arguments that he made and in the interactional positions he adopted. While the class was discussing the first curricular theme, Maurice sometimes made arguments in favor of individualism. At the same time, he acted individualistically by defending his own positions against the girls.

In the January 25 discussion of Rand's *Anthem*, for instance, Maurice both positioned himself as an individualist, separate from the girls, and he made an argument defending individualism. As described in Chapter 3, this class discussion centered around Rand's proposal for an "equality society," one in which individuals do not "owe anything to their brothers" but act only for themselves. The class discussed this issue, and other texts relevant to the individual/society theme, by analogy with the contemporary U.S. welfare system. To what extent should society support the disadvantaged through welfare programs? In responding to this question, Maurice did not argue for extreme individualism, like Rand, but his argument was more individualist than the collectivism defended by the girls.

During the discussion of Rand on January 25, Mrs. Bailey gave a participant example in which Brenna was a welfare mother and Mrs. Bailey was a "bum." Both were living off welfare. The class discussed whether those with money should be required to support such people. Early in the discussion Tyisha defends an individualist position while all the other students, including Maurice, defend a more collectivist one.

> **T/B:** why shouldn't I just? okay, if it's not a, what,
> 605 you know, what if it's not a disaster as in, in
> Brenna's case. I mean I don't have babies in diapers
> anymore. long past it. what happens if, you
> know, (3.0) what happens if I get to be old and [bell
> rings (3.0)] not if I, when I get to be old, what
> 610 happens if-
> **STS:** [laughter] (1.0)
> **T/B:** what happens if when I retire, I don't have any
> money to live on? are you then supposed to take
> care of me?
> 615 **STS:** [chatter]
> **TYI:** I don't think that's fair because I- I might be
> struggling too and they're taking taxes out of my
> money.
> **CAN:** when you get old, what's gonna happen to
> 620 you?
> **JAS:** you get old, and we gonna do the same thing
> for you.
> **TYI:** so what if everybody in this whole world was
> struggling and?
> 625 **STS:** [2 seconds of shouting]
> **MRC:** what if she, what if she didn't have to go
> through them when she got old? what if she had
> money when she got old and she didn't need that,
> she simply caring for these people?

Mrs. Bailey asks the question at lines 612–614, using herself as a participant example: Should others in the society take care of Mrs. Bailey when
she's old? Tyisha answers no, defending a more individualist position like
Rand's. Candace and Jasmine defend a more collectivist position, arguing that we should take care of each other. The vocal girls consistently
defended such a pro-welfare, collectivist position across many classes. It
is Tyisha the outcast who defends the individualist position in this class,
which might lead us to speculate about how her interactional position as an
outcast leads her to make individualist arguments. This speculation would
be premature, however, because Tyisha changes her position and defends
collectivism later in this same class. It turns out to be Maurice who defends
a somewhat individualist alternative against the vocal girls' collectivism.

Maurice's comment at lines 626–629 is hard to understand, but as the
discussion proceeds it becomes clear that he is for the moment defending
the collectivist position along with the vocal girls.

> **T/B:** you have no children. you get a super job. and
> now you're giving the government forty thousand
> 675 dollars a year, a large portion of which is going to
> support other people's kids going to school. how is
> that going to come back to you?
> **ERK:** it might not come back to me, but it's going
> to help society.
> 680 **MRC:** right.
> **ERK:** there's lots of poor people on the street [4
> unintelligible syllables]
> **FST:** she's helping herself too=
> **T/B:** okay, how do you see yourself?
> 685 **FST:** she's helping herself too because with some
> of that money, they helping the community too that
> she live in, so it will help her too.
> **MRC:** you owe the people that don't have it, so
> you're like really helping, you're helping your
> 690 community. and, uh, if you're not helping, then why
> you in this country?

At lines 673–677, Mrs. Bailey pushes the students to consider a more individualistic point of view by elaborating her example to include the students
as hypothetical wealthy people who must pay taxes to support welfare
recipients. But Erika and another student defend the collectivist position,
arguing at lines 681 and 685–687 that her taxes would be benefiting the
community and that an individual has an interest in a strong community.

Maurice supports this collectivist line of argument at lines 680 and 688–
691, suggesting that everyone in our country should be willing to help

others. He continues to support this point of view in subsequent discussion, arguing at one point that Rand's ideal "equality" society would be "a poor society. All these bums on the street, people that can't afford to feed their babies, and people dying constantly" (lines 757–760). In the first part of the discussion, then, Maurice opposes Rand's individualism. As the seminar proceeds, however, he objects to the collectivism advocated by the girls – although he never embraces an extreme individualism.

Maurice begins to develop his diverging argument while discussing whether welfare recipients should have the right to vote.

> **T/B:** what <u>gives</u> you the <u>right</u> to- to <u>speak</u>, though,
> I mean, what <u>gives</u> you the right? <u>you</u> guys are the
> ones with the <u>money</u>, I mean we're talking ten years
> from now, fifteen years ago, <u>you</u> guys have the
> 860   <u>money</u>. I mean, I'm out there starving on the corner=
> **FST:** [that's right (hh)
> **T/B:** =[and <u>Brenna</u>'s got the two babies. what, what
> (2.0) what says <u>we</u> have a <u>right</u> to be part of the
> 865   conversation, and our opinions <u>valued</u> and taken
> into ac<u>count</u>, and, if we're <u>voting</u>, our vote counts as
> much as <u>you</u> that is sup<u>port</u>ing the society as
> opposed to <u>us</u> that are just <u>in</u> the society? why?
> **TYI:** we supposed to all <u>be</u> equal, you know.
> 870   **MRC:** but you're <u>not</u> equal.
> **FST:** <u>she</u> is equal.
> **T/B:** [what's the problem, Maurice?
> **FST:** [she is equal.
> **MRC:** we the, the government is paying <u>them</u>
> 875   **FST:** that's because
> **MRC:** so why should they have the right
> to say something if <u>they</u> not paying anything to the
> <u>gove</u>rnment?

At line 869, Tyisha articulates the dominant student point of view, claiming that everyone is supposed to be equal and opposing Mrs. Bailey's claim that taxpayers should get to vote and welfare recipients should not. Maurice objects at line 870, arguing that taxpayers and welfare recipients are in fact not equal. He elaborates at lines 876–879, arguing that those who rely on the government for support should not have as much of a voice.

In response to the girls' subsequent criticisms, Maurice qualifies his position. He narrows his claim to welfare recipients who could work but choose not to, arguing that, "If you just, if you just don't wanna work, and we, the government has to pay you, why should you have a <u>right</u> to say something?" (lines 892–894).

> MRC: I'm not saying like if somebody's husband
> died and <u>they</u> can't support their children. I'm not
> 925 saying we shouldn't pay for stuff like that. I'm just
> saying if somebody just <u>chooses</u> not to [work=
> CAN: [yeah, I
> know a <u>lot</u> of people like that.
> MRC: =because they don't want to work, why
> 930 should they have a right to <u>say</u> something if they
> <u>could</u> get a job?

Maurice identifies himself and others ("we") as taxpayers, and opposes this group to welfare recipients who do not want to work. His identification with the taxpayers, and his distinction between taxpayers and welfare recipients who choose not to work, opposes the girls' view that we are all in the same boat, supporting each other when we need it. Maurice is not defending Rand's extreme individualist position because he agrees with the girls that society should support people with genuine needs. Later in the discussion he claims that if you really enacted Rand's ideal society, "you become beasts" (line 1159). But Maurice does defend a less collectivist position than the girls.

Toward the end of the discussion, Mrs. Bailey asks whether Rand's proposed society could really be "equal." Maurice is the only student to defend an affirmative answer.

> MRC: it <u>could</u> be equal.
> 1320 T/B: <u>Maurice</u>?
> MRC: society <u>could</u> be equal.
> T/B: how?
> MRC: because <u>people</u>, because all the <u>rich</u> people
> would go over there since they don't want to pay
> 1325 any, since they don't want to pay [for
> LIN: [but they not
> <u>all</u> rich people.
> MRC: I'm <u>talking</u> please. all the <u>rich</u> people would
> go over there instead of all the <u>poor</u> people who
> 1330 couldn't pay the taxes.
> LIN: what is <u>he</u> talking about?
> MRC: all right=
> FST: [the people in society-
> MRC: =[see the people, like, I know. she <u>said</u>,
> 1335 could the society be, could the society be <u>equal</u>? <u>his</u>
> society that he's building. and they <u>could</u> be equal.

Maurice argues here that Rand's society could be "equal," if only rich people lived in it. He is not necessarily condoning Rand's society, but he is articulating a sense in which it could involve equality: If everyone in a society was rich and they all agreed not to pay taxes, they would be equal. Linda interrupts him at line 1326, objecting to his point, but Maurice reclaims the floor at line 1328. Linda then belittles Maurice's point and treats him as a non-participant in the conversation, referring to him as "he" at line 1331. Maurice nonetheless defends his point of view by clarifying at lines 1334–1336 how he is answering the teacher's question.

Interactionally, we see Maurice in this segment responding to the habitual challenges made by the vocal girls. They objected to his arguments and tried to exclude him from the conversation. In response, he asserted his right to defend an alternative and he articulated a plausible argument. The girls put him in the interactional position of an outcast who stands alone and must defend his own point of view. But Maurice somewhat willingly adopted this position. He could have continued to defend the collectivist view, together with the vocal girls, as he did early in the class. If he had done so, he might have been allowed to remain part of the girls' group. Or he could have remained silent, as the other boys did. He chose instead to defend unpopular positions, and he thus adopted the position of someone on the margins of the vocal girls' group. His own actions thus became another factor in his emerging identity as an outcast. Sociohistorical and local models of gender played an important role, but Maurice's own actions were important as well.

Despite the girls' efforts to ostracize him, Maurice remained on the teachers' good side. While discussing the example of herself as a welfare recipient, Mrs. Bailey had been pushing students to consider the merits of an individualist position (e.g., at line 678), and Maurice helped her develop this argument. At the end of the discussion, Mrs. Bailey then praised Maurice's argument.

1485 **T/B:**   I think
       that Maurice came up with a very good <u>point</u> there
       when he says that it's <u>possible</u> to have a society
       where everyone is <u>equal</u> if everyone is able to take
       <u>care</u> of themselves and <u>do</u> what they <u>need</u> to do to
1490 sus<u>tain</u> themselves without worrying about what
       most of you were pointing out to Gary or without
       <u>need</u>ing the little people to to give you what you
       need to get through life. okay? umm, I don't know if
       that sums it up very well, but I think, you've got an
1495 issue to <u>deal</u> with. you know, how <u>equal</u> can you
       be? how <u>free</u> can you be in a society? okay?

Mrs. Bailey probably praises Maurice's "very good point" because he has done what Paideia teachers value. He has defended an unpopular point of view, and in the process he has helped Mrs. Bailey give other students "an issue to deal with" (line 1495). Now students must reconsider their own positions and think more deeply about fundamental human questions like "how equal" and "how free can you be in a society."

Maurice both defended individualism and willingly adopted the interactional position of an outcast on other occasions as well. On February 21, for instance, they discussed Pericles' *Funeral Oration*, in which Pericles praises Athenian soldiers who died in the Peloponnesian War. The teachers raised the question of why Athenian men went to fight in the war if their society did not force them to fight. Mr. Smith offered himself as a participant example of an Athenian soldier.

> **T/S:** you send me into battle.
> **TYI:** what'd you say?
> **T/S:** I can always turn around and run like heck and get
> 280 out of that battle. (2.0) I don't have to die.
> **TYI:** but you part of my so- you part of my, um- society,
> so you have to do it.
> **T/B:** do I have to do it if I'm part of your society?
> **FST:** °[5 unintelligible syllables]°
> 285 **MRC:** no, you don't have to
> **T/B:** I'm an outcast. what does that mean to you, Maurice?
> **MRC:** you can do anything you want to, you're not
> obligated to do it if you don't want to.
> **T/B:** ah. interesting idea. if you're in Athens, you don't
> 290 have to be in the military if you don't want to? where did
> you see that in the reading?
> **MRC:** I didn't. Mr. Smith told me.
> **STS:** [1 second of laughter]

Mrs. Bailey includes herself in the participant example as another hypothetical Athenian soldier, together with Mr. Smith, and she identifies her hypothetical soldier as "an outcast" at line 286. She draws this concept from earlier discussions of the individual/society theme. She then asks Maurice what that means. It could be a coincidence that she singles out Maurice, but she might do this because of his own identity as something of an outcast in the classroom. Maurice responds to her question at lines 287–288 by characterizing the outcast positively. Instead of dwelling on the isolation or the beast-like characteristics of outcasts, Maurice emphasizes that they can do what they want. As he was on January 25, Maurice is sympathetic to individualism here.

There may have been a parallel between Maurice's interactional position in the classes on January 25 and February 21 and the argument he made about the curriculum. The group of vocal girls defended a collectivist position while Maurice the partial outcast defended a partly individualist position. But this parallel did not involve systematic overlap between the local metapragmatic model that teachers and students used to identify him and the local cognitive model of the curricular theme. In Tyisha's case, teachers and students used categories of identity from the curriculum to identify Tyisha herself. Participant examples that include the student being identified, as in the case of Tyisha the beast, can allow the use of curricular categories to identify students directly – because the student does in fact get characterized using those categories. But the parallel between the girls' defense of collectivism and their interactional solidarity in the classroom, although one might speculate about connections, did not involve the same sort of overlap between local cognitive and metapragmatic models. Teachers and students may have opportunistically used the category of "beast" to identify Maurice, but they did not systematically build metapragmatic models for him using this curricular category. Such systematic overlap between metapragmatic and cognitive models did happen to Maurice with respect to the second curricular theme, as described in the next section.

MAURICE IN THE MIDDLE

Maurice went from being just another good student to being the only vocal boy and an outcast whom the vocal girls marginalized in class discussion. This exclusion may have been uncomfortable for Maurice at times, but he defended himself effectively and sometimes even embraced the role of an outcast who argued against the vocal girls. Later in the year, however, the teachers sometimes joined the vocal girls in treating Maurice as an outcast and putting interactional pressure on him. The teachers did this by asking Maurice to choose between his identity as a good student and his identity as a male. I will review two examples. The first occurred before the class began discussing the second curricular theme. This example illustrates how tension between the two salient aspects of Maurice's classroom identity was building even without the systematic use of curricular categories – as teachers and students drew on the local metapragmatic model of promising girls and unpromising boys, on sociohistorical expectations about gender and on other resources to identify him as being caught between his gender and his desire to be a good student. The second example shows how teachers and students used categories from the second curricular theme to put even more pressure on the tension in Maurice's identity.

Male Resistance

In order to understand how the boys were successfully cast as resistant during discussions of the second curricular theme, we first need to understand the depth of the split between boys and girls. Before they began discussing the second curricular theme, gender became an explicit curricular category

again on February 18. Maurice and others became participant examples in
this class because of their gender, and they enacted the curriculum in revealing ways. The following analysis of this class discussion illustrates how
deep the split between boys and girls had become in this classroom, how
Maurice sometimes sided with the boys, and how discussions of gender
as a curricular category facilitated the split – especially when the curricular category of gender was mediated through participant examples and
applied to students' own identities.

On February 18, Mrs. Bailey and the students discussed the scene from
the *Odyssey* in which Odysseus encounters the Sirens. The Sirens were
female creatures who lured seafaring men to their island with enchanting
songs. Upon arriving, however, men discovered that the Sirens were in
fact hideous carnivores. The Sirens then ate them. Having been warned,
Odysseus makes his men plug their ears and tie him to the mast, and he
is thus able to enjoy the Sirens' song while his men keep the ship safely
away from the island. In their seminar discussion the teacher and students
explored the implicit messages of this episode – for example, the representation of women as seductive but dangerous.

Mrs. Bailey began the discussion by disciplining Gary, one of the male
students who generally refused to participate.

> **T/B:** <u>watch</u> out. okay. Gary, I am <u>going</u> to tear that up,
> which is something I <u>haven</u>'t done in a classroom in a
> couple of years but <u>when</u> you are repeatedly asked <u>not</u> to
> 75   do something, then you are forcing me to do some <u>more</u>
> <u>drastic</u> things. (4.0) o<u>kay</u>, women are dangerous. what do
> <u>we</u> do?
> **STS:** [laughter]

Students may be laughing at line 78 out of schadenfreude, enjoying
Gary's distress. But they may also be appreciating the parallel between
Mrs. Bailey's interactional position and the curricular topic. She is acting
rather dangerously toward Gary, and thus she may be answering her own
question.

This brief parallel between the participants' gendered identities and the
curricular topic recurs as the discussion proceeds. The parallel is facilitated
by a participant example, which begins at lines 76–77 when Mrs. Bailey uses
"we" to ask her question about women. As they continue to talk about
how women are dangerous, she continues to connect the curricular topic
to students' own experiences with gender.

> **T/B:** what do <u>we</u> do? <u>William</u>, what do <u>women</u> <u>do</u> that's
> 80   dangerous?
> (8.0)
> **FST:** °we're <u>waiting</u>°

T/B: Maurice, what do women do that's dangerous?
FST: when you're surrounded by them you better watch out.
85 [laughter from female students and T/B]
T/B: what do the girls in this room do to create a danger
for you?

At line 79, Mrs. Bailey singles out William. Characteristically, she gets no response. At line 83, she singles out Maurice and uncharacteristically gets no response. Maurice may be silent here because Mrs. Bailey connects the curricular topic so clearly to the gender split in the classroom. He has repeatedly been positioned as an outcast from the female-dominated class, and the example may make his interactional isolation so salient that he judges silence to be the wisest course.

Mrs. Bailey uses "we" at lines 77 and 79, which positions herself and the girls as characters in an example that they will use to discuss the curriculum. At line 82, a female student identifies herself as a member of this "we." She also speaks like a teacher (perhaps like a dangerous teacher) by telling William that "we're waiting." At line 84 another female student makes a joke and continues to identify women as dangerous. Only the females laugh. In her comment at line 84, this unidentified girl switches from "we" to "them" in referring to dangerous women. This momentarily moves the discussion away from the girls themselves. But at line 86, Mrs. Bailey explicitly connects the topic to "the girls in this room" and asks what makes them dangerous. This makes clear that they are discussing the curricular topic of gender with reference to the girls themselves.

Mrs. Bailey goes on to include Maurice in this participant example, as the girls' victim.

CAN: think you like somebody else on purpose. pretend to
like somebody else on purpose.
90 **T/B:** okay, that could hurt Maurice, that kind of thing. they
could play with his affections and then toss him overboard.
okay, what else c- could the ladies in the room do?
FST: we can become obsessed
T/B: not, not the women being obsessed with him, wh-
95 what might happen to Maurice? I want your opinion. what,
what might happen to you, Maurice? (10.0) Maurice, is
this thing in this classroom full of women a distraction?
[female laughter] would you do better in a classroom full of
boys? (4.0)
100 **MRC:** °I don't know°
T/B: Maurice, I'm asking you a question.
MRC: I don't know.
T/B: you don't know.

Candace responds to Mrs. Bailey's question by describing an indefinite male who might be hurt by the dangerous girls. At line 90, however, Mrs. Bailey explicitly introduces Maurice as the subject of discussion. This adds Maurice as another character in the participant example, with Mrs. Bailey and the girls as the dangerous females and Maurice as their potential victim.

Mrs. Bailey also refers to Maurice in the third person at line 91. Because he has failed to respond when addressed as "you," Mrs. Bailey continues the discussion without him. Mrs. Bailey also makes him the object of the girls' actions – they could hurt him, "play with his affections and then toss him overboard." Maurice has thus become an object in two ways. He refused to participate in the conversation and now the females have excluded him as an interactional participant. Mrs. Bailey has also described him, within the example, as an object of the girls' actions. As shown at line 93, the girls continue to position themselves as first-person participants, referring to themselves as "we."

In her comments at lines 94ff., however, Mrs. Bailey makes it clear that she does not want to focus on the women's "obsessions." She wants to focus on Maurice. She turns to him at line 95, referring to him again as "you." But Maurice, again uncharacteristically, does not respond at all. At lines 95–101, Mrs. Bailey increases the pressure on Maurice to respond, escalating to the explicit statement, "Maurice, I'm asking you a question." The teachers had spoken like this to other boys when they refuse to participate, but I had never observed them talking like this to Maurice. Maurice responds with "I don't know," twice, which is the only thing he says in this whole discussion.

The class could have discussed gender and the *Odyssey* in various ways. As she did with many other texts, however, Mrs. Bailey chose to use a participant example. This choice foregrounded the division between the boys and girls in the classroom because it applied gendered categories of identity from the curriculum to teachers and students themselves. It thus brought into play the robust local metapragmatic model of promising girls and unpromising boys. William enacted the typical male response that fit with this model when he refused to say anything. Mrs. Bailey then asked Maurice, perhaps hoping that he would be the one boy who would respond. But because Mrs. Bailey and the girls were teasing him, Maurice probably suspected that this would not be a dispassionate discussion of the curriculum. Thus Mrs. Bailey put Maurice in an awkward position. He generally cooperated with the teachers, but he could see that this would be a dangerous topic, through which Mrs. Bailey and the girls could tease and marginalize him. So he chose to act like a stereotypical male and refused to participate.

Mrs. Bailey and the girls responded by explicitly characterizing the boys as unpromising.

JAS: you <u>would</u> because they are able to take [4
105   unintelligible syllables] stupid things because if more <u>boys</u>
than girls
T/B: <u>oh</u> the place would get <u>stup</u>ider.
[laughter from female students]
T/B: that's how boys are, they're kind of <u>stup</u>id. maybe,
110   maybe the boys in this room are a little bit [2 unintelligible
syllables]. <u>o</u>kay, ahh, (6.0) I am going to have to ask this
question to the girls because the boys aren't very
<u>forth</u>coming. any<u>bo</u>dy in here ever have a <u>crush</u> on
somebody?

At line 105 Jasmine seems to be saying that a predominantly male class
would produce more "stupid" comments. Mrs. Bailey picks this up at lines
107 and 109, explicitly labeling the boys as stupid. She may be teasing here,
trying to entice the boys to participate and defend themselves. However,
because this characterization fits with her general attitude toward the boys,
her blunt statement is not just teasing. The message about the boys' identities is clear: They are not cooperative or promising students. Mrs. Bailey
then directs her instruction exclusively to the girls at lines 111ff. Thus she
not only *describes* but also *enacts* the difference between promising girls and
unpromising boys. She acts as if it is not worth teaching the boys because
they do not respond anyway.

Various acts and resources contributed to this robust identification of
the boys as unpromising on February 18: Gender was a central concept in
the curriculum for that day; Mrs. Bailey used the boys and girls' own identities in a participant example; William and the other boys were explicitly
asked but refused to participate, and they thus enacted the local metapragmatic model of unpromising boys; students and teachers also drew on the
sociohistorical models of boys' lack of academic success and black boys'
resistance to school. In this context, Maurice had to choose between enter-
ing the dangerous discussion and himself refusing to participate. When he
chose the latter, Mrs. Bailey and the girls identified him as unpromising
and uncooperative like the other boys. In this way the teacher joined the
vocal girls in foregrounding the tension in Maurice's local identity. They
did not let him remain a promising boy, but instead made him choose
between being a promising student and being one of the boys.

Mrs. Bailey's analogy between Odysseus' encounter with the Sirens and
the boys and girls themselves was fitting in several ways. The Sirens' song
surrounded male sailors, and if men went to their island the Sirens harmed
them. In this classroom there were twice as many girls as boys. On this particular day there were only three boys and a dozen girls present, so the girls
did surround the boys. The vocal girls also controlled classroom discussion, and they harmed the boys by teasing and insulting them. In addition,

Mrs. Bailey herself acted like the Sirens in some respects. She tried to lure William and Maurice into participating in this class, and she joined the girls in teasing the boys. Like the Sirens, she acted dangerously at lines 72–76 and 107–114. Furthermore, it is also fitting that Mrs. Bailey singled out Maurice as an example in this discussion of Odysseus. Odysseus was able both to enjoy the Sirens' song and protect himself against them. Although Maurice withdrew in this discussion on February 18, in most classes he managed to participate successfully in class and retain his identity as one of the boys – by, for example, championing unpopular opinions against the girl majority and sometimes against the teachers. In the end, somewhat like Odysseus, Maurice cunningly and successfully behaved both like a successful male and a good student. But the girls, and sometimes the teachers, did not make it easy for him.

Caught Between Loyalty and Resistance

The discussion on February 18 shows how Maurice occupied a precarious position in the classroom. His position became even more precarious when they began discussing the second curricular theme, because the teachers and the girls used categories from that theme as resources to put pressure on the pre-existing tension in Maurice's local identity. As teachers and students discussed the loyalty/resistance theme in the spring, the social identification of Maurice and students' learning about the curriculum began to mesh. The local cognitive model of the second theme co-developed and overlapped with the local metapragmatic model they were using to identify Maurice, in the same way as the local cognitive model of the first curricular theme co-developed and overlapped with the metapragmatic model teachers and students used to identify Tyisha in January and February.

The second curricular theme asked whether an individual should remain loyal to or resist an imperfect political order. This theme provided a cognitive model of society that easily became analogous to the social organization of the classroom. Teachers have power in a classroom, like those who rule society, and students can decide whether to support or resist the teachers' agenda. The vocal girls were like loyalists who followed the teachers' agenda of running intellectually productive Paideia classes. The addition of "resistance" as a curricular category allowed the other boys into the analogy between the classroom and the curriculum, as students who refused to participate in the teachers' goals for the classroom "society." This analogy between the curriculum and the classroom itself was created through several examples, some of which have already been discussed, and through the interactional positions tacitly adopted by and forced on boys and girls in classroom discussions.

But where did Maurice fall in this classroom "society?" Because the girls were on the side of the powerful, Maurice's identity as an outcast from the girls' group might have made him analogous to an individual resisting the social order. But Maurice was not really opposed to the teachers, who continued to treat him like a successful student. Because he was the only vocal boy, Maurice was caught in between the two groups. As they developed their local cognitive model of loyalty and resistance, the teachers and the girls used categories of identity from the second theme to model the tensions in Maurice's own identity and they used their emerging model of Maurice's identity to understand the curriculum. As these cognitive and metapragmatic models co-developed, Maurice was caught between the "loyal" girls and the "resistant" boys. With this joint metapragmatic/cognitive model as a resource, teachers and students forced Maurice to choose between his identity as a boy and his identity as a good student.

During a seminar discussion on May 10, this analogy between Maurice's own identity and the curricular theme crystallized. This discussion thus accomplished for Maurice what the January 24 discussion of beasts did for Tyisha. Maurice's awkward position, caught between his identity as a boy and his identity as a good student, had been developing for some time. The May 10 discussion crystallized that tension when teachers and students drew the cognitive model of someone caught "in the middle" from the curriculum and used it as a resource to identify Maurice. Just as the concept of "disruptive outcast" became central to the joint metapragmatic/cognitive model that was applied to Tyisha on January 24, the concept of someone caught "in the middle" between the powerful and the resistance became central to the joint metapragmatic/cognitive model that was applied to Maurice on May 10. Curricular categories by themselves did not suffice to establish Maurice's local identity. Many other resources were relevant, as described above, including sociohistorical models of gender and schooling, the emerging local model of promising boys and unpromising girls, the emergent structure of particular events and the girls' work identifying Maurice earlier in the year. But the second curricular theme helped "thicken" the developing metapragmatic model teachers and students had been building with other resources.

For the discussion on May 10, the class had read Cicero's letter to Atticus. In this letter Cicero ponders what he should do about the tyranny of Caesar and the plot (by Cassius, Brutus and others) to overthrow him. Should he tell Caesar? Should he join the plotters? Or should he just keep quiet? The text presents a cognitive model with three crucial characters: Caesar the tyrant, those plotting against him and Cicero caught between the two. Mr. Smith gives a participant example to illustrate Cicero's dilemma.

T/S: Mau<u>rice</u> let's give a good example, you'll love this.
sup<u>pose</u> this dictator, <u>me</u>. there was a plot going on.
150   and <u>you</u> found out about it. and you <u>knew</u> it was gonna-
it's existing (3.0) among the people you knew. would
you tell me. (5.0)
MRC: you said <u>they</u> know about it.
T/S: the <u>plot</u>ters, against me. they're planning to push me
155   down the stairs. [and <u>you</u> know about it
STS: [hnhhahahaha
T/S: now we <u>all</u> know Maurice and I have ha(hh)d
arguments all year. <u>would</u> you tell me about it.
MRC: well- I <u>might</u> but uh what if they- what if they found
160   out that I <u>told</u> you then they want to kill me. (5.0) so I'm
putting <u>my</u>self in trouble to save you, and I'm not going to
<u>do</u> it.
STS: hnh hahahaha

The example describes a role structure analogous to that in Rome:
Mr. Smith the hypothetical tyrant, the conspirators plotting to push him
down the stairs and Maurice the potential informer caught between the
two.

Figure 5.1 represents the analogy among the roles described in the text,
the roles described in the example and the positions enacted in the classroom interaction itself. The innermost rectangle represents the cognitive
model described by the text, with the three types of characters. The rectangle labeled "Denoted Events" represents the analogous triad of characters
in Mr. Smith's participant example. Together, these two rectangles represent the "denotational text" (Silverstein, 1992) or the events described as the
cognitive content of Mr. Smith's utterances. The outermost rectangle represents the "interactional text," the events that teachers and students enact
in the classroom. At this point in the conversation, Mr. Smith and Maurice
appear to be occupying conventional positions as teacher and student discussing the curriculum. But Mr. Smith's comment at line 157 indicates that
their own relationship may also be analogous to the one between Caesar
and Cicero. There is no line between Maurice and the students because
in this interaction his relationship with them has not yet taken any clear
form.

Like most participant examples, this one might have implications for
Maurice and Mr. Smith themselves in the classroom. If characteristics
attributed to participants' characters in the example have implications for
their own interactional positions, categories from the curriculum might be
used to identify Maurice and Mr. Smith. For instance, by asking whether
Maurice would side with him against the student plotters, Mr. Smith may
be raising an interactional question: Is Maurice on the teachers' side or

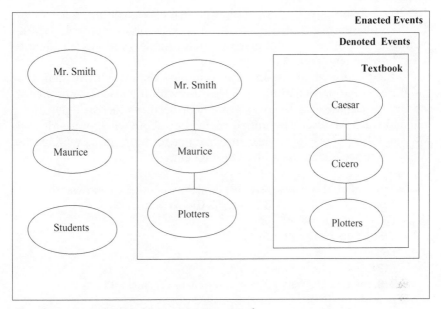

FIGURE 5.1. Introducing the participant example.

not? So when Mr. Smith asks Maurice whether he would side with him against the student "conspirators," the discussion may have implications for Maurice's own in-between position – a position that is in fact partly analogous to Cicero's. By giving an example that puts Maurice in between the teacher and the plotters, Mr. Smith indexes Maurice's months-long struggle as a male student caught between his desire to be one of the boys and his desire to participate with the teachers and the girls in classroom discussion. We cannot conclude at this early point that Maurice's own identity will in fact turn out to be relevant in their discussion of this example. But the possibility has been opened up, such that later discussion could presuppose and strengthen the parallel between Maurice's hypothetical position as a potential informer caught between a tyrant and the plotters and his actual position as a boy caught between a desire to engage in classroom discussion and his male peers' refusal to participate.

Mr. Smith gave this example in order to help students learn about Cicero's predicament and the curricular theme of loyalty and resistance. The class has been discussing the question of when citizens owe loyalty to their leaders and when they should resist unreasonable authority. By making Maurice a hypothetical Cicero, caught between loyalty to and resistance against the hypothetical tyrant, Mr. Smith hopes to discuss how a citizen like Cicero might decide between loyalty to and resistance against authority. Maurice begins to engage with this issue at lines 159–162 when his initial reaction cites his own safety as the primary consideration in deciding between loyalty and resistance. As the class continues to discuss the example, and as Maurice's own identity becomes increasingly relevant, students use their local metapragmatic model of Maurice's identity to explore the larger curricular question.

As they continue discussing the example, Maurice's own identity – caught between participating in discussion with the teachers and avoiding that discussion like the resistant boys – becomes increasingly salient and awkward. Maurice's hypothetical decision about whether to side with Mr. Smith has increasingly clear implications for Maurice's own identity. We begin to see this in the following segment:

> T/S: well that was my next question, do you think Caesar was
> a tyrant.[do you think Cicero thought=
> 185   FST: [I don't think so.
> T/S: =Caesar was a tyrant.
> FST: no
> MRC: yes
> T/S: then what's his problem. if the man- you just told me
> 190   point blank [that we could be pushed down stairs=
> MRC: [so.
> T/S: =and you wouldn't feel a thing about it. what's his big
> deal, if he believes Caesar is a tyrant, so what.
> MRC: well- he- if u:h he [4 unintelligible syllables] that they're
> 195   making some kind of plot against him, but he doesn't want to get
> involved. he doesn't know if he should get involved, he could get
> himself in more trouble. since he's already [3 unintelligible syllables]=
> T/S: well if Caesar's a tyrant why shouldn't you get
> involved. tyrants are generally dictatorial nasty people,
> 200   that prevent peo:ple from being at their ease.

When Mr. Smith says, "You just told me point blank that we could be pushed down stairs and you wouldn't feel a thing about it" (lines 189–192), both the volume and tempo of his speech increase. He seems angry. This contrasts with his light-hearted tone and laughter at line 157 above, where he seemed more clearly to be teasing. By line 192, Mr. Smith has escalated his emotional involvement, and thus he may be raising the stakes of the interaction. It used to be a joke, but now he is taking Maurice's choice more seriously. Even though they are just speaking about the example, Mr. Smith treats Maurice's choice not to tell him as a betrayal. (Mr. Smith uses "we" at line 190 because by this point Mrs. Bailey has become another hypothetical tyrant in the example.)

This starts to put the same sort of pressure on Maurice himself that was applied to Cicero and is being applied to Maurice in his hypothetical role as a potential informer. Maurice-the-student has begun to occupy

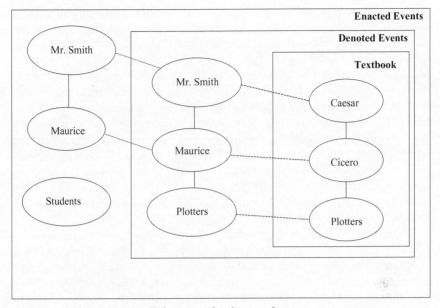

FIGURE 5.2. Emerging parallels across the three realms.

Maurice-the-potential-informer's role, as it is described in the example. He is caught between someone in power (the teacher) and others who resist. In the metapragmatic model that teachers and students have developed of the classroom, the opposition group includes the male students who refuse to participate. This yields an emerging three-way parallel between the events described in the text, the example and the classroom itself. Cicero was caught between those in power and those in opposition. In the hypothetical example, Maurice gets caught between the tyrannical teachers and those planning to push them down the stairs. In the classroom, Maurice is getting caught between the teachers and the unresponsive male students.

Figure 5.2 represents this emerging parallel between the example and Maurice's own identity in the classroom, with the dotted lines connecting the three analogous realms. The figure uses different types of dotted lines to represent the different character of the two analogies. The parallel between the text and the example involves iconism between two cognitive models. The parallel between these and the enacted events of the interactional text involves emerging iconism between cognitive and metapragmatic models. As the discussion proceeds, these cognitive and metapragmatic models start to co-develop and the boundary between them blurs. (Although it is available in the structure of the models, the male students have not yet been placed into the analogous role of plotters in the classroom, so that part of the parallel is still missing.)

In addition to reinforcing Maurice's social identity as a boy caught between the teachers and the other boys, the parallel across these three domains also has the potential to help students build more complex cognitive models of the curriculum. In the first segment at lines 159–162, Maurice presented his own safety as the primary consideration in his decision not to warn the tyrant. At lines 198–200, Mr. Smith points out that, if Maurice is really dealing with a tyrant, he should join the resistance. The teacher is arguing that decisions about loyalty and resistance should not be made solely out of self-interest. Sometimes a citizen must act against those in power. As the students explore this and related arguments about Cicero's predicament and about loyalty and resistance, the analogy between classroom relations and the loyalty/resistance theme allows them to use their emerging metapragmatic model of Maurice's own identity as a resource.

Mr. Smith's comment at lines 198–200 also seems to lessen the interactional pressure on Maurice. At lines 189–193, Mr. Smith put interactional pressure on Maurice to side with the teachers by speaking in an angry tone. But at lines 198–200, he seems to be arguing that Maurice should oppose the hypothetical tyrants. This shift shows that the interactional positions in this classroom event have not yet solidified. Despite the potential parallel between Maurice's in-between position and Cicero's, after line 200 teachers and students might have gone on to position Maurice as just another student discussing the topic of tyranny and resistance. Mr. Smith's apparent anger could have been merely a pedagogical device to get Maurice involved in the discussion. Despite the power of sociohistorical and local models to frame events, the social identification and academic learning that actually occur in any event are contingent accomplishments.

As this event proceeds, however, teachers and students continue to develop the overlap between Maurice's own in-between identity in the classroom and the second curricular theme. Thus they make the analogy among the text, the example and Maurice's identity stronger and more salient. Teachers and students use categories from the curriculum to crystallize the metapragmatic model of Maurice's identity "in the middle" and to put increasing interactional pressure on him. This begins to happen a few minutes later in the discussion when several girls volunteer to tell the teachers about the plot. Up to this point the example has contained only Mr. Smith and Maurice as characters. When the girls enter the example as loyalists, however, the local metapragmatic model that sharply separates girls from boys becomes more readily available as a resource for both academic learning and social identification. This gendered model of loyalty and resistance in the classroom becomes available as a resource for making sense of Cicero's text and the curricular theme. Once it includes the loyal girls, discussion of the example for academic purposes also allows teachers and students to refine their metapragmatic model of Maurice's identity in the classroom. They take advantage of the curricular distinction between the powerful, the loyal and the resistant to reinforce Maurice's awkward dual identity.

At this point, in the following segment, these cognitive and metapragmatic models begin to co-develop.

> **T/S:** gee you sound terribly confused Maurice. sort of like Cicero here.
> **T/B:** what w- if you knew that they actually- you know there's a group of kids that are actually going to do: this
> 225   dastardly deed. and you know that there's going to be some reaction. what might you do th- and you kn- you know basically wh:ile you might not be- enamored totally of Mr. Smith or myself you- basically: don't wish that we were crippled for life or whatever, what might
> 230   you do that day. you know that's going to come- that this is all going to happen on Wednesday. what are you going to do that day.
> **CAN:** I would try to warn you.
> **FSTs:** right. I would ((* overlapping [comments *))
> 235   **T/B:**   [he's- he's not- he's not going to warn us though.
> **T/S:** no.
> **T/B:** what- what are you going to do that day Maurice. (1.0)
> **MRC:** stay away. [2 unintelligible syllables]
> 240   **T/B:** what are you going to do?
> **MRC:** I'm going to stay away so I won't be- be:
> **T/B:** so you're not going to come to school on Wednesday.
> **MRC:** °no°
> **CAN:** that way he's a coward.
> 245   **FST:** what would you do.
> **MRC:** what would you do.
> **T/S:** a coward.
> **CAN:** yeah 'cause he's scared.

This segment decreases the distance between the events described by the participant example and the classroom interaction itself. Several times they start making a point in the conditional, or with a modal that indicates the events of the participant example are hypothetical (lines 223, 229, 233, 245) – saying "if he knew," he "might," and he "would." But then they move toward the present indicative, talking about Maurice's actions as if they are happening in the here and now – "there's a group of kids," "he's not going to warn us" and "he's scared." Maurice himself describes his hypothetical actions in the indicative ("I'm going to stay away"), thereby also moving the events of the example closer to those occurring among the teachers and students themselves in the classroom.

This decreasing distance between the example and the classroom itself brings the girls' own identities into play. Because of the developing analogy between the classroom and the curriculum – an analogy that has been further elaborated through the discussion of Mr. Smith the hypothetical tyrant and Maurice the potential informer – the girls' appearance in the example raises the question of how they are positioning themselves in the classroom. If Mr. Smith himself has power in the classroom, somewhat like a tyrant, how do the girls relate to this power? At lines 233–234, Candace and other female students indicate that they would affiliate with the teachers in the example. This adds another group to the emerging cognitive model being developed in the example: loyal subjects. But it also reinforces the girls' position as students loyal to the teachers' agenda and opposed to the boys' resistance in the classroom itself. By making their own classroom identities salient in this way, the girls also intensify Maurice's predicament. When Candace, and then Mr. Smith, call Maurice a coward at lines 244 and 247, Candace begins to speak as Candace-the-student and not as a hypothetical Roman. She is not only elaborating the example but also challenging Maurice himself. Like their characters in the example, the girls in the classroom affiliate with the teachers and exclude Maurice.

As we have seen, the vocal girls have been doing this for several months now. They take advantage of the cognitive model brought by the textbook and the example to push even harder on the tension in Maurice's identity. Insofar as he wants to be a good student, Maurice might want to affiliate with Mr. Smith-the-tyrant and thus, by implication, with Mr. Smith-the-teacher. But once the girls enter the participant example, Maurice would have to affiliate with both the girls and the teachers. This would damage his standing with the boys. Mr. Smith and Candace have thus put Maurice into a Cicero-like predicament – one that has implications for his social identity as a "good" student and as "one of the boys" – by mobilizing categories from the curriculum.

Figure 5.3 represents how teachers and students are beginning to *enact* the participant example at this point. This enactment involves an elaborate analogy among (1) Caesar, Cicero and the Roman plotters; (2) Mr. Smith-the-tyrant, Candace-the-loyalist, Maurice-the-potential-informer and the student plotters; and (3) the teachers, the "loyal" girls, Maurice and the "resistant" boys. The figure represents this analogy with dotted lines across the three realms. The analogy, facilitated by the participant example, allows the co-development of local cognitive and metapragmatic models. Teachers and students identify Maurice and intensify his interactional predicament by using a model of identity borrowed from the curriculum, one that represents Cicero caught in the middle between those in power and those who

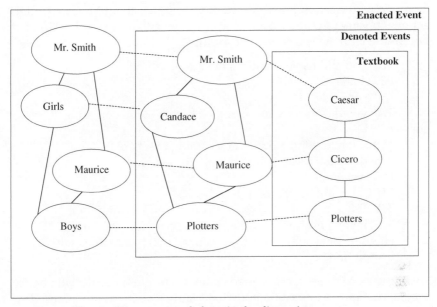

FIGURE 5.3. The participant example later in the discussion.

resist. At the same time, they develop a local cognitive model of the curriculum borrowing from metapragmatic models of their own identity. The resistant boys, for instance, are routinely identified as unpromising and inappropriate. This negative evaluation seeps into their cognitive model of the curriculum, as teachers and female students represent the tyrant as more sympathetic than the plotters.

Like Maurice-the-potential-informer, and like Cicero, Maurice-the-student gets excluded from the classroom interaction as he thinks about what to do. The teachers and the vocal girls accomplish this marginalization in part through pronoun usage. For much of the remaining discussion after line 244, other speakers exclude Maurice from the conversation, referring to him as *he*, whereas before they had referred to him as *you*. Maurice started out participating with the teachers in the discussion of the example. But immediately after Candace has said that she, unlike Maurice, would warn the teachers about the plot, the teachers and girls start to exclude Maurice, referring to him as *he*. They could have continued to refer to him as *you*, as they do while discussing Mr. Smith and Candace as characters in the hypothetical example. The switch to *he* sends an interactional message: Maurice no longer belongs to the group that dominates classroom discussion, the group that includes the teachers and the vocal girls. In both the example and the classroom, Maurice is caught on the outside.

As the conversation proceeds, Mr. Smith speaks about Maurice's inter-actional position in the past tense, as if Maurice had irrevocably decided not to side with the teachers in the example.

> **T/S:** you told <u>us</u> you wouldn't tell us <u>a</u>nything.
> **FST:** haha
> **FST:** °<u>I</u> wouldn't.°
> **T/S:** you'd rather see our mangled <u>bo</u>dies at the bottom of
365 the staircase.
> **MRC:** I: told you I wouldn't be coming to <u>school</u> that day.
> **T/S:** does that mean you're not part of the plot.
> **FST:** yeah
> **MRC:** I'd <u>still</u> be part of it. I- [if I
370 **T/B:**   [if you- if you <u>know</u> about it=
> **T/S:** if you <u>know</u> about it that's: an ac<u>com</u>plice. you <u>knew</u>
> about it. you could have <u>stopped</u> it. all you had to do is say-
> it shouldn't be done, it's wrong.

At line 366, Maurice faces a predicament. He must decide whether to accept Mr. Smith's description of what Maurice's actions have caused, or whether to change course and affiliate with the teachers in the classroom. In response, Maurice tries to cast himself as a potential victim of the plot-ters, just as the teachers are. At lines 196, 241 and in this segment at line 366, he says that he is going to stay away from school because he could face retribution from the plotters if he joined the teachers and face retribution from the teachers if he joined the plotters.

Discussing his hypothetical character within the example, Maurice adopts a strategy similar to the one he has himself been using in the classroom. He has tried to maintain his identity as both a good student and a respectable boy by refusing to identify himself completely with either the teachers or the boys. As described above, he has tried to position himself as something of an individualist – participating in dis-cussion with the girls, but opposing their arguments in many cases and thus maintaining his distance. Within the example, he makes his hypothet-ical character adopt an analogous strategy. It turns out that Cicero himself did this – he stayed out of the way, did not choose a side and waited for the conflict to get resolved. Both Maurice-the-potential-informer and Maurice-the-student adopt a similar strategy. Maurice thus tries to main-tain a stance that had been largely successful, siding neither with the girls and the teachers nor with the boys.

On May 10, however, the girls and the teachers make this strategy impos-sible. Candace and the girls have labeled him a coward. And Mr. Smith does not accept his hypothetical choice to stay away from school. He accuses Maurice of wishing for the teachers' violent demise. Mr. Smith's colorful comment at lines 364–365 might be taken as a joke, but Maurice's tone at line 366 is earnest. Mr. Smith seems angry again at line 371. By using the word "accomplice" to refer to Maurice-the-potential-informer, Mr. Smith casts Maurice's hypothetical character as morally questionable. Choosing to stay away, Mr. Smith implies, is tantamount to joining the plotters. Mr. Smith thus denies Maurice the middle ground of staying away, and he thereby puts more pressure on Maurice to choose one side or the other.

Maurice makes his decision, saying that his hypothetical character will stay away and then by withdrawing himself from the conversation. After line 373 the teachers and students consistently refer to Maurice as *he* for about six minutes. Maurice has been excluded from the teachers and the vocal girls' group in the classroom. He can still be a member of the boys' group, but the other boys almost never participate in class. So by joining that group he seems to be giving up on classroom participation. Maurice tried to maintain an identity both as a student who makes valuable contributions in class and as an adolescent male respected by his peers. But through the example, Mr. Smith and the girls made his balancing act difficult, and for the moment they have forced him to choose one of his identities over the other.

Catalyzed by the discussion on May 10, teachers and students solidified their analogy between the second curricular theme and the social organization of the classroom. The power relationships described in the curriculum became analogous to power relationships in the classroom. Using this analogy, teachers and students further developed their local metapragmatic/cognitive model of Maurice's identity as caught "in the middle" between the powerful and the resistance. The teachers and the girls used the three-part distinction between those in power, those caught in-between and those opposed in order to identify Maurice himself as caught between being a good student and being a male student respected by the other boys. Before May 10, the vocal girls had tried to exclude Maurice from classroom discussion, and they had occasionally forced him to withdraw and join the boys. On May 10, joined by the teachers, the girls used their emerging local cognitive model of the second curricular theme to do this more effectively.

Later in the discussion on May 10, however, Mrs. Bailey and the girls invited Maurice back into the conversation – this time as a potential ally on their side against Mr. Smith. The following segment, from later in the May 10 discussion of Cicero, shows how Maurice re-entered the conversation. This discussion also illustrates how, at the same time as teachers and students used their cognitive model of the curriculum to identity Maurice, Maurice's emerging identity also helped students develop their local cognitive model. The teachers wanted students to learn about Cicero's predicament through Maurice's, and in fact teachers and students explicitly articulated the analogy between Maurice's position in the classroom "society" and Cicero's position in Roman society. In the following segment,

Mrs. Bailey leads students through the first of ten questions that Cicero explicitly asks his friend Atticus in the text.

> **T/B:** okay so <u>now</u> let's see how we can compare
> 455 Maurice's situation at this point to the <u>options</u> that
> Cicero is articulating or lining out for his friend
> Atticus. take the <u>first</u> one would you Gary. (4.0) just
> take the <u>first</u> one. <u>read</u> it and let's see what we can
> <u>do</u> with it. how does Maurice's situation compare with
> 460 Ci- Cicero's situation.
> **GAR:** [reading] should a man continue to live in his
> own country under a dic- tatorship.
> **T/B:** okay, what would <u>that</u> mean as far as Maurice.
> **CAN:** shou- should he stay in the room even though Mr.
> 465 Smith's been a <u>bad</u>- a <u>hard</u> teacher.

Without hesitation, Candace re-phrases one of Cicero's questions in terms of the "Maurice in the middle" example. Other students are able to do this with the questions that follow, showing that at least some of them understand the analogy between the hypothetical Maurice and Cicero's text.

As described in Chapter 3, one of these teachers' central Paideia goals was to have students draw analogies between their own experiences and the essentially contestable questions raised in the curriculum. The teachers wanted students to use their own experiences to formulate arguments about curricular topics. As they discuss Cicero's text, students begin to do this.

> **T/B:** okay so- should Maurice, <u>continue</u> in this room, quietly
> 470 going along (2.0) with the situation. okay do number <u>two</u>
> Ivory.
> **IVR:** °should he do everything possible to overthrow the
> dictatorship do th-°
> **T/B:** could you read it <u>louder</u> and <u>slower</u>.
> 475 **IVR:** [reading] should <u>he</u> do everything <u>possible</u> to
> overthrow the dictatorship. do the ends justify the
> means even if it place the <u>state</u> <u>itself</u> in danger.
> **T/B:** okay. now what does <u>that</u> mean Ivory.
> **IVR:** should he do everything- (6.0)
> 480 everything that- [(5.0)   should he do=
> **T/B:**   [<u>Maurice.</u>
> **IVR:** =everything he c- he <u>could</u> to make Mr. S- Mr. Smith
> reconsider his a- as<u>sign</u>ment even if it means putting-
> the class in danger.

485 **T/B:** o:kay. even if it means putting the class it<u>self</u> in
danger, <u>nice</u>ly done. okay now what are some of the things
he could have done. (2.0)
IVR: um (2.0) he could have a meeting with Mr. Smith
or something.
490 **T/B:** have a <u>meet</u>ing with Mr. Smith. what would be the <u>dan</u>ger
of talking to Mr. Smith about the imp<u>oss</u>ibility of this
assignment.
IVR: they could get into an <u>arg</u>ument. he can [3 unintelligible
syllables]
T/B: he gets into an <u>arg</u>ument. and what might result for the
495 rest of the class. one of you just said <u>state</u> equals
class
STS: [unintelligible comments]
T/B: you don't <u>like</u> this. do <u>twice</u> as much. right? you've
certainly've all run across <u>that</u> line at different
500 points. okay <u>that</u> might put you in danger. what <u>al</u>so
might put you in danger. more extreme danger.
FST: he could just nail the whole class.

In this segment, Ivory, considered by the teachers to be one of the weaker students, successfully uses the analogy between the text and the example. At line 482, for instance, she re-states Cicero's second question in terms of the Maurice example. And at line 493 she begins to use what she knows about Maurice and Mr. Smith to extend her thinking about the issues in Cicero's text. At line 495, Mrs. Bailey re-states a comment that she attributes to a student, a comment that makes explicit the analogy that they have been working with: "state equals class."

At line 502, we see a student continue using the analogy. All the students know about Mr. Smith's "tyrannical" tendencies. He did in fact "nail the whole class" on occasion. When provoked by students' misbehavior or lack of preparation, he would sometimes drag them line by line through a text and point out students' misunderstandings. The student speaking at line 502 also knows that Maurice has often challenged Mr. Smith, disagreeing with his arguments as a way of both participating in class and maintaining his distance from the teachers. The local metapragmatic model of Maurice and Mr. Smith's identities in the classroom thus provides resources that students use to develop a cognitive model of Cicero's predicament. Students do not articulate a full argument about this second curricular theme during the "Maurice in the middle" class, but over the year they formulated such arguments about curricular themes in more sophisticated ways (as described in Chapter 3).

In addition to helping the students reason about the curriculum, in this part of the discussion Mrs. Bailey also pursued another interactional strategy – one that moved Maurice out of his awkward position in the

middle. Mrs. Bailey and Mr. Smith did not get along well. This was
Mr. Smith's first year at Colleoni High. He had used his seniority as a vet-
eran teacher to displace the prior history teacher, who had been a friend of
Mrs. Bailey's. In addition, Mrs. Bailey considered him to be harsh and too
demanding as a teacher. She tried to build relationships and form alliances
with the students, while Mr. Smith did not seem to care what the students thought and remained a distant authority figure. The example of
Mr. Smith the tyrant thus gave Mrs. Bailey an opportunity to criticize him
as too demanding, by mobilizing the curricular category of "tyrant" to
identify Mr. Smith himself. This is apparent at line 491, where she describes
Mr. Smith's assignment as "impossible." Because this is a participant example one could ask: Is Mr. Smith himself tyrannical in class? There has been
evidence earlier in the discussion that Mr. Smith's own identity is in fact
relevant.

> **T/B:** let's- Maurice is our Cicero character here. okay, a:nd
> the issue °I- I'm going to leave myself out of this one.° the-
> 430 the issue is Mr. Smith who we all know has been
> oppressing you all year.
> **FST:** mmhmm.
> **T/B:** o[kay.
> **MRC:** [mmhmm.
> 435 **T/B:** a:nd a group of people have decided that (1.0) it is
> time to end the oppression. especially when you've said
> look at how much is left in the history book, you are to go
> home and in the next two weeks learn everything, and your
> final exam and last grade will be based on mastery of all of
> 440 the stuff that's left in the history book that we haven't done
> this year. you know what your history books have left in
> them [right?
> **T/S:** [centuries.
> **T/B:** okay. so that's the oppression. he's got total control
> 445 over your grade. if you don't do that you know you're
> going to end up in summer school, wonderful way to spend
> the summer, so, some- some of you get together and say this
> will end and we'll end it by doing in Mr.- Smith, between
> class periods on the stairs.

At line 429, Mrs. Bailey excludes herself from the example. She and
Mr. Smith had both been hypothetical tyrants, but she removes herself
from the example and leaves Mr. Smith-the-tyrant as the topic of discussion. Mrs. Bailey then takes the opportunity to exaggerate the harshness of
Mr. Smith's teaching and discipline. She is speaking about the example,
which is merely hypothetical. As she describes the hypothetical Mr. Smith

as tyrannical, however, her complaints echo those that both she and the students sometimes made about Mr. Smith himself.

As the class keeps discussing the example, Mrs. Bailey not only ratchets up her negative characterization of Mr. Smith, but she also encourages the students to imagine an even more gruesome end for Mr. Smith the tyrant. She thus shifts the interactional focus away from Maurice and onto Mr. Smith. In this context, she invites Maurice back into the classroom interaction.

> **T/B:** okay that- that could be another danger the class
> could face. okay- what's another thing you could do that
> 505 might put the whole class in danger. (5.0) Mr. Smith is in
> the room and he's talking away, he's got his back to you
> because he's writing on the blackboard. what do you do
> Maurice? you're evil, now remember [do the=
> **STS:**   [hahahaha
> 510 **T/B:** =most extreme thing, get rid of Mi- get rid of Mr.
> Smith, his back is to you at the blackboard, what can you
> do.
> **CAS:** throw something at him. I don't know.
> **T/B:** throw something at him? like a- an eraser? is that
> 515 going to do much good?
> **FST:** or a chair
> **FST:** a book
> **T/B:** a book?

At line 508, Mrs. Bailey gives Maurice an opportunity to imagine that he might do something to Mr. Smith. She encourages Maurice to do something "extreme" and reminds him that he is "evil." Earlier in the discussion Maurice was not "evil" at all – he was an unfortunate potential informer caught between the tyrants and the plotters. But now Mrs. Bailey has invited him back into the example with a different role, as the assassin selected to eliminate the tyrannical Mr. Smith.

This affects Maurice's identity in two ways. First, he is no longer interactionally positioned between the girls and the boys. He has been invited to join Mrs. Bailey and the girls as they use the example to tease and complain about Mr. Smith. Maurice willingly accepts the invitation. At line 434, he had returned to the classroom discussion to complain briefly about Mr. Smith, and after line 518 he joins subsequent discussions of the example. But Maurice is still singled out. He is not just another one of the group because he is now the "dangerous" one who can assassinate Mr. Smith. Mrs. Bailey enlists him on her side, but as someone to do the girls' dirty work. So Maurice is once again a member of the group participating in class, but he has a special status. It may be that his maleness makes him "dangerous," but they do not pursue this possibility.

Maurice also plays an important role a few minutes later, as Mrs. Bailey's plot against Mr. Smith backfires.

> **T/B:** okay. Maurice takes care of the <u>prob</u>lem. Mr. Smith
> 600   is <u>gone</u>. what's the <u>next</u> problem you're going to face.
>   **CAS:** another <u>teacher</u>.
>   **T/B:** who- comes in and he looks at Mr. Smith's <u>lesson</u>
>   plans and says, <u>that's</u> what you guys are doing. (1.0) how
>   you- what kind of pre<u>cau</u>tions ca:n you all take to keep <u>that</u>
> 605   from happening.
>   **MRC:** destroy the lesson plans.
>   **STS:** hnhnh hahahahahaha
>   **T/S:** ah but suppose Mrs. <u>Bai</u>ley, who now knows I was
>   pushed down the stairs begins to worry she's the <u>next</u> one.
> 610   what happens to sweet Mrs. <u>Bai</u>ley.
>   **MRC:** hnh she gets killed.
>   **T/S:** hahaha you get <u>killed</u>. O:h?
>   **STS:** [1 second overlapping comments]
>   **MAR:** no more <u>Ju</u>lius Caesar.
> 615   **T/B:** n(hh)o more Julius Caesar.

At line 606, Maurice willingly imagines the sort of havoc students might create after eliminating Mr. Smith-the-tyrant. But at line 608, Mr. Smith turns the tables on Mrs. Bailey. His hypothetical character has been killed, and thus the students may have (analogically) expressed their dislike toward Mr. Smith himself. But Mr. Smith then entices the students to do the same to Mrs. Bailey. Maurice obliges at line 611, imagining that she would be killed too. Mr. Smith laughs heartily. Mrs. Bailey used the curricular category of tyrant to identify Mr. Smith himself as tyrannical, and she successfully enticed the students to express their dislike for Mr. Smith. But then Mr. Smith leads the students to apply the category to Mrs. Bailey too.

This shift in Maurice's identity, from being "in the middle" to joining Mrs. Bailey and the girls in criticizing Mr. Smith, illustrates the contingency and multiplicity of his identity. Maurice was not simply a typical African American boy whose identity was determined by familiar sociohistorical categories. The girls did draw on the sociohistorical stereotype of resistant, unpromising black males as they worked to exclude him from classroom conversations, but this stereotype did not suffice to describe Maurice's identity because teachers and students applied it in unexpected ways in the local context of Mrs. Bailey and Mr. Smith's classroom and in the even more local contexts of particular events. Neither was Maurice's social identity determined by the emerging local model of Maurice in the middle or the pervasive local model of promising girls and unpromising boys. Both sociohistorical and local models played an important role in constraining his identity, but they were sometimes overridden or modified within and across contingent events.

The example of Mr. Smith being pushed down the stairs made such an impact on teachers and students that they referred to it in subsequent classes. On May 17, for instance, they discussed Antony's speech to the Romans, as described in Shakespeare's *Julius Caesar*. In the following segment from May 17, Mrs. Bailey refers back to the example of Mr. Smith the tyrant that they had developed on May 10. "He" at the beginning of the segment refers to Antony.

> **JAS:** no. cause he know he got u:m, the plebians on his side they gon' stick <u>up</u> for him.
> **T/B:** so he's- he's got them- he's <u>play</u>ing them. and he's got- he's pretty sure he's got them on- on a <u>line</u> now. [I =
> 845 **STS:**   [[overlapping comments]
> **T/B:** mean just a- we got, remember, what was it <u>last</u> week? we got into that whole thing a few weeks ago with Mr. Smith being <u>pushed</u> down the stairs.
> 850 **STS:** hahahh [ahaa Mr. Smith
> **T/B:**   [I can- I can't remember the- the- the <u>in</u>tricacies of that whole thing floating around but- and, you know, <u>I</u> come to Mr. Smith's funeral and I say. I <u>fea:r</u> I <u>wro:ng</u> these good students who:se actions have killed Mr.
> 855 Smith. [I do fear it.
> **FSTs:** [and we say <u>yeah</u>(hh)
> **T/B:** okay- give [me a break guys.
> **MRC:**   [he can read the will there-
> **T/B:** pardon?
> 860 **MRC:** he can read the will there even if he <u>is</u> wrong then because he has them on his side. they started [3 unintelligible syllables] and if uh. <u>Bru</u>tus and whoever it was, if they go <u>up</u> there, and try to make him <u>stop</u>, the- everybody else is gonna at<u>tack</u> them.

At line 849, Mrs. Bailey refers back to the example, and she tries to use the example to discuss Antony's speech. This does not work, because the students just laugh about the example instead of engaging with the subject matter. Maurice's response at line 861 is characteristic, however. He offers a sensible and serious interpretation of the text here, acting like a good student in the same way that he has all year.

The May 17 class also contains instances of Maurice's other characteristic interactional position – being ostracized by the girls.

T/B: what about this- this- part here? (2.0)
this last part about ninety two. (5.0) bear with me my heart
645   is in the coffin there with Caesar and I must pause till it
come back to me. what's that about?
MRC: it means it's- he's grievin' about Caesar. and he
can't, uh, finish talking until he's finished.
FSTs: [1 second of laughter]
650   **NAT:** but that doesn't make sense
MRC: what?
T/B: what's the problem Natasha?
NAT: I don't understand what he said. he said you can't
finish until he's finished. [laughter among female students]
655   **MRC:** I mean. he can't finish breathing. I mean he can't
finish talking until he's finished breathing.
NAT: I don't, see that (3.0) [laughter again among FSTs]
T/B: do you think that's what's going on? he's so
overcome by emotion he can't speak anymore?
660   **FSTs:** no.
FST: I think
NAT: I think like he, he sayin', you know, feels be<u>lie</u>ved.
you know, he still. (2.0) you know like he still, his heart is
in the coffin with Caesar, I think like, he's mad, he still,
665   be<u>lie</u>ve, you know he still [4 unintelligible syllables]

At line 649, several girls laugh at Maurice's answer. Maurice tries to clarify his point at line 655, but the girls continue to object and laugh at lines 657 and 660. This is the familiar pattern: Despite the fact that Maurice makes a sensible point, the girls ridicule and marginalize him. In this class on May 17, then, we see two of Maurice's three characteristic interactional positions. He answers questions seriously and intelligently, and the teachers treat him as a good student. He also gets teased and attacked by the girls, who marginalize him as an outcast from their group.

CONCLUSIONS

Like Tyisha, Maurice's social identity changed in unpredictable ways across the academic year. He started off as just another good student. When the local metapragmatic model of promising girls and unpromising boys became robust in October and November, he became the one boy who nonetheless acted like a promising student. At first this did not cause problems for Maurice. He acted like both a promising student and a respectable boy, and no one challenged either of these identities. But starting in December, the vocal girls regularly challenged his academic contributions and marginalized him in class discussions. The girls' attempts to marginalize him gained more traction when the class began discussing the first curricular theme, with its category of "beast" or outcast. Using the analogy between the classroom and a "society," teachers and students applied the curricular category of outcast to Maurice several times. This reinforced Maurice's awkward in-between position as the only boy who participated in class discussions with the teachers and the girls.

Maurice responded by embracing his individuality. He defended unpopular positions against the vocal girls and the teachers, and he maintained some distance from the teachers and the girls by challenging them. But he continued to participate constructively and refused to let the girls silence him. The teachers generally supported Maurice, treating him like a cooperative, promising student. During some discussions, however, like those on February 18 and May 10, the teachers joined the vocal girls and forced Maurice to withdraw into silence as the other boys habitually did. The second curricular theme provided the teachers and vocal girls with an important resource that they used to foreground Maurice's awkward in-between position and force him into silence: Categories of identity drawn from the curriculum and from the analogy between the classroom and a hierarchical society.

As they used these categories of identity from the curriculum to develop Maurice's social identity – catalyzed by the May 10 discussion of Maurice as a participant example – teachers and students constructed systematic overlap between their local cognitive models of the curriculum and their local metapragmatic models of Maurice's identity. The analogy between the classroom and a society was central to this overlap. Categories such as "loyalist," "resistant" and "in the middle" both facilitated teachers and students' thinking about the curricular question of when citizens should resist against the powerful and their social identification of Maurice as caught between the loyal girls and the resistant boys. As was the case with Tyisha, the social identification of Maurice in this classroom meshed with and became inextricable from students' learning about the loyalty/resistance theme.

Despite the importance of the local metapragmatic/cognitive model in this case, however, Maurice's emerging in-between identity did not depend solely on local models. Teachers and students used sociohistorical models of students like Maurice as another resource in identifying Maurice and creating his predicament. African American males who want to engage with school face a balancing act in many urban U.S. classrooms, as they are caught between the often-opposed roles of "good" student and "respectable" male (Anderson, 1999; Ferguson, 2000; Fordham, 1996). If they consistently position themselves as opposed to the teachers, they may no longer qualify as good students. But if they position themselves on the same side as the teachers, they may no longer qualify as respectable African American males. Students and teachers were able to develop Maurice's identity "in the middle" in part because they at least tacitly drew on the sociohistorical predicament of many African American males in contemporary American schools.

As I have argued, however, Maurice was not simply another example of this predicament. Just like Tyisha, Maurice's local identity drew on sociohistorical models but modified these in local context and in particular events. The teachers and students in this classroom drew categories like "outcast," "potential informer" and "in the middle" from a distinctive curriculum to model Maurice's identity, and his identity took shape against the robust local stereotype of promising girls and unpromising boys. Teachers and students used resources from various timescales as they identified Maurice in shifting ways across the year, and thus we cannot explain Maurice's classroom identity primarily with reference to sociohistorical processes. The outcome of Maurice's social identification also differed from the typical case. Unlike many African American boys (and girls) faced with a similar dilemma, in Mrs. Bailey and Mr. Smith's classroom Maurice managed to retain both aspects of his identity. On February 18 and May 10, Maurice's interactional position became so awkward that he withdrew from the conversation for a while, but he never stayed silent for long. Maurice continued to participate in class and to defend himself most of the time, despite the awkward position created by his in-between identity. In this regard, too, Maurice did not fit the sociohistorical stereotype.

6

Denaturalizing Identity, Learning and Schooling

In *The Paideia Proposal*, Adler argues that American schools are failing to fulfill their central mission of preparing students to participate in democracy. Now that the United States has progressed to universal suffrage, he argues, our educational system must prepare all students for their rights and responsibilities as citizens. We must overcome "the cultural inequality of homes and environments" (Adler, 1982: p. 39) and provide truly equal educational opportunity to all, such that we become "an educationally classless society." To accomplish this, Adler prescribes the Paideia curriculum in which all students have the opportunity to read classic texts and relate these texts to their own lives through seminar discussion. A Paideia education will give disadvantaged students equal access to the powerful ideas found in classic texts, and it will show these students how such ideas can be connected to their own lives. This will not only enrich their lives, but it will also allow them to participate fully in democracy and accomplish social mobility.

Tyisha and Maurice's trajectories of identification can be read as ironic commentaries on this educational vision. Mrs. Bailey, Mr. Smith and their students used ideas from classic texts, together with other resources, to identify Tyisha and Maurice as disempowered outcasts from the classroom community. Teachers and students used classic models of the relation between an individual and society, for instance, like Aristotle's account of anti-social "beasts," as resources when they excluded Tyisha and identifed her as disruptive. Using classic models of the relation between loyalty and resistance, they forced Maurice to choose between his desire to do well in school and his desire to affiliate with the other boys. Instead of finding the ideas in classic texts empowering, then, Tyisha and Maurice had to fight against the disempowerment and exclusion that some of these ideas facilitated.

Classic texts became disempowering for these students, against Adler's expectations, because some of these texts describe hierarchy and exclusion.

Mrs. Bailey and Mr. Smith followed the Paideia practice of connecting classic texts to students' own lives. When those texts described hierarchy and exclusion, the teachers used instances of hierarchy and exclusion from the students' lives to illuminate the texts. The students responded well to this pedagogical technique because hierarchy, exclusion and many other ideas from classic texts do in fact apply to working-class African American students like Tyisha and Maurice. As Adler would have predicted, these classic ideas were both cognitively and interactionally powerful for the students – even though the texts were written by Aristotle, Hammurabi, Shakespeare and others from different cultural traditions. Despite their relevance and power for the students, however, these classic ideas did not benefit all of the students as Adler intended. Instead, some ideas helped teachers and students disempower Tyisha and Maurice in the classroom, as they applied classic models of hierarchy and exclusion to these two students. So Adler was right about the power of classic texts, but in this case he was wrong that the power of the ideas would benefit students.

The cases of Tyisha and Maurice can also be read as ironic commentaries on another common pedagogical injunction – that teachers should give students "voice" by allowing them to connect curriculum to their own experiences. Bushnell and Henry (2003), Maher and Tetreault (2001) and others have argued that students should not simply internalize authoritative knowledge. Instead, students should be exposed to the multiple voices that could legitimately speak on curricular topics. One favored technique involves students articulating their own perspectives on curricular topics. Teachers often accomplish this by having students relate the curriculum to their own experiences through autobiography, accounts of personal experience, participant examples and similar pedagogical devices. Mrs. Bailey and Mr. Smith followed this pedagogical strategy, insofar as they encouraged students to develop their own arguments and connect the curriculum to their own experiences. Tyisha and Maurice certainly related their experiences to the curriculum, but this did not allow them to articulate their own voices. On the contrary, teachers and students used discussions of these students' experiences to exclude them from classroom conversations and deny them voice. So advocates of student "voice" are right that students' experiences can be connected to the curriculum in powerful ways, but in some cases this does not include and empower students.

Why did the Paideia curriculum and the pedagogical use of students' experiences misfire in this case? Perhaps Adler and advocates of "experience-near" teaching are simply wrong. Perhaps connecting ideas from classic texts to students' own experiences does not help disadvantaged students achieve social mobility or articulate their own voices. From the single classroom analyzed in this book we can conclude only that Adler and advocates of student "voice" did not fully anticipate the consequences of their pedagogical strategies. Despite what happened to Tyisha and

Maurice, however, I would not argue against the goals of making students better citizens and giving them voice, nor against the method of having them relate classic texts to their own experiences. I have seen these pedagogical approaches work for many students, including some in Mrs. Bailey and Mr. Smith's classroom, and I believe that Paideia seminar discussions and experience-near teaching are often valuable for students.

I would like to draw a different lesson from Tyisha and Maurice's ironic exclusion and loss of voice. Adler and advocates of student "voice" recommend useful pedagogical techniques, but they make a common mistake in predicting the outcome of these techniques. They propose too-simple theories of education and social identification, assuming that curricular concepts and student experiences will always function in the same way. They fail to see how students' identities depend on processes and resources at various timescales and how these resources are combined in contingent ways that often produce unexpected outcomes. I do not deny that Adler and the other pedagogical theories describe how education and social identification sometimes work. Some Paideia students do increase their stock of symbolic capital and accomplish social mobility, and some students do find voice through experience-near teaching. Adler's mistake – one common to both folk and academic theories – is to overgeneralize from a special case, treating a contingent configuration of cross-timescale processes as the natural way that education and social identification work.

GENERALIZABILITY AND CROSS-TIMESCALE RELATIONS

In response, Adler and advocates of student "voice" would offer an alternative explanation for Tyisha and Maurice's ironic disempowerment. Their theories do not claim to predict every possible outcome, and Tyisha and Maurice may simply be unusual cases in which the students' social identities got tangled up with the curriculum in unproductive ways. In other words, Adler's theory may be generally correct and the cases described in this book may not generalize. At first glance, it seems plausible that Tyisha and Maurice represent unusual cases. The overlap between social identification and academic learning in Mrs. Bailey and Mr. Smith's classroom was accomplished in significant part through participant examples and analogies between curricular themes and the classroom itself, and most classrooms do not involve so many participant examples and such extensive analogies. So perhaps this classroom was an atypical case.

In one sense it is true that the cases described here are unusual, but it is false in two other senses. My analyses of this classroom do describe how participant examples and local analogies allowed systematic overlap between social identification and academic learning. I discuss other types of speech events besides participant examples, like explicit descriptions of students' identities and the tacit interactional positioning of students,

and I show how these also played an important role in the social identification and academic learning that teachers and students accomplished.
But I claim that participant examples played a key role in creating overlap
between local metapragmatic and local cognitive models. And I acknowledge that many classrooms do not involve so many participant examples
or the extensive analogies between the classroom and the curriculum that
Mrs. Bailey and Mr. Smith developed.

However, even though Mrs. Bailey, Mr. Smith and their students discussed many participant examples, the sort of overlap between social
identification and academic learning that I describe likely occurs more
widely. Participant examples are only one member of a very widespread
class of discursive and pedagogical tools. My analysis may generalize
to a broad range of discourse that involves human subject matter and
"personalization" as a pedagogical or rhetorical strategy. Other discursive devices besides participant examples can personalize subject matter
and connect it to students' identities. Narratives of personal experience,
for instance, can facilitate similar overlap between categories used to
describe particular students and categories used to describe the curriculum (Wortham, 2001a). Quoted speech can also function like participant
examples when it allows a speaker to bring the words of a participant into
an ongoing discussion of subject matter.

Teachers commonly use devices like these in classroom discussion.
Many language arts teachers, for instance, help students interpret their
own experience through reading. Dyson (1989), McKinley and Kamberelis
(1996), Wilhelm (1997) and others describe how teachers often help students connect their own experiences to the language arts curriculum,
such that students use literature to explore themselves and their worlds.
Heathcote (1984) and O'Neill (1995) describe teachers and students creating "dramas" that involve students themselves in scenarios modeled
on curricular topics. In these and many similar cases, contemporary educators are creating classroom events that link students' own experiences
to the curriculum. All these types of personalization can do what I have
shown participant examples doing: facilitate overlap between social identification and academic learning, as metapragmatic models of students'
identities and cognitive models of the subject matter come to share certain
categories. The analyses in this book describe one case in which personalizing discourse can create interconnections between social identification
and academic learning, but other types of personalizing pedagogy probably accomplish similar overlap.

Mrs. Bailey and Mr. Smith's classroom might seem unusual in another
respect. These teachers followed a particular pedagogical tradition, the
"great books" or "Paideia" tradition. As such, they encouraged students
to develop and defend their own opinions and gave students unusual
freedom to articulate their own points of view. This pedagogical strategy

is not as unusual as one might think, however. Hatano and Inagaki (1991), Michaels and Sohmer (2001) and O'Connor (2001), for instance, describe "position-driven" classroom discussions, in which teachers present challenging questions and encourage students to develop their own answers. Many teachers give students space to articulate their own points of view. When coupled with personalizing discourse, these sorts of discussions make possible the metapragmatic/cognitive overlap that I have described.

Such overlap will not always disempower students. The vocal girls in Mrs. Bailey and Mr. Smith's classroom were empowered by the analogies between their classroom relations and the curriculum. Even Tyisha and Maurice themselves were not completely disempowered, insofar as both of them continued to defend themselves and to participate in classroom discussions throughout the year. Furthermore, there is no reason to expect that metapragmatic/cognitive models in other classrooms would always involve problematic social relations like hierarchy and exclusion. Depending on the models facilitated by the curriculum in other cases, metapragmatic/cognitive overlap could have various effects on students' identities – empowerment as well as disempowerment, inclusion as well as exclusion, respect as well as disrespect. We need more empirical work to explore the types of metapragmatic/cognitive models that emerge in classrooms and how teachers might use such models to encourage more productive social identification.

Because many classroom discussions involve both personalizing discourse and extensive student participation, then, I argue that Tyisha and Maurice are not just special cases. Not all classrooms involve personalizing discourse and human subject matter, and not all teachers give students space to participate extensively in discussion. The processes I have described in Mrs. Bailey and Mr. Smith's classroom will not occur everywhere. But this classroom does resemble others in many respects. Thus, social identification and academic learning may well overlap elsewhere. How much other cases will resemble this one is an empirical question. Mrs. Bailey and Mr. Smith's classroom resembles others enough that we should look for and expect similar processes in other places.

There is a second sense in which my analysis of Mrs. Bailey and Mr. Smith's classroom cannot simply be dismissed as a special case. This way of framing the issue – as if mine is either a representative or unrepresentative case and Adler's predictions for the Paideia curriculum either succeed in general or do not – misses a central point of my analysis. My account of Tyisha and Maurice shows that we should not construe processes like social identification simply in terms of general theories and events that do or do not support those theories. In order to explain the social identification that happens in Mrs. Bailey and Mr. Smith's classroom, we must do more than invoke general theories about the Paideia curriculum as a route to social mobility or the social reproduction of disadvantage in American high schools. Any such general theory will not capture the varied configurations of cross-timescale relations that actually accomplish social identification. Even my claim that social identification and academic learning often overlap masks heterogeneity in how this happens across cases.

We cannot understand how the Paideia curriculum works in practice, nor how social identification and academic learning work, without analyzing relevant processes at various timescales. In order to understand the social identification and academic learning that occurred in Mrs. Bailey and Mr. Smith's classroom, we need to know about the robust local metapragmatic model of promising girls and unpromising boys that emerged across several months. We need to know about the unusual trajectories of identification traveled by Tyisha and Maurice, trajectories that made them exceptions to the local gendered model. We need to know about the actions and reactions of Tyisha and Maurice themselves and the actions of the vocal girls and the teachers as they struggled with and against the emerging local model and individual trajectories. The social identification and academic learning that occurred in this classroom depended on interrelations among these sociohistorical, ontogenetic, local and event-level processes. Tyisha and Maurice, then, are not simply cases that support or disprove general theories about Paideia instruction, social identification and academic learning. These cases illustrate how resources from unexpected timescales can be crucial. In general, different configurations of resources do essential work in different cases. It would be a mistake to overgeneralize from any particular case and conclude that a fixed set of resources always suffices to explain social identification, academic learning and other basic human processes.

Hacking (1990), Foucault (1975/1977) and others denaturalize sociohistorical categories of identity and universal social theories that depend on such categories. "Deviant" is not a universal category of identity, but instead emerged in a particular sociohistorical context and only appears natural to those of us living in that context. We should apply the same denaturalization to sociohistorical categories of identity and the social theories that depend on them. Just as "deviant" is a contingent category that emerged sociohistorically across years and decades, taken-for-granted sociohistorical categories also come to have meaning across months and years in local contexts and across individual trajectories. "Deviant," "male," "black" and other categories of social identity do not mean the same thing throughout a society, until decades later when the categories shift through the kinds of processes described by Hacking and Foucault. Instead, sociohistorical categories of identity come to mean different things in context. "Unpromising boy," for instance, meant something particular in Mrs. Bailey and Mr. Smith's classroom and something even more particular with respect to Maurice's trajectory of identification.

For three or four decades now, people have been denaturalizing socio-historical categories of identity in this way – pointing out the contingency and context-dependence of taken-for-granted social categories and the theories that depend on them. Garfinkel (1967) and Goffman (1974) show how people must work to apply sociohistorical categories of identity in everyday life and how the relevant categories for understanding a case cannot be determined out of local context. Bourdieu's (1972/1977) and subsequent versions of "practice" theory have shown how categories of identity only take effect through a process of structured but contingent improvisation. Willis (1977), de Certeau (1984) and others describe how people resist and reorganize sociohistorical categories of identity, from below. Such work has done to apparently natural sociohistorical categories what Hacking and Foucault did to the apparently natural categories unreflectively employed by governments and many social scientists.

However sophisticated the theories from which they come, these critiques of naturalized sociohistorical categories have often devolved into an antinomy between "macro and micro," or a "dialectic" between "structure and agency." This sort of account reduces the complexity of heterogeneous resources and cross-timescale relations to two apparently homogeneous levels: constraining structures and creative actions. On such accounts contingency and change are explained by unexpected individual actions or anomalous events in which sociohistorical patterns do not reproduce themselves as expected. I would certainly agree that individuals sometimes behave and events sometimes unfold in unexpected ways. But the cases of Tyisha and Maurice have shown how contingency and change do not occur only through allegedly autonomous individual action or through seminal events. Contingency happens when unpredictable configurations of resources from across multiple timescales play a role in processes like social identification.

Tyisha and Maurice's social identities emerged as resources from sociohistorical, ontological, local, event-based and other timescales facilitated the creation of unexpected metapragmatic models. As shown in Chapters 2 and 4, Tyisha was not simply a "loud black girl," unproblematically filling this sociohistorical category of identity. Sociohistorical categories were relevant, but only as mediated through local metapragmatic models and as enacted across an atypical trajectory of identification. On the other hand, Tyisha did not become the prototypical unpromising girl just because of something that she or someone else did, acting as an autonomous "agent" and reacting against sociohistorical structures. Her behavior only became identified as something a disruptive student would do when teachers and students construed that behavior using contingent metapragmatic models of identity developed at the local timescale – borrowing concepts from emerging local cognitive models of the curriculum – and as these metapragmatic models solidified along Tyisha's distinctive trajectory of identification. Accounting for the contingent, unexpected character of Tyisha and Maurice's identities in this classroom requires not only an account of their individual actions, not only an account of the events in which both expected and unexpected models of identity emerged, and not only an account of the sociohistorical categories that helped to identify them. It also requires an account of how relevant categories and models emerged at several timescales and intersected so as to create the distinctive identities that developed for these students.

In general, there is no one adequate account of how people get socially identified – neither in prescriptions for social change like Adler's nor in universalizing social and psychological theories. To describe a process like social identification as if one set of sociohistorical and other resources always plays the essential role is to naturalize particular instances of a contingent, heterogeneous process. Models of identity can emerge contingently at each of many potentially relevant timescales, from sociohistorical to ontogenetic to local to event-based, and no one timescale nor one universally applicable set of timescales suffices to describe how all individuals become socially identified. An adequate account will capture how processes at several relevant timescales together establish a contingent social identity for any individual in a given context. In order to explain social identification in other contexts, we may need to cite somewhat different processes and timescales.

Overly general accounts thus fail to grasp the heterogeneity of social identification in practice. Instead of describing the way that social identification supposedly happens in all cases, and instead of trying to find cases that represent this supposedly universal process, we need detailed empirical descriptions of how heterogeneous resources do the work of social identification in different contexts. This book provides one such case. Tyisha and Maurice disprove simple accounts that "macro" and "micro" processes always play the preeminent roles in social identification. Sociohistorical categories and contingent events were important to the cases of social identification analyzed here, but local models and trajectories were just as crucial to Tyisha and Maurice's emerging social identities. The cases analyzed in this book also illustrate how contingent processes at several timescales come together to establish social identities. Instead of overgeneralizing from one type of case and concluding that a given set of resources is naturally appropriate for explaining social identification and academic learning, we need to approach these processes inductively and explore how different sets of resources contribute to different types of cases.

It would thus miss the point to claim that Tyisha and Maurice are atypical cases that will not help us understand social identification in Paideia and other classrooms. All social identification involves the contingent use of heterogeneous resources from many potentially relevant timescales. In order to understand how such contingent sets of resources solidify into durable, apparently natural social identities, we must do more than create theories that rely on a fixed set of timescales. The relevant question is not whether a general social theory is right or wrong or whether a particular case represents the correct general theory. We must ask instead how the sociohistorical categories proposed by such a theory interconnect with processes at other timescales to take effect in various types of cases. We must examine how contingent processes at several timescales work together to create stabilities and patterns both within and beyond individual cases.

I am not arguing for the uniqueness of each context and claiming that social science can only amass a series of case studies. Patterned cross-timescale regularities do occur, and we can describe common patterns in social identification and academic learning across cases. These regularities, however, will not involve a fixed set of resources that apply to most cases in the same way, nor will they involve only one or two timescales. We need careful analyses of cross-timescale relations in particular cases, and comparison of these with potentially similar cases, in order to see which generalizations are empirically warranted. This book analyzes one case, and it models the sort of detailed cross-timescale analysis we will need to explain complex human processes like social identification. Subsequent work will be able to compare this case with others to see how widely this configuration of processes occurs.

In order to understand what went wrong with Adler's vision of how Paideia instruction can empower students, then, we must do more than judge whether or not Mrs. Bailey and Mr. Smith's classroom was typical. Adler failed to anticipate how cognitive models of identity from classic texts could, through the Paideia technique of connecting students' experiences to the texts, be used to disempower and exclude students like Tyisha and Maurice. This failure does not necessarily mean that his theory is wrong, although it clearly fails to predict all cases. Nor does it mean that I have selected an unrepresentative example, although it may be unrepresentative in some respects. It means that Adler – like many other theorists – failed to see how students' social identities emerge through the complex intersection of contingent processes at several timescales. In order to assess the utility of Adler's theory, or any general theory, we will need to examine how heterogeneous resources facilitate trajectories of identification in both similar and different ways across cases.

KNOWLEDGE, POWER AND HUMAN NATURE

The analyses in this book have shown how local cognitive models of the curriculum became one important resource for identifying Tyisha and Maurice. Local cognitive models that represented the curriculum in certain ways – like the model of "beasts" and social outcasts that teachers and students developed in discussions of the first curricular theme – contributed to Tyisha and Maurice's emerging identities. Teachers and students need not have modeled beasts or outcasts as they did, and if they had developed different cognitive models of the curriculum then the students' identities would have developed in somewhat different ways. On the other hand, social identification might have occurred relatively independent of curricular categories, with other resources making the crucial contributions. As it was, however, local cognitive models of the two curricular themes became important resources for the social identification of Tyisha and Maurice. The reverse was also true, as the analogies between curricular themes and classroom relationships allowed metapragmatic models to serve as resources for academic learning.

As argued in Chapter 3 and shown in Chapters 4 and 5, social identification and academic learning were not independent processes that later overlapped. Instead, the metapragmatic and cognitive models that facilitated social identification and academic learning co-developed in key respects. Tyisha was already being identified as a difficult student before they began discussing the first curricular theme, but the curricular category of "beast" and the cognitive model of a society whose members ideally contribute to the common good helped teachers and students develop the more specific local identity of "disruptive outcast" for her. This cognitive model did not exist fully formed before teachers and students applied it to Tyisha in late January. Instead, they developed their cognitive model as they developed the metapragmatic model used to identify Tyisha. It was a joint metapragmatic/cognitive model. One contribution of the book has been to describe how "self/knowledge" like this can emerge at the local timescale. The intertwining of social identification and academic learning in this case resembles "ontological learning" and "power/knowledge," but my analyses have shown how these more general processes can involve unexpected configurations of resources, including local ones.

The cases of Tyisha and Maurice show that social identification and academic learning can do more than go on simultaneously. In cases like this they are better conceptualized as part of larger processes that involve subject matter, argument, evidence and academic learning as well as social identification, power relations and interpersonal struggles. In some ways, this should not be surprising. Chapters 2 and 3 described essential similarities between social identification and academic learning: Both face the problem of indeterminate relevant context, and both overcome this indeterminacy with reference to models that limit relevant context and constrain inferences. The process of identifying someone socially is, after all, a broadly cognitive process. It involves the development of metapragmatic models and the use of these models to make sense of experience. Metapragmatic models are just a particular type of cognitive model – one applied to make sense of people themselves as they participate in discursive interaction. This does not make social identification subordinate to cognition, unless we construe "cognition" in a very broad sense. For one thing, metapragmatic models are most often tacit and enacted, not explicitly represented, so we cannot reduce social identification to the special case of distanced, reflective academic cognition. For another, cognition is itself just a type of embodied social action.

Given that people socially identify themselves and others using models that are broadly cognitive, and given that people do academic cognition as part of embodied social action, it should not be surprising when cognition about local identities overlaps with cognition about the curriculum. Nonetheless, it is often surprising. This surprise happens because of our "purified" conception of academic learning (Latour, 1993). We tend to use a special case of decontextualized academic learning as a prototype (Dreier, 2003). Academic learning, we imagine, ideally involves pure representation of ideas – untainted by the particular contexts in which we learn them, facts about the social positions of the teachers and learners, and the instrumental intentions of learners (to get grades, to avoid punishment, etc.). This unrealistic ideal of decontextualized academic learning has been described by many others, in terms of "learning transfer" (Lave, 1988), in terms of "foundational" assumptions about academic rationality (Falmagne, 2000) and so on. Based on this ideal, we have created schools that strive to decontextualize knowledge as much as possible. No school ever realizes the ideal of pure academic learning, but schools often succeed in decontextualizing academic knowledge to some extent. Attempts to realize this ideal of decontextualized learning have both positive and negative consequences in practice (Varenne and McDermott, 1998; Vygotsky, 1934/1987). Conceptually, the ideal of decontextualized learning generates misleading overgeneralization. When we use a small set of decontextualized cases as the model for all academic cognition, we fail to see how heterogeneous resources more often play an important role in facilitating academic learning.

The analyses in this book show, as many others have done, that even apparently "pure" academic discourse is thoroughly interwoven with allegedly irrelevant processes like social identification. Social identification, power relations and interpersonal struggles routinely overlap with subject matter, argument, evidence and academic learning. Using data from Mrs. Bailey and Mr. Smith's classroom across an academic year, I have been able to show in detail how academic and non-academic processes from various timescales came together to constitute both social identification and academic learning in this classroom. Through the same processes that students and teachers used to make sense of academic subject matter, they struggled with and against social identifications of each other. This did not happen on a separate but concurrent track as a part of "classroom management" or some other non-academic function of classroom talk. Social identification and academic learning can be interwoven. Those who are interested in academic learning must acknowledge that such learning does not happen in some decontextualized realm of pure cognition. Teachers and students develop cognitive models not only for the sake of making academic sense but also for the sake of doing social action. Sometimes the social action cannot be separated from the academic cognition because the relevant metapragmatic and cognitive models cannot be separated.

In some respects, this metapragmatic/cognitive overlap should be welcomed by cognitive scientists. Chapter 3 described what Goodman (1955) called the "new riddle of induction," which afflicts all cognitive accounts of non-deductive inference. Goodman showed that people's inductive inferences must be constrained by more than the data and general rules of rational inference, because different pieces of potentially relevant background knowledge could lead to widely varying inferences from the same data set. Cognitive psychologists have struggled to explain how people limit potentially relevant context and overcome Goodman's riddle. They have been forced to propose increasingly elaborate innate constraints and theories that limit relevant context (e.g., Astuti et al., 2004; Keil, 1989). It seems implausible, however, that people are born with universal innate theories of sufficient complexity. The overlap of academic learning with processes like social identification suggests another strategy for solving Goodman's riddle. Once we acknowledge that cognition takes place in context, overlapping with processes like social identification, we need not propose as many innate cognitive constraints. If metapragmatic models become available to support academic learning, as they did in Mrs. Bailey and Mr. Smith's classroom, they can provide some of the constraints that would have to be built into innate models or otherwise accounted for.

It would take much more work to support this proposal that analyses of metapragmatic models and other non-academic resources might help solve the new riddle of induction. Whether that strategy would work or not, however, many educators and cognitive psychologists would resist the idea – partly to defend an unreasonable ideal of pure academic cognition, but also partly because of the poor treatment they have received in sociocultural analyses of schooling. Over the past few decades, sociologists and anthropologists have often unmasked the false purity of academic learning, showing how power relationships, cultural beliefs, social routines and other non-academic processes penetrate into the heart of schooling (e.g., Bowles and Gintis, 1976; Cazden, John and Hymes, 1972; Heath, 1983; Levinson, Foley and Holland, 1996; Mehan et al., 1996). This body of work has convincingly and overwhelmingly shown that academic learning takes place alongside and often bound up with social processes that do not fit into the ideal of "pure" academic learning. But the sociocultural accounts have also been accompanied – sometimes as intended by the authors and sometimes as inferred by readers – with a claim that educators' purified conceptions of academic learning mask the underlying social processes that are the real business of schooling. This is a very common inference, drawn as a conclusion to studies like mine that show overlap between social identification and academic learning: By showing that academic learning is bound up with social processes, I must be showing that academic learning is not happening, or that beliefs about academic learning represent an ideology that facilitates the social functions of schooling.

I do not want to draw this conclusion, however. It is certainly the case that academic learning cannot be divorced from processes like social identification. But this does not mean that academic learning does not happen or that it serves primarily to mask underlying social processes. As Latour (1999) argues, the social nature of an apparently pure cognitive activity, like science or academic learning, does not undercut its claim to be cognitively productive. Both science and academic learning enrich people's experience and help them discover things about the world. In order to accomplish these things, cognitive activities depend in part on social processes and structures. Many students in Mrs. Bailey and Mr. Smith's class, for instance, learned something about individualism and collectivism in part because of their metapragmatic model of Tyisha's identity. The fact that a social process contributed to their insights does not invalidate those insights.

Latour argues that we must avoid a common but unproductive opposition between allegedly pure learning and allegedly pure social process – as if the presence of one within the other would invalidate it. In fact, science and academic learning are shot through with social identification, power relations and interpersonal struggles that sometimes overlap with and partly constitute academic accomplishments. At the same time, social processes almost always rely on cognitive models like those found in science and academic learning. The interdependence of these two types of processes does not mean that students fail to learn in classrooms or that people fail to get socially identified. Human processes like learning about the world and identifying other people involve both social and cognitive aspects – not in one stable configuration, but as changing sets of heterogeneous resources. The heterogeneity of these processes only causes problems if we allow false, purified ideals to guide our thinking.

Latour calls for a revised conception of human nature, one that moves beyond counterproductive ideals of purity. We should not idealize the special case of a decontextualized thinker who builds representations of the world independent of surrounding social processes – partly because this limited ideal would encourage us to ignore the complex social aspects of scientific, academic and other human cognitive activity and partly because this would rob our thinker of many social resources that people use to complete cognitive tasks. There may be times and places where an ideal of relatively autonomous cognition serves an important social or ritual function – perhaps when justifying certain kinds of political or academic institutions. But in general we should not oppose the pure and heroic autonomous rational thinker to the tainted social actor or social system. As articulated by Falmagne (2000), Geertz (1973), Tomasello (1999), Vygotsky (1934/1987) and others, it is human nature to draw on heterogeneous academic and non-academic resources to accomplish aims that simultaneously involve cognition and social action.

I started the book by offering separate accounts of social identification and academic learning. This made the argument easier to follow because our folk theories and our institutionalized practices cast these as separate processes. I end the book by claiming that humans by nature do both at once. Some human phenomena are better explained with reference to relatively decontextualized cognitive models, although even these phenomena will also rely on some non-cognitive resources. Other phenomena are better explained with reference to tacit, embodied dispositions and social actions, although even these phenomena will also rely on some relatively decontextualized representations. Complex human activities generally involve many types of resources, overlapping in more or less systematic ways. This book has described the unexpected, heterogeneous set of resources that facilitated "self/knowledge" in one case. Other cases will probably involve the same sort of local metapragmatic/cognitive overlap, but academic and non-academic resources will also overlap in different ways. Instead of taking one case to represent the paradigm of all human activity, we must explore how heterogeneous resources work together to facilitate complex processes like social identification and academic learning. This book provides one model for how to do the cross-timescale analysis required for this work. We need more analyses of how subject matter, argument, evidence and academic learning mesh with social identification, power relations and interpersonal struggles. From such empirical analyses we will be able to describe the various ways in which apparently academic and apparently non-academic processes overlap.

MORAL VISIONS OF SCHOOLING

Once we acknowledge that schooling is not purely academic but is instead one of many human activities that draw on heterogeneous resources, we need to change both our scientific and our normative accounts of it. Scientifically, we need to study how non-academic processes such as social identification can contribute to cognitive accomplishments in the classroom (and vice versa). Normatively, we need to reconceptualize the goals of schooling and confront the fact that it is a moral enterprise. If schooling were merely about decontextualized ideas and purely academic practices, educators would not need to ask what kinds of students they are working to create. In fact, however, social identification, power relations and interpersonal struggles inevitably occur in schools and can often be inextricable from academic content. Given that schooling is inevitably also about building communities and changing who students are, educators face questions about what kinds of students, communities and practices they should aim to create.

As Hansen (2004) argues, the fact that schools do moral work increases teachers' responsibilities. With respect to Tyisha, Maurice and William, this raises the question of Mrs. Bailey and Mr. Smith's responsibility for the social identities they helped assign these students. The analyses in this book have described Mrs. Bailey and Mr. Smith treating students in ways that sometimes seem inappropriate. Did they go too far when they teased Tyisha, imagining that she was "like an animal," or in other cases when they explicitly called her a bad and disruptive student? Did they go too far when they treated William like the prototypical unpromising boy, or when they forced Maurice to choose between his identities as a respectable boy and a good student? I will argue that the teachers do bear responsibility for some of these acts. Before drawing this conclusion, however, we must consider the various resources that contributed to these students' social identities. We cannot simply blame the teachers, for both theoretical and ethical reasons. We cannot explain what happened to Tyisha and Maurice by citing the teachers' unethical behavior or lack of skill. Resources from several timescales made essential contributions to Tyisha and Maurice's trajectories of identification, and it would be poor analysis to attribute the bulk of it to the teachers' actions.

Mrs. Bailey and Mr. Smith had several decades of teaching experience between them. Mrs. Bailey was identified by faculty and administrators at Colleoni High as a particularly strong teacher – pedagogically successful, respected by students and active in curriculum development for the whole school. Mrs. Bailey managed to be both pedagogically challenging and sympathetic to the students. Many students recognized that she cared about them and sought out her counsel at times of emotional crisis. While I was doing my ethnographic work in her classroom, for instance, Mrs. Bailey spent many hours counseling a pregnant ninth grade student who had asked for her help. Mr. Smith was also an accomplished teacher. He had extensive pedagogical experience with various forms of student-centered discussion, and he had a graduate degree from an Ivy League university.

The teachers had created and implemented an unusual and promising curriculum, built around Paideia principles. They intended to expose students to classic texts from European and other traditions in order to empower their ethnically diverse working-class students. By giving students access to the texts and ideas that have been central to the development of our society, and that are available to the children of elites, the teachers hoped to provide resources that would help these students overcome social barriers. I do not know whether these students did in fact experience more social mobility than their peers. But the teachers successfully engaged the students with difficult, classic texts and with recurring, essentially contestable issues raised by these texts. Ninth graders, especially in comprehensive urban U.S. high schools, do not normally read Aristotle. Mrs. Bailey and Mr. Smith not only had the students reading Aristotle and similar texts, but they also engaged the students with Aristotelian arguments that still concern politicians, scholars and other educated people. In addition, the teachers were skilled discussion leaders, and they gave students freedom to develop their own arguments while guiding them toward central issues in the texts.

The empirical analyses have shown the teachers giving participant examples that sometimes identified students in unflattering ways. The teachers used these examples and other strategies for sound pedagogical reasons, and their strategies helped some students learn about the curriculum. My analyses show that participant examples can be multifunctional, simultaneously contributing to both social identification and academic learning. The teachers were concerned primarily with academic learning, and they did not notice the social functions that some of their examples served. Personalization in the classroom offers both risks and rewards. The teachers focused on the potential rewards, using students' own experiences to help illuminate the curriculum. In most of the cases I analyze, I do not believe that the teachers were aware of the simultaneous implications that their discussions had for students' identities.

Nonetheless, one might argue, they should have noticed when their examples had serious negative implications for students' own identities. In the few cases where I noticed these implications myself while I still had access to these teachers, I asked them about this issue. They made two arguments: that I was exaggerating the amount and depth of social identification that was occurring; and that they were simply teasing the students, not really identifying them in unpleasant or inappropriate ways. The empirical analyses in this book show how teachers and students did in fact engage in extensive social identification of students like Tyisha and Maurice, and how this identification went beyond teasing to have serious implications for their identities in the classroom. So I argue that the teachers were wrong to claim that the social identification done to Tyisha, Maurice and William was not serious. I do not know whether this social identification had any lasting consequences beyond the students' year in ninth grade. But teachers and students clearly noticed and reacted to it in the classroom, and some of the social identification seemed to be painful for Tyisha, Maurice and William.

We cannot simply blame the teachers, however. Processes at several timescales contributed to the social identification of these students. There were sociohistorical expectations about how students should behave, local metapragmatic models about types of students, actions by the vocal girls and the silent boys, actions and reactions by Tyisha, Maurice and William themselves, as well as actions by the teachers that contributed to the social identification. How can we assign responsibility in a case like this, in which so many processes and actions contributed to the outcome? We clearly cannot blame the teachers for more widely circulating sociohistorical models of identity that disadvantage certain kinds of students and contributed to painful social identifications in this case. Boys, and especially black boys, are stereotyped as resistant to school, and this gendered expectation is a collective responsibility. In this respect teachers and students were vehicles for longer timescale processes that operated through them. We cannot expect teachers always to be aware of such processes – given that their training often does not prepare them for this aspect of classroom life and given that they must attend to so many different things that occur simultaneously in any classroom discussion.

Furthermore, in Mrs. Bailey and Mr. Smith's classroom the students themselves contributed to the social identification that occurred. The vocal girls did as much work as Mrs. Bailey in establishing the stereotype of "promising girls and unpromising boys," and they did most of the work of forcing Maurice to choose between his identities as a respectable boy and a good student. Both Tyisha and Maurice themselves created and embraced aspects of their "outcast" identities. Tyisha, in particular, chose to disrupt classroom activities and to revel in her position as an outcast. Perhaps she was resisting the unjust social arrangements of schooling, but she nonetheless bears some responsibility for the identity that she eventually occupied.

So we cannot just blame the teachers for the painful and inappropriate social identification that occurred in their classroom. They do bear significant responsibility for what happened to these students, however. Mrs. Bailey introduced the robust local stereotype of promising girls and unpromising boys, a stereotype that played a central role in the painful social identification that happened to William and Maurice. She should have realized that this stereotype could influence boys' conceptions of themselves and that it could potentially close off educational opportunities for them. Mrs. Bailey and Mr. Smith discussed Tyisha and Maurice in many of the pivotal participant examples for innocuous or laudable reasons – to tease them and to help them learn the curriculum. But they should have realized that these examples had the potential for more serious effects, especially for students like Tyisha and Maurice who were already in precarious social positions. The teachers also labeled Tyisha and William as problematic students too quickly, too bluntly and too publicly. Both were frustrating students, in different ways, but a teacher should not give up on a student as "disruptive" or "unpromising," at least not so publicly.

I do not judge these teachers lightly. Teaching is extremely difficult, given the many processes occurring simultaneously in classrooms, the lack of time, the grinding schedule and the lack of resources in a high-need urban district. And we all, teachers or not, can be faulted for sometimes

missing the interpersonal implications of what we say and socially identifying others in potentially damaging ways. But teachers have the authority and the responsibility to organize classrooms in ethical ways, and so
we must hold them to a high standard. We must ask them to notice the
moral as well as the academic implications of their actions in the classroom. Mrs. Bailey and Mr. Smith were not responsible for everything that
happened to Tyisha, Maurice and William. The larger society, students
themselves, and the serendipitous configuration of resources from various
timescales played as important a role as the teachers. They were nonetheless responsible for the classroom. They should have seen more than they
did about what was happening to these students, and they should have
done more to interrupt it.

In response to these mistakes by the teachers, some might be tempted
to hide behind an unreasonable ideal of pure academic learning and deny
that such moral and interpersonal matters touch the core of schooling. I
have argued, however, that moral and interpersonal aspects of schooling
cannot be extricated from its academic mission. On the other hand, some
might be tempted to revel in the unmasking of schools' apparently non-
academic, seamy social side. This reaction also fails to confront the intertwining of subject matter, argument, evidence and academic learning with
social identification, power relations and interpersonal struggles. We face
instead the more complex task of developing a moral vision for schooling,
given the heterogeneous processes and resources that inevitably appear in
classrooms. In developing such a vision I would follow Wineberg's (2001)
argument that schools should encourage students to reflect deeply on what
it means to be human, to learn from others who think differently than we
do, and to develop the intellectual virtues of "discernment, judgment and
caution" with respect to the stories we tell about ourselves and others. I
would also follow Hansen's (2004) argument that human cognitive activities are aesthetic, moral and relational as well as intellectual, and that we
should aim to help students "see," not just "know," with aesthetic insight
and moral concern as well as intellectual rigor. Full development of such
a vision is beyond the scope of this book, and is, in any case, an ongoing project for each of us. This book has provided a case to think with,
as we develop our moral visions of schooling. If we want to grapple with
what actually occurs in schools, our visions should acknowledge the complex and contingent interconnections among academic and non-academic
resources that contribute to educational processes.

Appendix A

Teachers

Mrs. Bailey	T/B
Mr. Smith	T/S

Students

Brenna	BRE
Candace	CAN
Cassandra	CAS
Cordell	COR
Erika	ERK
Eugene	EUG
Gary	GAR
Germaine	GER
Ivory	IVR
Jasmine	JAS
Katie	KAT
Katina	KTN
Linda	LIN
Martha	MAR
Maurice	MRC
Natasha	NAT
Tyisha	TYI
William	WIL

Unidentified Students

Female Student	FST
Male Student	MST
Students	STS

Appendix B

'-'	abrupt breaks or stops (if several, stammering)
'?'	rising intonation
'.'	falling intonation
'_'	(underline) stress
(1.0)	silences, timed to the nearest second
'['	indicates simultaneous talk by two speakers, with one utterance represented on top of the other and the moment of overlap marked by left brackets
'='	interruption or next utterance following immediately, or continuous talk represented on separate lines because of need to represent overlapping comment on intervening line
'[...]'	transcriber comment
':'	elongated vowel
'° ...°'	segment quieter than surrounding talk
','	pause or breath without marked intonation
'(hh)'	laughter breaking into words while speaking

References

Adler, Mortimer. 1982. *The Paideia Proposal*. New York: Macmillan.

Agha, Asif. 2003. "The Social Life of Cultural Value." *Language and Communication*, 23(3–4): 231–273.

Agha, Asif. 2004. "Registers of Language." In *A Companion to Linguistic Anthropology*, ed. A. Duranti, 23–45. Oxford: Blackwell.

Agha, Asif. In press. *Language and Social Relations*. New York: Cambridge University Press.

Anderson, Elijah. 1999. *Code of the Street*. New York: W. W. Norton.

Appiah, Kwame. 1992. Identity, Authenticity, Survival. In *Multiculturalism*, ed. Amy Gutmann, 149–163. Princeton, NJ: Princeton University Press.

Apple, Michael. 1986. *Teachers and Texts: A Political Economy of Class and Gender Relations in Education*. New York: Routledge & Kegan Paul.

Astuti, Rita, Gregg Solomon, and Susan Carey. 2004. *Constraints on Conceptual Development: A Case Study of the Acquisition of Folkbiological and Folksociological Knowledge in Madagascar*. Boston, MA: Blackwell Publishers.

Austin, John. 1956/1975. *How to Do Things with Words*, 2nd ed. Cambridge, MA: Harvard University Press.

Bakhtin, Mikhail. 1935/1981. "Discourse in the Novel" (Trans. by Caryl Emerson and Michael Holquist.) In *The Dialogic Imagination*, ed. M. Bakhtin, 259–422. Austin: University of Texas Press.

Bakhtin, Mikhail. 1953/1986. "The Problem of Speech Genres" (Trans. By V. McGee.) In *Speech Genres and Other Late Essays*, ed. C. Emerson and M. Holquist, 60–102. Austin: University of Texas Press.

Bateson, Gregory. 1972. *Steps to an Ecology of Mind*. New York: Ballantine.

Bickhard, Mark. 1980. *Cognition, Convention, and Communication*. New York: Praeger Publishers.

Bickhard, Mark. 1993. "Representational Content in Humans and Machines." *Journal of Experimental and Theoretical Artificial Intelligence*, 5: 285–333.

Billings, Laura, and Jill Fitzgerald. 2002. "Dialogic Discussion and the Paideia Seminar." *American Educational Research Journal*, 39(4): 907–941.

Blommaert, Jan, and Chris Bulcaen. 2000. "Critical Discourse Analysis." *Annual Review of Anthropology*, 29: 447–466.

Blommaert, Jan, James Collins, and Stef Slembrouck. 2004. Spaces of Multilingualism. Working paper on Language, Power, and Identity, No. 18, Gent University. http://bank.rug.ac.be/lpi/.

Bourdieu, Pierre. 1972/1977. *Outline of a Theory of Practice*. (Trans. by Richard Nice.) New York: Cambridge University Press.

Bourdieu, Pierre. 1979/1984. *A Social Critique of the Judgment of Taste* (Trans. by Richard Nice.) Cambridge, MA: Harvard University Press.

Bowker, Geoffrey, and Susan Leigh Star. 2000. *Sorting Thing Out: Classification and Its Consequences*. Cambridge, MA: MIT Press.

Bowles, Samuel, and Herbert Gintis. 1976. *Schooling in Capitalist America*. New York: Basic Books.

Brickhouse, Nancy. 2001. "Embodying Science: A Feminist Perspective on Learning." *Journal of Research in Science Teaching, 38*: 282–295.

Bronfenbrenner, Urie. 1979. *Ecology of Human Development*. Cambridge, MA: Harvard University Press.

Brown, Lyn, and Carol Gilligan. 1992. *Meeting at the Crossroads*. Cambridge, MA: Harvard University Press.

Bruner, Jerome, Jacqueline Goodnow, and George Austin. 1956. *A Study of Thinking*. New York: Wiley.

Bucholtz, Mary. 1999. "Why Be Normal?" *Language in Society, 28*: 203–223.

Bushnell, Mary, and Sue Ellen Henry (2003). "The Role of Reflection in Epistemological Change." *Educational Studies, 34*: 38–61.

Cavell, Stanley. 1979. *The Claim of Reason: Wittgenstein, Skepticism, Morality and Tragedy*. Oxford, UK: Oxford University Press.

Cazden, Courtney, Vera John, and Dell Hymes., eds. 1972. *Functions of Language in the Classroom*. New York: Teachers College Press.

Certeau, Michel de. (1984). *The Practice of Everyday Life*. (Trans. by Steven Rendall.) Berkeley: University of California Press.

Christensen, Wayne. 2004. "Self-Directedness: A Process Approach to Cognition." *Axiomathes, 14*: 171–189.

Christensen, Wayne, and Mark Bickhard. 2002. "The Process Dynamics of Normative Function." *Monist, 85*(1): 3–28.

Cohen, Anthony. 1994. *Self Consciousness: An Alternative Anthropology of Identity*. New York: Routledge.

Cohen, David, Stephen Raudenbush, and Deborah Ball. (2001). "Resources, Instruction, and Research." In *Evidence Matters: Randomized Trials in Education Research*, ed. R. Boruch and F. Mosteller. Washington, DC: Brookings Institute Press.

Cole, Michael. 1996. *Cultural Psychology: A Once and Future Discipline*. Cambridge, MA: Harvard University Press.

Cole, Nancy. 1997. *The ETS Gender Study: How Females and Males Perform in Educational Settings*. Princeton, NJ: ETS Technical Report.

Cole, Michael, Yrjö Engeström, and Olga Vasquez, eds. 1997. *Mind, Culture, and Activity: Seminal Papers from the Laboratory of Comparative Human Cognition*. New York: Cambridge University Press.

Coulter, Jeffrey. 1989. *Mind in Action*. Atlantic Highlands, NJ: Humanities Press Interactional.

Criscoula, M. 1994. "Read, Discuss, Reread." *Educational Leadership, 51*: 58–61.

Dreier, Ole. 2000. "Psychotherapy in Clients' Trajectories across Contexts." In *Narrative and the Cultural Construction of Illness and Healing*, ed. Cheryl Mattingly and Linda Garro, 237–258. Berkeley: University of California Press.

Dreier, Ole. 2003. "Learning and Personal Trajectories of Participation." In *Theoretical Psychology: Critical Contributions*, ed. Niamh Stevenson, Hazel Radtke, René Jorna, and Henderikus Stam, 20–29. Toronto: Captus Press.

Dreyfus, Hubert. 1979. *What Computers Can't Do: The Limits of Artificial Intelligence*, rev. ed. New York: Harper & Row.

Dreyfus, Hubert, and Paul Rabinow. 1993. "Can There Be a Science of Existential Structure and Social Meaning?" In *Bourdieu: Critical Perspectives*, ed. Craig Calhoun, Edward LiPuma, and Moishe Postone, 35–44. Chicago, IL: University of Chicago Press.

Dyson, Anne. 1989. *Multiple Worlds of Child Writers: Friends Learning to Write*. New York: Teacher College Press.

Eckert, Penelope. 1989. *Jocks and Burnouts: Social Categories and Identity in the High School*. New York: Teachers College Press.

Eckert, Penelope. 2000. *Linguistic Variation as Social Practice: The Linguistic Construction of Identity in Belten High*. Malden, MA: Blackwell Publishers.

Engeström, Yrjö. 1987. *Learning by Expanding: An Activity-Theoretical Approach to Developmental Research*. Helsinki, Finland: Orienta-Konsultit Oy.

Engeström, Yrjö. 1993. "Developmental Studies of Work as a Testbench of Activity Theory." In *Situated Cognition*, ed. Seth Chaiklin and Jean Lave. Mahwah, NJ: Lawrence Erlbaum.

Engeström, Yrjö. 1999. "Activity Theory and Individual and Social Transformation." In *Perspectives on Activity Theory*, ed. Yrjö Engeström, Reijo Miettinen and Raija-Leena Punanāki, 19–38. New York: Cambridge University Press.

Falmagne, Rachel J. 2000. "Positionality and Thought." In *Toward a Feminist Developmental Psychology*, ed. Patricia Miller and Ellin Scholick, 191–213. New York: Routledge.

Falmagne, Rachel J. 2001. The Dialectic of Critique, Theory and Method in Developing Feminist Research on Inference. In *Theoretical Issues in Psychology*, ed. John Morss, Niamh Stevenson, and Hans Van Rappard, 145–157. Kluwer.

Ferguson, Ann. 2000. *Bad Boys: Public Schools in the Making of Black Masculinity*. Ann Arbor, MI: University of Michigan Press.

Flax, Jane. 1993. *Disputed Subjects: Essays on Psychoanalysis, Politics, and Philosophy*. New York: Routledge.

Foley, Douglas. 1996. "The Silent Indian as a Cultural Production." In *The Cultural Production of the Educated Person*, ed. Bradley Levinson, Douglas Foley, and Dorothy Holland, 79–91. Albany: State University of New York Press.

Fordham, Signithia. 1996. *Blacked Out: Dilemmas of Race, Identity, and Success at Capital High*. Chicago: University of Chicago Press.

Fordham, Signithia, and John Ogbu. 1986. "Black Students' School Success: Coping with the 'Burden of Acting White'." *Urban Review, 18*: 176–206.

Foucault, Michel. 1966/1971. *The Order of Things: An Archaeology of the Human Sciences*. New York: Pantheon Books.

Foucault, Michel. 1975/1977. *Discipline and Punish: The Birth of the Prison*. (Trans. by Alan Sheridan.) New York: Pantheon Books.

Foucault, Michel. 1994/2000. *Power*, Vol. 3: Essential Works of Foucault 1954–1984. (Trans. by Robert Hurley et al.) New York: The New Press.

Gadsden, Vivian, Stanton Wortham, and Herbert Turner. 2003. "Situated Identities of Young, African American Fathers in Low-Income Urban Settings." *Family Court Review, 41*: 381–399.

Garfinkel, Harold. 1967. *Studies in Ethnomethodology*. New York: Prentice-Hall.

Garfinkel, Harold, and Harvey Sacks. 1970. "On Formal Structure of Practical Actions." In *Theoretical Sociology*, ed. J. McKinney and A. Tiryakian, 337–366. New York: Appleton Century Crofts.

Gee, James. 1989. "Two Styles of Narrative Construction and Their Linguistic and Educational Implications." *Discourse Processes, 12*: 287–307.

Gee, James. 1999. *An Introduction to Discourse Analysis: Theory and Method*. London/New York: Routledge.

Gee, James. 2001. "Identity as an Analytic Lens for Research in Education." *Review of Research in Education, 25*, 99–125. Washington, DC: American Education Research Association.

Geertz, Clifford. 1973. *The Interpretation of Cultures*. New York: Basic Books.

Gergen, Keneth. 1982. *Toward Transformation in Social Knowledge*. New York: Springer-Verlag.

Giddens, Anthony. 1976. *New Rules of Sociological Method*. New York: Basic Books.

Goffman, Erving. 1959. *Presentation of Self in Everyday Life*. Garden City, NY: Doubleday.

Goffman, Erving. 1974. *Frame Analysis*. New York: Harper and Row.

Goodman, Nelson. 1955. *Fact, Fiction and Forecast*. Cambridge: Harvard University Press.

Goodwin, Charles. 1995. "Seeing in Depth." *Social Studies of Science, 25*: 237–274.

Great Books Foundation. 1991. *An Introduction to Shared Inquiry*, 2nd ed. Chicago: The Great Books Foundation.

Greeno, James. 1997. "On Claims That Answer the Wrong Questions." *Educational Researcher, 26*, 5–17.

Greeno, James., and the Middle School Mathematics through Applications Project Group. 1998. "The situativity of knowing, learning and research." *American Psychologist, 53*: 5–26.

Gregory, Steven. 2001. "Placing the Politics of Black Class Formation." In *History in Person*, ed. D. Holland and J. Lave, 137–170. Santa Fe: SAR Press.

Gumperz, John. 1982. *Discourse Strategies*. Cambridge: Cambridge University Press.

Hacking, Ian. 1990. *The Taming of Chance*. New York: Cambridge University Press.

Hansen, David. 2004. "A Poetics of Teaching." *Education Theory, 54*: 119–142.

Haraway, Donna. 1991. *Simians, Cyborgs and Women: The Reinvention of Nature*. London: Free Association Books.

Haroutunian-Gordon, Sophie. 1983. *Equilibrium in the Balance*. New York: Springer-Verlag.

Haroutunian-Gordon, Sophie. 1991. *Turning the Soul: Teaching Through Conversation in the High School*. Chicago, IL: University of Chicago Press.

Hatano, Giyoo, and Kayoko Inagaki. 1991. "Sharing Cognition through Collective Comprehension Activity." In *Perspectives and Socially Shared Cognition*, ed. Lauren Resnick, John Levine, and Stephanie Teasley, 331–348. Washington, DC: APA Press.

Hatgis, Christina. 2003. "Agency and the Deconstructed Subject." In *Theoretical Psychology: Critical Contributions*, ed. Niamh Stephenson, Hagel Radtke, René Jorna, and Henderikus Stam, 183–191. Toronto: Captus Press.

Heath, Shirley Brice. 1983. *Ways with Words: Language, Life and Work in Communities and Classrooms*. New York: Cambridge University Press.

Heath, Shirley Brice, and Milbrey McLaughlin, eds. 1993. *Identity and Inner-City Youth: Beyond Ethnicity and Gender*. New York: Teachers College Press.

Heathcote, Dorothy. 1984. *Dorothy Heathcote: Collected Writings on Education and Drama*, ed. Liz Johnson and Cecily O'Neill. London: Hutchinson.

Hedegaard, Mariane. 2002. *Learning and Child Development: A Cultural-Historical Study*. Aarhus, Denmark/Aokville, CT: Aarhus University Press.

Holland, Dorothy, and Margaret Eisenhart. 1990. *Educated in Romance*. Chicago, IL: University of Chicago Press.

Holland, Dorothy, William Lachicotte, Debra Skinner, and Carole Cain. 1998. *Identity and Agency in Cultural Worlds*. Cambridge, MA: Harvard University Press.

Holland, Dorothy, and Jean Lave, eds. 2001. *History in Person*. Santa Fe: School of American Research Press.

Holyoak, Keith, Dedre Gentner, and Boicho Kokinov. 2001. "Introduction: The Place of Analogy in Cognition." In *The Analogical Mind: Perspectives from Cognitive Science*, ed. D. Gentner, K. J. Holyoak, and B. N. Kokinov, 1–19. Cambridge, MA: MIT Press.

Honora, Detris. 2003. "Urban African American Adolescents and School Identification." *Urban Education, 38*: 58–76.

Hutchins, Edwin. 1995. *Cognition in the Wild*. Cambridge: MIT Press.

Jackson, Philip. 1968. *Life in Classrooms*. New York: Holt, Rinehart and Winston.

Johnson-Laird, Philip. 1983. *Mental Models*. Cambridge, MA: Harvard University Press.

Jordan, Will, and Robert Cooper. 2003. "High School Reform and Black Male Students: Limits and Possibilities of Policy and Practice." *Urban Education 38*(2): 196–216.

Keil, Frank. 1989. *Concepts, Kinds and Cognitive Development*. Cambridge, MA: MIT Press.

Kirshner, David, and James Whitson. 1997. "Introduction." In *Situated Cognition: Social, Semiotic, and Psychological Perspectives*, ed. David Kirshner and James Whitson. Mahwah, NJ: Lawrence Erlbaum.

Knorr-Cetina, Karin. 1999. *Epistemic Cultures: How the Sciences Make Knowledge*. Cambridge, MA: Harvard University Press.

Latour, Bruno. 1993. *We Have Never Been Modern*. (Trans. by Catherine Porter.) Cambridge, MA: Harvard University Press.

Latour, Bruno. 1999. *Pandora's Hope: Essays on the Reality of Science Studies*. (Trans. by Catherine Porter.) Cambridge, MA: Harvard University Press.

Lave, Jean. 1988. *Cognition in Practice*. New York: Cambridge University Press.

Lave, Jean. 1993. "The Practice of Learning." In *Understanding Practice*, ed. Seth Chaiklin and Jean Lave. New York: Cambridge University Press.

Lave, Jean, and Etienne Wenger. 1991. *Situated Learning: Legitimate Peripheral Participation*. New York: Cambridge University Press.

Leander, Kevin. 2002. "Locating Latanya: The Situated Production of Identity Artifacts in Classroom Interaction." *Research in the Teaching of English, 37*: 198–250.

Lemke, Jay. 1990. *Talking Science*. Norwood, NJ: Ablex.

Lemke, Jay. 2000. "Across the Scales of Time." *Mind, Culture, and Activity, 7*: 273–290.

Lensmire, Timothy. 1994. *When Children Write: Critical Re-Visions of the Writing Workshop*. New York: Teachers College Press.

Lensmire, Timothy. 2000. *Powerful Writing, Responsible Teaching*. New York: Teachers College Press.

Leont'ev, A. 1978. *Activity, Consciousness, and Personality*. (Trans. by Marie Hall.) New York: Prentice-Hall.

Levinson, Bradley, and Dorothy Holland. 1996. The Cultural Production of the Educated Person: An Introduction. In *The Cultural Production of the Educated Person: Critical Ethnographies of Schooling and Local Practice*, ed. Bradley Levinson, Douglas Foley, & Dorothy Holland. Albany: SUNY Press.

Levinson, Bradley, Douglas Foley, and Dorothy Holland, eds. 1996. *The Cultural Production of the Educated Person: Critical Ethnographies of Schooling and Local Practice*. Albany: SUNY Press.

Linger, Daniel. 2001. "The Identity Path of Edwardo Mori." In *History in Person*, ed. Dorothy Holland and Jean Lave, 217–244. Santa Fe: School of American Research Press.

Lopez, N. 2003. *Hopeful Girls, Troubled Boys*. New York: Routledge/Falmer.

Luke, Allen, and Peter Freebody. 1997. "Shaping the Social Practices of Reading." In *Constructing Critical Literacies: Teaching and Learning Textual Practice*, ed. S. Muspratt, A. Luke, and P. Freebody. Cresskill, NJ: Hampton Press.

Maher, Frances S., and Mary Kay Thompson Tetreault. 2001. *The Feminist Classroom*. New York: Rowman & Littlefield.

McDermott, Raymond. 1997. "Achieving School Failure: 1972–1997." In *Education and Cultural Process: Anthropological Approaches*, ed. George Spindler. 3rd ed., 110–135. Prospect Heights, IL: Waveland Press.

McGinley, William, and George Kamberelis. 1996. "Maniac Magee and Ragtime Tumpie: Children Negotiating Self and World through Reading and Writing." *Research in the Teaching of English, 30*: 75–113.

Mehan, Hugh. 1979. *Learning Lessons*. Cambridge, MA: Harvard University Press.

Mehan, Hugh, Irene Villanueva, Lea Hubbard, and Angela Lintz. 1996. *Constructing School Success: The Consequences of Untracking Low Achieving Students*. New York: Cambridge University Press.

Michaels, Sarah, and Rebecca Sohmer. 2001. "'Discourses' that Promote Academic Identities." In *Discourses in Search of Members*, ed. David Li, 171–219. New York: University Press of America.

Muldoon, P. 1991. Citizenship as shared inquiry. *English Journal, 80*: 61–8.

Murphy, Gregory, and Douglas Medin. 1985. "The Role of Theories in Conceptual Coherence." *Psychological Review, 92*: 289–316.

Newell, Allen, and Herbert Simon. 1972. *Human Problem Solving*. Englewood Cliffs, NJ: Prentice-Hall.

Newkirk, Thomas. 2002. *Misreading Masculinity*. Portsmouth, NH: Heinemann.

Nightingale, Carl. 1993. *On the Edge: A History of Poor Black Children and Their American Dreams*. New York: Basic Books.

O'Connor, Mary Catherine. 2001. "Can Any Fraction Be Turned into a Decimal?" *Educational Studies in Mathematics, 46*: 143–185.

O'Connor, Kevin, and Arthur Glenberg. 2003. "Situated Cognition" in *Encyclopedia of Cognitive Science*, L. Nadel. New York: Macmillan.

O'Neill, Cecily. 1995. *Drama Worlds: A Framework for Process Drama.* Portsmouth, NH: Heinemann.

Packer, Martin. 2001. *Changing Classes: School Reform and the New Economy.* New York: Cambridge University Press.

Packer, Martin, and Jesse Goicoechea. 2000. "Sociocultural and Constructivist Theories of Learning. Ontology, Not Just Epistemology." *Educational Psychologist, 35*: 227–241.

Piaget, Jean, and B. Barbel Inhelder. 1969. *The Early Growth of Logic in the Child: Classification and Seriation* (Trans. by E. A. Lunzer and D. Papert.) New York: W. W. Norton.

Pole, Jack. 1992. *The Pursuit of Equality in American History*, rev. ed. Berkeley: University of California Press.

Popkewitz, Thomas. 2004. "The Alchemy of the Mathematics Curriculum." *American Educational Research Journal, 41*: 3–34.

Pottorff, D., D. Phelps-Zientarski, and M. Skovera. 1996. "Gender Perceptions of Elementary and Middle School Students about Literacy at School and at Home." *Journal of Research and Development in Education, 29*: 203–211.

Prior, Paul. 2001. "Voices in Text, Mind and Society." *Journal of Secondary Language Writing, 10*: 55–81.

Putnam, Hilary. 1998. *The Threefold Cord: Mind, Body and World.* New York: Columbia University Press.

Rampton, Benjamín. 1999. "Sociolinguistics and Cultural Studies." *Social Semiotics, 9*: 355–374.

Rapport, Nigel. 1997. *Transcendent Individual.* New York: Routledge.

Rogoff, Barbara. 1990. *Apprenticeship in Thinking: Cognitive Development in Social Context.* New York: Oxford University Press.

Rogoff, Barbara. 1998. "Cognition as a Collaborative Process." In *Handbook of Child Psychology*, vol. 2: *Cognition, Perception and Learning*, ed. D. Kuhn and R. Siegler, 679–744. New York: Wiley.

Rogoff, Barbara. 2003. *The Cultural Nature of Human Development.* New York: Oxford University Press.

Rogoff, Barbara, Jacqueline Baker-Sennett, Pilar Lacasa, and D. Goldsmith. 1995. "Development through Participation in Sociocultural Activity." In *Cultural Practices as Contexts for Development*, ed. J. Goodenow, Peggy Miller, and Frank Kessel, 45–65. San Francisco: Jossey-Bass.

Ryle, Gilbert. 1949. *The Concept of Mind.* London/New York: Hutchinson's University Library.

Sadker, Myra, and Sadker, David. 1994. *Failing at Fairness: How America's Schools Cheat Girls.* New York: Maxwell MacMillan International.

Sapir, Edward. 1931/1949. "Communication." In *Selected Writings of Edward Sapir in Language, Culture and Personality*, ed. David Mandelbaum, 104–109. Berkeley: University of California Press.

Sapir, Edward. 1934b/1949. "Personality." In *Selected Writings of Edward Sapir in Language, Culture and Personality*, ed. David Mandelbaum, 560–563. Berkeley: University of California Press.

Schatzki, Theodore, Karin Knorr Cetina, and Eike von Savigny, eds. 2001. *The Practice Turn in Contemporary Theory*. London/New York: Routledge.

Schegloff, Emmanuel. 1988. "Goffman and the Analysis of Conversation." In *Erving Goffman*, ed. P. Drew and Anthony Wootton, 89–135. Boston: Northeastern University.

Schwartz, Barry. 1986. *The Battle for Human Nature: Science, Morality, and Modern Life*. New York: W. W. Norton.

Searle, John. 1969. *Speech Acts*. New York: Cambridge University Press.

Searle, John. 1983. *Intentionality*. New York: Cambridge University Press.

Shweder, Richard. 1991. *Thinking through Cultures: Expeditions in Cultural Psychology*. Cambridge, MA: Harvard University Press.

Silverstein, Michael. 1976. "Shifters, Linguistic Categories, and Cultural Description." In *Meaning in Anthropology*, ed. Keith Basso and H. Selby, 11–55. Albuquerque, NM: University of New Mexico Press.

Silverstein, Michael. 1992. "The Indeterminacy of Contextualization: When is Enough Enough?" In *The Contextualization of Language*, ed. Aldo DiLuzio and Peter Auer, 55–75. Amsterdam: John Benjamins.

Silverstein, Michael. 1993. "Metapragmatic Discourse and Metapragmatic Function." In *Reflexive Language*, ed. John Lucy. New York: Cambridge University Press.

Silverstein, Michael. 2003. "Indexical Order and the Dialectics of Sociolinguistic Life." *Language and Communication, 23*: 193–229.

Silverstein, Michael, and Greg Urban, eds. 1996. *Natural Histories of Discourse*. Chicago, IL: University of Chicago Press.

Sinclair, John, and Malcolm Coulthard. 1975. *Towards an analysis of discourse: The English used by teachers and pupils*. London: Oxford University Press.

Sökefeld, Martin. 1999. "Debating Self, Identity, and Culture in Anthropology." *Current Anthropology, 40*(4): 417–447.

Sperber, Dan, and Dedre Wilson. 1986. *Relevance*. Cambridge, MA: Harvard University Press.

Star, Susan Leigh, and J. Griesemer. 1989. "Institutional Ecology, 'Translations' and Boundary Objects: Amateurs and Professionals in Berkeley's Museum of Vertebrate Zoology, 1907–39." *Social Studies of Science, 19*: 387–420.

Sum, Andrew, and Paul Harrington, with Charles Bartishevich, Neeta Fogg, Ishwar Khatiwada, Jacqui Motroni, Sheila Palma, Nathan Pond, Paulo Tobar, and Myklaylo Trub'skyy. 2003, February. The Hidden Crisis in the High School Dropout Problems of Young Adults in the U.S.: Recent Trends in Overall School Dropout Rates and Gender Differences in Dropout Behavior. Conducted by the Center for Labor Market Studies (CLMS) at Northeastern University. Available on the Web at: http://www.nupr.neu.edu/5-03/dropout.html. Downloaded 5/20/03.

Taylor, Charles. 1985. "The Concept of a Person." In *Human Agency and Language*, ed. C. Taylor, 97–114. New York: Cambridge University Press.

Tomasello, Michael. 1999. *The Cultural Origins of Human Cognition*. Cambridge, MA: Harvard University Press.

Trabasso, Thomas, T. Secco, and Paul van den Broek. 1984. "Causal Cohesion and Story Coherence." In *Learning and Comprehension of Text*, ed. H. Mandl, Nancy Stein, and Thomes Trabasso, 83–111. Hillsdale, NJ: Lawrence Erlbaum.

Urban, Greg. 1996. *Metaphysical Community*. Austin: University of Texas Press.
Urban, Greg. 2001. *Metaculture: How Culture Moves through the World*. Minneapolis, MN: University of Minnesota Press.
Varenne, Herve, and Raymond McDermott. 1998. *Successful Failure: The School America Builds*. Boulder, CO: Westview Press.
Vygotsky, Lev Semenovich. 1924/1971. *The Psychology of Art*. (Trans. by Scripta Technica.) Cambridge, MA: MIT Press.
Vygotsky, Lev Semenovich. 1934/1987. *Thought and Language* (Trans. by A. Kozulin.) Cambridge, MA: MIT Press.
Walkerdine, Valerie. 1988. *The Mastery of Reason*. New York: Routledge.
Weltman, Burton. 2002. "Individualism versus Socialism in American Education." *Educational Theory, 52*: 61–79.
Wenger, Etienne. 1998. *Communities of Practice: Learning, Meaning and Identity*. New York: Cambridge University Press.
Wertsch, James. 1998. *Mind as Action*. New York: Oxford University Press.
Wertsch, James. 2001. *Voices of Collective Remembering*. New York: Cambridge University Press.
Wheelock, Ann. 2000. The Junior Great Books Program. A Report Prepared for the Junior Great Books Program. ERIC.
Wilhelm, Jeffrey. 1997. *You Gotta BE the Book*. New York: Teachers College Press.
Williams, Meredith. 1999. *Wittgenstein, Mind and Meaning: Toward a Social Conception of Mind*. London/New York: Routledge.
Willis, Paul. 1977. *Learning to Labour*. Farnborough: Saxon House.
Wineburg, Sam. 2001. *Historical Thinking and Other Unnatural Acts*. Philadelphia: Temple University Press.
Wittgenstein, Ludwig. 1953. *Philosophical Investigations*, 3rd ed. (Trans. by G. E. M. Anscombe.) New York: Macmillan.
Woolard, Kathryn. 1989. *Double Talk: Bilingualism and the Politics of Ethnicity in Catalonia*. Stanford, CA: Stanford University Press.
Wortham, Stanton E. F. 1994. *Acting Out Participant Examples in the Classroom*. Philadelphia: John Benjamins.
Wortham, Stanton E. F. 1997. "Denotationally Cued Interactional Events: A Special Case." *Semiotica, 114*, 295–317.
Wortham, Stanton E. F. 2001a. *Narratives in Action*. New York: Teachers College Press.
Wortham, Stanton E. F. 2001b. "Interactionally Situated Cognition: A Classroom Example." *Cognitive Science, 25*: 37–66.
Wortham, Stanton E. F. 2001c. "Gender and School Success in the Latino Diaspora." In *Education in the New Latino Diaspora: Policy and the Politics of Identity*, ed. S. Wortham, Enrique Murillo, and Edmund Hamann, 117–141. Westport, CT: Ablex.
Wortham, Stanton E. F. 2003. "Learning in Education." In *Encyclopedia of Cognitive Science*, ed. L. Nadel, volume 1, 1079–1082. New York: Macmillan/Nature Publishing Group.
Wortham, Stanton E. F. 2005. "Socialization Beyond the Speech Event." *Journal of Linguistic Anthropology, 15*, 95–112.
Zack, V. , and B. Graves. 2001. "Making Mathematical Meaning Through Dialogue: 'Once You Think of It, The Z Minus Three Seems Pretty Weird.'" *Educational Studies in Mathematics, 46*: 229–271.

Index